Advance Praise for *Microsoft Pr*
2010 Project Management

"Robert Happy has written a book that the novice and the expert both can benefit from reading. He explains how to use Microsoft Project throughout the life cycle of a project in a practical, straight forward manner that will help make any Project Manager more successful in using the tool."

—Laura Pease, EPM Program Manager, Varian Medical Systems

"Thankfully I was referred to Robert Happy and the Project Management Practice after asking the question: isn't there someone who can understand my projects and then teach me how to use this software to manage them? Please help me find a way to use this software in the "real" world! Robert's approach effectively taught me how to break down a project into manageable steps and then link them together to effectively manage results. Robert was able to tie in the right level of project management process and concepts with the tools to make it work best for me. All of this and more is captured in this book which I am sure you will find as an invaluable resource to learning Project 2010."

—Carol S. Myers, Vice President, Project Planning and Management, Takeda Global Research and Development Center

"Rob truly has a talent for training Project Managers. He knows how to bring together the theories of Project Management practices and the capabilities of project tools. I have used Robert to train several groups of Project Managers with varying levels of ability and he is always able to position the training in a way that strengthens their skills. In this book he does a thorough job of filling the gap between Project Management process and the use of Microsoft Project as a tool. His use of real-world examples and the hands-on exercises in the book help to solidify the techniques and tips that he delivers in each chapter. I think this book will be a useful guide to anyone trying to improve their knowledge of Project 2010."

—Annie Fitzgerald, MBA, MCTS, Project MPUG Board Member, Phoenix

The combination of Project Management theory, scheduling best practices, hands-on exercises, tips, and Real World Scenarios make this book an excellent scheduling primer, instructional guide, and reference for schedulers at all levels. Robert Happy is not only an excellent instructor and presenter, but he has done a phenomenal job of blending all these elements together into his new book, based on the new release of Microsoft Project 2010. Highly recommended reading, if you want to learn how to properly develop and maintain a schedule using Microsoft Project. The exercises thoroughly reinforce the knowledge presented; the Real World Scenarios provide excellent anecdotal evidence of the importance behind the best practices, presented throughout the book; and the material is logically organized making this an excellent reference text.

—Doc Dochtermann, PMP, PMI-SP, PMI Technology Member Advisory Group

Robert understands the blend and importance of linking process, people, tools, and purpose. Most organizational representatives have a biased perspective according to their role and expertise. Robert's training and consulting have a way of bringing them together successfully and helping organizations, teams, and individuals successfully transform into a holistic Project Management environment. Robert has now accomplished the same thing with this book. When Robert says that using Microsoft Project is easy, he is absolutely correct. What it takes, however, is an understanding of the process to plug into the tool. You follow the process, the tool does the work. Robert's book will bring it together, from purpose, vision, people, process, tools, and finally to results. I highly recommend this book to those who want to significantly improve an important competency.

—G. Lynne Snead, President, Insight Systems Consulting and Talent Evolution Systems

Microsoft®
Project 2010 Project Management

Microsoft®
Project 2010 Project Management:
Real World Skills for Certification and Beyond

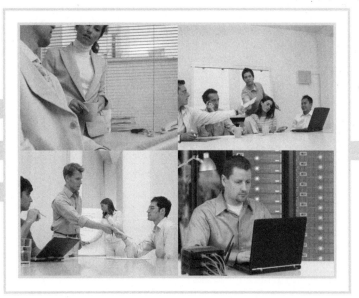

Robert Happy, PMP, MCT

WILEY

Wiley Publishing, Inc.

Acquisitions Editor: Jeff Kellum
Development Editor: Dick Margulis
Technical Editors: David Blair and Christine Flora
Production Editor: Christine O'Connor
Copy Editor: Tiffany Taylor
Editorial Manager: Pete Gaughan
Production Manager: Tim Tate
Vice President and Executive Group Publisher: Richard Swadley
Vice President and Publisher: Neil Edde
Project Manager I: Laura Moss-Hollister
Associate Producer: Josh Frank
Quality Assurance: Marilyn Hummel
Book Designers: Judy Fung and Bill Gibson
Compositor: Craig Woods, Happenstance Type-O-Rama
Proofreader: Publication Services, Inc.
Indexer: Robert Swanson
Project Coordinator, Cover: Lynsey Stanford
Cover Designer: Ryan Sneed

For general information on our other products and services or to obtain technical support, please contact our Customer Care Department within the U.S. at (877) 762-2974, outside the U.S. at (317) 572-3993 or fax (317) 572-4002.

Wiley also publishes its books in a variety of electronic formats. Some content that appears in print may not be available in electronic books.

Library of Congress Cataloging-in-Publication Data
Happy, Robert, 1965-
  Microsoft Project 2010 project management : real world skills for certification and beyond / Robert Happy.
— 1st ed.
     p. cm.
   ISBN 978-0-470-56110-2 (pbk.)
   ISBN 978-0-470-91716-9 (ebk.)
   ISBN 978-0-470-91718-3 (ebk.)
   ISBN 978-0-470-91717-6 (ebk.)
 1. Microsoft Project. 2. Project management—Computer programs. I. Title.
HD69.P75H3575 2010
658.4'04028553—dc22
                              2010019279

Dear Reader,

Thank you for choosing *Microsoft Project 2010 Project Management: Real World Skills for Certification and Beyond*. This book is part of a family of premium-quality Sybex books, all of which are written by outstanding authors who combine practical experience with a gift for teaching.

Sybex was founded in 1976. More than 30 years later, we're still committed to producing consistently exceptional books. With each of our titles, we're working hard to set a new standard for the industry. From the paper we print on, to the authors we work with, our goal is to bring you the best books available.

I hope you see all that reflected in these pages. I'd be very interested to hear your comments and get your feedback on how we're doing. Feel free to let me know what you think about this or any other Sybex book by sending me an email at nedde@wiley.com. If you think you've found a technical error in this book, please visit http://sybex.custhelp.com. Customer feedback is critical to our efforts at Sybex.

Best regards,

Neil Edde
Vice President and Publisher
Sybex, an Imprint of Wiley

To my loving wife, Charlotte, and three sons, Nicholas, Alexander, and Lucas. You make my life complete, gratifying, and out of the ordinary. And to my Mother, who would be proud.

Acknowledgments

I would like to first acknowledge my family, who completes my life and motivates me to always want to do better and never settle for mediocrity. Charlotte, Nicholas, Alexander, and Lucas—I love you with with all of my heart, and our family makes us stronger every day.

I would also like to acknowledge my business partners from our company, Project Management Practice, Inc., with whom I have been consulting and training in project management for many years. Keith Wilson, whom I have been working with for almost 20 years now: thank you for all you do—you're the king of execution, which is always key to our success. Sean Creaghan is the eternal optimist and relationship builder extraordinaire, who understands our business and keeps us glued together. David Blair takes patience and expertise to new levels. David has been there for me in many challenging client situations and always comes through with phenomenal solutions where no one else can. Charity Howder makes sure I stay on track and allows me to focus on what is important while ensuring the details are well looked after.

I want to thank Jeff Kellum from Wiley, who has been there for me since the beginning of this book to provide direction and balance to the writing process, and without whom this book would not have been written. Also, thanks to all the editors who have played such a significant role, particularly Dick Margulis and David Blair. I would also like to give a special thanks to David Blair for contributing to Chapter 3 of this book, providing the technical input to better describe Microsoft Project Server 2010 and the enterprise project-management solution.

Finally, I want to acknowledge all of the clients and organizations who have let me into their professional lives to help with project management. For nearly 20 years, I have had the honor and privilege to work with hundreds of organizations and thousands of people with one mission in mind: to improve their lives with better project management. I am always thankful for the opportunities to share my experiences with new people and build lasting relationships as they continue to be rewarding, challenging, and always intriguing.

About the Author

 For almost 20 years, Robert Happy has consulted with hundreds of organizations involving thousands of employees to establish effective project management practices. This includes both private and public-sector organizations spanning many industries, working with all levels of staff members from project teams to senior executives. Robert continues to consult with organizations with one mission in mind: optimizing the application of project management customized to meet each organization's unique requirements. Over the years, Robert has focused much of his time on working with a variety of organizations, such as 3M, Honda, Abbott Labs, US Marine Corps, Leapfrog, Royal Canadian Mounted Police, Bell Helicopter-Textron, Fifth Third Bank, Takeda Pharmaceuticals, United Way, Dow Pharmaceuticals, Amgen, Genentech, and many more. Examples of work included developing project management offices (PMOs), project management organizations, methodologies, processes, and custom PM systems to support a variety of application areas.

Robert is currently president and senior consultant for Project Management Practice, Inc. and an authorized senior-level consultant with Franklin Covey Corporation, where he previously held the position of director of project management. Prior to joining PMPI, he was founder and president of Project Consulting Group, specializing in complete custom project-management solutions. Before that, Robert was executive vice president for Time Line Solutions Corporation, a Symantec subsidiary, specializing in automated project-management solutions, and was a founding partner for the Project Management Center, which is a consulting organization specializing in project management. Currently, Robert has responsibility to lead and build the consulting and technology programs within Project Management Practice, Inc.

Robert is the author of Implementing an Effective Project Management Culture, which was presented and published at the 2001 Project Management Institute's (PMI) international symposium and proceedings. He presented a case study with Abbott Labs at the prestigious international Drug Information Association symposium. Robert has also published a number of articles for Microsoft Corporation, which are posted on Office Online, and he is a contributor to The Project Management Scorecard.

Robert graduated with a Bachelor of Business Administration from the University of New Brunswick, was on the dean's list, and attended Carleton University for Graduate Studies in Management. Robert has been a member of PMI for over 15 years and is fluent with A Guide to the Project Management Body of Knowledge (PMBOK). He is a Microsoft Certified Trainer (MCT) and Technology Specialist (MCTS). He is also part of an elite company, which is a Microsoft Gold Certified Partner organization. Robert continues to work with organizations around the world to implement successful project-management solutions by applying proven effective techniques.

Contents at a Glance

Contents

Table of Exercises

Introduction

This is a practical book for all users of Microsoft Project who need to plan, track, and communicate effectively for any type of project. Whether you're a more casual project manager or a professional project manager, this book delivers a sensible approach to using Project 2010 based on best practices around project management. It embodies proven effective learning techniques gleaned from years of consulting and teaching experience.

Whether you need to build simple plans or more complex plans with Project, this book shows you how to use powerful tools and techniques to better manage your projects. I've been training and consulting with Microsoft Project since the release of earlier versions nearly 20 years ago and as such have perfected the optimal approach to transfer knowledge efficiently so you can get the most out of the software.

Working with Project isn't like using other Microsoft Office products—such as Word, Excel, or PowerPoint—in that it requires you to have some core knowledge and understanding of project management in conjunction with the application. This book ties the primary project-management concepts to the appropriate functions in Microsoft Project, resulting in your increased productivity and effectiveness. This is neither a beginner, an intermediate, nor an advanced course but rather a comprehensive program with the core building blocks to support your projects from planning, monitoring, and controlling through closing. So, no matter what level of expertise you have with Microsoft Project, this book will help you optimize your use of the tool.

Although this book is a practical, hands-on guide, it's also designed to prepare you for the Microsoft Certifications 77-178 Exam—Microsoft Project 2010, Managing Projects. Candidates for this exam should have experience effectively scheduling, communicating, and tracking projects using the desktop version of Project 2010 Standard and Professional (excluding Project Server features). The exam will be a live-app or performance-based exam designed to measure your skill based on outcome and not necessarily on how you perform the tasks. The attached CD provides video based demonstrations and examples of key objective domains for the exam.

Who Should Read This Book

This book is written for people who need to optimize their use of Microsoft Project 2010 in a practical and sensible way. Whether you consider yourself a professional project manager or a casual user, this book will help you understand what is important to you when using Project 2010 and how to use the relevant tools and functions to meet your exact needs.

Your title may or may not be Project Manager, but many of us today are responsible for managing project activities in conjunction with our day-to-day routine tasks. This book is a practical guide for project managers who want to get the most out of using Project 2010 to manage project workloads in the most efficient and effective manner possible.

This book is also designed for candidates who want to get certified and take the 77-178 exam—Microsoft Project 2010, Managing Projects. Candidates for this exam use Project Standard 2010 and Project Professional 2010 desktop features to manage (plan and track) a project schedule and communicate the project to various stakeholders, and they must demonstrate that they understand relevant project-management concepts.

What You'll Learn

As you progress through this book, you'll learn how to use Project 2010 to help you succeed in managing projects. You'll first understand how Project 2010 fits into project management and where it will and won't help as a tool.

The first part of this book provides guidance on getting started the right way. This includes understanding the strategic relevance of using a tool like Project and how it fits into each stage of the project-management process. You'll also learn the differences between Project Standard 2010 and Project Professional 2010 while learning about how Project Server 2010 and Enterprise Project Management (EPM) fits into the overall scheme of things. I also cover important aspects of the tool that you need to know to get started building your schedule, such as starting a new project, using calendars, defining the project start date, and key option settings.

As you move to the second part of the book, you'll learn about important planning essentials. This section is based on a proven four-step planning process that includes building your work breakdown structure; estimating duration; setting dependencies; and assigning resources, work, and costs. You'll also learn about user-controlled scheduling and automatic scheduling and when and how to apply each scheduling technique. I cover important concepts such as understanding the critical path, using constraints, and deadlines. By the end of this part, you'll understand Project's calculation engine and the key drivers that affect the calculation of time and costs.

After you've learned how to build your plan effectively, you need to communicate it to many different types of stakeholders. The third part of the book teaches you about communicating and collaborating essentials. You'll learn how to use and customize the different views, tables, fields, filters, groups, and formats to develop more meaningful reports and presentations. You'll also learn how to collaborate with other applications, such as SharePoint, and easily move project data into applications like Excel, PowerPoint, Word, and email. In addition, this part deals with creating and maintaining master schedules or consolidated schedules using inserted subprojects. This includes creating integrated schedules with cross-project (external) links and shared resources.

In the last part of the book, you'll learn the essentials of tracking and analyzing. After a project is created and the schedule has been communicated to stakeholders for buy-in and signoff, you don't just put away the plan and forget about it. In this section, you'll learn how to use Project 2010 to keep your project on track; manage the impact of change; understand variances; make better decisions about the tradeoffs between scope, time, and resources; and take the most appropriate corrective action. You'll also learn about the basics of earned value management and how Project supports this technique.

Throughout the book, you'll find real-world case studies and exercises that walk you through the processes of building a plan from scratch, communicating it effectively, and tracking and analyzing it to help keep you on track. You'll also find notes scattered throughout the book to help you understand more detailed concepts. In addition, real-world scenarios provide you with insights into the daily life of a project manager using Project 2010.

This book was also written to address the core functional domain areas that will be covered in the MCTS 77-178 Project 2010, Managing Projects exam. This live-application, performance-based exam maps to this book, and understanding the topics covered in this book will effectively prepare you to write and pass the exam. Because the exam is a live-app exam, the book's CD includes an overview of what will be covered in the exam, with real-time recordings to help you simulate the functional domains that you may be tested on. The exam isn't meant to be a catch-all for every feature in Project 2010, so neither is this book. It was designed using the same approach as the exam, applying the 80/20 rule: it covers the important features and functions that you use 80% of the time to effectively manage your project schedules with Project 2010 and not the obscure or rarely used features used only 20% of the time by a smaller group of users.

What You Need

The exercises in this book assume that you're running Microsoft Project 2010 for the desktop. You don't need nor does this book cover Project Server 2010. As discussed in Chapter 3, "Overview of Enterprise Project Management," Project 2010 comes in two varieties: Standard and Professional. This book covers the primary features of Standard plus the additional features of Professional, which include the following:

- Team Planner
- SharePoint synchronization
- Inactive Task feature

These features may be covered on the exam. So, even if you have the standard version, if you plan to take the exam, please review these features in this book; doing so should suffice. There will be no questions regarding the collaboration functionality between Project Professional and Project Server; again, Project Server isn't needed for this book or the exam.

If you don't have a copy of Project 2010, you can download a trial version from the following site:

`www.microsoft.com/project`

If you want more eLearning to supplement this book and help you prepare further, you can go to the following site:

`www.pm-practice.com`

What Is Covered in This Book

The following list provides an overview of the topics covered in each chapter.

Part I: Getting Started the Right Way

Chapter 1: Project 2010 as an Enabling Tool for Project Managers: In this chapter, you'll learn about Project 2010's role in the life of a project manager: where it will and won't enable you to be more effective and its overall strategic and tactical relevance in project management.

Chapter 2: Mapping the Project-Management Process Groups to Microsoft Project 2010: Understand how Project fits into *A Guide to the Project Management Body of Knowledge* (PMBOK), Fourth Edition, and its associated project-management stages: initiating, planning, monitoring and controlling, executing, and closing. You'll learn where and when Project provides support in each stage of the project-management process and a project's life cycle.

Chapter 3: Overview of Enterprise Project Management: Understand the key components of the EPM solution that Microsoft offers in conjunction with Project and when it's most appropriate to make the investment in a Project Server 2010 solution. You'll also learn the differences between Project Standard 2010 and Project Professional 2010.

Chapter 4: Getting Started and Setting Up the Microsoft Project Environment: Before building your schedule, you need to learn about how to initiate a new plan and define some key settings. This includes starting from a template, defining the project start date, using calendars, and other option settings important for your successful use of the tool.

Part II: Planning Essentials

Chapter 5: Creating and Entering the Work Breakdown Structure and Task Arrangement: The cornerstone of any good project plan is having a good WBS and task structure. In this chapter, you'll learn how to develop a WBS and enter the task structure into Microsoft Project 2010. This is the first step in a four-step process to creating schedules effectively in Project.

Chapter 6: Estimating and Entering Duration or Work: Step 2 of the four-step planning process includes estimating duration. In this chapter, you'll learn about various estimating techniques and how to enter them into Project. You'll also start to learn how to use either manually scheduled tasks or auto-scheduled tasks and how they differ in this step.

Chapter 7: Setting Dependencies and the Critical Path: Step 3 of the four-step planning process focuses on setting dependencies and setting up the network for the schedule. After it's set up, you'll learn about the critical path and how to use this in Project. You'll also learn about using constraints and deadlines, and you'll continue to study the differences between manually scheduled tasks and auto-scheduled tasks.

Chapter 8: Assigning Resources and Costs: The last step in the four-step planning resources is all about assigning resources and costs. You'll learn how to set up a resource pool and assigning resources to the various tasks in the schedule, including using the Team Planner view, which is only available for Professional users. You'll also learn in detail how the scheduling engine works, based on the scheduling formula and various task types: fixed duration, fixed work, and fixed units. You'll continue to study the differences between manually scheduled tasks and auto-scheduled tasks.

Chapter 9: Understanding the Calculation Engine for Automatic Scheduling: At any time, you can switch to auto scheduling to take advantage of the efficiencies of Project's powerful calculation engine. This chapter is a synopsis of the primary drivers that impact the calculation of time (start and finish dates) and costs, which are touched on throughout the planning process.

Part III: Communicating and Reporting Essentials

Chapter 10: Understanding Views: Project comes equipped with many different ways to look at schedule information. The default view is the Gantt Chart view with the new Timeline view on top. In this chapter, you'll learn how to navigate from one view to another, including the new views for the Timeline and the Team Planner view.

Chapter 11: Using Tables and Custom Fields: You can control what you see in each view by changing or modifying tables. This includes creating new custom fields complete with drop-down lists, formulas, and/or graphical indicators. You'll learn how to change tables and customize fields for more effective communicating and reporting.

Chapter 12: Using Filters, Groups, and Sorts: In this chapter, you'll learn about powerful tools that can help you focus on specific data and manage your project more effectively. This includes learning about filtering, highlighting, grouping, and sorting to slice and dice information in ways that will lead to better decision making and more meaningful communication.

Chapter 13: Creating Custom Views, Formatting, and Reporting: After you learn about the various tools for communication and decision making, you can customize views to apply specific tables with custom fields, filters, groups, and formatting. You'll also learn how to format the text and bar areas for more eye-catching communication and how to use Project 2010's reporting tools.

Chapter 14: Creating Master Schedules with Inserted Projects: In this chapter, you'll learn how to create an integrated master schedule with inserted subprojects. You'll also learn how to create cross-project dependencies as well as share resources across multiple projects. This will include looking at the critical path across multiple projects.

Part IV: Tracking and Analyzing Essentials

Chapter 15: Setting and Maintaining Baselines: You'll learn about the importance of setting baselines and how this works in Project, including which fields are baselined. You'll also learn how to maintain baselines and set multiple baselines if needed. You'll be introduced to various views and tables that are set up specifically for you to view the baseline.

Chapter 16: Updating and Tracking Status: In this chapter, you'll learn about updating and tracking techniques and strategies. This includes learning about the different types of percent completes in Project and how to capture status and actuals. You'll learn how to capture actuals for start, finish, duration, work, and costs.

Chapter 17: Variance Analysis and Taking Corrective Action: After you learn how to capture and enter actuals into Project, it's important to analyze the impact this may have on your schedule. In this chapter, you'll learn about using the variance fields in Project to analyze your plan and then take advantage of various tools to take corrective action. This chapter includes an overview of earned-value management and Project's earned-value fields.

Appendixes

Appendix A: Appendix A provides an objectives map for exam 77-178, Microsoft Project 2010, Managing Projects. If you're studying for the exams, use this appendix to find the portion of the book that covers the objectives you're currently studying.

Appendix B: About the Companion CD.

What's on the CD

With this book, we're including an array of training resources. The CD offers sample templates with formulas for graphical indicators, sample videos with an overview of key areas covered on the certification 77-178 exam, live application simulations, a PDF of the book, and an overview of what's new in Project 2010. The CD's resources are described here:

Sample Templates   In the book, I refer to two powerful custom columns with graphical indicators based on formulas. The CD includes two files as follows:

- Formula Needs Updating for 2010.mpp
- Formula Task Finish Status for 2010.mpp

Sample Videos and Exam Domain Examples   Throughout the book, I include numerous hands-on exercises showing you how to perform a variety of tasks. The CD includes videos to support some of these important concepts examples of the primary domain areas that will be covered on the live-application performance-based exam. Consolidation of Exercises and Results: you will find a consolidation of all the hands-on exercises in one place with matching mpp files which illustrate the completed results for each exercise making it easy for you to practice and learn at your own pace.

The Sybex E-book   Many people like the convenience of being able to carry their book on a CD. They also like being able to search the text via computer to find specific information quickly and easily. For these reasons, the entire contents of this book are supplied on the CD, in PDF form. We've also included Adobe Acrobat Reader, which provides the interface for the PDF contents as well as search capabilities.

Overview of What's New In Project 2010   Project 2010 comes equipped with many new and powerful features. A series of videos highlights important new features in Project 2010, including the differences between the Standard and Professional versions.

How to Contact the Author

If you have any questions about using Project 2010 or this book, feel free to contact me any time at rhappy@pm-practice.com. Also, if you have any training or consulting needs regarding custom project-management solutions, you can check out our website at www.pm-practice.com or email me at your convenience. We have a team of best in class, cost-efficient experts ready to respond to meet your exact needs—including myself.

Getting Started the Right Way

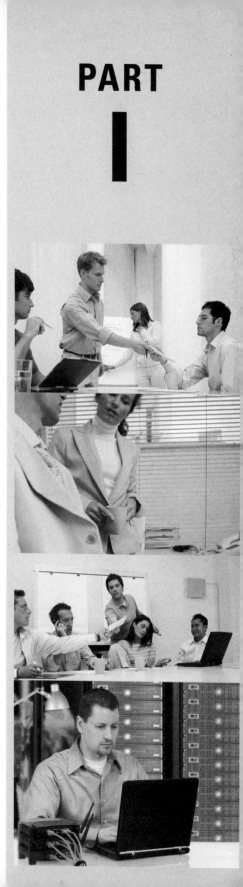

Using the right tool for the right job in the right way seems simple enough, right? Well, it isn't always the case. Microsoft Project users often jump into the tool, using it the wrong way or for the wrong reasons, paying little or no attention to important project-management concepts and key settings, and creating poor or ineffective project plans. This book will help ensure your success as a project manager by focusing on the most essential concepts and functionality in Project.

This book isn't a catchall that describes each and every obscure function in Project. Nor is it a catchall for project-management theory. It's the most important parts of each, chosen based on experience, for you to apply as you navigate through your real-world projects.

The first part of this book discusses when to use Project and why it's an essential enabling tool for creating project schedules. It also covers some of the key settings that have a significant effect on your schedule before you enter any task information.

Chapter

1

Project 2010 as an Enabling Tool for Project Managers

IN THIS CHAPTER, YOU'LL LEARN ABOUT THE FOLLOWING:

- ✓ The knowledge gap between using Microsoft Project and understanding project management
- ✓ How key credentials can help your career
- ✓ When to use Project
- ✓ The strategic relevance of project management and Microsoft Project
- ✓ A proven, effective approach to learning Microsoft Project

In this chapter, you'll explore how Project is often misunderstood as being difficult or to complex too use. I'll walk you through why this belief is misplaced and how Project is an enabler, designed to help you succeed in project management. We'll also look at some key project-management concepts and walk through a proven approach to learning Project.

Why Do People Think Project Is Hard to Use?

Project isn't difficult to use. Closing the knowledge gap between project-management concepts and using Project will be important to your success.

Accidental or Not, Knowledge Is Important

Approximately 20 years ago, I began my project-management career—like most other project managers during that time frame, by accident. Even in today's project-focused world, with so much more emphasis on education, certification, and project management as a career, far too many organizations and project managers take an ad hoc approach when it comes to managing projects. I'm not sure who coined the phrase "project management—the accidental profession," but given my experience as a consultant and trainer, and having worked with hundreds of organizations and thousands of people, I can attest to its reality.

How many project managers today thought, "When I grow up I want to be a project manager"? Far too often, we're plunged into managing or leading projects without the right set of skills, training, knowledge, processes, and tools, not to mention organizational support with regard to roles, responsibility, and authority. I'm sure you can relate in one way or another.

But all isn't lost. Over the past few decades, great strides have been taken by organizations such as the *Project Management Institute (PMI)* and accredited educational institutions to enhance skills, knowledge, standards, and credentials. They've provided a clearer path that legitimizes project management as a career and provides a significantly greater level of professionalism. For example, PMI offers certification as a *Project Management*

Professional (PMP); and you can become a *Microsoft Certified Technology Specialist (MCTS)* for *Microsoft Project.* Over that same period, project-management tools—in this case, software—have moved from mainframe to desktop, from DOS to Windows, and from very difficult to easy-to-use.

You may be thinking, "Microsoft Project, easy to use? I don't think so!" But Project 2010 *is* easy to use, and my primary purpose for writing this book is to prove it to you. I've worked with most of the mainstream project-management applications over the years—some have come and gone, and some are still around. I can assure you that Project 2010 is not only easy to use, especially considering all it can do, but also, in my opinion, one of the best versions of project-management software ever put on the market.

Credentials Will Help Close the Gap

At first glance, it may seem self-serving for Microsoft to offer MCTS credentials in using a tool like Project. However, this and other credentialing programs serve the project-management community. Let's look at the numbers.

I've been told that there are approximately 250,000 credentialed PMPs in the world at this time—give or take a few (thousands, maybe). Compare that to the estimated over 20 million, and growing, Microsoft Project users. You can see the order of magnitude between the number of people using Project (and managing projects) and those who are certified PMPs.

Why is this important to you?

There are two key reasons. First, it illustrates that a large knowledge gap exists. Far more people use Project than understand the core concepts of project management. To use this tool effectively, you should be well versed in project-management techniques and knowledge regardless of how you obtain it. However, I think that if we tested PMPs and non-PMPs, the PMP population would beat out the non-PMPs in comprehension and effectiveness with using Project. (I don't mean that the only people who understand the core concepts of project management are credentialed PMPs.)

Second, it's hard for organizations to assess the skill level of project managers. In the past, you could perhaps get away with writing Project Manager on a résumé and list a knowledge of Project with your skills. But over time, the truth came out as employees struggled not only to manage projects effectively but also to demonstrate their ability to use a tool like Project. I've spent most of my career working with professionals, and times are changing. Organizations are requesting more credentials because they have been burned too many times. Certifications such as PMP and MCTS are becoming common requirements and can be key differentiators for you and your career. Just because you're certified doesn't mean you'll be a good project manager, just as passing the bar doesn't guarantee you'll be a good lawyer—there are many other factors to consider. However, it does allow a benchmark to be set for core knowledge of theory, concepts, and the use of Project.

⊕ **Real World Scenario**

Credentials and Consistency in Career Development

I was working with a good-sized pharmaceutical company. Their project-management department had grown quickly because of success on some recently launched products and a growing pipeline. Included in the department were positions ranging from junior and senior project managers to director level.

The group was experiencing dissension around a lack of clearly defined roles, responsibilities, experience, and required skills for each level. Many on staff felt that they had been misplaced or incorrectly categorized in their position. There was no effective way to demonstrate why each person had been placed in their job classification.

Our job was to map out the roles, responsibilities, experience, and required skills for each position. We broke skills into both soft (leadership-type) and hard (such as creating plans in Project effectively). With input from each group member, we developed a comprehensive list of skills and requirements. After these were defined, we were able to map those positions to the existing staff and look for gaps and inequalities.

Subsequently, each person was given a tailored roadmap to success that outlined their respective career-development path and included information about the specific knowledge and skills they needed to obtain. Part of the roadmap included certification requirements. In order to advance, both internal organizational certifications and external credentials were required, including knowing how to use Project. Credentials such as PMP and MCTS helped us level the playing field and ensure consistency and standards around project-management knowledge and skills.

Is It Me, or Is It the Software?

I train and consult with Project today and plan to do so for the foreseeable future. And I still run into the same old grumbling: this software is too hard to use.

Consider another situation: accounting. Buying accounting software doesn't make you an accountant. Accountants need to bring knowledge to the table. Having the key concepts—understanding balance sheets, income statements, debits, credits, and so on—is essential to be effective with accounting software.

The same principle applies to Project 2010. Project requires you to have some grasp of core concepts and to understand project management before you use the application. The problem isn't the tool but the knowledge gap between understanding fundamental project-management concepts and knowing how to apply them in Project 2010—or any project-management software.

The more you know about the essential concepts of project management, the more success you'll have in managing projects and optimizing Project 2010. You may even find yourself enjoying it. So, ask yourself: "Is it me, or is it the software?"

This book incorporates the core project-management concepts you need to know to be successful with Project 2010. I'll give you a proven, effective approach that has been refined and optimized over many years. You'll learn how Project can be an enabling tool throughout the life cycle of any project. And, in particular, you'll learn to map the key project-management process groups and knowledge areas outlined in *A Guide to the Project Management Body of Knowledge, Fourth Edition* (PMBOK; PMI, 2008) to the tool.

How can Project assist you, as a project manager, through the initiating, planning, executing, controlling, and closing stages of a project while supporting you in key project-management areas such as scope, time, cost, resource, and communication? This question will be the primary focus for this book. Finding the answer will help you be more successful with managing your projects.

🌐 Real World Scenario

Understanding Project-Management Concepts Will Help with Using Microsoft Project

One of my very early consulting engagements involved a government research organization that was managing and coordinating a number of important projects. The group I was working with were scientists who were responsible for leading each research initiative. They had chosen to put their plans into Project, and I was tasked to teach them how to use the software.

Right away, it became obvious that their troubles had more to do with not understanding key project-management concepts than with learning how to use the tool. Among other things, they weren't familiar with scope management and constructing a well-organized work-breakdown structure. Their lack of awareness of these techniques (and many others) and subsequent difficulties with Project made it clear to me that if you don't have the right understanding of project-management concepts and techniques, you'll be unsuccessful in using Project or any other project-management software. It would be like trying to use Word without knowing how to write or Excel without a basic understanding of numbers.

When to Use Project

Throughout many client engagements, I've seen Project used in some fascinating ways. To understand when it's most appropriate to use a tool like Project, it's important to first differentiate between the types of work that take place in organizations. Project is for projects.

As organizations perform work, it can be characterized into two major categories: operations and projects. Although these work categories share many common traits, they differ in some key ways. Consider a *project* as defined in PMBOK: "A project is a temporary endeavor undertaken to create a unique produce, service, or result."

Three key characteristics define a project and differentiate projects from operations. See if you can fill in the blanks with these differentiating characteristics:

1. _____

2. _____

3. _____

If you chose *unique*, *temporary*, and *result* (or *deliverable*), you're on the right path. In contrast, operations focus on ongoing, repetitive activities, geared toward optimizing the value and utilization of existing assets. Projects focus on the creation of new value or unique *deliverables* in the form of tangible or intangible *results*. Based on the PMBOK definition, projects come from all levels in an organization and from any function, department, or group. Project management is no longer limited to traditional engineering, IT, or big research-and-development type projects, but now extends across most industries, departments, and functions.

Look at the first keyword in the definition of a project. Zero in on that word: *temporary*. Every project has a well-defined beginning and a well-defined end. In other words, there is no such thing as an ongoing project (see Figure 1.1).

FIGURE 1.1   No Such Thing as an Ongoing Project

🌐 Real World Scenario

How Long Is Temporary?

Temporary doesn't mean projects can't be long or vary in length. I've worked on projects in R&D organizations, particularly in the pharmaceutical and aerospace industries, that went on for years. The typical life cycle of drug-development projects, for example, may range from five to seven years, depending on the stage of development and how many phases are being carried in the project plan.

I've also worked on plans for projects that were less than a week in length and yet had all the complexity of longer-duration projects. An extreme example was a plant shutdown for a large mining company that took place over a three-day period. The team worked 24 hours a day in 12-hour shifts. In that time, we had to plan to complete more than 500 work orders and task items. This required detailed planning of tasks, timing, and resources—a great use of a tool like Project. Most projects lie somewhere between these drastically different examples.

Projects Are Supposed to End—Really

If you're working on a project and the end is unclear, stop and take the time to define the finishing point. Too often, confusion exists about when a project stops being a project and becomes part of operations or ongoing support. Even if you do a good job developing the result of a project, if there is confusion during hand-off or putting the result of the project into production, there may the misplaced perception of a poorly managed project. Your project may even be considered a failure. This isn't a good situation to be in, especially after working hard on a project.

PMBOK does a wonderful job differentiating not only between projects and operations but also between *project* life cycles and *product* life cycles. It states that every project has a beginning, a middle, and an end, with a cycle time that can be represented by some version of the curve shown in Figure 1.2.

FIGURE 1.2   Project life cycle bell curve

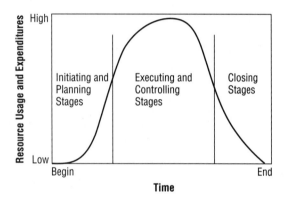

As the project moves through the initial stages, they're often broken down into phases. PMBOK directs us to organize and structure these phases by deliverables, or what I refer to as *interim deliverables*, which together will constitute the completion of the project and delivery of the final deliverables (the *result*).

As you move through the project life cycle and project phases, the impact of change on time, cost, and scope becomes increasingly worse and is sometimes catastrophic. If you don't have good initiating and planning processes, supported with the right tools—including Project—then the cost of rework, false starts, do-overs, and canceled or failed projects will be far greater to your organization (and your career) than the cost of the relatively small amount of time it takes to initiate and plan well.

Projects vs. Product Life Cycles

Keeping in mind that projects have defined life cycles, we need to clearly distinguish those life cycles from the life cycle of the product, service, or result that is being created from the project. Projects are unique undertakings that come with some level of uncertainty. As a result of that uniqueness, they eventually move into production or to the operations side of an organization, to be maintained in a non-unique or routine manner. As I mentioned, PMBOK differentiates project versus product life cycles, to help you know when to apply project-management techniques and tools. Consider Figure 1.3.

FIGURE 1.3   Product vs. project life cycles

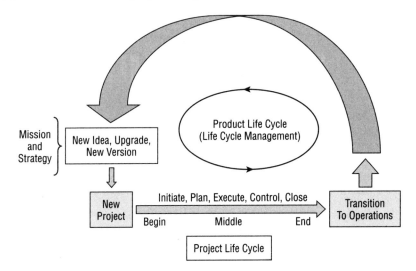

The figure clearly illustrates that product life cycles contain project life cycles and that products may constitute multiple projects, such as new versions or improvements. Often this is referred to as *life cycle management* (LCM). It's easy to draw a parallel to when it's appropriate to use a tool such as Project. During the project life cycle, you should apply project-management techniques and tools. This is where Project becomes an enabling tool.

Figure 1.4 illustrates that for Project to be used in the right way, for its primary intention, it should be applied to the project-activity side of work, leaving other systems and processes to support ongoing, operational activities. It's also becoming more important to pay attention to the need for integration of systems in overlapping areas of operations and projects, such as enterprise resource planning (ERP), financial, and customer relationship management (CRM) systems. Knowing when to use Project and recognizing that it's an enabling tool when used for the right type of activities will go a long way toward enhancing organizational success.

Consider the Impact

Often, we're given tasks that seem to meet the definition of a project but don't appear to warrant the creation of a detailed or even high-level plan in Project. The size of the project does become a differentiating factor for determining when and how to use a tool like Project, but it's important to combine common sense with guidelines.

FIGURE 1.4   Operations vs. projects

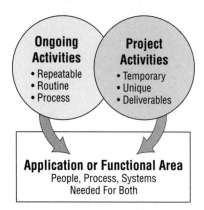

I've worked with many project management offices (PMOs) that use criteria such as the number of person hours (effort or work hours) to determine whether an activity warrants the creation of a plan in Project. Other considerations may include duration or the number of tasks involved. It isn't uncommon to see a mixed set of these criteria used to determine not only whether the activity warrants a separate project plan but also whether an appointed project manager is needed.

Keeping your categorization process simple will help ensure your success in implementing a policy around what makes a project a project and when to employ a tool like Project 2010. Always consider the impact that implementing the project will have on the organization.

 **Real World Scenario**

Person Hours as a Guideline

Working with a PMO for an organization that develops custom software solutions, we set up a custom enterprise project-management system using Microsoft Project Professional and Project Server. To facilitate project planning, we created many enterprise templates.

To determine whether a project was to be planned out in detail, we first put the project through a fairly rigorous initiation process. This evaluation determined whether the project was to be deemed a strategic or long-term project or considered a tactical or short-term project.

Project templates were only used to plan strategic or long-term projects that consumed more than 120 person hours. Short-term or tactical projects were also planned in Project but were tracked only as individual line items in a consolidated master plan. This allowed the organization to keep track of all work related to projects.

Another large financial institution used 40 person hours as the discerning factor for whether an activity was large enough to warrant a plan in Microsoft Project.

Strategic Importance of Project 2010

Understanding that Project is an enabling tool to support project-type activities is important. It's also important to understand not only where your projects come from but their strategic relevance to your organization.

Strategy Drives Projects

Strategic decision making may be outside your sphere or responsibilities as a project manager, but understanding which work is mission critical isn't. That information needs to be communicated up and down your organization. Consider Figure 1.5.

FIGURE 1.5 Mission, strategy, projects

Every organization has a *mission*. Some are more formal than others; but generally speaking, the mission defines why an organization exists or what its primary purpose is. A well-defined mission, perhaps in a well-thought-out mission statement, provides high-level direction to the organization. It's hard to tie that directly to the low-level questions we have to answer every day.

To help with the process of tying mission to *strategy*, and ultimately to projects and operational activities, organizations create business plans or strategic plans. These further define an organization's direction for spending its valuable resources to create and support products or services. This process of moving an organization's mission into strategy is critical and essential for providing the framework in which to make decisions about which projects to work on. Well-defined, strategic goals provide the next level in determining what an organization should do to accomplish its mission.

Consider this definition from *The Strategy Process*, by Henry Mintzberg and James Brian Quinn: "A strategy is the pattern or plan that integrates an organization's major goals, policies and action sequences into a cohesive whole. A well-formulated strategy helps to marshal and allocate an organization's resources into a unique and viable posture based on its relative internal competencies and shortcomings, anticipated changes in the environment, and contingent moves by intelligent opponents." (Prentice Hall, 1991).

It's important to understand that strategic goals aren't projects. Referring to the previous definition, it's easy to make the connection between strategy and projects. The components of strategy, action sequences, marshaling and allocating the organization's resources, and achieving major goals all create a need for projects. Generally, many projects go into achieving one strategic goal.

The other important component of this definition is that a strategy can be a pattern or a plan. If you don't have a well-formulated or documented strategy, such a strategy still exists based on the choices you make every day. A significant number of those choices determine which projects to work on and which tasks within those projects to work on. If priorities aren't set and strategy isn't well-directed, your organization may drift.

You can think of a mission statement as being at the 40,000-foot level, which is hard to link directly to your daily task list. Strategic goals are at the 20,000-foot level: they're essential for direction and priority-setting but need to be broken into more manageable pieces to get to a more tactical level. This next level is where projects come into play. Projects are the tactical components of strategy: key mechanisms to take strategy and move it into actionable components.

In practice, all projects should tie directly back to strategic goals. In many organizations, score cards or some form of management by objectives (which can also be derivatives or representations of strategic goals) result in the formation of projects. Projects become the 10,000-foot level view. Your daily task load, which may be a combination of project and operational work, reflects the ground level.

Your perception of the scale of action will depend on your level within the organization. If you're at the 40,000-foot level—say, a CEO or an executive director—a project is a tactical or granular level of detail. However, if you're on a project team with specific tasks assigned to you, the project level is your high-level or big-picture view.

Working on the Right Projects in the Right Way

Strategy helps drive which project to work on, which in turn feeds into the concept of portfolio project management. The processes and tools employed in portfolio management help to determine the right projects to work on, whereas project management deals with how to work on projects the right way. PMI defines a *portfolio* as "a collection of projects or programs and other work that are grouped together to facilitate effective management of that work to meet strategic business objectives." Strategy drives portfolios, and portfolios drive projects.

Let's consider what portfolio management and project management are all about. It's important to discuss portfolio management first, so we can determine the fit for Project 2010.

Here is PMI's definition of *portfolio management*: "The centralized management of one or more portfolios, which includes identifying, prioritizing, authorizing, managing and controlling projects, programs and other related work, to achieve specific strategic business objectives."

Although there may be some overlap between portfolio management and project management's initiation of processes, Project 2010 isn't specifically designed to support portfolio management. But again, all isn't lost. Microsoft provides Project Server as its enterprise project-management solution. Project Server 2010 provides the necessary tools to conduct portfolio management and integrate with your project-management processes and system.

Now, let's look at a definition of project management, which is the primary focus on this book. Again, I'll turn to PMBOK. (Perhaps you're getting the hint that it may pay to read PMBOK, if you haven't already.) PMI defines project management as follows: "The application of knowledge, skills, tools and techniques to project activities to meet the project requirements."

This definition embodies the foundation for this book. It states that project management combines knowledge, techniques, skills, and tools. What better way to illustrate the necessity of combining project-management knowledge with the power of a software tool such as Project 2010? Considering that PMI and PMBOK represent the current, predominant standard, particularly in the US, given that other methodologies do exist such as Prince2, it is very useful to map how PMBOK relates to the use of Project 2010.

To be clear about when to use Project and its strategic relevance, consider Figure 1.6.

FIGURE 1.6   Strategic Relevance

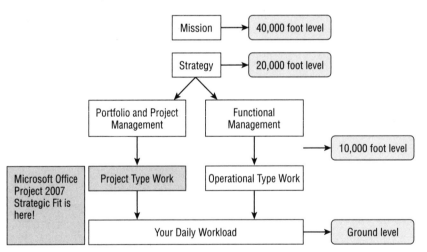

Ensuring that everyone in your organization is doing mission-critical work is no easy task. Obviously, the bigger the organization, the harder this job becomes. From senior executives to the team-member level, it depends not only on how well *functional management*

or department heads execute on business plans and strategic goals but also on how well portfolio and project management are implemented. The larger the portfolio of projects, the greater the need to invest in project-management people, processes, and tools. The strategic relevance directly correlates to the strategic value of successfully implementing the projects.

🌐 Real World Scenario

Strategic Value of Projects

An organization I worked with once estimated the strategic value of successfully completing mission-critical projects at $500 million. Understanding this value made it easy to justify an investment in a tool like Project and also in the people and processes to support the projects. Until that point, the company employed a "just do it" approach. It was able to get away with this ad hoc way of doing things as a smaller company, before growing and reaching a critical mass. Then, it started to feel the pain that comes with aligning mission-critical activities to daily workload in an ad hoc, less-than-organized manner.

Understanding the value of successful project completion leads to support and buy-in to implement a project-management solution. In this situation, much more was involved in the solution than just implementing Project. This company set up a PMO and developed effective portfolio- and project-management processes and systems.

Improving Results with a Proven, Effective Approach

My colleagues and I have refined our approach to teaching Project 2010 over the past 15 years and have proven this approach with thousands of trainees. We've been fortunate enough to work with some of the largest and most successful organizations in the world, as well as hundreds of small to medium-sized companies. We've practiced our approach with private-sector and public-sector organizations with great success, and we want to share it with you so you can experience the same success with Project.

Many of the techniques and approaches discussed in this book are based on best practices around scheduling and apply to previous versions of Project, although I highlight the new and powerful features of Project 2010. If you don't already have Project 2010, you'll want to get it, based on the key new features.

Planning, Communicating, and Tracking

In Chapter 2, "Mapping the Project-Management Process Groups to Project," I map out specifically how Project syncs up with PMBOK, and that is essential to your success. Basically, you're doing one of three things when using Project: planning, communicating, or tracking and analyzing. Knowing the essentials of each of these will enhance your experience with Project and your career as a project manager, coordinator, or leader.

In the planning stages, you should consider the key components of the plan relating to scope, time, resources, and costs and how these will be integrated. After your plan is built, you need to communicate it effectively to the stakeholders: project customers, sponsors, senior management, team members, and functional managers. Communication is key, and Project augments this function significantly. Finally, when a project begins, it's important to monitor and control its execution. Project 2010 has some powerful capabilities to help you manage change, take corrective actions, and stay on track.

Thus the heart and soul of this book, and of using Project, boils down the following:

1. Planning essentials

2. Communicating and reporting essentials

3. Tracking and analyzing essentials

Proven Effective over Time

This approach to using Project and framing your interaction with the software is tried and true. Each of the three major sections listed in the previous section will be broken down into more detailed steps. First, you need to know Project's planning essentials. I'll walk you through proven effective planning processes with Project to ensure that you create the most effective and operational plans possible. I'll tie in best practices related to planning, following a five-step process that will optimize your experience with building plans in Project.

Project 2010 will greatly enhance your ability to ensure alignment among your stakeholders. Project has some incredible new features for reporting, and I'll walk you through the most important ones. You know that communication is a key to success, so why not take advantage of the reporting tools in Project to improve your effectiveness? Too often, Project users get stuck using the default Gantt view as the only communication tool, when its usefulness is limited. This book will open your eyes to new communication techniques available through Project. Even if you don't know what you're doing, you'll look good doing it! Yes, that's a joke. But why not get the recognition you deserve, appear professional, stay on top of communications, and manage them well? Doing so will go along way to developing your successful career.

Finally, I'll discuss tracking and analyzing. After a plan is built and communicated effectively to everyone involved for buy-in and sign-off, the project will begin. During the execution stage, work will be performed by team members, as you outlined in the plan.

At this point, people have a tendency to put the tool aside and forget about it. This isn't the right approach. During execution, you should not only continue to manage communications but also manage change, status, issues, risks, and so on. People put Project aside due to a lack of understanding of how to use it during this stage of a project. The perception is that it's too hard or takes too much time to use Project. Given the right framework for updating, tracking, and analyzing project information using Project (see Figure 1.7), you'll find that there are some powerful, easy-to-use tools that you won't want to be without during your next project.

FIGURE 1.7   Proven, effective, driven results

Summary

The more you learn about project management, the better off you'll be when selecting and applying the right tools at the right time. This is particularly true with Microsoft Project 2010. Although Project is easy to use and equipped with powerful tools to help you manage throughout a project's life cycle, the more you learn about the key concepts that support using the tool, the more effective you'll be as a project manager using Project.

In this chapter, I discussed the importance of credentials and how they can help advance your career. Two key organizations, PMI and Microsoft, offer certifications that help close the knowledge gap between project management and Microsoft Project.

It's important to understand where Project is strategically relevant in its application. Knowing when to use Project is as important as understanding how to use it.

Mission drives strategy, which drives portfolios and projects. Both project activities and operational activities need to be supported by people, processes, and systems relevant to the projects' strategic value. This helps ensure that you're working on mission-critical activities.

My approach to teaching Project has been developed over the past 15 years and has proven effective over and over again. I know you'll benefit from it as thousands of Project users already have.

Key Terms

deliverable

functional management

A Guide to the Project Management Body of Knowledge, Fourth Edition (PMBOK)

Microsoft Certified Technology Specialist (MCTS)

Microsoft Project

mission

Project Management Institute (PMI)

portfolio

portfolio management

project

Project Management Professional (PMP)

result

strategy

Chapter

2

Mapping the Project-Management Process Groups to Microsoft Project 2010

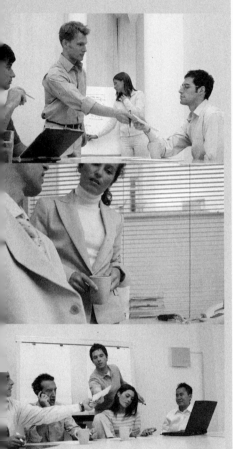

IN THE CHAPTER, YOU'LL LEARN ABOUT THE FOLLOWING:

- ✓ Five key project-management process groups

- ✓ Initiating process activities and Project usage

- ✓ Planning process activities and Project usage

- ✓ Executing process activities and Project usage

- ✓ Monitoring and controlling process activities and Project usage

- ✓ Closing process activities and Project usage

Every project has a life cycle with a beginning, a middle, and an end. Each goes through a series of processes, formally recognized or not. The organizations I've worked with have had varying degrees of maturity and depth with regard to project-management processes. Regardless of where you are with your project-management maturity, you should have a clear understanding of how a tool like Project can help in each of the project-management process groups. This chapter deals with how Project maps to each process group and where it will be a significant help, will only help a little, or will be no help at all.

Mapping Project to Your Methodology Will Increase Effectiveness

I've worked with many different methodologies and project-management processes over the years, but I always come back to *A Guide to the Project Management Body of Knowledge, Fourth Edition* (PMBOK), published by the Project Management Institute (PMI). It's come out on top as the generally accepted approach to project management and one of the predominant project management standards.

Other methodologies are available, such as PRINCE2, a widely used project-management methodology in the United Kingdom. The approach we take in teaching Project is flexible and not definitively tied to any one methodology. And at a very high level, the *process groups* in PMBOK can easily be mapped to other methodologies or project-management frameworks. As is the case with the *software development life cycle* (SDLC) methodologies I've worked with, the high-level activities are comparable in many aspects; differences become apparent in the way they're implemented. Sometimes it's a matter of semantics. In other instances, there are fundamental differences in approach, particularly at the detail level. All that being said, in this book I'll focus on mapping to PMBOK, to clearly illustrate where Project plays a role in supporting a project manager as you navigate through a project.

Whether you map to PMBOK or not, it will be beneficial for you to take some time and map how you'll use Project in your environment for the specific application area you work in. For example, if you work in an IT environment, it will be worthwhile to map how Project can support your IT projects and related processes. Regardless of whether you use a standard SDLC, you can determine how Project will support you through the requirements, design, develop, testing, and implementation stages of your projects. This can be said for all project types: product development, construction, facilities, operations, HR, marketing, finance, and so on. Mapping the use of a tool like Project to your project-management methodology and the type of projects you work on will increase your effectiveness in using the tool and also your overall efficiency as you move from on stage to another.

An Overview of the PM Process Groups

This is in no way meant to be a general project-management book that replaces your need to read and learn PMBOK or other project-management materials. An abundance of good material is available to choose from, so it won't be hard to expand your knowledge. Most major universities offer some form of project-management curriculum, plenty of organizations offer project-management training and materials, and a variety of books are on the market. This book is geared toward tying a tool—Project—into the necessary project-management concepts.

Let's quickly review the main project-management process groups and discuss how these groups map to using Project. Most project-management methodologies I've worked with and customized have had some type of initiating/planning stage followed by an execution/implementation stage and ending with a close-out stage. Phraseology may vary, subprocesses and techniques may vary, but at a high level, similarities usually exist. Let's start there.

PMBOK defines five project-management process groups:

- Initiating

- Planning

- Executing

- Monitoring and controlling

- Closing

Each of these main process groups breaks down into smaller, more detailed processes, which collectively make up the entire process. First, let's map these main groups and follow up with a more detailed focus on where to apply Project. We also need to consider how these groups interact, because they aren't linear in nature.

In Figure 2.1, you can see the overlap and circular relationship between planning, executing, and monitoring and controlling. One of the new features in PMBOK is a greater emphasis on how monitoring and controlling overlays the planning and executing stages, with partial overlap into initiating and closing.

FIGURE 2.1   Project-management process groups

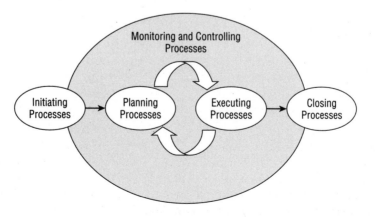

Recognize that the connection between planning and executing isn't a one-way link. When you finish formulating your plan in Project, and the work begins, you don't put aside the plan and forget about it: you use it to help manage change, track status, and take corrective action. It's up to the project manager to keep tabs on the "doing" part or the execution stage of a project, to incorporate new information into the plan to reflect the impact of changes and current status, and to communicate back to stakeholders. This is why monitoring and controlling overlaps planning and execution and is a big part of what a project manager does. And this is where Project can help you succeed.

At a very high level, Table 2.1 maps out where Project 2010 will be the most help as you manage individual projects.

TABLE 2.1 Where Project Is the Most Help

PM Stage	Project Usage Level	Comments
Initiation	Low	May help develop high-level order of magnitude estimates for schedule, scope, and cost.
Planning	High	Helps define, integrate, and communicate scope, time, cost, and resource plans. Some support for risk planning.
Executing	Med-High	Helps direct who does what when, in terms of execution. Provides the roadmap and clear path to the final deliverable or result.
Monitoring & controlling	High	Helps monitor and control change and measure the impact on scope, time, cost, and resources. Allows for effective variance analysis and decision-making for taking corrective action.
Closing	Low-Med	Useful for final variance analysis, lessons learned, developing future forecasting abilities, best practices, and benchmarking.

In the following section, I'll make a deeper assessment, showing precisely how Project will help you at each of the project-management stages. Note that we're solely looking at how Microsoft Project 2010 can be used as a standalone or desktop solution. If you're using Project in an enterprise solution, its usefulness will be significantly different. The Microsoft Office *Enterprise Project Management* (EPM) solution will be discussed in more detail in Chapter 3, "Enterprise Project Management and Other Key Considerations." EPM has much more robust usage in all areas of each project-management process group and includes portfolio project management. Regardless of whether you're using Project Standard or Project Professional in an EPM environment, it's important to understand its role with or without the complete EPM tool set.

Initiating Processes and Project Usage

PMBOK defines *initiating* as follows: "The Initiating Process Group consists of those processes performed to define a new project or a new phase of an existing project by obtaining authorization to start the project or phase."

The activities or work of the initiation process generally include these:

- Authorize a project (or phase) to begin.

- Identify the project manager.

- Describe the project goals/objectives.

- Define order-of-magnitude size estimates for scope, cost, duration, and resource effort.

- Identify high-risk items.

- Document these items in a project charter and preliminary scope statement.

It isn't hard to see that the initiating processes aren't the primary application for Project. Until a project manager is identified, there may not be anyone to put together a project plan. And often, the lines are blurred between portfolio management, initiation, and planning. For example, a portfolio-management process may include identifying a project manager prior to the beginning of the initiating processes; in other organizations, a project manager may not be identified until the planning process. (I'm not suggesting this as a best practice—ideally, the project manager should be identified as early as possible.)

But a key objective during initiating is to get some idea of the order of magnitude of the project size. Project can help by creating a high-level plan, perhaps with just key milestones at first, along with high-level estimates of major scope elements for cost, duration, and effort.

> Even if you're using Microsoft Word to capture your project charter, you can easily formulate a high-level plan in Project and effortlessly inject it into your project charter document. I'll show you how in Part 3 of this book, "Communicating and Reporting Essentials." This way, as you move from initiating to planning, you'll have a consistent tool and approach throughout the project life cycle.

Often, as you move from one stage of a project to another, there is no consistency or reference back to the initiation document and decisions. That is why it's a good idea to create a preliminary scope statement during initiation to help define the order of magnitude of the final result.

People are frequently overwhelmed at the prospect of having to plan an entire project—particularly if the project is likely to span months, let alone years. We've found that using traditional *rolling-wave planning* works very well to calm the nerves and produce a more effective plan. With this approach, you plan the detailed tasks and activities out as far as you can see on the horizon. In the project plan, leave placeholders for those future phases. Toward the end of each phase, plan for the next horizon. You'll learn more about planning in this manner and creating phases, tasks, and milestones in Chapter 5, "Creating and Entering the Work Breakdown Structure."

You must also consider the concept of *progressive elaboration*. Using this approach, you plan the details of what is in front of your immediate horizon—for example, the next phase—and create high-level placeholders for future phases. The high-level placeholders capture the order of magnitude of how long subsequent phases will last and possibly their approximate budget, without going into detail.

With rolling-wave planning and progressive elaboration, you can use Project to plan in as much or as little detail as required for the current project stage. You don't have to carry every detail in Project from the onset. (Don't confuse progressive elaboration with *scope creep* and *change requests*. These need to be managed differently, using other tools in Project such as baselines and variance-analysis tools. I'll cover these in Part 4, "Tracking Essentials.")

Also, as I'll discuss in part in Chapter 3, if you're working with the EPM suite of tools, aspects of Project Server are devoted heavily to the project initiation and selection process. After the appropriate project is chosen, Project (desktop or client) is then used to carry the work into its detailed initiation and planning activities.

🌐 Real World Scenario

Progressive Elaboration and Project Initiation

One client site I worked at used a gating process to move from one stage of a project to the next. We developed a complete Project template that mapped out the entire development process, including a project kick-off gateway. The kick-off gateway was part of the initiation process and included the development of a project charter, which was presented to the project review board before proceeding to a more in-depth proof-of-concept stage. The concept stage subsequently led to the more robust, detailed phases of the project. As it turned out, the completed template was much too large (number of line items) to carry in this first stage, so we created a subtemplate or template library that held the complete details for each stage.

The approach we took was to initiate the plan with a very high-level scheme outlining the order of magnitude for each phase. Just one or two key tasks and milestones captured the work, duration, and cost estimates. This plan was then included in the project charter and presented to the board for formal approval to move onto the proof-of-concept stage. If the project was approved, the details of the next phase were inserted into the project plan and presented at the next gateway meeting. As it moved through each gateway, the plan was progressively elaborated. The details for each phase were incorporated using the appropriate subtemplate.

Including the project-initiation activities in the template allowed the client to capture the work that was being performed to develop the project charter, which was robust in this case, and include it in the project pipeline. Keeping it at a high level and elaborating the details as the project moved through each stage made planning and using Project much more manageable and more efficient for the project managers.

Another significant benefit of this approach was that it maintained consistency throughout each stage of the project-management process. The same plan in Project was used in initiation, planning, executing, and closing, even if the project manager and the owner of the plan changed.

Table 2.2 outlines in more detail where Project may be useful in the initial stages of a project.

TABLE 2.2   Project Initiation and Project 2010

Initiating Activity	Project* Usage Level	Comments
Authorize project to begin	Low	Client and desktop aren't used, but other EPM tools can help.
Identify project manager	Low	No direct help.
Describe goals/objectives	Low	No direct help, although later Project may help with revisions or modifications.
Define order of magnitude for scope, duration, cost, and resource effort	High	An initial high-level plan can be developed in Project and inserted into the project charter.
Identify high-level risk items	Low	Not very helpful at this stage. (A complete risk-management tool set is available in EPM.)
Write project charter	Medium	Some inputs are possible from Project into the charter document.
Write preliminary scope statement	Low	No help other than some input from the high-level plan.

*Project as a standalone or desktop; other EPM tools will help with initiation.

Planning Processes and Project Usage

PMBOK defines *planning* as follows: "The Planning Process Group consists of those processes performed to establish the total scope of the effort, define and refine the objectives, and develop a course of action required to attain those objectives."

The activities of the planning process generally include the following:

- Define who will work on which parts of the project.
- Define a specific project budget and cost management approach.
- Describe the deliverables to be produced during the project.
- Document goals/objectives in a concise scope statement.
- Define completion criteria and owners for project deliverables.
- Define the scope of the project in a work breakdown structure (WBS).
- Define the series and relationship of tasks to complete for each deliverable.
- Define the duration and effort for each task.
- Document these items in a schedule.
- Identify and assess risks to the project, and define risk-response criteria.
- Define how the execution of the project will be monitored and controlled.

It becomes obvious when looking at the general activities of project planning that using Project is a natural fit. Project planning can be considered one of the core reasons for using Project 2010; Project is specifically designed for this purpose. Unlike other tools such as Word, which is great for word processing, and Excel, which is an excellent tool for number crunching and analysis, Project has very specific and effective tools to help you with most of the key planning activities.

In Chapter 1, "Project 2010 as an Enabling Tool for Project Managers," I discussed our proven, effective approach to learning Project; planning essentials are one of three core components. Planning is still done very poorly in many of the organizations I've worked with, and it generally has little to do with the tool.

⊕ Real World Scenario

Why Don't People Plan?

In most of the training classes I offer on project management or Microsoft Project, I ask the participants, "Why don't people plan?" Usually, I get responses like these:

- I don't have time.
- Around here, we don't get rewarded for plans; we get rewarded for results.
- I would like to, I just don't know where to start or how to do it.
- Everything changes or moves so fast. Why bother?
- I know the theory, but around here I never get a chance to exercise it.

Much of the problem stems from not understanding the true value of good project planning. You may get away with this approach once in a while, or perhaps you don't realize the benefits that good planning techniques bring to projects. Those who don't plan inevitably fall into a do it–fix it cycle, which always lead to inefficiencies, rework, false starts, do-overs, or outright project failure. Good planning results in high returns with respect to faster completion times, increased efficiencies in resource and cost management, and increased satisfaction—not just for the project customer but for everyone affected by the project.

My colleagues and I use the following rule of thumb to help motivate us to plan better: *For every minute you spend doing good project planning, you'll get five back during execution.* It's like giving someone a one-dollar bill and getting back a five-dollar bill. That makes it worth the time to learn good project-planning techniques.

Planning is critical to the success of any project, big or small, particularly because all projects involve doing something that is unique—something that has never been done before. Consider, too, that it's significantly more challenging to make changes to scope, the deeper into execution you get. So, planning involves more processes or subprocesses than initiation does. You don't need to conduct the same level of planning for all projects; the amount of planning should be commensurate with the scope and impact of the project. You can't skip critical planning steps like devising a scope statement, risk plan, WBS, and schedule, but they may not need the same detail.

It's also important to recognize that the primary output of the planning process is a project-management plan that consists of more than what you can produce in Project alone. Here are some elements you may include in a project-management plan:

- Scope statement
- Risk plan
- Scope and work breakdown structure (WBS)
- Schedule, activity sequencing, and critical path
- Cost and budget plan
- Resource plan and defined project team
- Change-management plan
- Other management plans such as quality, communications, purchases and acquisitions, and contracting

With these elements in mind, you can see that Project will be an enormous help. Most important, it's a highly effective tool for scope planning, documenting and managing the WBS, scheduling, activity sequencing, defining the critical path, cost and budget planning, and resource planning.

If you think of the core components of any project plan, they boil down to scope, time, and cost (resources), otherwise known as your *triple constraint.* I'll discuss the triple constraint in more detail in Chapter 3. For any project-management methodology, using Project to help in the planning stage is a no-brainer. The challenge is to ensure that you first understand good project-planning techniques and then understand how to apply them to Project.

One of the key things I've learned over the years is that not only is every project unique by definition, but every organization is unique as well. Every off-the-shelf solution needs some type of customization or tailoring at some level. You should develop planning processes that suit your project, your culture, and the needs of your stakeholders, whether with a tool like Project or the processes put forth in PMBOK. Luckily, both are flexible enough that they can be adapted to meet this challenge.

Many organizations fail because they either try to do too much too fast, which can lead to disastrous results; or they do too little, which doesn't add any significant results. As illustrated in Figure 2.2; this balancing act of implementing the right amount of process and technology with the project types and culture of an organization is tricky.

FIGURE 2.2   Balancing the process and technology with the unique needs of the project and organization

Process   vs.   Project Types
and Technology   and Culture

🌐 **Real World Scenario**

Too Much Too Fast—Not Always a Good Thing

I was working with a large financial institution's IT department in the early stages of implementing project management and using tools such as Project to help them start moving past the "just do it," ad hoc approach to getting things done. During this process, they went through a significant merger. Both of the merging IT departments were of a similar size, but the new IT organization had a highly defined and stringent project-management methodology—complete with very thick three-ring binders. When the directive came down that all IT projects were to follow this methodology, a culture clash resulted that ultimately brought most IT projects to a grinding halt on the side of the organization that had no methodology in place.

It seemed as though the "just do it" organization was trying to learn to run before learning how to walk (which can cause a lot of bruised knees and even broken legs). After many months of negotiations, power struggles, and compromises, the two sides came to an understanding that resulted in a more balanced approach to project management. Combining the best of both worlds, the solution allowed more flexibility based on type, size, and impact of a project. The more stringent requirements for each project-management process were phased in over time, coupled with the right level of training and support.

Although every project by definition is unique, the process of delivering and/or managing the project maybe be patterned after a proven approach. Project enables you to subsequently turn successful approaches and processes into reusable templates. For example, an IT organization may develop a template based on its SDLC methodology, or a pharmaceutical company by develop a template based on its drug-development methodology. The more mature an organization is with regard to project management, the more mature these templates and project-management processes become. I'll cover templates in Chapter 5.

Table 2.3 lists the key activities that happen during project planning and indicates how Project 2010 can help you.

TABLE 2.3   Planning Activities and Project 2010 Utilization

Planning Activity	Project 2010 Usage Level	Comments
Create scope statement	Low	May provide input with regard to scope, timing, and cost later.
Scope plan and WBS	High	Has powerful, easy-to-use features to help you plan, organize, and manage WBS elements.
Activity and schedule development	High	Provides strong functionality in creating and maintaining activities, project schedules, and networks.
Critical-path analysis	High	Based on the critical-path method, easily calculates, highlights, filters, or groups critical-path items and total slack.
Resource and staffing plan	High	Easily creates and defines resource assignments and load requirements for both human and non-human resources.
Cost and budget plan	High	Lets you plan and track costs and budgets with powerful and flexible tools.
Risk plan	Low to medium	No direct help initially. Can help with risk-response planning if the action or contingency plan requires adding items to WBS or if you need to assess risk to a schedule.
Change-management plan	Low (initially)	Won't help with creating a change-management plan but will play a significant role in managing changes to scope, time, and cost after a project begins.
Quality plan	Medium	Not the primary tool for defining a quality plan, but quality activities can be built into the WBS and project schedule and can become part of the quality plan.

TABLE 2.3   Planning Activities and Project 2010 Utilization *(continued)*

Planning Activity	Project 2010 Usage Level	Comments
Communications plan	Medium	Not the primary tool for defining a communications plan, but much communication is based on output from Project and can be incorporated into the plan.
Purchases and acquisitions plan	Medium to high	Can be used to identify resources and costs related to purchases and acquisitions and built into the WBS and resource pool. These can be filtered and used as the primary input for a P&A plan.
Contracting plan	Medium	Lets you map contracting requirements as part of the resource pool. The new feature, cost type resources, can be useful, depending on the contracted resource type.
Project control system	High	Can be a primary tool for project control to manage scope, time, and cost/resources. You can use the baselining tools, track actuals, and control variance and the impact of change.

Executing Processes and Project Usage

PMBOK defines *executing* as follows: "The Executing Process Group consist of those processes to complete the work defined in the project-management plan to satisfy the project specifications."

This stage is about executing the work defined in the WBS and coordinating the resources (including people) necessary to carry out the plan. These activities are application- or product-process specific, as opposed to the activities defined in the each project-management process group. I'll state the obvious: It's hard to execute against a plan if there is no plan.

I refer to organizations that move from idea to execution in 60 seconds flat as "just do it" organizations. Although you may get away with this approach once in a while, it isn't sustainable over time. I am fully aware that we live and work in an increasingly competitive environment with intense pressure to get results faster. But *faster* doesn't mean *poorly* or *the wrong way*. Besides, good project-management planning equals faster execution.

The activities involved during the execution phase include but aren't limited to these:

- Direct and manage the activities defined in the project-management plan.

- Acquire and develop a project team, and enhance the project team's performance.

- Communicate and distribute project information, such as progress and status, to project stakeholders.
- Perform quality assurance.
- Manage contracts and relationships with contracted resources.

From a project-management standpoint, if you have a good plan, good resources, and a good tool set, managing the execution process activities will be enjoyable. If you have a bad plan and the wrong resources, and you aren't using tools effectively, execution will be a painful experience.

In the executing stage of a project, you obtain a significant return on investment for the time you spent during the planning stage. But how much will Project help? Look at Table 2.4.

TABLE 2.4   Executing Activities and Project Usage

Executing Activity	Project Usage Level	Comments
Direct and manage activities.	High	Defines who does what when. Although Project won't perform the work, it will help you direct and manage the work to be performed.
Acquire a project team.	Medium	Helps communicate resource needs and obtain resources with the right skills and in the amounts required to successfully complete the project.
Develop the project team.	Low	Little help.
Communicate and distribute project information.	High	Provides easy-to-use, powerful communication and reporting tools.
Perform quality assurance.	Low to medium	Lets you plan QA activities into Project to show when they will occur and who will do them. QA activities are performed outside the tool.
Manage contracts and relationships.	Low to medium	Not used, with the exception of planning contracting activities. Managing relationships is enhanced with effective communication tools but requires strong interpersonal skills.

Considering that you spend a significant amount of time communicating and reporting during the execution stage of a project, a tool like Project 2010 can be an enormous help. I've heard estimates that project managers spend as much as 90 percent of their time communicating during this timeframe. You'd better do it well, or things can get out of control in a hurry.

It's also important during this stage that project managers spend a majority of their time managing the *project* and not the *project plan*. A well-developed project plan—with an effective use of the tool—lets you quickly visualize and report progress to stakeholders. A *poorly* designed plan—or ineffective use of the tool—results in you spending far too much time playing with the plan rather than effectively managing the project.

Let's look at the lines of communications that can exist between project stakeholders, using the following recombination formula:

Lines of communication = $n (n - 1) \div 2$

The letter *n* stands for the number of stakeholders involved in the project, including project team members, project customers (internal or external), project sponsors, resource managers, senior management, and so on. For example, if you had to communicate with only three project stakeholders, life would be pretty easy because you'd have only three lines of communication to manage. However, most projects have many more than that. Even on a relatively small project, you may have to communicate with as many as 10 stakeholders. That means you have 45 potential lines of communication, as illustrated in Figure 2.3.

FIGURE 2.3   Lines of communication

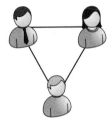

Three stakeholders = three lines of communication which is easy to manage.

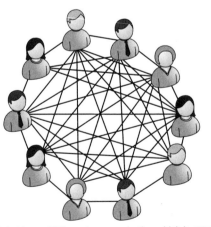

Ten stakeholders = 45 lines of communication which is more challenging to manage.

This example makes clear that effective communication is critical to your success as a project manager. That is why Part 3 of this book is dedicated entirely to this Project functionality, providing information about views, tables, filters, groups, and custom fields with stoplight reports, all geared toward the needs of various parties involved. I feel that it's the most under-utilized part of the software and can potentially provide some of the greatest return to you.

Monitoring and Controlling Processes and Project Usage

PMBOK defines *monitoring and controlling* as follows: "The Monitoring and Controlling Process Group consists of those processes required to track, review, and regulate the progress and performance of the project; identify any areas in which changes to the plan are required; and initiate the corresponding changes."

Activities in this process group may include the following:

- Monitoring and controlling project work
- Change management
- Scope verification and control
- Schedule control
- Cost control
- Quality control
- Project team management
- Performance and variance reporting
- Stakeholder management
- Risk monitoring and control
- Contract management

The key in this group is to ensure that project goals are met, by applying different techniques and using tools such as Project. I find it remarkable how many project managers don't use tools during this stage. This is a big part of the value that a good project manager can bring to the table; using a tool like Project will help significantly because it's designed specifically for this purpose. It has the built-in capabilities to set a baseline, track progress, measure the impact of change, report variances, and help you make better decisions about corrective action.

How many times have you created (or been on a team where the project manager created) a Gantt chart at the beginning stages of a project, only to put it aside after the project started? Project is much more than just a pretty Gantt chart; that's why I'll spend an entire section in this book exploring how you can use some of the key tools to help with monitoring and controlling.

Monitoring and controlling activities result in the need to use Project a number of different ways, including updating the project plan with actual data and revising it as required. Measuring project performance and reporting variances in scope, time (schedule), cost, and quality are all important factors in reaching your objectives on any project. Consider Table 2.5, which outlines where Project will be the most help during this stage of a project.

TABLE 2.5   Monitoring and Controlling Activities and Project Usage

Monitoring and Controlling Activity	Project Usage Level	Comments
Monitoring and controlling project work	High	Provides powerful tools to help track project work and compare actual vs. planned work.
Change management	High	Equipped with tools for variance reporting, to let you quickly assess the impact of change. Allows for what-if scenario planning.
Scope verification and control	High	Includes many WBS tools to effectively manage scope and support verification and control.
Schedule control	High	Provides flexible tools for managing schedule components and variances.
Cost control	High	Equipped with many effective tools to help you plan and control cost.
Quality control	Low to medium	Limited use, other than building quality activities into your plan and perhaps capturing quality issues in a text or note field.
Project team management	Medium	Helps provide direction in terms of who does what when. This element requires skills outside of Project.
Performance and variance reporting	High	Has many specific tools and reports for this purpose.
Stakeholder management	Medium	Helps with effective communications and managing expectations.
Risk monitoring and control	Medium	If a risk occurs, can communicate the impact on scope (new or changed WBS items), time, and cost.
Contract management	Low to medium	Not much help other than indicating the impact changes may have on the project plan.

Most people use Project to develop the major components of a project-management plan but fail to use it effectively for monitoring and controlling (or updating and tracking) purposes. If your project-management process requires a project plan in the planning stage, then why not apply the same principle to the execution and controlling stage?

At many client sites, project-management processes note the importance of project status reviews but fall short of clearly defining these steps. I suggest building the requirement into the process to set a baseline and then tracking actual data to compare what was planned to what is really taking place. Build project-review meetings into the process, and use Project to communicate performance and variance analysis. Standard tracking views can be customized and built directly into Project based on the key measures that are important to you.

Real World Scenario

Manage to the Plan: Updating and Tracking

I've developed templates for many different types of projects. The majority of them include custom views, fields, tables, filters, and groups to match the uniqueness of the project-management methodology being used. There is usually one template for planning, one (or more) for key stakeholder reports, and one for updating and tracking. Each view can be tailored to the processes and stakeholders you communicate with in each stage of your project life cycle. The notion is to enhance monitoring and controlling and to use Project to help achieve your goals. Many organizations I've worked with fall short in this respect, but they soon learn that managing to the plan and using effective tracking and updating techniques is a recipe for success.

Closing Processes and Project Usage

PMBOK defines *closing* as follows: "The Closing Process Group consists of those processes performed to finalize all activities across all project-management process groups to formally complete the project, phase or contractual obligations."

Activities in the process group usually involve the following:

- Tie up loose ends, and resolve outstanding issues.
- Prepare and submit final reports.
- Complete and close out contracting relationships.
- Finalize and archive project plans and records.
- Communicate final results to key project stakeholders.
- Capture and document lessons learned, and generate recommendations and best practices for future projects.
- Reward and recognize project team members and major contributors.

It's safe to say that of all the process groups in project management, this one is most often overlooked or bypassed. How often do you take the time to properly archive your files? More important, how often do you hold a lessons-learned event to capture what went well and what didn't? In my experience, very few organizations place value on implementing good closeout processes.

I believe one of the key activities during this stage of a project is to conduct a lessons-learned event. Here, you can capture important input from team members and other stakeholders and learn what you and your team did well and what can be done better next time.

You can then take that information and use it to generate best practices and recommendations for improvement.

Lessons-learned events should not involve personal and character attacks on project team members or other participants. They can focus on predefined topics specific to the project and an evaluation of the project-management process groups. For example, you can break down the lessons-learned event by phase or deliverables, facilitate the event, and obtain feedback based on the major components of the project. This may help with obtaining more organized feedback. If you're using standard methodology or a project template, you can use that as the basis to form a template for lessons-learned topics.

One easy-to-use tool is a plus/delta T structure, as shown in Figure 2.4.

FIGURE 2.4 Plus/Delta T structure for lessons learned

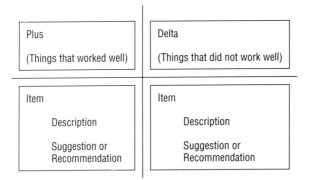

🌐 Real World Scenario

Lessons-Learned Categories Should Include Project Usage

It's sometimes appropriate to categorize your plus/delta T structures into various major topics. The topics you choose depend on the nature of your work. For example, while working with a large pharmaceutical company, we held a lessons-learned off-site event with the core project team. In advance of the meeting, we defined various workgroups based on the specific application area for each of the team members involved. We categorized the topics into major components, such as clinical, manufacturing (CMC), regulatory, quality, and so on. We also included a major category for project management and the use of Microsoft Project. Each workgroup mapped out their respective plus/delta and presented their best practice suggestions and recommendations for improvement. Providing direction enabled the groups to keep the sessions nonpersonal, and the feedback was remarkable.

I've used this approach with other types of projects. For an IT project, we broke the major categories into requirements, design, develop, testing, QA, and implementation or rollout. Whatever your project, it's important to include an evaluation of the project-management function; I suggest you include the use of tools, particularly Project.

You can use the plus/delta T approach in a group environment or in one-on-one meetings. The idea is to gather good-quality, nonpersonal input. Part of your overall enterprise project-management system should be a knowledge base for capturing lessons learned, best practices, and recommendations for improvement.

Considering the activities involved in closing out projects, it's obvious that Project will play a more limited role in this stage. Project is useful for illustrating key items and providing evidence and a record of where things went well or not so well. Table 2.6 lists where Project can be useful during closing activities.

TABLE 2.6   Closing Activities and Project Usage

Closing Activity	Project Usage Level	Comments
Resolve outstanding issues	Low to medium	May provide some direction into where issues are occurring or if they're related to the schedule
Prepare and submit final reports.	High	Provides output for key project reports
Close out contracting relationships.	Low	No help other than to illustrate when this activity should occur
Finalize and archive plans and records.	Low	Is one of the many files archived
Communicate final results.	Medium	Provides significant input
Document lessons learned.	Low to medium	May provide input for some of the items discussed
Reward and recognize team members.	Low	No direct help

Closing projects effectively is important, but this stage is often undervalued or overlooked by project managers and organizations. If you take the time to capture important information, suggestions for best practices, benchmarks, and recommendations for improvement at the end of each project, the return on your investment will be significant. You can avoid reinventing the wheel and repeating mistakes, and your projects can gain from efficiencies learned from others.

It's difficult for project managers to take the time for these types of activities; they're usually stressed from starting other projects or working on more than one project at a time. And if the organization doesn't value or support closing processes, including lessons-learned events, there is little chance that proper closing activities will be conducted. But without proper closing processes in place, valuable historical information will be lost and therefore won't benefit future projects.

Summary

In this chapter, we looked at how to apply Project during the five key project-management process groups defined in PMBOK. I provided a brief overview of each of the process group and their corresponding activities and key deliverables. Of the five process groups, Project plays a significant role in planning, executing, and monitoring and controlling; it plays a much more limited role in initiation and closing. As a result, it's easy to understand our approach to learning Project based on the three core modules of planning, communicating (the biggest role for a project manager), and tracking and analyzing (monitoring and controlling processes).

Analyzing each project group in more detail, I demonstrated whether Project usage is low, medium, or high. You learned that Project's use depends on the activity or output required for each process.

This book focuses on Project Standard and the client portion of Project in an EPM environment. You get a completely different picture if you consider Project Professional. Most of the activities that Project 2010 doesn't support as a standalone tool can be handled by the functionality you gain in an EPM environment. We'll discuss what EPM is all about in the next chapter.

Key Terms

closing

Enterprise Project Management (EPM)

executing

initiating

monitoring and controlling

planning

process groups

software development life cycle (SDLC)

Chapter

3

Overview of Enterprise Project Management

IN THIS CHAPTER, YOU'LL LEARN ABOUT THE FOLLOWING:

- ✓ Understanding Enterprise Project Management (EPM)
- ✓ Comparing Project Standard with Project Professional
- ✓ Mapping EPM to the PMBOK

Having a clear understanding of when to use Project in a desktop environment versus an enterprise, shared database environment is important. This chapter covers how Project fits into the Enterprise Project Management (EPM) puzzle and when to implement a solution like EPM in your organization. It also addresses the difference between Project Standard and Project Professional.

What Is EPM?

Because two versions of Project are available—one that works in an EPM environment (Project Professional) and one that doesn't (Project Standard)—it's important to understand the difference. Therefore, you need to have at least a brief understanding of what EPM is all about.

You may want to consider an investment in Project Professional even if you don't plan to implement an EPM solution. Here is a synopsis of the key features you gain by obtaining Project Professional instead of Project Standard:

Team Planner View   Lets you manage the right mix of people and workloads in a visual and intuitive manner. Click and drag tasks to resources for easy assignments and resource management. If you need to plan and manage resources on projects, you'll find this view to be invaluable.

Direct Project to SharePoint Synchronization   Lets you synchronize your tasks to SharePoint Foundation 2010 or SharePoint Server 2010 directly from Project and receive updates from team members from SharePoint back into Project.

Inactive Tasks Function   Lets you render a task inactive without deleting it from the plan. You can conduct what-if analyses or see the impact on the timeline, resource work, or cost if a task or group of tasks were no longer included, with the ability to turn them back on at any time.

Enterprise Project Management Overview

EPM is what Microsoft calls its complete project-management solution set. Obviously, the phrase *Enterprise Project Management* was in play long before Microsoft decided to use it to describe and market its project-management tool set, so it may have different meanings to different organizations. This book refers to EPM in the same context that Microsoft does. Keep in mind that this chapter isn't meant to be an in-depth technical analysis or even a how-to discussion of EPM, but rather a brief overview to provide you with direction regarding what EPM is about and when it makes sense to use it.

The Microsoft EPM solution is essentially a project and portfolio management (PPM) platform, which organizations across a broad range of industries can use to automate primary PPM processes with a variety of tools and configurations. The Microsoft EPM solution components help organizations accomplish the following:

Demand Management   Capture all project requests in a centralized system, and have those requests governed by a workflow process

Portfolio Selection and Analytics   Prioritize and select project portfolios that align with business strategy.

Resource Management   Manage resources across the organization.

Schedule Management   Create simple and complex project schedules.

Time and Task Management   Collect task status updates from resources.

Team Collaboration   Work on a SharePoint platform for team site creation, including issue and risk management.

Business Intelligence and Reporting   Gain visibility across all projects, portfolios, and programs.

This book focuses primarily on how to use Microsoft Project 2010 (the client), which is a key component of the EPM solution for schedule management. Most of the concepts and techniques described in this book apply to using Project, whether you use it with or without the EPM solution. EPM brings together client, server, and web-based technology to give you everything you need to manage organization-wide projects. With that in mind, let's explore the primary components of the EPM solution.

The core products of the Microsoft Project 2010 EPM solution set consist of the following:

- Microsoft Project Professional 2010
- Microsoft Project Server 2010
- Microsoft Project Web App (PWA) 2010

One major consideration when deploying an EPM solution, as opposed to Project for the desktop, is that the system requires more consideration for stakeholders other than project managers. These stakeholders most likely include executive and senior managers, functional (resource) managers, portfolio managers, project managers, team members, and potentially even contractors and vendors. For these roles to be effective within the EPM system, it's vital to have well-defined project-management processes to ensure that the EPM system is optimized and tailored for each role. You also need effective project- and portfolio-management processes, particularly if you're using the Demand Management and Portfolio Selection components of the system. That being said, a significant amount of time and resources are needed to ensure the proper design, configuration, and rollout of an EPM solution. EPM is much more than simply installing a desktop solution. Consider Figure 3.1, which highlights the important components and application layers for an EPM solution.

FIGURE 3.1   EPM 2010 solution architecture

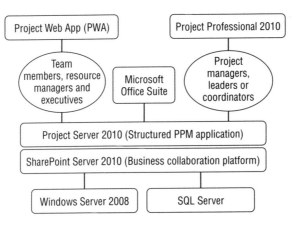

Note: Project Server 2010 runs as a service application to
SharePoint Server 2010.

Project Professional 2010 is the primary scheduling tool that project managers use to build
and manage project plans; but PWA, accessed with Internet Explorer as a web application, is
capable of editing project schedules with an interface similar to that of Project Professional.
Senior management, resource managers, team members, and other stakeholders can use PWA
to view and communicate project information in various ways.

As I pointed out in Chapter 2, Project 2010 is an enabling tool for project managers.
Project as a standalone product comes up short in key areas of the project life cycle. However,
in an EPM environment, you're equipped with tools to help manage the entire life of a project
from initiation to closing in a more robust manner.

Enterprise project-management features are based on a three-tiered architecture. The
client tier is provided by Project Professional 2010 and Project Web App, which uses
Internet Explorer to connect to Project Server 2010. The middle tier of the architecture is
provided by Project Server 2010 running on SharePoint Server 2010. The database tier of
the solution is provided by Microsoft SQL Server. The total EPM solution includes functionality to support end-to-end PPM and collaboration among all project stakeholders.

Enterprise Standards and Controls

One advantage of using EPM is the ability to establish enterprise standards and controls
around your project-management processes and the way the system is used. The system has
the flexibility and power to control who gets to see what type of project information and also
what they can do with that information. You can also customize the entire environment in
which these various roles participate in the PPM system. Demand management from project
initiation through customized business-strategy priorities and portfolio selection based on
cost or resource constraints allows simulation of enterprise process standards. Enterprise-level

project and resource information creates standard and consistent views and reports. Add custom fields, complete with formulas, look-up tables and graphical indicators, filters, groups, and tables, and you can see how much value a properly configured EPM system can bring to an organization.

EPM standards and controls are typically maintained by an EPM administrator. This person may come from the project management office (PMO), group, or department and works closely with the IT department to configure the system to meet the organization's requirements. In an EPM environment, when you see a component identified as an enterprise component (such as an enterprise Gantt chart), that means end users, including project managers, can't change or edit that component. Only the EPM administrator usually has permission to modify enterprise components. Figure 3.2 displays the various EPM administrative functions that are maintained by a few individuals with the EPM administrator role. This role isn't always provided by IT. Often it's a shared role, usually with a project-management function such as a PMO or related group.

FIGURE 3.2   EPM administrative functions

Security	Enterprise Data	Database Administration	Look and Feel
Manage Users	Enterprise Custom Fields and Lookup Tables	Delete Enterprise Objects	Manage Views
Manage Groups	Enterprise Global	Force Check-in Enterprise Objects	Grouping Formats
Manage Categories	Enterprise Calendars	Daily Schedule Backup	Gantt Chart Formats
Manage Security Templates	Resource Center	Administrative Backup	Quick Launch
Project Web Access Permissions	About Project Server	Administrative Restore	
Manage Delegates		OLAP Database Management	

Time and Task Management	Queue	Operational Policies	Workflow and Project Detail Pages
Fiscal Periods	Manage Queue Jobs	Alerts and Reminders	Enterprise Project Types
Time Reporting Periods	Queue Settings	Additional Server Settings	Workflow Phases
Timesheet Adjustment		Server Side Event Handlers	Workflow Stages
Line Classifications		Active Directory Resource Pool Synchronization	Change or Restart Workflows
Timesheet Settings and Defaults		Project Sites	Project Detail Pages
Administrative Time		Project Site Provisioning Settings	Project Workflow Settings
Task Settings and Display		Bulk Update Project Sites	
Close Tasks to Update			

The nice thing about using the enterprise functionality is that the system automatically pushes out these standards to the end-user community. So, if the administrator creates a project-level status indicator that is new to the system, the next time a project manager logs on, they will automatically inherit that and any other new enterprise functionality that has been created.

Even though enterprise standards and controls are managed by an EPM administrator and can't be changed by project managers, you can create local changes within your own project plans to meet your own unique needs. For example, if a stakeholder would like a milestone report in green, and that report isn't part of the enterprise standard, you can create a green milestone report that resides within your plan and that doesn't affect anyone else's. This ability is referred to as *local functionality*. It gives an organization and a project manager the best of both worlds. You can impose enterprise standards where needed through Project Server, yet allow project managers to create local components such as views, tables, fields, groups, filters, reports, and even local resources that aren't part of an enterprise resource pool.

EPM as a Central Repository for Resources and Projects

Sharing resources effectively—across projects and across an organization—has always been a challenge. Developing and implementing easy-to-use and cost-effective systems to support this has historically been elusive. EPM goes a long way toward solving this problem.

Enterprise Resource Capabilities

One important consideration for moving to an EPM solution is the need to share and track resources across projects and across a department or organization. You may be interested in comparing capacity versus demand or planned work versus actual work, not for just one project but across all projects, within one department or across many. If so, consider moving to an EPM solution. This is one of the primary reasons to switch to EPM.

Microsoft's EPM solution has tools you can use to define named or generic resources and associate them with the appropriate permissions and roles. Depending on your role, you can have a completely different experience and set of permissions to access the system. For example, a group of senior managers may log on and see high-level dashboard views with sensitive financial information; team members may log on and see detailed tasks that they have been assigned, with no financial information. After the enterprise resource pool is set up, as new projects are created, project managers build their project teams by using powerful match-and-replace tools for generic skills for named resources, as shown in Figure 3.3.

Prior to selecting resources, you can view resource availability directly from the team builder tool. In the Resource Center, you can view not only availability but also the tasks resources have been assigned across the enterprise. In Figure 3.4, you can see an example of the View Assignments area.

You can also dynamically analyze one or more resources to see what their respective availability profiles look like, as shown in Figure 3.5.

The EPM solutions effectively allow you to consolidate and centralize resource information, which can be easily tailored to custom requirements pertaining to roles, skills, locations, organizational structure, permissions, and so on.

Team members and task updaters can provide updates via PWA and Project Server for all types of work, project and non-project, in a single view. Figure 3.6 shows the interface for task and timesheet communication and updating.

FIGURE 3.3   Building a team from enterprise resources

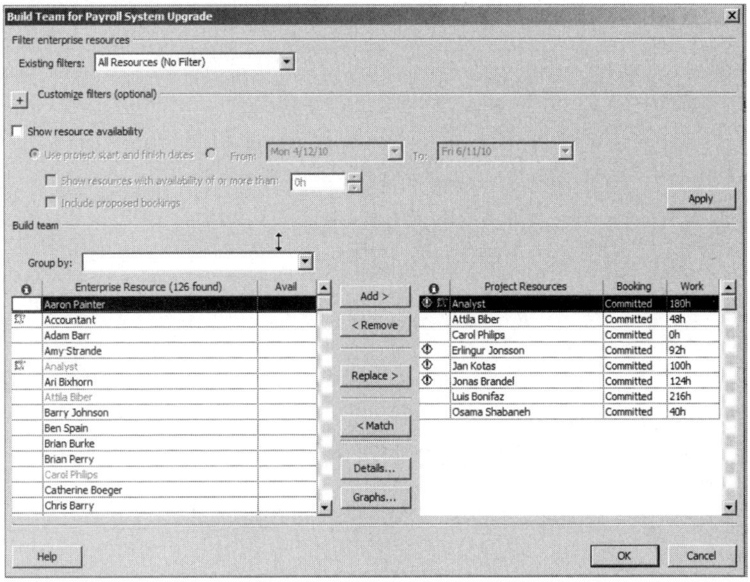

FIGURE 3.4   Resource assignments view

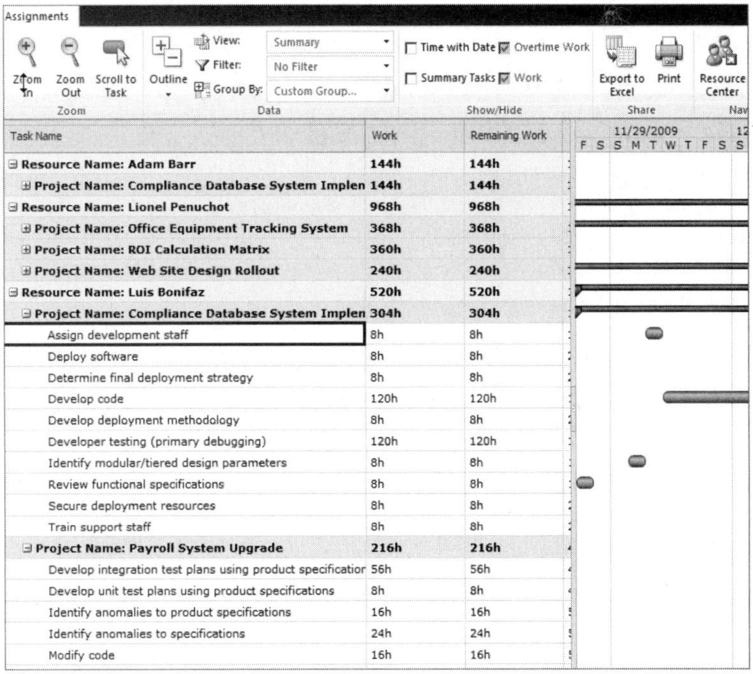

FIGURE 3.5   Viewing resource availability

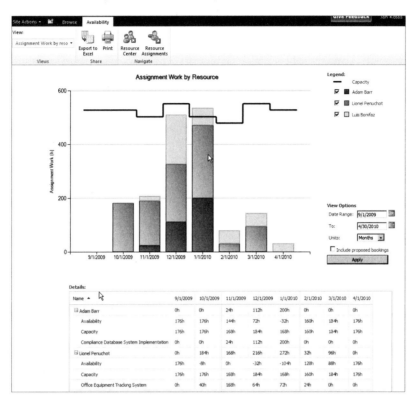

FIGURE 3.6   Timesheets view in Project Server

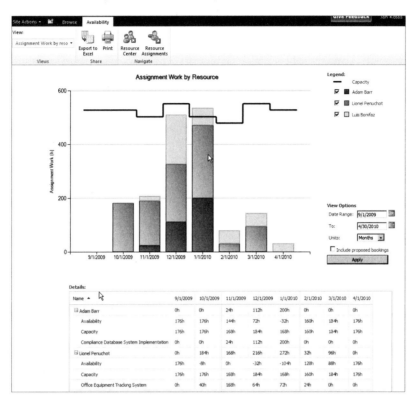

Central Repository for Projects

Another main reason to implement an EPM solution is to establish and maintain a central repository for all projects across an organization. You can easily imagine how having many project managers saving many project plans on desktops or all over the network can get out of control. When project managers use Project for the desktop, they save their plans as .mpp files on their hard disk, in personal folders, or in a shared network. It's very easy to create islands of project information or disparate data that floats around an organization with no easy way to access it, communicate it, or create meaningful reports.

Project Server solves these problems by allowing all projects to be stored in one place with easy and effective access through powerful collaboration views via PWA or directly from within Project Professional. By combining that accessibility with the ability to control who gets to see what projects based on their role, Project Server provides a robust solution to housing the portfolio of your projects in a way that makes sense for your organization. You can tailor the system to group projects by owner, strategic goal, project type, and so on with project-level status indicators for such things as schedule, budget, business, technical, or any other indicator you require. As mentioned earlier, these indicators can be created using formulas to automate color changes; or they can be kept manual, allowing project managers to change the indicators based on their perception. Figure 3.7 is an example of what this may look like in the Project Center of Project Server.

Creating a central repository for projects in an EPM environment isn't the same as creating a central repository in a shared folder or directory on a network. When you use Project Server, the project information is stored in a common SQL Server database. This gives you more effective access to project information while providing the ability to cross-reference data.

FIGURE 3.7 Project Center view with status indicators

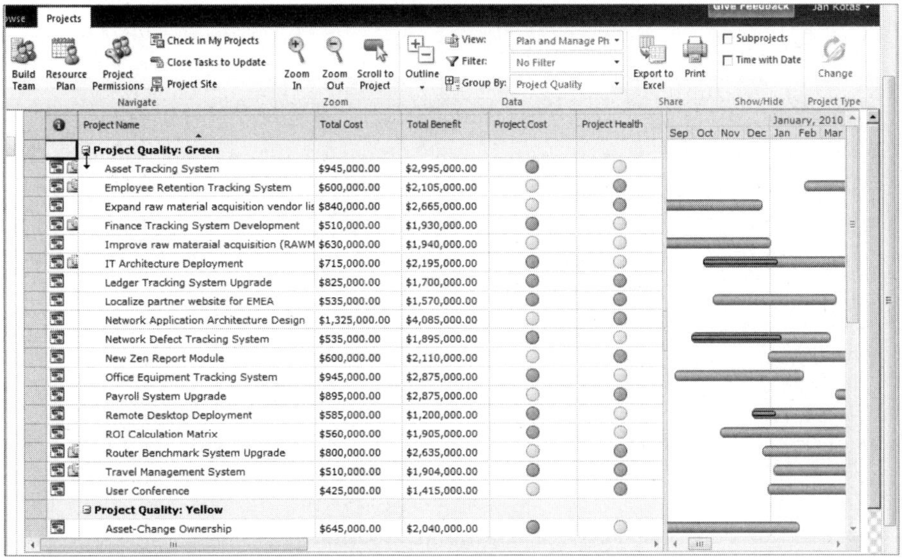

> ### ⊕ Real World Scenario
>
> #### Using EPM for Just Projects, Not Resources
>
> One client needed to publish project plans without resources or assignments. The primary goal was to establish dashboard views for milestones across projects for executives while providing the rest of the organization access to various levels of project details. After the projects were stored in the Project Server database, we integrated that data with the client's resource-modeling system to apply various resource-modeling algorithms and calculate resource budgeting needs for a specific time period. Project Server proved to be the most efficient system to perform this data consolidation in a common database.
>
> In this situation, without loading up resource assignments, we were able to customize the EPM views and reports to meet the needs of all the stakeholders and create quick and easy access, in real time, to important project information, complete with colorful status indicators and benchmarks. An EPM solution can provide significant value even without taking advantage of assigning enterprise resources.

When to Consider EPM

Project for the desktop without EPM allows for some sharing of resources and consolidation of projects. For example, you can create a master plan with inserted projects (.mpp files); after it's established, you can view the details of all the source plans. Furthermore, every time you open the master plan, it displays any updated information from the source plans. You can even update the source plans from the master plan, providing a two-way dynamic link. Also, a separate file with just the resources loaded can be used as your resource pool to share resources across projects. Consider Figure 3.8.

However, this solution has some serious limitations. First, everyone who accesses the master, consolidated plan needs to have a license and understanding of how to use Project. Second, it isn't a multiuser system, so it limits how many people can access the data at the same time, even though more than one person can open data in read-only mode. Finally, it's only a good solution for a small group of projects and a small group of users. This scenario will become uncontrollable if the number of users and projects reaches any real size. It isn't uncommon for people to get locked out of their own plans and have information change without their knowledge. Furthermore, as the data grows (particularly resource assignments), the master and resource files expand significantly, which eventually causes performance issues.

Given the relatively low cost of implementing Microsoft's EPM solution versus its value, it doesn't take much in terms of the strategic value of the projects your organization needs to manage and deliver before you should start considering adopting EPM or a similar solution. It's difficult to define a threshold in terms of processes, collaboration benefits, portfolio management, or the number of projects or resources involved, because it varies from one organization to another. In general, if you have more than 10 projects with more than 25 resources, you should consider EPM. But I've implemented an EPM solution for a single project—in that case, a program that resulted in a new business venture. That single project was so strategically significant, and had so many subprojects and resources involved, that the client benefited greatly from installing and configuring an instance of EPM.

FIGURE 3.8   Using the desktop to share resources and projects

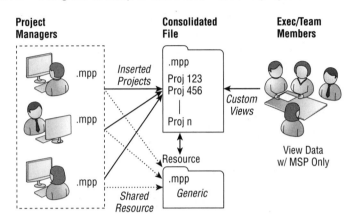

The following list outlines some of the primary considerations of whether to move to EPM:

- Multiple projects need to be stored in a central repository.

- Resources are across projects, or your organization has a centrally located resource pool.

- You need to make better assignment decisions based on skills and availability.

- Project information needs to be accessed without using Microsoft Project.

- Executives, senior management, team members, resource or functional managers, contractors, and vendors need role- and permission-based interaction with project information.

- You need to provide access key project information, such as dashboard views for better insight and control.

- Team members need permission to provide updates and input into tasks on a project plan.

- The organization needs to make better decisions about resource needs for capacity planning and availability.

- You need a central collaboration and communication point for all project stakeholders.

- Project information must be integrated with other corporate databases.

- Portfolio management must be integrated with project management.

It may be that only one of these considerations drives your decision to move to EPM, or it may be a combination of these and others.

🌐 Real World Scenario

Scale Down or Scale Up—It Doesn't Take Much to Get Started

Given that implementing an EPM solution is relatively cost effective, it may not take much to tip you into implementing a scaled-down version. One client I worked with had an immediate need to integrate project task and schedule information, but not resource assignments, with another database application. That requirement alone made the case for moving projects into an EPM solution.

The client's primary rationale for installing Project Server was to make it easier to access project information in SQL. When end users were able to access the information with PWA, the use of other tools and features began to increase.

Understanding Roles within EPM

Access to both functions and data in Project Server is governed by roles. Each role has associated permissions that let you view project information (what you can see) and interact with project information (what you can do). This section describes the typical roles within an EPM environment.

Executives and EPM

Executives and senior management play a significant role in any EPM solution. Because the solution can easily provide consolidated and centralized access to enterprise-wide project information, EPM can add a great deal of value for the executive stakeholder group. EPM is customizable, and you can configure a variety of views to create big-picture or dashboard reports complete with pivot tables, graphs, and other performance indicators.

Executives have easy access to resource information to allow comparisons of such things as capacity versus planned versus actual. Because you can control enterprise-level settings, you can also ensure that strategic goals are met and enterprise standards are followed. Figure 3.9 shows an executive dashboard view of performance indicators and other project information.

Resource or Functional Managers and EPM

With an EPM solution in place, resource managers can access resource information across a department or for an individual resource. They can use PWA to actively participate in the resource planning process by changing or replacing resource assignments or matching generic resources with named resources. All of this can be accomplished without ever opening Microsoft Project. Figure 3.10 shows how this is done with PWA.

FIGURE 3.9   Executive performance indicator dashboard view

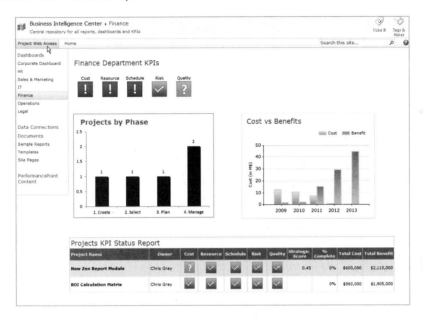

FIGURE 3.10   Editing resource assignments with PWA

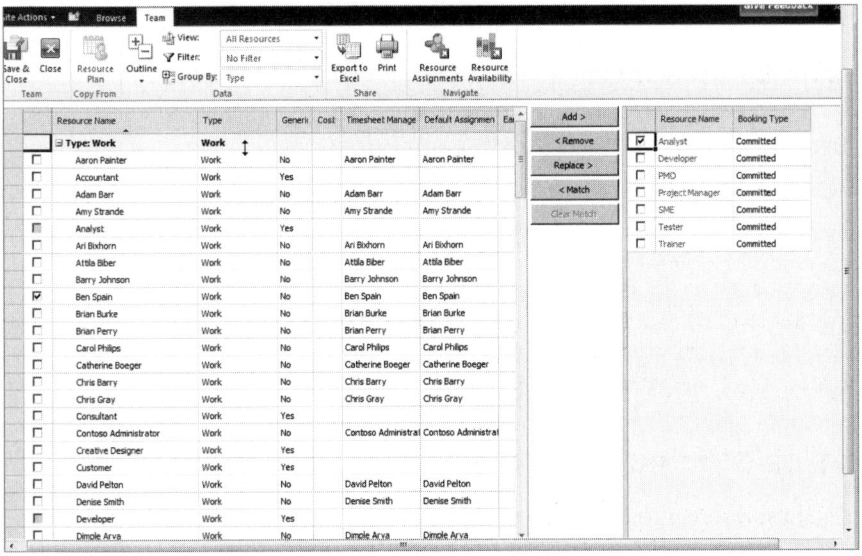

Team Members and EPM

Team members can access project information in real time whenever they need to. They can view their respective task assignments or see the entire project. Team members can be assigned a set of permissions defining what they can see and what they can do with the information when they see it. Because projects can also have project workspace SharePoint sites, communication and collaboration become a natural part of working on a project.

One benefit of using Project is that team members can log on and update task information for such things as percentage complete, hours worked, hours remaining, actual start and end dates, and proposed new dates. In Project Server 2010, team members have significantly more ability to interact with task information, including completing and submitting timesheets for both project and non-project work. Figure 3.11 shows the interface that team members typically use for task updates.

FIGURE 3.11 Task update page

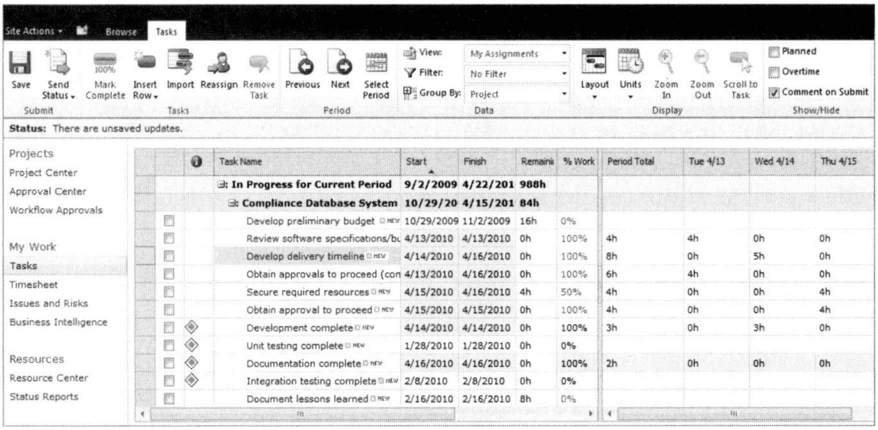

Project Managers and EPM

Project managers continue to use Project Professional to create plans, except that instead of saving plans as .mpp files, they publish plans to Project Server, where they reside in the Project Server database. The nice thing about using Project Server is that there is a two-step process for saving and publishing. If you simply save the project plan, it resides in a separate draft database and isn't available for PWA users to view. After you publish the plan, the project information makes itself available for general viewing through the various PWA views based on the roles and permissions of the end user community.

Another important difference in using Project Professional is the way project plans are maintained. After the plan is published with resource assignments, team members can log on to Project Server and update their tasks for status, including percent complete, hours worked, and remaining hours or actual start and finish dates. These updated tasks are then routed back to project manager for review and approval. You can preview the impact of updates before accepting them into your plan. Figure 3.12 shows Project Server's preview function.

🌐 Real World Scenario

Is It the Solution or the Culture?

I've worked on implementing custom EPM solutions for many types of organizations. The most successful solutions foster a culture that provides both top-down and bottom-up support and feedback on using the system at all levels.

One client installed EPM and called us in after the fact to provide training. We found that the culture didn't foster the support of team members to provide updates. They weren't held accountable; nor did all senior managers buy in and encourage team members to provide updates. Due to the lack of cultural support or incentive for team members to provide input, the system was failing.

Training was only part of the solution. We needed to clearly communicate the problem and obtain buy-in and support at all levels of the organization. In this case, it took significant effort to change the culture and behavior, including adding to each user's quarterly objectives the requirement to use the system. The point is that even the best EPM system can fail if the culture doesn't support it or if the culture isn't set up for success.

FIGURE 3.12   Previewing updates before acceptance

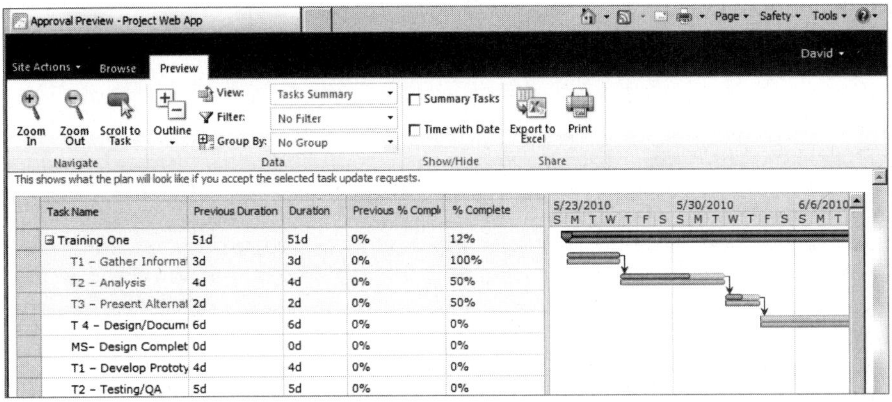

After the project plan is approved, it's automatically updated based on the information received from the team members. The project manager can be given the ability to modify the updates and make any necessary adjustments.

The first and most important element in ensuring success with an EPM implementation is to make sure good project plans are published to the server. For this to happen, project managers must be proficient in the use of good scheduling practices and how to use Project. So, whether you're switching to EPM, using Project for the desktop, or using Project in conjunction with some other solution, the contents of this book still apply and are essential to learn.

Portfolio Managers and EPM

Portfolio managers guide the process of comparing proposals against business needs, financial constraints, and other deciding factors. You can use EPM to set up project-proposal templates, configure workflow phases and stages, and set up and perform portfolio analyses using business drivers, cost constraints, and resource constraints. Using Project Server 2010 what-if analysis capabilities, portfolio analysts can easily model different scenarios by refining resource or cost constraints or by forcing projects into or out of the portfolio. Figure 3.13 shows a portfolio of projects with cost constraints compared to budget and what it might look like if some projects were forced out of the portfolio.

FIGURE 3.13   Selected and unselected projects analyzed

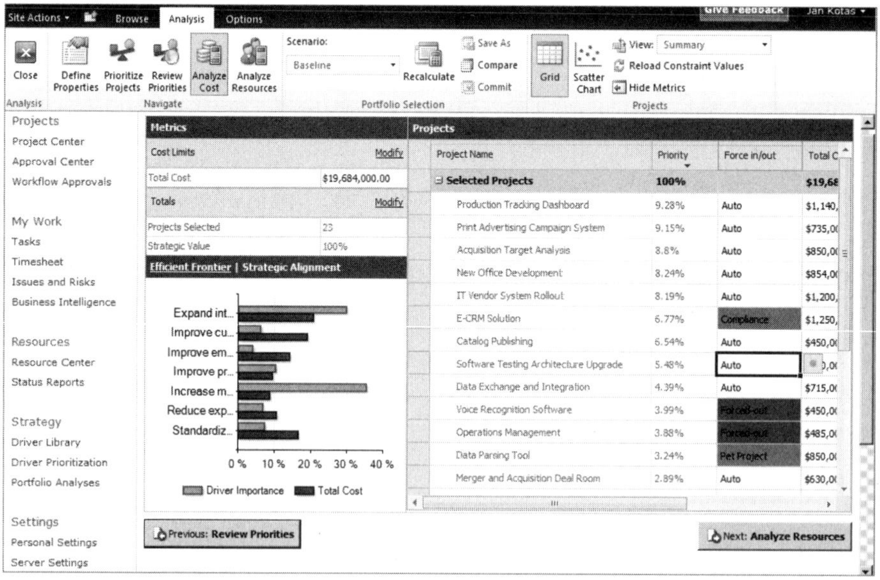

Project Server includes a robust governance and workflow tool to help guide the portfolio- and project-management processes, including creating, selecting, planning, and managing projects. Figure 3.14 shows the high-level governance that can be followed.

FIGURE 3.14   Project Server governance stages and workflow

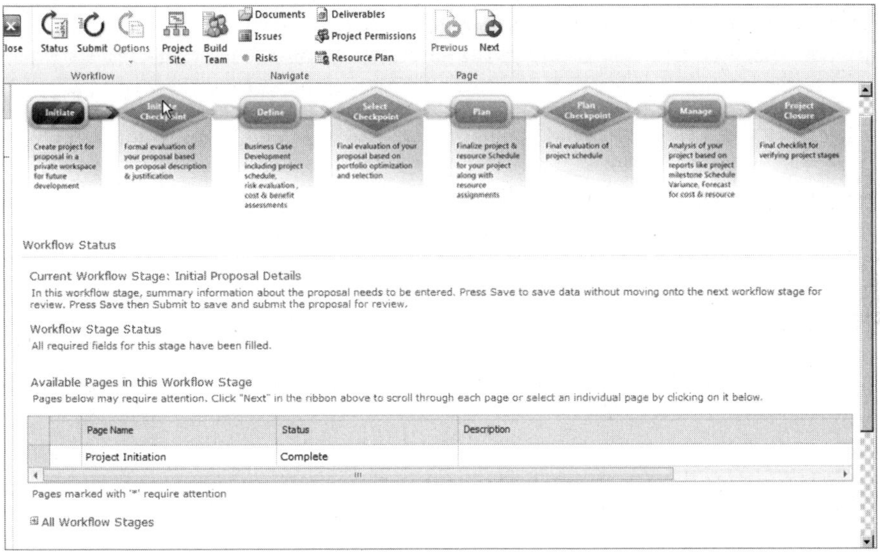

Mapping EPM to PMBOK

If you consider the complete EPM solution, then you cover the gamut in terms of supporting the project-management process groups and knowledge areas put forth by *A Guide to the Project Management Body of Knowledge*, Fourth Edition (PMBOK). Although portfolio management falls outside of the project-management process groups, with some overlap or blurred lines particularly around initiation, it's still a vital concern to organizations and the Project Management Institute (PMI). Consider Table 3.1.

TABLE 3.1   EPM Mapping to PMBOK and PPM

Portfolio- and Project-Management Process Groups	EPM
Strategic valuation	Strong
Prioritization	Strong
Selection	Strong
Initiating processes	Strong
Planning processes	Strong
Executing processes	Strong

TABLE 3.1   EPM Mapping to PMBOK and PPM *(continued)*

Portfolio- and Project-Management Process Groups	EPM
Monitoring and controlling processes	Strong
Closing processes	Strong

The portfolio-management processes of defining strategic value, prioritizing, and selecting projects are highly supported by Project Server. All five stages of the project process groups are also highly supported when Project is used in conjunction with Project Server. With all the collaborative tools (document management, issue tracking, risk management, and other customizable components), the full EPM suite is, in effect, a total project- and portfolio-management solution.

Summary

In this chapter, you learned the key components of an EPM solution, which includes connecting Microsoft Project Professional to Project Server. This allows non–project managers to connect to, view, and interact with data using a thin client called Project Web App. Access is based on roles and assigned permissions. Team members, portfolio managers, executives, resource managers, and others can all log on using Internet Explorer to access project data.

You learned when it's appropriate to consider implementing an EPM-type solution. Items discussed included capturing all requested proposals and moving them through a workflow process, consolidating multiple projects in a central repository, accessing and sharing resources across projects and the organization, automating the updating process, and providing timely access to project information in a format suitable for the project audience.

EPM also supports complete portfolio-type activities, such as tying in to strategic drivers, prioritizing projects, and selecting the optimal project portfolio. You saw how the EPM solution maps to the PMBOK and concluded that it does highly support all of the major project portfolio process groups. The lines between portfolio project management and individual project management are often blurred, but the EPM solution provides a true cradle-to-grave solution for project management.

I also hope you learned from this chapter that regardless of whether you're using Project for the desktop or in an EPM environment, you need to know the concepts in this book to build effective project plans. Remember, garbage into the EPM system results in garbage out.

Chapter

4

Getting Started and Setting Up the Microsoft Project Environment

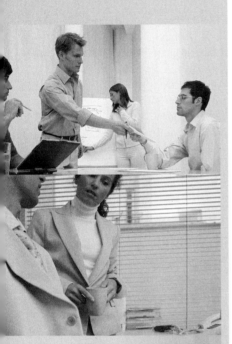

IN THIS CHAPTER, YOU'LL LEARN ABOUT THE FOLLOWING:

- ✓ Moving around default Microsoft Project views and using the ribbon

- ✓ Using the Project 2010 backstage and templates, importing plans from Excel, and opening plans from older versions

- ✓ Understanding and defining key option settings

- ✓ Understanding, creating, and assigning calendars at the project, task, or resource level

- ✓ Defining the project start or finish date and other key project information

- ✓ Formatting current-date and start-date gridlines

- ✓ Saving MPP files vs. publishing plans to the server

In this chapter, you'll learn about the new look and feel Microsoft Project 2010 has to offer, starting from the new Timeline view, the ribbon, and the improved interface, all of which have dramatically enhanced how you see and work with your project schedules. You'll see how the ribbon is organized to facilitate more efficient scheduling activities.

In this chapter, I'll also focus on the key settings and tools that are unique to Project 2010 and that help you get up and running fast—and in the right way. Often, Project users accept the defaults, not realizing that this isn't how they want the tool to operate. Understanding some important option settings before you start planning will go a long way toward helping you use Project more effectively.

Getting Started, and Moving Around Project

In these sections, we'll explore the basics of the Project 2010 environment, using the ribbon and moving around the default Gantt Chart with Timeline view. You'll see how to set up Project so you can easily change from one view to another. You'll also look at how to get started quickly from predefined templates, creating your own templates and taking advantage of powerful planning tools.

The default view for this version of Project combines the more traditional Gantt Chart view with the new Timeline view, as illustrated in Figure 4.1.

Quick view switching and zoom: Quickly switches to another view or zooms the timescale in or out. The Timeline view is displayed by default above other views but can be easily turned on or off. It's basically a concise overview of the entire schedule. The Gantt chart, named after Henry Gantt, who popularized this chart for planning in the early part of the 20th century, is one of the most widely used views in project management today. Therefore, it's important to master working and communicating with this view. We'll also explore how to use the other views and create and customize your own views in Chapter 14, "Custom Stakeholder Views and Reports."

You should avoid getting stuck in the default view, which displays a default table called the Entry table. The Entry table is good for planning but not necessarily for communicating and reporting or for updating and tracking.

Another mistake people often make is referring to the Gantt chart as the project plan. The Gantt chart is simply a bar chart that represents the length of a task based on a defined timescale—a day, month, quarter, or year. As discussed in Chapter 1, "Project 2010 as an Enabling Tool for Project Managers," and Chapter 2, "Mapping the Project-Management Process Groups to Project," there is much more to Project and project management than just the Gantt chart.

FIGURE 4.1   The default view: Gantt Chart with Timeline

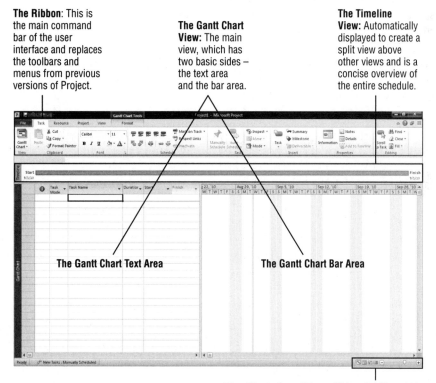

The Ribbon: This is the main command bar of the user interface and replaces the toolbars and menus from previous versions of Project.

The Gantt Chart View: The main view, which has two basic sides – the text area and the bar area.

The Timeline View: Automatically displayed to create a split view above other views and is a concise overview of the entire schedule.

The Gantt Chart Text Area

The Gantt Chart Bar Area

View Shortcuts and Zoom Slider: Quickly switch to another view or zoom timescale in or out.

Welcome to the Ribbon

If you've used any previous versions of Project, you may be surprised by what you see. Previous versions were based on menus and toolbars, but these have been replaced with the ribbon. I've heard both positive and negative feedback regarding the ribbon, but I believe it will add significant value as you go through each stage of managing your project.

By the time Project 2010 was released, I had been using the ribbon in other Office 2007 products like Word, Excel, and PowerPoint; I got used to this new approach to activating features and commands. (The ribbon wasn't included in Project 2007.) If you're new to using the ribbon, it may take some getting used to. I think you'll find that in Project 2010, the ribbon organizes the way you plan, track, and manage tasks and resources in a much more effective manner. Even if you prefer the menu and toolbar approach, the organization of commands in this version is better suited for project management than in previous versions.

Commands are organized in logical groupings that are collected under tabs; this will help you be more efficient about getting things done in any stage of your project life cycle. Figure 4.2 illustrates the new look and feel of the ribbon.

FIGURE 4.2   The ribbon

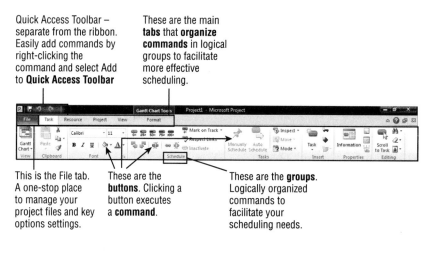

Quick Access Toolbar –
separate from the ribbon.
Easily add commands by
right-clicking the
command and select Add
to **Quick Access Toolbar**

These are the main
tabs that **organize
commands** in logical
groups to facilitate
more effective
scheduling.

This is the File tab.
A one-stop place
to manage your
project files and key
options settings.

These are the
buttons. Clicking a
button executes
a **command**.

These are the **groups**.
Logically organized
commands to
facilitate your
scheduling needs.

The look and feel of the ribbon or how it appears on your screen may vary depending on the screen resolution settings you have defined. Throughout this book I will generally use a lower resolution to capture screen shots, which may truncate some of the commands in each of the groups in the ribbon. Therefore, even though the commands and groups are the same, the ribbon is designed to adjust automatically to better fit the commands to your screen thus resulting in a different look and feel with different screen resolution settings.

The ribbon has five main parts, as follows:

Tabs   Tabs are organized logically to make it easy to navigate to specific types of commands as they relate to tasks, resources, projects, views, and formatting. This will prove more intuitive than the old menu and toolbar approach as you navigate through planning, communicating, and tracking processes.

Groups   Groups are logically organized commands under each tab. They're designed to put related commands together to make it easier and quicker for you to get things done in Project.

Quick Access Toolbar   This is the small command section at the top of the ribbon. You can customize it to enable one-click access to commands regardless of the current ribbon state. To add the commands you use the most, right-click the command and choose Add to Quick Access Toolbar.

Buttons   Buttons represent commands that can be executed by clicking. They're organized into logical groups for quicker access. For example, the Font group located under the Task tab has commands such as Bold, Italics, and Underline.

Boolean buttons toggle on and off, depending on whether they're activated. There are also check boxes. For example, under the Format tab in the Show/Hide group, you can select Project Summary Task. There are also flyout anchors, split buttons, and combo buttons:

Flyout anchors   These display a drop-down list of commands to choose from, such as the Task Mode command under the Tasks tab in the Schedule group.

Split buttons   These are composed of two parts. The top part executes an action; the bottom part, with the arrow, opens a menu of more choices, such as a list of additional fonts from the Font command.

Combo buttons   These give you the choice to activate a command, with an additional list of other selections: for example, the Paste command under the Tasks tab in the Clipboard group.

These are all useful buttons and are easier to work with than in previous versions, so take time to browse the commands and get to know them.

File tab and the backstage view   You'll access the backstage view frequently. This is the interface that appears when you click the File tab in the upper-left corner. It fills the screen and contains features related to working with project files (many of which were on the File menu in previous versions of Project). For example, commands for opening, saving, and printing files are located here. You can also manage Project Server connections if you're using Project Professional connected to Server 2010. (If you don't have Project Server, then don't pay attention to this function.)

You'll also find the Options command here, which was on the Tools menu in Project 2007. Project Options control many preferences about how Project works and will be discussed in more detail later in this chapter. Figure 4.3 shows the backstage area.

One other key tool in the backstage is the Organizer, which allows you to move elements such as custom views, tables, fields, and calendars easily from one project to another. For example, if you create a company calendar and you want to share it with another project manager, you can use the Organizer to move it. You simply need to have both project files open to swap elements.

FIGURE 4.3   Access the Backstage view by Clicking on the File tab

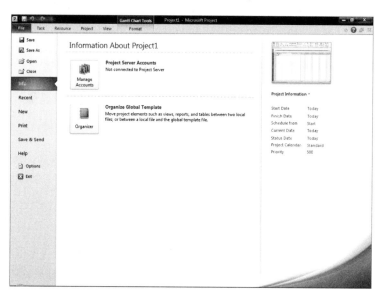

The Default Gantt Chart with Timeline View

In Project 2010, the Timeline view is automatically displayed on top of the Gantt chart—or any other view, for that matter. When you open Project, you see that the Gantt chart is intact, with new features and an improved look and feel. Together, the Timeline view and the Gantt chart make a powerful combination and act as the default starting point for your Project experience. In this section, you'll learn about both of these views. In Part 3 of the book, "Communicating and Reporting Essentials," I'll go into more detail about using and customizing views.

The Timeline View

The Timeline view is brand new to Project and is a concise overview of the entire schedule in one rolled-up summary bar. It automatically adjusts as your schedule changes and can be customized to include existing milestones or tasks (you can also add new tasks while in the Timeline view). It allows you to quickly see the big picture, share it in Word or PowerPoint, and email it to other stakeholders. Figure 4.4 shows the Timeline view.

To turn the Timeline view on or off, follow these steps:

1.   Click the View tab.

2.   In the Split Screen group, uncheck (clear) the Timeline box.

     You can check it back on anytime you want, in any view.

FIGURE 4.4   The Timeline view

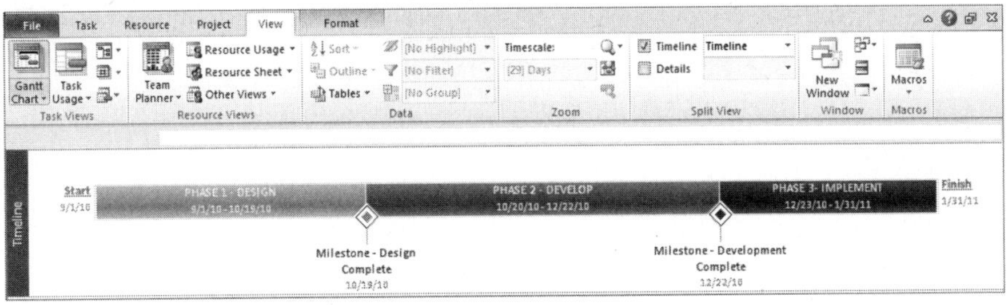

To share the Timeline view in email or add it to a presentation, do the following:

1. Click anywhere on the Timeline view area, and click the Format tab.

2. In the Copy group, click Copy Timeline.

3. Choose the option for email, presentation, or full size.

    After you make the selection, you can paste the Timeline view directly into your email, PowerPoint, or other application document.

As you build your plan by adding tasks and scheduling them accordingly, the Timeline view automatically adjusts to represent your most current information. At any time, you can add tasks or milestones to (or remove them from) your Timeline view by right-clicking the task or milestone in the Gantt chart and selecting Add to Timeline. In Figure 4.4, I've added two key milestones.

The Gantt Chart View

The Gantt chart consists of two distinct sides. The left side is known as the *text area*, and the right side is known as the *bar area*. Each side has its own scroll bars, and each side can be formatted separately. For example, if you want to format critical tasks to be displayed in red, you need to format both the text area (text styles) and bar area (bar styles)—formatting the text area doesn't automatically format the bar area, and vice versa. This will be covered in more detail in Chapter 13, "Formatting Text and Bars." Figure 4.5 shows the default Gantt Chart view in Project.

> If you've used earlier versions of Project, you'll notice that the look and feel of the graphical user interface (GUI) has been significantly enhanced in Project 2010 in all the views and in both the text and bar areas.

Other Views

As you become more proficient with Project, you'll want to plan, track, and communicate in various views. Think of a view as the way you see project data and the format in which it's served up to you. Views are divided into two main categories: *task-related views*, which focus on task-related information such as start dates, finish dates, durations, and which resource is assigned to do a task; and *resource-related views*, which focus on resource-related information such as cost rate, availability, resource group, and which tasks have been assigned to a resource. For example, the Task Usage view lists tasks with resource assignments; this is a task-related view. The Resource Usage view, which lists resources with tasks underneath, is a resource-related view. We'll explore views in depth in Part 3.

FIGURE 4.5   Default Gantt Chart view

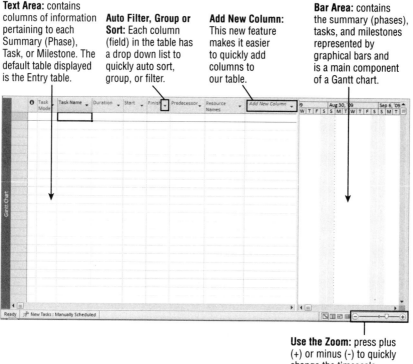

Text Area: contains columns of information pertaining to each Summary (Phase), Task, or Milestone. The default table displayed is the Entry table.

Auto Filter, Group or Sort: Each column (field) in the table has a drop down list to quickly auto sort, group, or filter.

Add New Column: This new feature makes it easier to quickly add columns to our table.

Bar Area: contains the summary (phases), tasks, and milestones represented by graphical bars and is a main component of a Gantt chart.

Use the Zoom: press plus (+) or minus (-) to quickly change the timescale.

Project has made it simple and fluid to move from one view to another. Depending on which tab you selected, you'll have different options.

Changing Views from the Task and Resource Tabs

Clicking the top part of the Gantt Chart button on the Task tab or the Team Planner button on the Resource tab lets you switch views from the drop-down list. Whether you're working with the Task tab activated or the Resource tab activated, you're presented with the same list of views to choose from, as illustrated in Figure 4.6.

You can apply any view in the list. Or, you can access more views by selecting More Views from the bottom of the menu; then select the view you wish to apply or edit.

FIGURE 4.6   View list from the Task or Resource tab

Changing Views from the View Tab

On the View tab, the views are divided by type (task or resource); see Figure 4.7. Clicking the top part of a button takes you to the most recently used view of that type, and clicking the bottom part of the button allows you to apply any view of that type. These views are much better organized than in previous versions, to let you quickly identify more useful ways to view project information.

FIGURE 4.7   Views available on the View tab

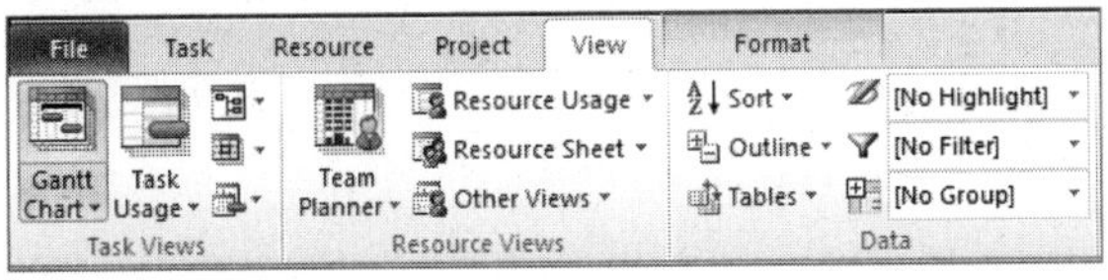

Quick View Switching

Quick view switching allows you to quickly switch to another view no matter what table you've activated in Project. (A *table* is a collection of columns [fields] displayed in the text area of the Gantt chart on the right side of the view.) As shown in Figure 4.8, this option is located in the bottom-right corner of the window. The view icons from left to right are Gantt Chart, Task Usage, Team Planner, and Resource Sheet.

FIGURE 4.8   Using quick view switching to change views

Notice that the quick view switching options are co-located with the zoom function, which lets you quickly change the scale of the timeline by zooming in or out.

Split Screens

The default view for Project is a split view with the Gantt Chart view as the primary view and the Timeline view as the secondary view (this is called Gantt with Timeline in the list of views). But this split view is different from previous versions of Project, because it puts the secondary view on top of the primary view.

You can apply split-screen views with the secondary view below the primary view. To do so, right-click in the bar area to activate a split screen. But it's easier to activate a top split with the Timeline view or a bottom split with a Details form view.

To display the task or resource form in a split-screen view, click Details on the Task tab or the Resource tab in the Properties group, as shown in Figure 4.9.

You can also control the Timeline split view and details split view: on the View tab, in the Split View group, select the Timeline check box to display a Timeline view on top, or select the Details check box to display various form views on the bottom. If you click in the bottom view and right-click, you'll have even more form views to choose from, as shown in Figure 4.10.

FIGURE 4.9   Displaying a split-screen view

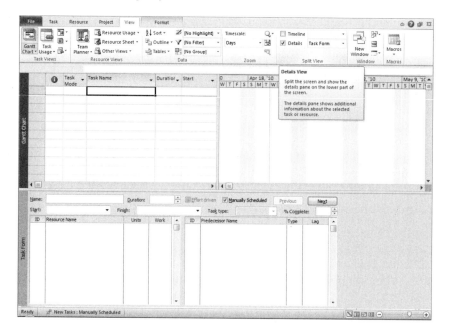

FIGURE 4.10   Changing the bottom form view

All these different views may be overwhelming, given that we haven't covered the fundamentals of planning, communicating, and tracking yet. As we move into Part 2, "Planning Essentials," Part 3, and finally Part 4, "Tracking Essentials," these views will start to make more sense.

Using Project Templates to Get Started

You may be working on projects that can be patterned after a common methodology, process, or approach. In this context, you may be able to start your project-planning process from a template. Templates provide consistency and give project managers a more efficient approach to project planning.

A template may have a predefined work breakdown structure (phases, tasks, and milestones), task relationships and links, duration estimates, generic resource assignments, and even custom views. You can also use portions of templates by using standard cut-and-paste functionality.

If you or your organization hasn't created any templates, Project comes equipped with many predefined templates that are worth exploring. You can find other templates on Office Online, where new templates are uploaded and published regularly. You'll find templates designed for projects ranging from construction to new product development, and everything in between. Don't be afraid to open and move around within a template: you won't do any harm to other settings in other plans, and you can close it without saving if you don't want to use it.

The training examples in this book are based on a simple template from a basic development project with three main phases: Design, Develop, and Implement. This template can be easily understood regardless of the types of projects you'll be managing. It's based on the list of phases, tasks, and milestones, shown in Figure 4.11, which we'll discuss in more detail in Chapter 5, "Creating and Entering the Work Breakdown Structure."

Until you finish this book, knowing what goes into a good plan and therefore a good template may be a mystery. For now, just know that using templates can make your planning process more efficient.

FIGURE 4.11 Training template example

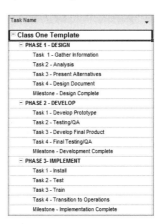

 Real World Scenario

Creating Effective Templates

Most organizations I work with create their own templates to more accurately reflect the way they work. Beware! Creating good templates is harder than you may think. The following list provides some considerations to guide you in your template development initiatives:

- Take the time to create a well-defined, well-thought-out work breakdown structure (WBS). See Chapter 5.

- Avoid using constraints or deadlines in a template, because doing so diminishes its reusability. See Chapter 7, "Setting Dependencies and the Critical Path."

- Avoid using named resources.

- If you assign resources to tasks, make sure the resources are generic.

- Set task and resource dependencies to make scheduling easier.

- Include rough estimates for duration or work to make planning easier.

- It may be necessary to create different templates for different-sized projects. Small, medium, and large projects have different planning and tracking needs.

- When you save a template, make sure there is no baseline or actual data, such as percent complete, anywhere on the plan. An option comes up automatically to remove this type of data.

- Templates can include custom features such as views, tables, filters, groups, fields, and calendars.

- Templates can include custom option settings, as explained later in this chapter, as well as any custom formats you may want to use for communicating.

As you can see in Figure 4.12, when you start a new project, you can start from a blank project, an existing project, or a template. This is similar to how other Microsoft Office applications work. In Project, templates often contain not only predefined formats and settings but also reusable project phases, tasks, and milestone information.

You can select from Recent Templates; Sample Templates, which come with Project; or My Templates, which you create yourself. You can also explore templates online by selecting Office.com Templates.

To start a new plan using a template, follow these steps:

1. Go to the backstage by clicking the File tab . The New Project task pane opens to the left of the text area and the View bar.

2. Click New. As shown in Figure 4.12, there are a variety of template options to choose from. My Templates lists any custom templates you've saved, and Office.com Templates includes many additional templates to choose from.

3. Double-click a template to load it.

FIGURE 4.12   Starting a new plan from a template

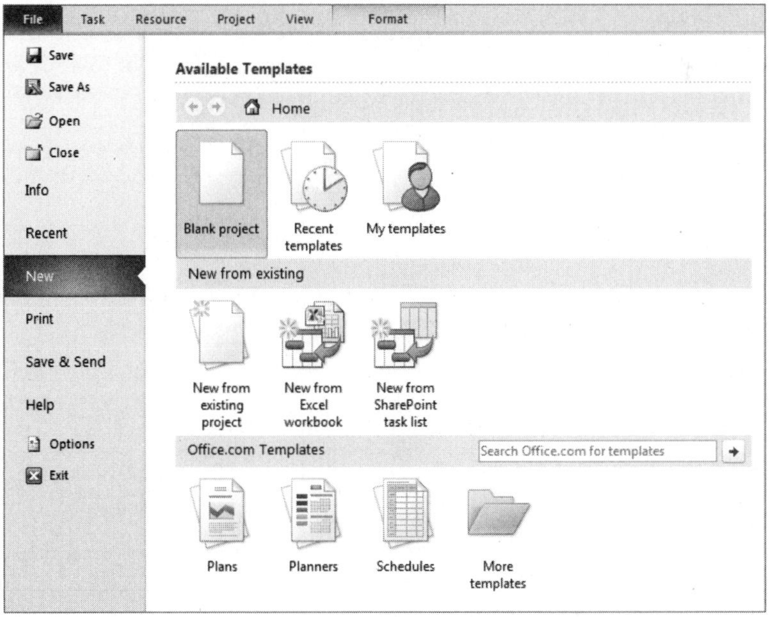

In Chapter 3, "Enterprise Project Management and Other Key Considerations," I discussed some of the benefits of implementing an enterprise project-management solution using Project Server. Creating Enterprise templates is one of those key benefits. Enterprise templates allow you to quickly deploy new or updated templates to any user connected to the server. In an Enterprise Project Management (EPM) solution, when you access templates, you see a tab specifically for enterprise templates. Enterprise templates let you ensure consistency in planning across an organization and also report progress across common phases, tasks, or milestones against a common life-cycle methodology.

Importing Plans from Excel

One of Microsoft Project's biggest competitors isn't project-management software from another manufacturer but Microsoft Excel. Before Project 2010 was released, I thought people used Excel instead of Project to manage projects because of two fundamental factors:

- *Familiarity*—Users are more comfortable with Excel and therefore may believe it's easier to use than Project. They have used Excel for a long time, even though they may be using only a fraction of its features. To use Project effectively, you must take the time to learn both the functionality of the tool and project-management concepts.

- *Availability*—Project 2010 doesn't ship with the Office 2010 suite of applications. Because Project is sold separately and at a significant price, availability may be an issue for many people.

When you've been through this book, you'll realize that this version of Project has made tremendous strides in familiarity and ease of use. If you want a more Excel-like approach to scheduling, you can have it; and when you're ready to employ best practices around scheduling and project management, the software can accommodate that too. Excel is an excellent product for what it does, but Project is the right tool for managing projects. With that in mind, at some point you may need to bring Excel plans into Project.

New: Enhanced Copy and Paste

With Project 2010, you can copy and paste content to and from Office programs like Excel and retain formatting, outline levels, and column headings.

You can open Excel files directly in Project by following these steps:

1. Go to the backstage by clicking the File tab in the upper-left corner.
2. Click Open.
3. To the right of File Name, select the file type for Excel Workbook files in the drop-down list.
4. In the File Open box, select your Excel file, and click Open.
5. Follow the wizard instructions.

To map tasks from Excel into Project, map the tasks to the Name field in Project—this is where your tasks are managed. Figure 4.13 shows the Task Mapping function of the Import Wizard.

FIGURE 4.13   Importing files from Excel into Project

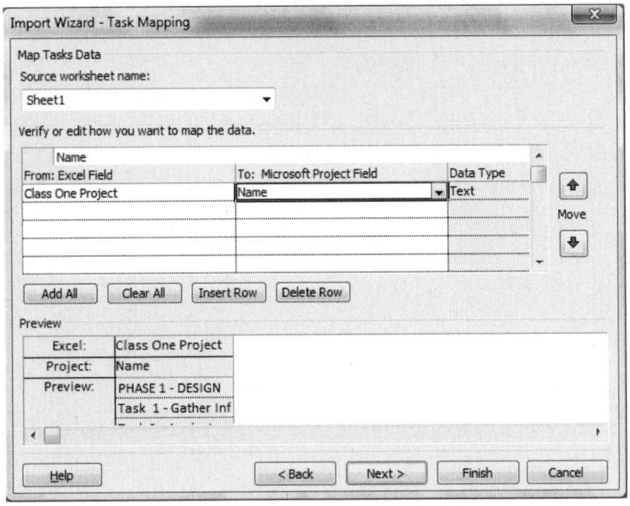

Key Options and Settings You Need to Know About

This section explores key options and settings that will help you succeed in understanding and working with Project. You'll also be introduced to a powerful new function in Project that gives you a choice between manual and automatic scheduling. You'll learn about outlining options, default task-type settings, and other settings that affect how Project works. Unlike other software products, where you can get by just fine without exploring option settings, it's important to take the time to review the various functions available to you in this area of the tool. You can find the Options dialog box in the backstage by clicking the File tab.

Manual or Automatic Scheduling

Manual or automatic scheduling is a powerful new functionality in Project 2010. It gives you flexibility in how Project handles the calculation of your tasks and milestones. In the past, when you added tasks to a plan or schedule, the duration and dates were automatically calculated and associated with the tasks regardless of whether you wanted them to be. Now you have a choice: you can turn the automatic scheduling feature on or off for new tasks you add or for existing tasks in your plan.

Automatic scheduling is designed to calculate the scheduled start and finish dates of summaries (phases), tasks, and milestones based on factors such as the project start date, calendars (working time versus nonworking times), duration estimates, dependencies (links between tasks), resource assignments, and constraints. When you select manual scheduling, Project 2010 ignores scheduling factors and lets you place tasks wherever you want. You can even type words into the Start and Finish date fields, such as "two weeks after delivery" or "one month after submission." In Part 2 of this book, you'll become fluent in both automatic scheduling and manual scheduling techniques. Figure 4.14 illustrates how to turn manual or automatic scheduling on or off.

Notice in Figure 4.14 that when you have a manually scheduled task, the Duration and Start and Finish fields are left blank. They will remain blank until you add information or change the Task Mode to Auto Scheduled. If you add words to the Start or Finish field, they will be replaced with dates if you switch from manual to automatic.

Project Summary Task and Outline Number

One of the first things I do when planning a project is turn on the Project Summary Task option. (You'll find this option on the Format tab in the Show/Hide group, as shown in Figure 4.15.) It accomplishes two key things. First, it automatically creates a roll-up that summarizes such things as start, finish, duration, work, costs, and so on for the entire project in one easy-to-read line. Second, it establishes and maintains the proper outline structure. This is particularly useful if you choose to use outline codes or WBS codes: Project creates a level-0 project-summary task.

FIGURE 4.14   Turning manual scheduling on or off

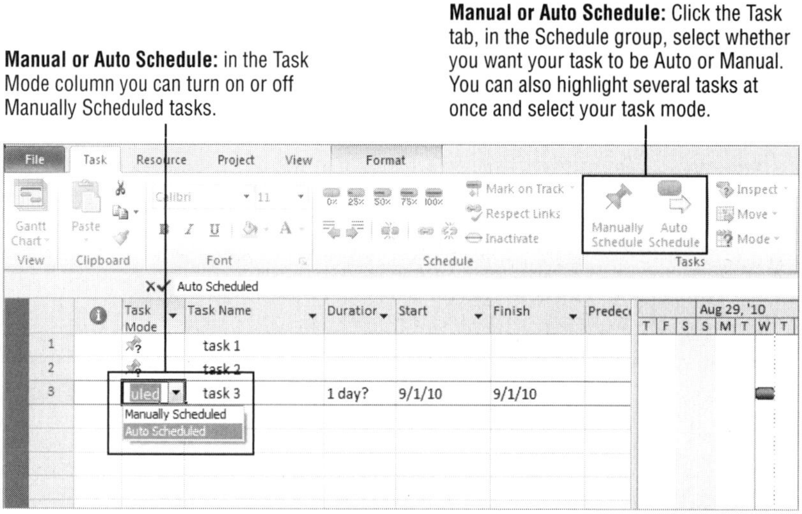

Manual or Auto Schedule: in the Task Mode column you can turn on or off Manually Scheduled tasks.

Manual or Auto Schedule: Click the Task tab, in the Schedule group, select whether you want your task to be Auto or Manual. You can also highlight several tasks at once and select your task mode.

FIGURE 4.15   Project Summary Task option

Let Project automatically insert a top level
project summary task. This will allow you
to summarize your entire project into one
line – Line 0. The default name will be
based file save name.

Project Summary Task: In the Format Tab,
Show/Hid group, you can click the Project
Summary Task on or off. You can also click
the **Outline Number** feature on or off, as well.

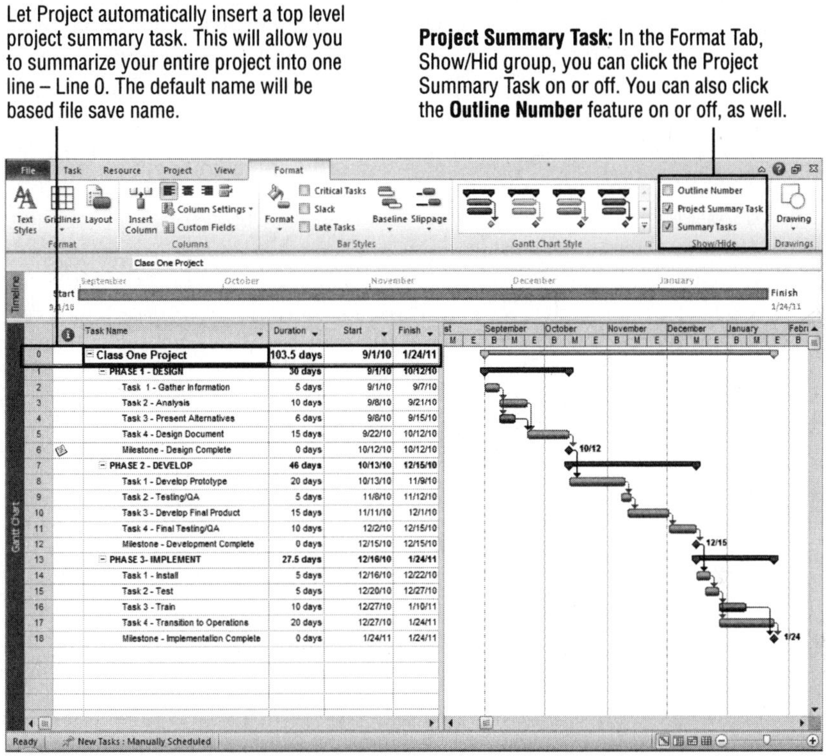

Working with clients, I'm often tasked with creating templates from existing plans or analyzing and improving existing plans. One of the first components of a plan that I review is the WBS. There are many considerations when establishing a good WBS, as discussed in more detail in Chapter 5. However, one piece of the puzzle in Project is to establish a project-level summary task.

A significant number of the plans I review have a manually created project-level summary task, which by default assumes WBS number 1.0. This subsequently causes all other WBS components to be included in level 1.0, and level 2.0 is never created. This is one of the first things I correct by switching on the Project Summary Task option. When the automated project-summary task is in place, it's then necessary to delete the manually created summary task without deleting any of its subtasks. I'll tell you how to do this in Chapter 5.

> Project can automate the outlining codes for all the phases, tasks, and milestones in your plan, based on your WBS hierarchy. Click the Format tab. Then, in the Show/Hide group, select the Outline Number check box shown in Figure 4.15. Use this option only if you want to display the outline codes for each phase, task, and milestone added to your schedule.

The project-summary task is also important because it's the line item that represents your project in master consolidated plans (or in Project Server), which I cover in Chapter 14, "Creating Master Schedules with Inserted Projects." If you create a summary task manually, you're in effect creating a redundant line item. (This will become more apparent when we discuss planning and the WBS in Chapter 5.) Whether you display it or not, the project-summary task becomes line item 0 in your WBS and automatically takes the name of the file when you save your plan. Therefore, it's important to give your file a meaningful name, because it will be reflected in the WBS and many reports and communications you generate.

If you want to break the link between the file name and the level-0 project summary task, you can type over the name in the Task Name field. However, I don't recommend doing this, because it will cause confusion for those looking at the master plan or published plan in Project Server. If you accidentally type over the name, you can reestablish the link between the line item 0 project-summary task and the file name by updating the file properties as follows:

1. Go to the backstage by clicking the File tab.

2. On the right side of the screen, click Project Information, and select Advanced Properties.

3. Type the file name into the Title area under Summary.

 If you switch to Project Server and publish plans, the plan line item displayed in the Project Center will be based on the project-summary task.

Real World Scenario

Automating the Project-Summary Task vs. Manually Creating One

Many years ago, I was tasked with putting together one of my first consolidated master plans for a client. More than 30 separate subproject plans were to be inserted into the master plan. The subproject plans were created by a variety of project managers. Many of these plans were created with a manual summary task, which seemed fine at first. However, after the consolidation process, I realized that Project automatically inserts a project-summary task. For subprojects with a manually inserted summary task, we ended up with two separate summary tasks in the consolidated plan. The consolidated plan not only appeared to be redundant but was also less efficient to use. And repeatedly explaining why some plans had two summary lines when we needed only one got old quickly.

The other negative factor about manually creating the summary task was that it ruined the outline numbering. Everything essentially fell under level 1, and subsequently all indented tasks started with the outline code 1. The moral of the story: let Project insert the project-level summary task for you.

Scheduling Approaches and Default Task Types

Project 2010 introduces a whole new approach to scheduling referred to as User Controlled Scheduling (UCS), which will be reviewed in detail in Part 2—"Planning Essentials." UCS is based on the task mode being set to Manually Schedule task which is the default setting for new tasks.. Auto scheduling is the approach that previous versions of Project used as the default to calculate your schedule automatically based on key drivers from the scheduling engine of Project. The rest of this chapter refers to options only when you use automatic scheduling.

In project management, you can take different scheduling approaches when creating your plan. This section introduces one of the more complex concepts of scheduling with Project. The overall scheduling approach Project takes depends on the default task type you select. It's better to set these defaults up front, prior to entering task information, which is why I discuss it in this chapter. But I cover the impact of these settings in more detail in Chapter 8, "Assigning Resources and Costs." The topics covered in this section will become clearer as we move through the next chapters. So, if you don't fully grasp them now, you will.

Your schedule can be either duration-based or effort-based. The approach you choose depends on your plan-management needs, your resources and time, and how you want the tool to behave.

Duration-Based Scheduling

Duration-based scheduling is estimated from a time standpoint (duration). That duration stays the same regardless of how many resources you assign. This is known as *fixed duration* in Project. Many of my clients prefer this approach; they have a requirement to track dates and duration, keeping the timing intact regardless of the resources assigned. This isn't to say that you can't load up resources and work and track them in a duration-based plan; but duration-based scheduling changes how the tool behaves after you begin to assign resources and work.

To understand how the tool behavior changes, it's important to understand the difference between duration and work. *Duration* is the difference between the start and finish dates of a task. Duration is typically displayed in days, but it can be displayed in minutes, hours, weeks, or months.

Duration is based on available working times from the default standard calendar, which is based on a typical 5-day, 40-hour workweek that runs from Monday to Friday. As such, 1 day is equal to 8 hours, 5 days is equal to 1 week, and so on. When you're estimating duration, if you enter 7 days, the duration shown in Project will be closer to one and a half weeks. If you enter 30 days (thinking it's equal to 1 month), don't be surprised when your duration equals 6 weeks. The next section shows how to customize calendars.

A tradeshow is an example where duration-based scheduling is useful. If a tradeshow is 10 days long, and you assign 1 person to it, then Project calculates the work as follows:

Work = 10 days × 1 person (same as 100%) = 10 days or 80 hours

---

Fixed Duration and Fixed Dates

It's important to understand that fixed duration isn't the same as fixed dates. These are separate functions in Project.

Fixed duration means the duration doesn't change regardless of resource assignments; but the start and end dates are free to move based on other factors, such as the project start date, task dependencies, and calendars. Chapter 9, "Understanding the Calculation Engine for Automatic Scheduling," reviews the key drivers in the calculation of time (start and finish dates) in Project.

Fixed dates are different, and in Project they're referred to as *task constraints*. I cover this in Chapter 7. You can fix the start or finish date of a task with a constraint such as Must Start On or Must Finish On, and the date will remain fixed regardless of any other calculation factors.

For example, if you plan an off-site meeting with your team and book a facility for a specific date—say, June 15—that date is fixed regardless of any other factor in Project. On the other hand, you may have a fixed duration for a task such as printing, with no fixed dates. If the task is estimated to take three days and begins on Monday, it will end on Wednesday. If the start date moves to Tuesday, the task will end on Thursday.

In a duration-based or fixed-duration schedule, the duration of 10 days remains constant regardless of the resources assigned. So, if you assign 5 people to the tradeshow at 100 percent, then because the duration remains the length of the tradeshow, work is calculated as follows:

Work = 10 days × 5 people (same as 500%) = 50 days or 400 hours

Duration-based scheduling is a nice option when you want the timing of the schedule to stay intact as you change resource assignments.

Effort-Based Scheduling

Work, on the other hand, reflects the number of person-hours—the amount of labor or effort—required to complete tasks. Typically, this is the people power. The unit of work defaults to hours in Project, and scheduling is typically driven by resource assignments. Some clients I work with prefer to estimate the work or effort first, and then assign the resources and have Project calculate the duration, start, and finish dates based on the level of resource loading. This type of scheduling is generally referred to as *effort-based scheduling*.

To set up Project for this type of scheduling, you set the task type to Fixed Work or Fixed Units, with Effort Driven turned on. Note that *effort-driven* is synonymous with *fixed-work*.

🌐 **Real World Scenario**

Duration-Based (Fixed-Duration) Scheduling with Resources

I recently worked with a client that needed to keep the duration estimates for tasks fixed but understood the relationship between resource-loading requirements and capacity. We created project templates based on fixed-duration tasks, a strong dependency structure, and generic resource assignments.

Each plan was initiated by working with core team members to provide inputs. Core members provided not only information about the timing of events but also estimates of each resource assignment based on a percentage of the generic resource required. In this case, we were only interested in getting estimates for a particular role, such as statistician or programmer. After the role requirements were loaded, we could estimate the planned workload for each department and compare it to capacity across all projects. Using this template, the client could better plan for resource needs by month, quarter, and year and could do high-level planning, leaving the details of individual employee availability and resource leveling to the resource managers. In this case, the task-duration estimates and project start and end dates had to stay intact while we changed the resource loading, so fixed duration worked best.

The Relationship between Work and Duration

To really understand work and duration, consider the formula that Project uses to control scheduling:

$$Work = Duration \times Units$$

You can fix one component (based on the task type you choose) and enter the second variable, and Project calculates the third.

New in Project 2010, the units field behaves slightly different than in previous versions. Changes to the assignment units field is no longer automatically modified to be greater or less than the default value of 100%. It will only change if you change it manually yourself. Another field called Peak units will be used to reflect any variation across time-phased work if it varies from one day to another. This will be discussed further in Chapter 8, "Assigning Resources and Costs."

As shown in Figure 4.16, you can also choose a combination by selecting either Fixed Units or Fixed Duration as the Default Task Type and then turning the Effort-Driven function on or off. For example, if you choose both Fixed Duration and New Tasks Are Effort Driven, Project attempts to protect both the duration and the work as you make changes to your schedule. If you change the duration of a task, Project doesn't change the work but rather changes the unit assignments of the task.

FIGURE 4.16   Set the Default Task Type (Fixed Duration, Fixed Work, or Fixed Units).

Default task type: set the default task type before entering tasks so you do not have to go back and change task types after the fact. Remember, you can change this on a task-by-task basis at anytime.

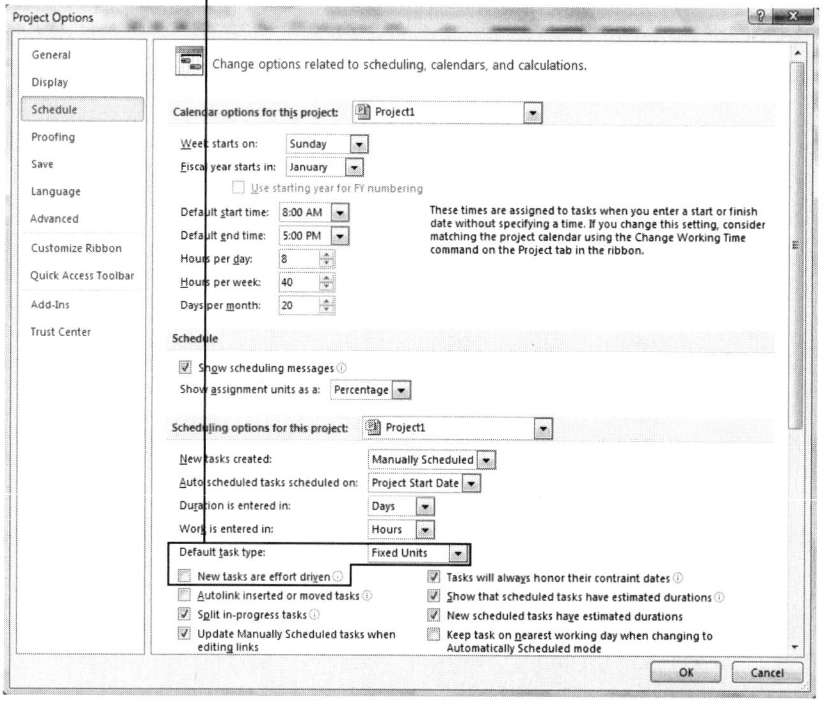

Assignment Units

Assignment units are an indicator of a resource's availability. For example, both your project and another may require work by a mechanical engineer. Only 50 percent of that engineer's time may be available for your project. (Usually, the maximum is 100 percent when referring to a single person.) I discuss this in more detail when I review resource assignments in Chapter 8.

A painting task is a good candidate for effort-based scheduling. You may estimate that the work will take 10 days or 80 hours, but depending on how many resources (painters) you assign, the duration will vary. If you assign

- One person at 100%, then the duration will be 10 days.

- One person at 50%, then the duration will be 20 days.

- Two people at 100% each, then the duration will be 5 days.

Project calculates the start and finish dates accordingly. So, although the total work remains constant, your timeline fluctuates based on the resources you assign.

Either way, it's important to think carefully about how you work and which approach is best suited to your project and organization. You can set up the default for the project, but the requirements can change from one project to the next and from one task to the next. You must consider the implications on the schedule as you make changes to resource assignments.

🌐 Real World Scenario

Effort-Driven Scheduling Approach

While working with an IT department, we were asked to implement a solution that allowed for collaboration between the project manager and the resource managers to help with scheduling based on resource availabilities. We set up a template with the Default Task Type set to Fixed Units and New Tasks Are Effort Driven turned on. The template included generic resource assignments with estimated work, not duration, for each task along with the most likely dependency (network) structure.

The planning process included working with the resource managers to replace the generic resources with named resources and unit (percentage) estimates. Each unit estimate was based on availability of that particular resource. The resource managers were the keepers and coordinators for their respective team members. As the generic resources were replaced with the named resources and the units were entered into Project for each resource assignment, the duration and start and finish dates were automatically calculated, resulting in a purely effort-driven schedule.

It's also fine to use Project just for the scheduling component of time and not assign resources. In that case, you don't have to worry about resource assignments. However, if you assign even one resource to a task, then whether you like it or not, work will be calculated by the formula, and changes to resource assignment will have a significant impact on your plan.

The default for Project is an effort-driven scheduling approach based on fixed units. This means that as you assign resources, the duration is recalculated. The assignment units and work remain fixed unless you manually change them. As shown in Figure 4.16, you can change the Default Task Type settings by following these steps:

1. Go to the backstage by clicking the File tab.

2. Click Options (under Project), and select Schedule. Look for the section Scheduling Options in This Project.

3. From the Default Task Type drop-down list box, choose the most appropriate option (Fixed Duration, Fixed Work, or Fixed Units).

4. Click the New Tasks Are Effort Driven check box to turn the feature on or off. Remember that an effort-driven approach fixes the work in conjunction with the task type. By default, Fixed Work is effort-driven, and New Tasks Are Effort Driven is automatically selected.

Other Options

Take the time to review the rest of the tabs under Options. You'll find many of them useful. For example, if you're interested in auto save, review the Save tab. For spell-check options, review the Proofing tab. Most of the functions and options are self-explanatory.

Working with Calendars

Another key factor in getting started the right way is understanding that Project uses calendars in its calculations for start and finish date. You can set up and customize calendars to reflect your unique working times. Calendars can be applied at the project, task, or resource level.

Creating New Calendars

You can also use project calendars to simulate what-if scenarios. For example, if you were on a tight schedule and you wanted your staff to work on Saturdays, you could set up a new base calendar and apply it to the project to see the impact it would have on the timeline.

To create a new calendar, use the following approach, which uses the example of creating a custom calendar with working Saturdays:

1. Click the Project tab. In the Properties group, click Change Working Time. Figure 4.17 shows the Change Working Time dialog box.

2. Click Create New Calendar. In the Name field, type **Saturday Working Days**.

3. Click OK.

4. Click the Work Weeks tab.

5. Click Details, and select Saturday.

6. Click Set Day(s) to These Specific Working Times.

7. Enter the working times for Saturdays in the From and To fields, and click OK.

8. Click OK to create the new calendar.

Project has enhanced this dialog box to make it easier to create new calendars and exceptions and to modify working and nonworking times. After calendars are created, you can apply them not only at the project level but also at the task level and resource level. If you double-click a task in the Gantt chart, you can use the Advanced tab of the Task Information dialog to apply a different calendar to the selected task. On the resource sheet, you can change the base calendar or individual working time for each resource.

Real World Scenario

Specialized Calendars

Many of my clients maintain a project calendar that takes into consideration the main company holidays for the year—New Year's, Memorial Day, Independence Day, and so on. After that calendar is added to their project, by default, Project won't schedule any work to be done on these days for the entire plan.

You can create a working weekend calendar to apply to specific tasks that require work over the weekend. This is common for certain types of tasks, such as during release of a new product. One bank I worked with had specific tasks referred to as *bank conversions*. Whenever the bank acquired another bank, staff would go in on Friday after closing, and by Monday morning, the acquired bank could be opened under the new name, ready for business. In this situation, we added the weekend calendar only to the conversion tasks.

I also work with many multinational corporations that have projects involving global resources. In Project, you can assign a different calendar to each resource if you need to. One client had separate calendars for the United Kingdom, China, Canada, and Australia to cover each of the resources on the project. If a resource from Canada was assigned over Christmas, they also had a holiday for Boxing Day (the day after Christmas). Project by default considered that nonworking time and extended the end date of any task falling over that period.

FIGURE 4.17   Changing the working time and creating a new calendar

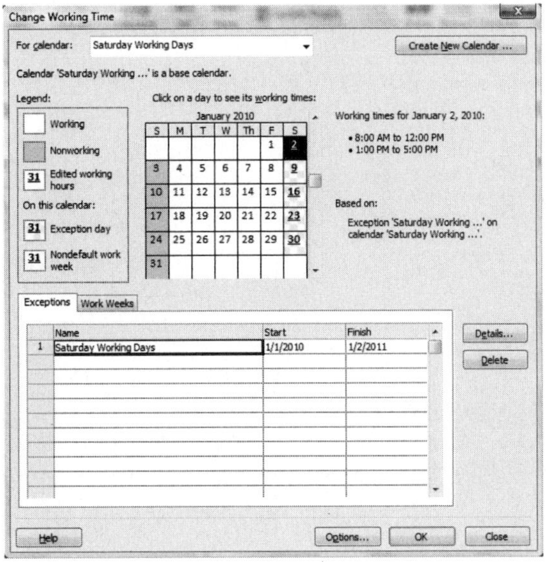

Whether you assign calendars at the project, task, or resource level, all your project calendars are taken into consideration when Project calculates the timeline of your plan. But remember, creating a calendar doesn't automatically assign it anywhere in your plan. Later in this chapter, I'll discuss the Project Information dialog box; that is where you assign the calendar that affects the entire project.

Keep in mind that the calendar directly affects the scheduling of start and finish dates. That is why when a task is set at 5 days' duration, it shows up as a week-long task. By default, Project considers weekends nonworking time—unless, of course, you change the default.

Instead of modifying the standard calendar, I suggest creating custom new calendars that can then be applied to the project, tasks, or resources.

Controlling Conversion Factors

You can also control the conversion factor that Project uses to convert days to hours or days to months. I strongly suggest that you align this with the working times in your calendars. To review or change the conversion factors, follow these steps (Figure 4.18 shows the Schedule tab):

1. Go to the backstage by clicking the File tab.

2. Select the Schedule tab.

3. Review the calendar options for this project: hours per day, hours per week, and days per month.

FIGURE 4.18 Review calendar options and conversion factors.

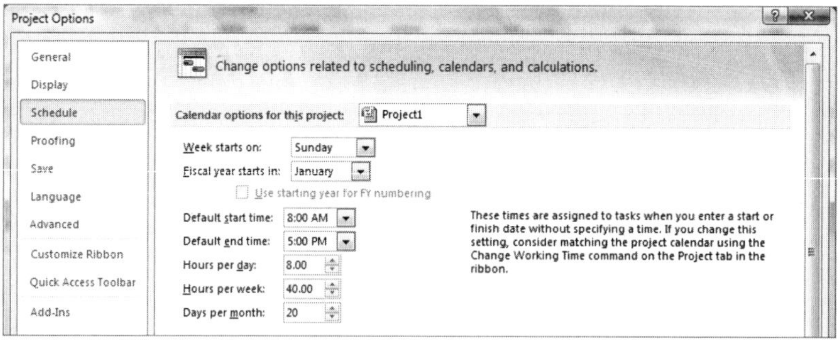

Project Start- and End-Date Options

Project bases its calculation of the start-date field for all new tasks on what is defined in the Start Date field in the Project Information box under the Project tab. When you start a new project, the current system date is, by default, applied as the project start date. It's important to define this date yourself to reflect the plan you're creating. You can change the project start date at any time to try what-if scenarios that delay or move up the start of a project.

Setting the start date accurately is not only a critical step in setting up project plans but also a powerful tool. You can recalculate your entire plan if a project start needs to be shifted and then easily communicate the changes to your project stakeholders. To define your project start date, follow these steps:

1. From the Project tab, in the Properties group, choose Project Information. Figure 4.19 shows the Project Information dialog box.

2. In the Start Date box, type or select the project start date.

 NOTE   You can change your project calendar from the Project Information dialog box. If you do so, remember that the new calendar will affect all tasks in the project schedule.

In Project, you can choose to schedule from the project end date and apply a backward scheduling technique. This may be useful for initial planning based on a deadline you've been given, but it creates a schedule based on an "as late as possible" constraint. I recommend that you change Project back to forward scheduling (scheduling from the project start date) before you begin the project. If you don't, as tasks begin to slip, they may continue to be pushed out to the left (starting earlier) rather than being pushed out to the right (starting later).

As an alternative to backward scheduling, you can apply a deadline or "must finish on" constraint to the milestone that signifies the end of the project. Then, when you want to run what-if scenarios, adjust the project start date and compare results. I cover this in more detail in Chapter 7.

FIGURE 4.19   Define your project start date.

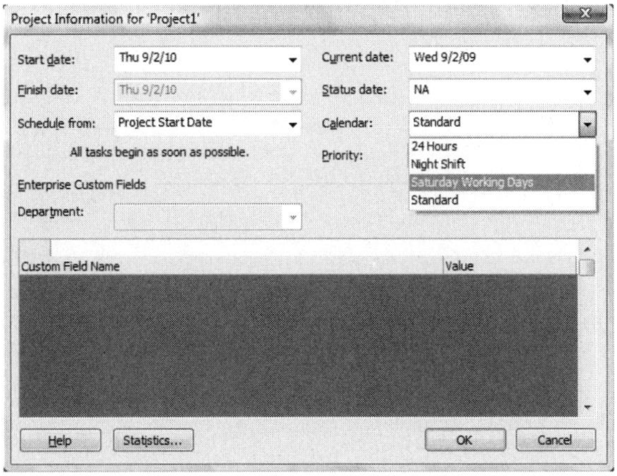

Displaying the Project Start and Current Dates in a Gantt Chart

After the project start date is defined, you can graphically display it and the current date in the Gantt chart. I use this feature on all project plans and templates.

It's a good idea to display both the start date and current date to visualize where you are in the project compared to when the project started. Choose a color combination that works for you. I usually choose red for the current date and blue for the project start date. The current date continues to move, while the project start date stays the same (unless, of course, you change it in Project Information). Follow these steps:

1. On the Format tab, in the Format group, click Gridlines. Figure 4.20 shows the Gridlines dialog box.

2. In the Line to Change list, select Project Start.

3. In the Normal section, select a solid line in the Type drop-down list.

4. In the Normal section, select blue in the Color drop-down list.

FIGURE 4.20   Format current-date and start-date gridlines.

5. In the Line to Change list, click Current Date.

6. In the Normal section, again select a solid line in the Type drop-down list.

7. Select red in the Color drop-down list. (The default is orange, but you can select any color you want.)

8. Click OK to save the changes and close the dialog box.

The result provides clear lines so you can easily compare where you are today versus the project start date, as shown in Figure 4.21. This is particularly helpful after the project starts, because everything to the left of the current date should be finished, and everything to the right should still need to be done.

NOTE   You can also change project information such as the start date or change project calendar by going to the backstage area by clicking on the File tab and then the Info tab. On the far right you will see the project information similar to the path described in Figure 4.19. You can also click on the drop down list beside Project Information and access Project Properties to change things such as title, manager, author, or add project level keywords or comments.

FIGURE 4.21   Gantt chart displaying current-date and start-date grid lines

Format Gridlines: Format your current date to be red and your project start date to be blue. Everything to the right of the red line (current date) is in the past and therefore should be done. The current date moves all by itself as time marches on.

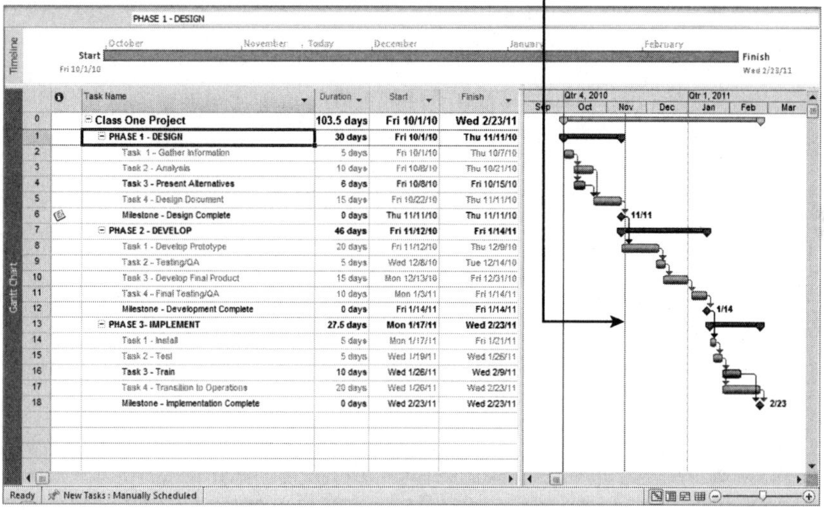

Summary

Getting off on the right foot is critical to your success with Project.

In this chapter, you first became familiar with the ribbon and the various views in Project, including the default Gantt Chart with Timeline view. Next, you reviewed how to use some key tools to help you get started. You learned the importance of using templates to help standardize your project-management approach and make new project setup more efficient. If you've been using Excel for planning, you now know how to bring Excel plans into Project.

You learned the importance of setting up projects to reflect the way you and your organization operate. One of the new features in Project lets you switch from manual scheduling to automatic scheduling. This includes understanding some important option settings, such as how the default task type drives scheduling. You also learned about effort-based and duration-based scheduling.

I encouraged you to turn on automatic generation of the project-summary task for every project. You learned that the project-summary task automatically injects a top-level summary of your project, which rolls up and calculates such things as start and finish dates, duration, work, and costs at the project level.

You learned about drivers that impact the calculation of your schedule's timing, including calendars and the project start date. Calendars define your working time and affect how Project calculates start and finish dates. They can be applied at the project, task, or resource level. The project start date defaults to the system date unless you specify a different date; it's up to you to define the project start date, because it's the starting point for your schedule.

Project also supports backward scheduling—scheduling from the finish date of project. But I recommend scheduling from the project start date and using other tools such as constraints and deadlines to control and manage to an end date.

All the concepts covered in this chapter will become progressively clearer as you move into the next part of the book. I'll walk you through a proven method for creating project plans in the most effective manner possible using Project.

Hands-On Exercises

The following hands-on exercises are designed to test your understanding of the topics discussed in this chapter. We've provided files on the companion CD that will show you what your project file should look like as you perform these exercises.

EXERCISE 1

Setting Up—Initializing a New Project

1. Enter a Start Date for the first working day of next month, and set Calendar to Standard (should be the default).

2. On the Project tab, click Project Information.

3. Enter a Start Date of two weeks from today, and set Calendar to Standard.

4. Click the Statistics button. Why are the current start and end dates the same? Why is there no data in fields other than 0? Click the Close button.

5. Save the File as Class One Project.mpp.

6. Click the Format tab.

7. In the Show/Hide group, select Project Summary Task.

8. Go to the backstage by clicking on the File tab, and click Options. In the dialog box, select Schedule.

9. In the Scheduling Options for This Project section, notice that that New Tasks Created is set to Manually Scheduled.

10. In the same section, change the Default Task Type to Fixed Duration, and uncheck the New Tasks Are Effort Driven check box.

11. In the Calendar Options for This Project section, make sure Hours Per Day is 8 and Hours Per Week is 40.

12. While in Project Options, Select the Save tab. Under Auto Save Every, enter a value of 30 minutes. Ensure that Prompt Before Saving is selected, and click OK.

EXERCISE 2

Change the Working Time—Working With Calendars

1. On the Project tab, in the Properties group, click Change Working Time.

2. Select 24 Hour from the For Calendar drop-down list box, and select Night Shift Calendar. Notice the difference in the working times and days for these two pre-built calendars.

3. In the Change Working Time dialog box, click the Create New Calendar button. In the Name field, type **Class One Project**. Make sure Make a Copy of Standard is selected, and click OK.

4. Click the drop-down list at the top of the dialog box. You now have four choices of calendars, including the new calendar you just created: Class One Project.

5. Click the drop-down list again, and choose the Class One Project calendar.

6. In November, make Thanksgiving and the day after holidays—nonworking days. To create a holiday, select the holiday dates in the calendar, and then enter the holiday name in the Exception text box.

7. In December, make December 25, the day before, and the day after holidays—nonworking days (if it falls on a weekend make the Friday and Monday nonworking days).

8. Answer this question: If a task starts today and is 10 days long, on what date will it end? Remember, duration is calculated using working days.

9. Under the Project tab, select Project Information. Change the Calendar to Class One Project.

As you add resources to the resource sheet (pool), calendars are created for each resource using the Standard calendar as the base. These calendars are automatically added to the drop-down list; you can modify them individually to reflect vacations and work hours, or select any new ones you've created. Resource calendars apply only to specific resources and affect only the tasks to which the resources have been assigned. Project calendars apply to the entire project. If resources are assigned, Project considers both as it calculates start and end dates for tasks.

Planning Essentials

In Part 2, I'll walk you through a tried-and-true planning process to set up your schedules in Project efficiently, following project-management best practices. You'll learn how to create useful plans that set you on the path to success not only in using Project for planning but also in using it for communicating and tracking. Each step is a building block, so it's important to understand the concepts as well as the functionality of the tool. The core planning steps are as follows:

1. Enter the work breakdown structure (WBS).

2. Estimate duration (or work).

3. Set dependencies/task relationships.

4. Assign resources (and costs if required).

These steps can be mapped back to the triple constraints of project management: scope, time, and cost and resources.

Scope is represented by the WBS (step 1). Steps 2 and 3 drive the timing of your schedule and therefore map to the constraint of time. Although step 4 may affect time, depending on your scheduling approach, it maps clearly to the constraint of cost and resources.

You'll try a standard project example, Class One Project, which I've made very generic. It's a simplified development project based on three major phases:

- Design

- Develop

- Implement

Although this example was originally based on a new-product development project, I've made it generic enough to be applicable to any new development initiative. I've also added the word *phase*, *task*, or *milestone* in front of each line item in the WBS to demonstrate how the tool may apply to any type of project. You'll progressively build the plan using the steps I've described. In Chapter 7, "Setting Dependencies and the Critical Path," you'll create another generic project plan called Class Two Project, with which I introduce the concept of creating master consolidated plans with more than one project.

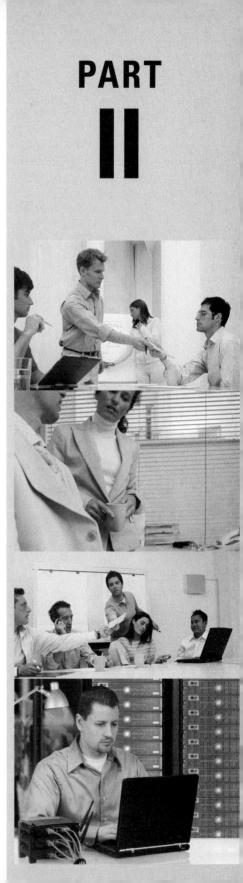

Chapter

5

Creating and Entering the Work Breakdown Structure and Task Arrangement

---

IN THIS CHAPTER, YOU'LL LEARN ABOUT THE FOLLOWING:

✓ A work breakdown structure (WBS) and why it's important

✓ How to enter the WBS and tasks into Project

✓ Key outlining tools for establishing the hierarchy of the WBS

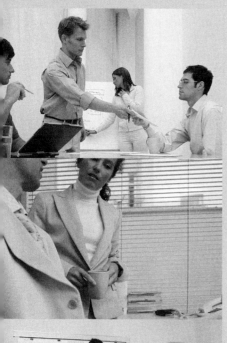

You should consider the WBS a cornerstone of any project plan. A good WBS helps define and organize all the work needed to complete your project. It's the first thing you'll construct in your schedule. After ensuring that you have the basic knowledge surrounding core WBS concepts, I'll walk you through some powerful tools to enter and maintain your WBS in Project.

This chapter uses a WBS example based on a generic development project, broken down into three major phases: Design, Develop, and Implement. Each phase has associated tasks that ultimately drive your timeline, resource requirements, and costs.

What Is a WBS, and Why Is It Important?

"Begin with the End in Mind is based on the principle that all things are created twice. There's a mental or first creation, and a physical or second creation to all things." (Stephen R. Covey, *The 7 Habits of Highly Effective People*.)

Clearly defined goals, no matter what type of project you're working on, are a key to success for managing projects. Studies by the Standish Group, IDC, and others lead to the same conclusion: one of the primary reasons projects fail is poorly defined or misunderstood goals. Defining goals in the context of projects translates into defining *scope*, which ultimately leads to delivering a project that meets or exceeds customer expectations. Between the mental creation and the physical creation, the "End in Mind" needs to be clearly documented and communicated throughout each stage of a project. To document scope in conjunction with other scope documents such as a clearly defined scope statement, you create a WBS, which defines all the work packages that make up the phases (summary tasks), tasks, and milestones. Applying the right techniques and tools to manage this information is essential to your success.

What Is a WBS?

A Guide to the Project Management Body of Knowledge, Fourth Edition (PMBOK), written by the Project Management Institute (PMI), defines the WBS as "a deliverable-oriented hierarchical decomposition of the work to be executed by the project team, to accomplish the project objectives and create the required deliverable."

You begin with the project goal or desired result, which ultimately represents the output or final deliverable and typically described in the scope statement prior to developing a schedule in Project. To create a WBS, you subdivide that goal (final deliverable) into smaller, more manageable pieces in a hierarchical format (much like an organization structure chart), to a level of detail that allows for effective management of the work. The WBS drives the creation of all phases, tasks, and milestones in a project schedule. These phases, tasks, and milestones subsequently can be scheduled for time, resources, and costs.

 The WBS represents the total scope of work in a project. Therefore, what isn't defined in the WBS is outside the scope of a project.

Creating a WBS, and Its Importance to Project

Creating, documenting, and managing a WBS well is imperative for anyone interested in using project-management software effectively. Choosing the right tool to support this effort is critical. Project is specifically designed for this purpose and is fully equipped with uncomplicated functionality to get you up and running fast with a WBS; it also includes more advanced features if you want or need them.

Sometimes, difficulty grasping the concepts behind creating a WBS creates misplaced frustration with using project-management software. Remember that the WBS represents all the work in your project, from start to finish. Project helps you represent the work, but the mental process of creating it is up to you regardless of the tool you use.

You can begin to create a WBS by focusing on the final deliverables. Then, ask yourself, "What are the key interim deliverables?" Each interim deliverable becomes a level 1 component in the WBS. If it's difficult to think of interim deliverables, think of important milestones—those are probably your level 1 activities. After you define each level 1 component, break these coarse-grained activities into finer-grained activities, as outlined in Table 5.1.

TABLE 5.1   Basic WBS Outline Format

WBS Item	Description
(0) Final deliverable	Project summary task
1.0 Interim deliverable 1	Summary task, phase, or major piece
1.1 Task 1	Lowest level of detail in the structure
1.2 Task 2	
1.3 Task *n*	
1.4 Key milestone	Deliverable achieved
2.0 Interim deliverable 2	
2.1 Task 1	

TABLE 5.1   Basic WBS Outline Format *(continued)*

WBS Item	Description
2.2 Task 2	
2.3 Task *n*	
2.4 Key milestone	Deliverable achieved
3.0 Interim deliverable *n*	

Developing a WBS is often a complex endeavor that requires understanding both the techniques for WBS development and the scope of the subject matter at hand. As a project manager, you'll often rely on subject matter experts (SMEs) for input into the WBS, to achieve better accuracy. Using a tool like Project with the right techniques allows greater involvement from SMEs. Their input leads to more complete scope definition, schedule development, and resource and budget estimates.

⊕ Real World Scenario

Developing a WBS with Input from the Team

I've helped many clients develop effective project plans, based on first developing a sound WBS. One situation involved a $70 million portion of a development project for a large pharmaceutical company. We brought a global project team together for a two-day offsite meeting. Working with core SMEs, I developed a high-level WBS as a starting point. Each functional area was given its own color of sticky notes. On a wall that represented their functional area (department), under each high-level item (phase or deliverable), each group added details using the sticky notes. By the end of the meeting, I was able to take the wall WBS and incorporate it into Project, ultimately leading to the creation of a complete cross-functional project plan that had 100 percent buy-in from the team.

The investment up front of developing the WBS with the core team was cited as one of the key reasons the project was considered successful; the WBS saved them significant money and time during implementation. One of the byproducts of this approach was that it allowed an incredible amount of collaboration among the participants and groups. The WBS also served as a template for future development projects.

I've since used similar techniques with project teams, using sticky notes or a technique called *mind mapping* to define a WBS on a wall or on paper before entering it into the tool.

After a WBS is developed, it needs to be supported by the right tool, and that of course is the focus of this book: Microsoft Project 2010. If your projects follow a standard methodology or approach, then the WBS can be templated, as discussed in Chapter 4, "Getting Started and Setting Up the Microsoft Project Environment." The key component to creating successful templates is the WBS. Therefore, to be successful using any template, you must be familiar with creating, modifying, and manipulating the WBS in Project.

A WBS can be displayed in many different formats, but it's commonly displayed in an outline structure, network diagram, or tree structure. The default in Project is the Gantt Chart view, which is based on using an outline format as described in Table 5.1. Many project managers like to view their WBS in a tree structure that's similar to an organization chart format, as shown in Figure 5.1. Unfortunately, such as tree structure isn't readily available in Project; but you can build a tree-structure diagram in Visio and import it into Project, which displays it in an outline format. You can also take your WBS outline from Project into Visio.

FIGURE 5.1   WBS in a tree structure

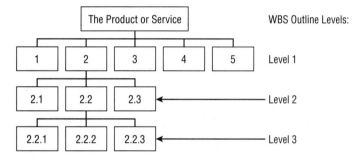

As each box is broken down into more detail, you can see new WBS levels being developed. Each level rolls up or collapses into the one above it. Level 0 represents the project level, and level 1 represents the coarsest level of detail. Usually, this level includes the big pieces or interim deliverables. For example, you may see things like requirements, design, development, testing and quality assurance (QA), and roll-out at level 1. Level 2 and beyond move the WBS from a coarse-grain view to a fine-grain view.

As you can see in Figure 5.1, the WBS coding structure corresponds to work packages the same way you may organize complex documents using section 1.0, paragraph 1.1.1; section 2.0, paragraph 2.1.1; and so on. You should also distinguish coarse-grain and fine-grain components in an outline format; the layout may look like that in Figure 5.2.

Project 2010 includes a feature called *manual scheduling*, discussed in more detail later in this chapter and in following chapters. Figure 5.2 displays duration, dates, and dependencies; but manual scheduling allows you to create a WBS without them. This lets you first focus on scope planning by creating a WBS without having Project automatically fill in durations, dates, and Gantt bars.

Remember, if you want outline codes to appear automatically in your plan, as discussed in Chapter 4, you can switch them on by going to the Format tab ➤ Show/Hide group ➤ Outline Number.

FIGURE 5.2   WBS example with outline codes in Project

Outline Numbers are automatically generated based on the level and position of the line item. As you move tasks around or insert new ones these numbers are automatically recalibrated.

Show Outline Number: Under the Format tab, Show/Hide group you can click on or off the Outline Number.

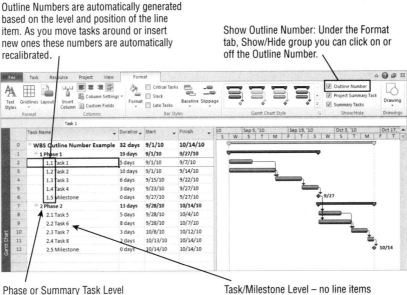

Phase or Summary Task Level

Task/Milestone Level – no line items indented directly under it.

Right-Sizing Your Plan

How many levels of detail can you have in Project, and how many details should you include in your WBS? The answer to the first part of the question is, "As many as you need." You can insert and indent as many levels of detail as necessary, as discussed later in this chapter. The second part of the question is slightly more complicated. Figure 5.2 shows a two-level WBS, but the majority of projects have between three and six levels of detail; larger-scale projects can have even more. It's up to the project manager to ensure that the WBS is right-sized to optimize productivity based on the specific type and size of the project.

If the WBS is too small (has too few details), it will add little value to the plan and won't provide clear direction or communicate the project scope well. On the other hand, if the WBS is too large (has too many details), it will leads to over-complication. You'll have too much overhead to carry and manage in the plan to optimize your return on investment during execution. Right-sizing is a balancing act between the team members doing the work and the project manager managing the work—between micro-managing (defining who does what when) and being able to report progress to your sponsor or project customer.

It's usually a challenge to choose the most appropriate level of WBS elements. You can use the following guidelines to help define the levels of detail for your plan:

- Is the WBS structure compatible with your organization's reporting requirements and management systems?

- What level of detail do team members require (as opposed to upper management, which generally requires less detail)?

- Is there enough detail to estimate resource requirements?

- Is there enough detail to estimate timeline requirements?

- Are all related items on the same vertical branch?

- Do lower-level elements fully describe the upper level?

- Does the WBS detail allow you to effectively manage project risks and drive key issues?

- Does the WBS provide the most effective way to plan for and track the project scope, timeline, and budget?

🌐 Real World Scenario

Too Much Can Be a Bad Thing

We were working at a client site to develop a detailed project template that would be used and reused to initiate the plans for new product-development initiatives. We started with some gung-ho SMEs who were very detailed-oriented and wanted to make sure everything was captured. By the time all the inputs had been collected for each phase or major component and deliverable, the template contained 3,000 line items. It seemed harmless enough, and everyone was proud of it when it was done—except some important stakeholders. The program managers and team members were overwhelmed with the amount of detail and found little value when planning that much detail into projects, especially because they knew many projects would be canceled before completion, not making it through all the stage gates.

This highly detailed template also complicated training, because users were learning the tool for the first time. Complexity became the issue of the day, and the template was met with much resistance. We ended up scaling back the template to about 500 line items, with the flexibility to add more details as a project progressed through each stage. You need to balance the needs of all the stakeholders—lesson learned!

Progressive Elaboration and Defining Project Phases and Milestones

Projects are usually divided into *phases*, which become the level 1 components of the WBS. Using project phases provides better management control and appropriate links to the operations at your organization. Each project phase is marked by completion of one or more milestones. *Milestones* are important completion points in a project that are often tied to a deliverable that is a tangible, verifiable work product, such as a study report, a detail design, a document, or a working prototype. The deliverables, and hence the phases, are part of a generally sequential logic designed to ensure proper definition of the product, service, or result of the project based on the WBS.

In more formalized project-management organizations or more significant projects, the conclusion of a project phase is often marked by a review of both key deliverables and project performance. This is done to determine whether the project should continue into its next phase and to detect and correct errors cost-effectively. Phase-end reviews are often called *phase exits*, *stage gates*, or *go/no-go decision points*.

Each project phase normally includes a set of defined work packages designed to establish the desired level of management control. The majority of these items are related to the primary phase deliverable, and the phases typically take their names from these: Product Design, Develop, Testing, Roll-out, and others as appropriate. Typically, the details of these components become more clearly defined or understood as you move through the project life cycle.

As a project manager, you can apply rolling-wave planning in Project to progressively elaborate the detail of the WBS and move from a coarse-grain view to a more detailed, fine-grain view. In Project, it's fine to elaborate on one phase and not another. You can add details at any time. In other words, you can begin with high-level estimates for all phases, major tasks, and milestones to provide a sense of the order of magnitude you're expecting and add the details later, as you move from one phase to the next.

Using manual scheduling, you can also do *top-down* scheduling. This means you put in estimates at the phase or summary-task level that remain separately calculated from the detailed roll-up tasks. I cover this concept in depth in Chapter 6, "Estimating and Entering Duration and Work." Consider Figure 5.3, which shows some detail mapped out in Phase 1 but only high-level activities for Phases 2 and 3. More detail will be added as you move from Design to Develop, after Design is closer to completion. You can capture the order of magnitude for Develop and Implement, with the idea that you'll elaborate on them as you move from one phase to the next.

FIGURE 5.3   Progressive elaboration timeline

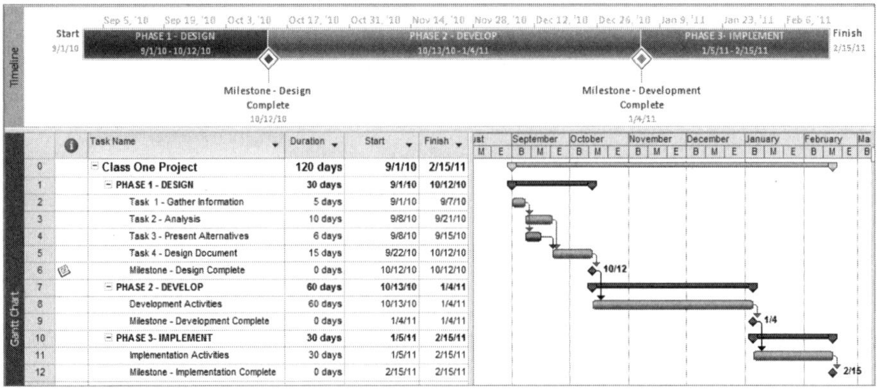

You have one high-level task in Phase 2 called Development Activities and one in Phase 3 called Implementation Activities. A new feature in Project 2010 allows you to create a top-down summary task, which supports the concept of progressive elaboration. Typically in Project the details indented under a summary task drive the calculation of duration and start and finish dates. But you can now create summary tasks first; they can have dates that don't exactly match the roll-up dates of the subtasks. This will be discussed in detail in Chapter 6.

Determining Your Project Tasks and Milestones

Schedules consist of tasks and their relationships. A *task* is a work activity or event that has a clear start, a clear end, and a duration; it typically produces a measurable result or end product. A task also implies action, so it's a best practice to name your tasks with a verb-noun combination such as "write draft," "review draft," or "approve draft."

Project presents WBS information on the screen in a hierarchical arrangement. In Project, a task is usually shown indented below a phase of the WBS know as the summary task, as in Figure 5.2. The last level of detail in your WBS—the line item that has nothing indented under it—always defaults to being a task or milestone. As soon as you indent a line item under it, that item is no longer considered a task but becomes a summary task (a phase or major piece of the WBS) automatically.

Here are two basic approaches you can follow to define tasks:

- Begin at the start of the phase or summary task, and lay out tasks until you reach the finish.

- Begin at the end of the phase or summary task, and work backward to the start. (What task or tasks must be completed before this task can begin?)

It's a best practice to add a finish task to the task list to wrap up the summary task or phase. These tasks are also referred to as *milestones*—tasks with zero duration. Milestones are important events or dates in a project but aren't tasks with work associated with them.

Milestone

When you assign a duration of zero to a task, it automatically changes to a milestone and is represented in the Gantt bar area by a diamond.

Milestones are incredibly useful for reporting, gating, decision-making, defining key handoff points, benchmarking, and tracking, so it's a good idea to add them to your plan. They don't have to be at the end of a summary task—they can be spread throughout your plan. But placing milestones at the end of summary tasks is a good starting point. Because milestones represent a completion point, it's a best practice to name them as a completed task, such as "draft completed" or "draft approved."

Where the Rubber Meets the Road

I'm always gratified when I help a client succeed who was struggling with developing a plan early in their project-management career. It sounds easy at first: put together a list of tasks, and create a schedule. No problem. But it isn't so easy.

At any given time, I'm usually working with four or five customers that are building project plans or developing templates after they've made a first attempt and haven't ended up where they wanted to be. Generally, they're in this situation for two reasons: they don't understand the techniques for creating a meaningful WBS, and they don't understand how to use the tool to create the structure. Someone like me can facilitate both the process and the tool knowledge, allowing the client to focus on the content and simultaneously transferring that knowledge so the client can take over the process and the tool.

This is where the rubber meets the road. The tool is ineffective without a good WBS and task structure, and you can't function efficiently in any project without a good WBS.

If you don't know what you're doing at this point, it will become obvious. Don't be afraid to ask for help. You can minimize your pain, frustration, and embarrassment by seeking assistance from experienced project managers internal or external to your organization, from the Web, from training, or, yes, even from a consultant. The information is becoming a commodity and is readily available; you only have yourself to blame if you don't act. The more you learn about WBS development and techniques, the more success you'll enjoy in managing any type of project, large or small.

Entering Your WBS: Phases, Tasks, and Milestones

In this section, you'll learn how to enter your WBS phases, tasks, and milestones into Project. You'll learn about the importance of the Task Name column and how to differentiate between a phase, a task, and a milestone in Project.

Getting to Know the Task Name Column

In Project 2010, you need to become thoroughly familiar with the Task Name column in the default Entry table in the default Gantt Chart view, which is under the View tab. Part 3,

"Communicating and Reporting Essentials," provides information about how to customize both views and tables in Chapter 10, "Understanding Views," and Chapter 11, "Using Tables and Custom Fields." For now, note that the root field for the task name in the field list is *name*; *task* is added as a custom title in the Entry table.

The Task Name column is important because this is where you enter and manage the WBS components, resulting in the definition of the phases, tasks, and milestones for your project. There are many ways to get the WBS components into the Task Name column, including starting from a template with a predefined WBS set. As mentioned in Chapter 4, you can create your own template or use one of the many existing templates that come with Project. To find these, go to the backstage under New, and choose Sample Templates.

If you don't have a template to start from or a list of tasks in another application to copy and paste, you need to enter your WBS directly into the Task Name column. The Task tab and groups are organized to enable this. Decide whether you want to start with the Manually Schedule option or the Auto Schedule option on the Task tab in the Schedule group, as discussed in Chapter 4. You can begin with manual scheduling, which allows you to focus 100 percent on the WBS without being distracted by automatic duration, start date, and finish date estimates.

To enter a WBS element into Project, follow these steps:

1. In the Task Name column, click the cell in line item 1.

2. Enter the name of the phase, task, or milestone.

3. Press Enter.

Repeat these steps for each WBS element. One technique is to enter all the WBS components first and then outline the details. Sometimes this can be more efficient if you have the complete list of tasks; but if you want to outline the tasks and create the hierarchy as you go, using a more brainstorming type of approach, you can.

When entering the WBS components, stay focused on completing the list. Don't worry about other columns in the Entry table; these will be important only after you've completed the WBS setup. Figure 5.4 shows the WBS elements before durations have been assigned.

As you enter a WBS element into the Task Name column, you don't have to put the word *task* or *milestone* in front of the item; Project detects phases (summary tasks), tasks, and milestones automatically when you indent a line item, as I'll explain in the next section. I've added these words to the example in Figure 5.4 so you can see where I'm heading.

Also as shown in Figure 5.4, on the Task tab, in the Insert group, you can quickly insert summary tasks (phases), milestones (tasks with zero duration), and tasks.

User-Controlled Scheduling

As discussed in Chapter 4, you can choose between manual scheduling and automatic scheduling. Throughout this book, you'll learn best practices for scheduling that lead to dynamic, effective project plans. However, early in the planning process, you may want to use manual scheduling, which ignores automatic scheduling tools when Project calculates start and finish dates for your plan until you're ready to turn them on.

FIGURE 5.4   Entering the WBS into the Task Name column

Enter the WBS (phases, tasks, and milestones) directly into the Task Name column in the default Gantt Chart view. Stay focused on completing the WBS prior to entering other schedule and resource information.

Under the Task tab in the Insert group, you can easily add new Summary tasks (phases), milestones (tasks with zero duration), and tasks to your WBS.

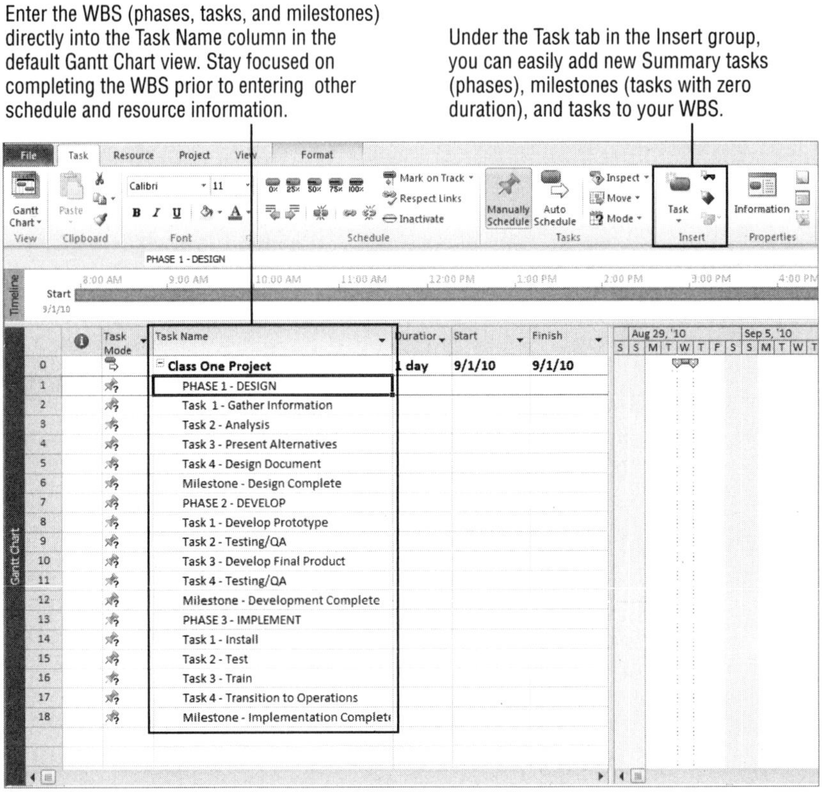

The default for Project is to start with manual scheduling turned on. This can easily be shifted to automatic scheduling when you're ready. To switch back and forth from manual to automatic, either use the Task Mode column in the Gantt chart Entry table or go to the Task tab; in the Schedule group, you can toggle back and forth from manual to automatic. One of the key benefits of using manual scheduling when you're defining your WBS is that you can begin with a blank slate and not be distracted by automatic duration estimates and start and finish dates. This allows you to stay focused on finishing your WBS before entering your schedule estimates. Figure 5.5 illustrates the difference between a section (Phase 1) with automatic scheduling turned on and a section (Phase 1) with manual scheduling turned on.

Outlining (Indenting and Outdenting) Tools

After you've entered the components of your WBS in the Task Name column, it's time to organize the phases, tasks, and milestones. Using the outlining tools shown in Figure 5.6 allows you to structure the information into the correct hierarchy so each task and milestone belongs to the appropriate summary task (which I use synonymously with the term *phase*). Task tab ➢ Insert group ➢ Summary automatically creates the initial hierarchy for you, as shown in Figure 5.6.

FIGURE 5.5   Automatic scheduling and manual scheduling examples

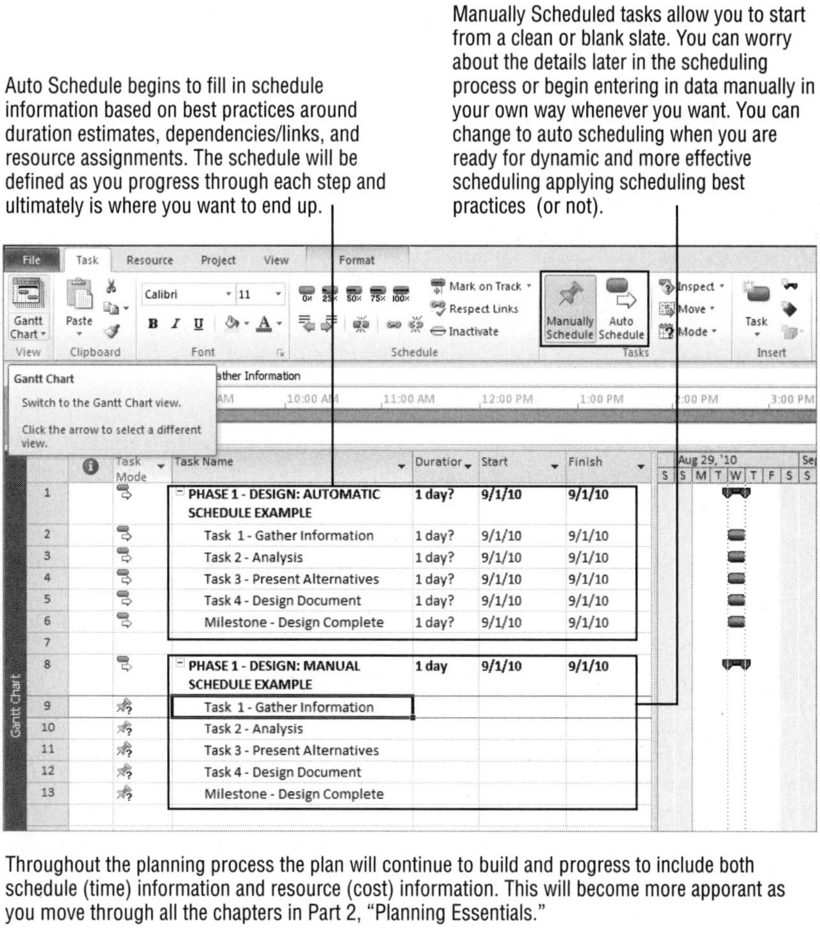

Auto Schedule begins to fill in schedule information based on best practices around duration estimates, dependencies/links, and resource assignments. The schedule will be defined as you progress through each step and ultimately is where you want to end up.

Manually Scheduled tasks allow you to start from a clean or blank slate. You can worry about the details later in the scheduling process or begin entering in data manually in your own way whenever you want. You can change to auto scheduling when you are ready for dynamic and more effective scheduling applying scheduling best practices (or not).

Throughout the planning process the plan will continue to build and progress to include both schedule (time) information and resource (cost) information. This will become more apporant as you move through all the chapters in Part 2, "Planning Essentials."

Summary Tasks

Summary tasks provide broad categories under which you can group tasks. The summary task represents the total work (effort), cost, duration, and start and finish dates of all the detailed tasks below it. In the Class One Project example, Design is the summary task. The totals across each column are calculated based on the roll-up of the detailed tasks: Gather Information, Analysis, Present Alternatives, Design Document, and the milestone Design Complete.

FIGURE 5.6   Inserting a summary task automatically

Project automatically creates an initial hierarchy
when you use the Insert Summary command.
Notice a placeholder has been created for you
to enter your first indented task.

Under the Task tab in the Insert
group, you can easily insert or add
a new Summary (phase)

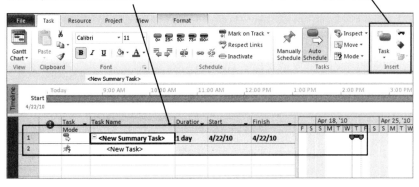

 Project 2010 includes a feature that lets you turn off the automatic roll-up
calculation of the summary row. If you turn the summary task to manual
scheduling, it no longer takes into account the detailed tasks below it.
This allows you to freely enter duration, start, finish, and any other project
information at the phase level. This approach, which is covered in more
detail in Chapter 6, supports *top-down scheduling* and is new to Project
2010. In previous versions of Project, you were forced into a bottom-up
estimating and couldn't freely enter information at the summary level.

This approach is particularly useful if you want to enter high-level estimates first for, say, an entire phase, such as **Develop—3 Months**, and
later enter the detail estimates. Even better, Project 2010 lets you have the
summary task maintain its manually entered estimate and compare it to
the roll-up of the detail tasks, giving you the best of both worlds. This is
covered in more detail in the next chapter.

Notice the difference between the way a task and a summary task (phase) are displayed
in the Gantt bar area. To differentiate between a phase (major piece or summary task) and
a detail task, follow these steps (see Figure 5.7):

1. Click the line item you wish to indent.

2. On the Task tab, in the Tasks group, click the Indent button to make it a detail task of
the summary task above it.

3. Repeat this process for each detail task and milestone associated with that phase or
summary task.

You can highlight several tasks and indent all at once. Stop indenting when you get to the next summary task.

> You can select a block of tasks and indent (or outdent) them all at once. Use the Ctrl or Shift key for multiple selections.

FIGURE 5.7 Outlining the WBS with Indent and Outdent tools

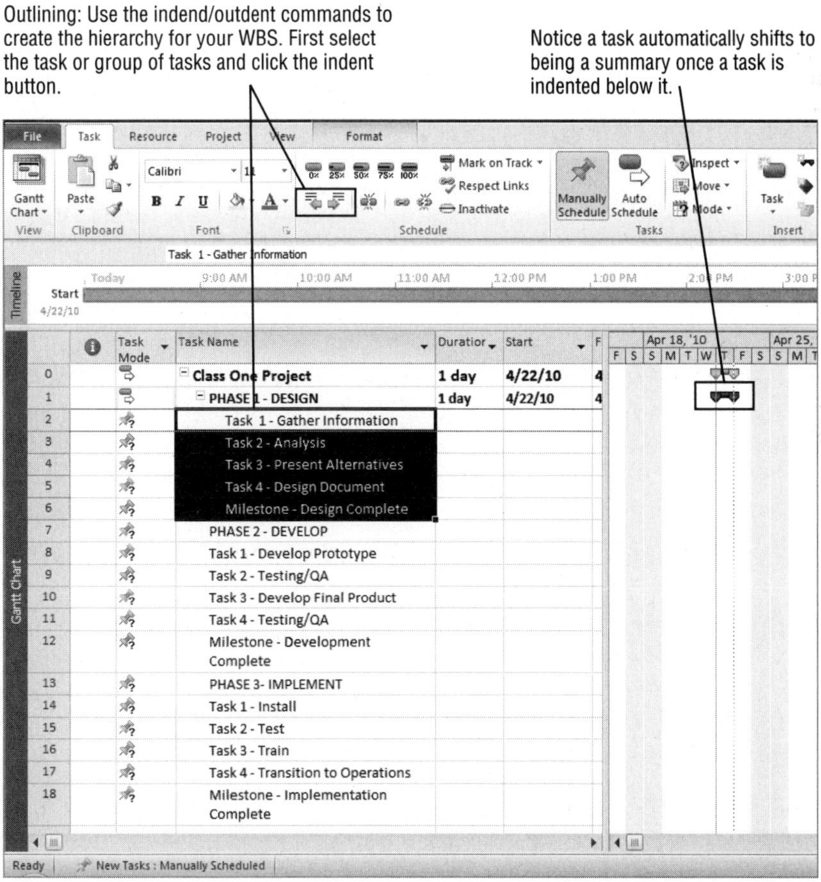

Outlining: Use the indend/outdent commands to create the hierarchy for your WBS. First select the task or group of tasks and click the indent button.

Notice a task automatically shifts to being a summary once a task is indented below it.

As each component is broken down into more detail, you can see new levels in the WBS being developed. Each level rolls up, or collapses, into the one above it. As a result, you get multiple levels of detail for each project. As noted previously, level 0 represents the project level, and level 1 represents the highest level or coarsest level of detail. Level 2 and beyond move the WBS from a coarse-grain view to a finer-grain view.

Collapse and Expand: Show Outline

After you begin outlining tasks, a minus sign appears beside each summary task in the Task Name cell. You can click it to collapse, or roll up, the detail tasks beneath the summary task. If a summary task is collapsed, a plus sign appears beside it; you can click the plus sign to expand the detail. This way, you can create roll-ups of your plan by collapsing and expanding various levels of detail.

WYSIWYG

As you get to know Project, you'll discover that it's a WYSIWYG (pronounced "wizzywig") product—what you see is what you get. This means that whatever you display on the screen is what's printed or communicated, including the levels of detail you've collapsed or expanded. As explained in Chapter 14, "Creating Master Schedules with Inserted Projects" Project 2010 includes enhancements to the print and page setup features to make it easier to preview, change, and fit Gantt charts for more effective printing.

You can also use the Show Outline tool, shown in Figure 5.8, to quickly expand and collapse various levels of detail in a plan. Using this tool allows you to display and report at the necessary level of detail for the group you're communicating with. Usually, stakeholders who are higher in the organization require less WBS detail; those at the team level require more. Show Outline lets you quickly generate a level 1 report or a level 2 report without having to collapse or expand the summary tasks one at a time.

FIGURE 5.8   Collapse and expand WBS with Show Outline.

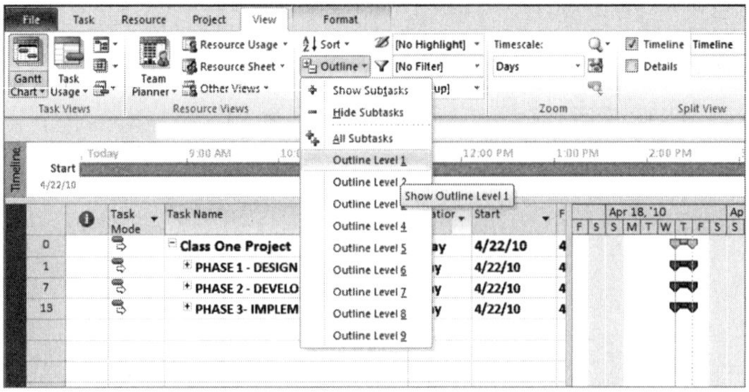

Follow these steps to generate a level 1 view:

1. Select View tab ➤ Data group ➤ Show Outline.
2. From the drop-down menu, select Outline Level 1.

   You can select any level of detail needed.

Managing Your WBS

Take advantage of the WBS coding tool to maintain and manage your WBS and easily move, copy, add, or delete phases, tasks, or milestones. Use the multilevel undo (MLU) feature to run what-if scenarios.

Using the WBS Coding Tool

As discussed in Chapter 4, you can turn on outline codes automatically by selecting Format tab ➤ Show/Hide group ➤ Outline Number. You can turn the Project Summary line on or off here as well; doing so automatically numbers line items based on their relative positions in the WBS.

As you add, delete, or move tasks or add more detail, the numbering automatically adjusts to reflect the new structure. Unfortunately, this isn't always good news. You may need to freeze your WBS codes so they don't change or automatically renumber. For example, if a large project has a number of vendors, or a project is charged to an external customer, the WBS represents the scope and statement of work; it reflects what is charged out to the customer. After a contract is signed and the scope is signed off (particularly if you're charging hours or dollars against a line item in the plan), you may want to freeze the WBS numbers so you can be consistent in reporting and referring to those line items.

Typically, adding line items reflects a change in scope and therefore may require adding a new unique WBS number without changing existing ones. Hence, the WBS becomes your primary tool to manage changes to scope, which generally have an impact on time and cost. If you want to manage your WBS in this fashion, you can take advantage of the WBS coding tool and apply the WBS field to your table. With this in mind, you need to first turn off the Outline Number option. (Be sure it's unchecked: Format tab ➤ Show/Hide group ➤ Outline Number.)

To insert a WBS field into the Entry table (the default table in the Gantt chart view), follow these steps:

1. In the Entry table, click the Task Name column header. Doing so highlights the entire column.

2. Select Format tab ➤ Columns group ➤ Column Settings, and then choose Insert Column. A list appears of fields that can be inserted into any table.

3. From the Field Name drop-down list, select WBS. As shown in Figure 5.9, the WBS column is inserted to the left of Task Name column with the WBS numbers automatically shown.

4. You can move a column by highlighting the column header and clicking and dragging to the right or left in the table.

In Project 2010, you can also go to the last column in the Gantt chart and click the Add New Column heading. Doing so opens the list of fields available to be inserted into the table. You can turn this option on or off on by selecting Format tab ➤ Columns group ➤ Column Settings ➤ Display Add New Column.

FIGURE 5.9   Insert WBS column

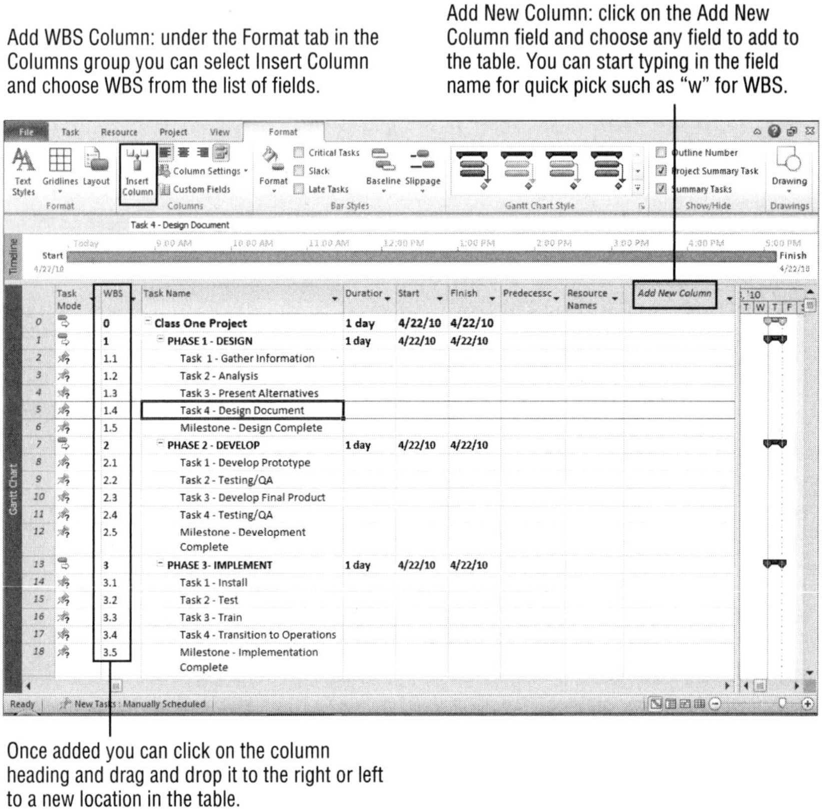

Add WBS Column: under the Format tab in the Columns group you can select Insert Column and choose WBS from the list of fields.

Add New Column: click on the Add New Column field and choose any field to add to the table. You can start typing in the field name for quick pick such as "w" for WBS.

Once added you can click on the column heading and drag and drop it to the right or left to a new location in the table.

Initially, the WBS number is equivalent to what the Outline Number option provides. The default WBS structure uses a numerical sequence (1, 1.1, 1.1.1, and so on), and this is often all you need. The default remains in place until you define the outline code using the WBS function. Using this tool, you can set up a WBS coding format and then renumber to freeze the codes. You can renumber the codes at any time.

When you renumber the WBS codes, Project applies a numbering scheme based on the current outline structure, in sequence. For example, you can choose a code that has numeric and alpha in combination, such as 1.1.a, 1.1.b, and so on.

To set up a WBS coding format and set your codes, follow these steps:

1. Select Project tab ➢ Properties group ➢ WBS.

2. Click Define Code. Figure 5.10 shows the WBS Code Definition dialog box.

3. Enter a prefix code, if needed, in the Project Code Prefix field. Prefix codes are often useful to identify a project or program name; they aren't required. Figure 5.10 shows the prefix Trn, to represent training.

4. In the Code Mask section, define the type of sequence for each outline level of your WBS code. Each level builds on the others to create the complete WBS code mask:

    Level   This indicates the outline level being defined. This field automatically increments as you enter additional code masks.

    Sequence   Select from a drop-down list of choices to define how successive WBS items are to be listed. The choices are Numbers (Ordered), Uppercase Letters (Ordered), Lowercase Letters (Ordered), and Characters (Unordered).

    Length   Enter a number representing the required length for this level of WBS code. Click Any if the WBS code can be any length. The maximum length of the entire WBS code is 255 characters.

    Separator   Enter a character to separate the WBS code levels. The default separator is a period.

5. Accept the default settings for Length and Separator. (You could customize Length or Separator if, for example, you wanted 1.0 instead of 1 for the first level.)

6. Press Enter for each WBS level. You need one code mask for each WBS level in your plan.

7. Click OK. Your WBS code is now set.

Working with WBS Codes

You can renumber your WBS codes at any time by selecting Project tab ➢ Properties group ➢ WBS ➢ Renumber. You're prompted to renumber for the entire project or just the selected tasks. After you set the WBS codes, whenever you add a new task, the WBS number will be unique regardless of its position in the task list.

Also remember that WBS codes are maintained in a separate WBS field, which isn't directly beside the task name, like the Outline Number option. If you still have the Outline Number option turned on, the outline renumbers automatically and continues to appear directly beside the task in the Task Name column regardless of the WBS codes you customize. These two identifiers may be different—automated outline numbers and WBS codes aren't synchronized.

Conducting What-if Scenarios with Multilevel Undo

Multilevel undo (MLU) allows you to conduct various what-if scenarios. What if a task is delayed by a week, or you want to try assigning different resources or inserting new tasks? MLU gives you peace of mind; you can try different approaches or apply different options, and easily undo them.

FIGURE 5.10 Define and set WBS codes.

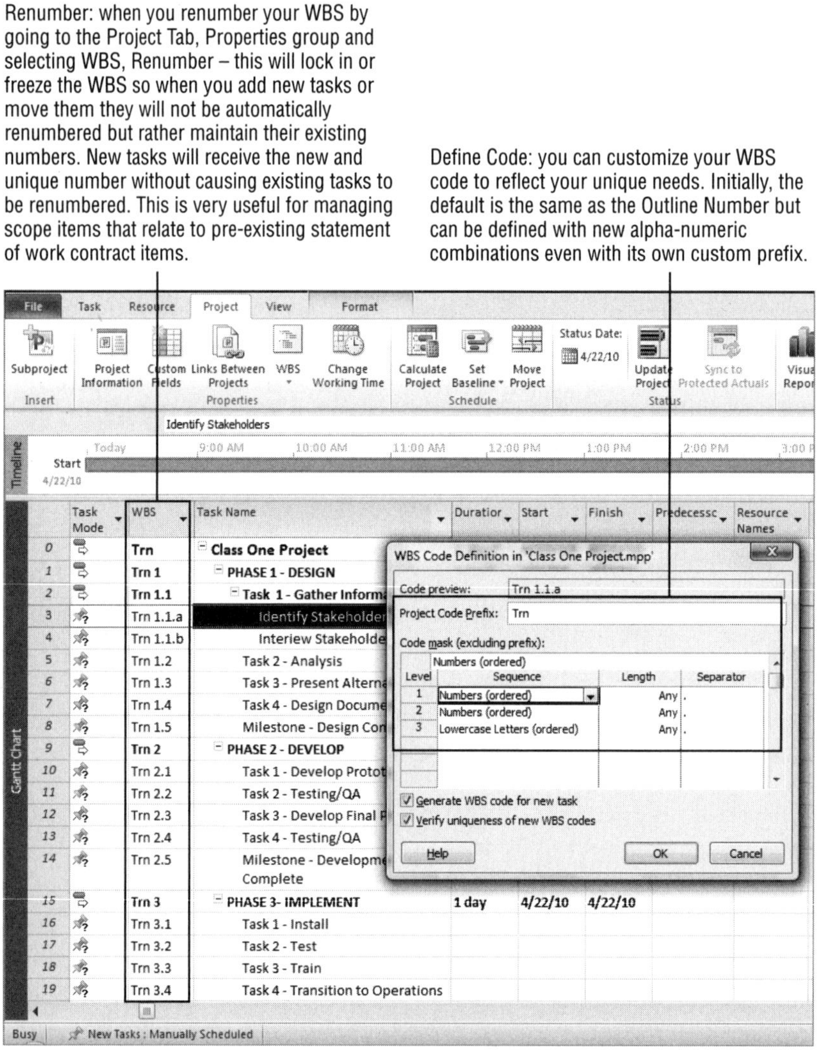
Renumber: when you renumber your WBS by going to the Project Tab, Properties group and selecting WBS, Renumber – this will lock in or freeze the WBS so when you add new tasks or move them they will not be automatically renumbered but rather maintain their existing numbers. New tasks will receive the new and unique number without causing existing tasks to be renumbered. This is very useful for managing scope items that relate to pre-existing statement of work contract items.
Define Code: you can customize your WBS code to reflect your unique needs. Initially, the default is the same as the Outline Number but can be defined with new alpha-numeric combinations even with its own custom prefix.
WBS Code Definition in 'Class One Project.mpp'
Code preview: Trn 1.1.a
Project Code Prefix: Trn
Code mask (excluding prefix):
Level
Sequence
Length
Separator
1 Numbers (ordered) Any .
2 Numbers (ordered) Any .
3 Lowercase Letters (ordered) Any .
Generate WBS code for new task
Verify uniqueness of new WBS codes
Help
OK
Cancel

In Project 2010, you don't have to click the Undo button multiple times. The MLU tool, shown in Figure 5.11, comes with a drop-down list that lets you pick how many actions you wish to undo. This feature is more useful, the larger and more complex your project is.

To use the MLU functionality, follow these steps:

1. On the Quick Access Toolbar, click the Undo button.
2. Click repeatedly to undo, or use the drop-down list to select the number of actions to undo.

You can also apply this technique for multiple redo.

FIGURE 5.11 Using Multilevel undo

Real World Scenario

Map the WBS to the Statement of Work

While working with a client to set up an integrated project schedule for a large government aerospace contract, I had to map the WBS to the statement of work (SOW). In this plan, we also needed to attach payments for each SOW item. Each SOW item ended in a milestone, which allowed us to create a milestone payment plan.

To manage the SOW, we defined the code mask accordingly; it mapped to the WBS. We also had to ensure that the WBS codes didn't change as we added more items to accommodate change requests (particularly major scope changes) or to move components around to accommodate more effective tracking.

Without a tool like the WBS coding tool, we would have had to customize a text or number field and type the numbers manually. The WBS coding tool saved us a significant amount of time by automating this process.

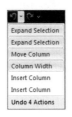

Summary

With or without a tool, creating and managing an effective WBS is a key technique to successfully manage projects. The WBS defines the total scope of a project and is the primary driver for establishing effective schedules and resource and cost plans. Project comes fully equipped with easy-to-use tools to get you up and running fast. Powerful tools are at your fingertips whenever you need them, for complete WBS management.

Creating and entering the WBS into Project is the first step toward scheduling success, and you should take ample time on any project to define the WBS properly. The larger the project and the more people involved in performing the work, the more complex the WBS will be, and the more time you'll need. Just because a project is small doesn't mean you shouldn't create a WBS; it means the WBS will be smaller. You need an effective tool to manage your WBS, big or small; and Project is the right tool for the job.

Hands-On Exercises

The following hands-on exercises are designed to test your understanding of the topics discussed in this chapter. We've provided files on the companion CD that will show you what your project file should look like as you perform these exercises.

EXERCISE 3

Outlining (Creating the WBS)

Using step 1 of the planning process enter the WBS (phases, tasks, and milestones), create the following WBS and try some of the features described in this chapter. Make sure you understand the value of entering tasks and outlining in two separate steps. Also make sure you understand the many reasons for developing your WBS prior to entering data in Project.

1. Enter the following in the Task Name column in your Class One Project fileL

    PHASE I – DESIGN
    >   Task 1 – Gather Information
    >   Task 2 – Analysis
    >   Task 3 – Present Alternatives
    >   Task 4 – Design/Document
    >   Milestone – Design Complete

    PHASE 2 – DEVELOP
    >   Task 1 – Develop Prototype
    >   Task 2 – Testing/QA
    >   Task 3 – Develop Final Product
    >   Task 4 – Final Testing/QA
    >   Milestone – Development Complete

    PHASE 3 – IMPLEMENT
    >   Task 1 – Install
    >   Task 2 – Test
    >   Task 3 – Train
    >   Task 4 – Transition to Operations
    >   Milestone – Implementation Complete

2. Use the Indent and Outdent tools to create the following hierarchy:

    PHASE I – DESIGN
    >   Task 1 – Gather Information
    >   Task 2 – Analysis

Task 3 – Present Alternatives

Task 4 – Design/Document

Milestone – Design Complete

PHASE 2 – DEVELOP

Task 1 – Develop Prototype

Task 2 – Testing/QA

Task 3 – Develop Final Product

Task 4 – Testing/QA

Milestone – Development Complete

PHASE 3 – IMPLEMENT

Task 1 – Install

Task 2 – Test

Task 3 – Train

Task 4 – Transition to Operations

Milestone – Implementation Complete

3. Select Format tab ➢ Show/Hide group ➢ Outline Number. Make sure Project Summary Task is checked as well.

4. Outline numbers appear next to the task names. Notice that level 0 is project summary task.

5. Select a phase, and use the + or – button for the View tab ➢ Data group ➢ Show Outline function to collapse and expand detail.

6. Use the + and – buttons to expand or collapse the entire project at the project summary task level.

7. Use the double-plus button for the View tab ➢ Data group ➢ Show Outline ➢ All Subtasks option to expand the entire project.

8. Save the Class One Project file.

 In a normal schedule, you do not need to add the word "task" or "milestone" in front of the name. You are doing it in this exercise just for practice and to help with networking in future exercises.

Chapter

6

Estimating and Entering Duration or Work

IN THIS CHAPTER, YOU'LL LEARN ABOUT THE FOLLOWING:

- ✓ Understanding the difference between duration and work in Project 2010

- ✓ Using duration conversion factors as they pertain to working time

- ✓ Estimating and entering duration and work in Project

- ✓ Performing top-down estimating vs. bottom up estimating

- ✓ Understanding and using the Performance Evaluation and Review Technique (PERT) in Project

Remember that you follow a four-step process to creating schedules effectively:

1. Enter the work breakdown structure.
2. Estimate duration (or work).
3. Set dependencies/task relationships.
4. Assign resources (and costs if required).

This chapter covers step 2 of the process. After you've established your work breakdown structure (WBS), which is all about defining your scope, as explained in Chapter 5, "Creating and Entering the Work Breakdown Structure," you can focus on establishing your timeline. This includes both estimating and entering duration, as explained in this chapter, followed by setting task dependencies as discussed in Chapter 7, "Setting Dependencies and the Critical Path." I'll explain the difference between work and duration and teach you how to enter this information in Project. Finally, I'll provide a brief overview of the concepts associated with the Program Evaluation and Review Technique (PERT) and how to use this functionality in Project.

Estimating Duration vs. Estimating Work—What's the Difference?

In Chapter 4, "Getting Started and Setting Up the Microsoft Project Environment," you learned about different task types and scheduling approaches. Effort-based scheduling is based on fixing your work estimates, causing duration to be recalculated based on resource assignments. In Project, effort-based scheduling is defined with a task type of *fixed work* or *fixed units* with the *Effort-driven* option turned on. An example of this is estimating the work (effort) of a task such as Testing/QA to be 40 hours (5 days). When you add one person at 100%, the duration is calculated based on the following formula (assuming the calendar hours/day = 8 hours):

Work = Duration × Units

or

Duration = Work ÷ Units

In the example,

Duration = 40 hours ÷ 100% = 40 hours or 5 days

Because the work portion is fixed at 40 hours, when you assign a second resource, the duration is split between the 2 resources sharing the 40 hours, resulting in 20 hours of work each; the duration is then recalculated as 20 hours or 2.5 days. As you assign more resources, the duration keeps getting shorter; and as you assign fewer resources, the duration gets longer, resulting in a recalculation of the finish date of that particular task.

In duration-based scheduling, you fix your duration estimate. Then, regardless of the resource assignments, the duration remains the same (fixed), and work is recalculated. For example, you may want to provide a one-week (five-day) review process for stakeholders to sign off on a design document even though they may only spend one hour each on the review. Another example might be going to a conference that lasts five days. The number of people going to the conference determines the work effort, but the duration remains at 5 days. In Project, duration-based scheduling is defined with a task type of *fixed duration*. Because duration and work are tied together by the formula of Work = Duration × Units, it's important to understand how to estimate and enter both duration and work in Project.

Estimating Duration for a Project

Entering duration is straightforward in Project. The challenge isn't with the tool but rather in determining how long a task will take, based on the uniqueness of the project. Life would be much easier for project managers if there was some foolproof way to estimate how long something may take. Many different models and methods are available for estimating, but none is entirely accurate. The principal reason is that projects vary significantly: even though a project may look like another one, significant differences may exist in organizational culture, technology, or user needs.

To prepare to estimate effectively, you may wish to consider the following key elements:

- Size
- Complexity
- Risk
- Experience
- Environment

I often work with organizations that categorize projects by using simple criteria such as small, medium, or large. Understanding the *size* of a project affects how you plan and manage it; this includes estimating. As important (or perhaps more important) than size is *complexity*. You should always consider the complexity of the solution the project is addressing. This includes understanding the requirements and how inherently difficult it may be to accomplish them. This also may have an impact on your estimates.

Risk generally refers to events that may occur that threaten your ability to achieve success on the project or a particular component of a project. At a high level, you can consider the likelihood that the project won't be complete, won't be used, or will come in over budget or not on time. Even when you're estimating for duration or work, you should carefully consider high-level risk factors and how they affect the project.

The *experience* of the team for the proposed project may also have an effect on your estimates. Experienced groups have a higher likelihood of completing projects with less risk and in less time than do inexperienced groups. You should also take into account the *environment* in which the project's work will be conducted. Things like culture, available tools, the methodology to be used, and the overall value your organization places on best practices pertaining to project management all may affect project performance.

Estimating Methods

You can use different models and techniques to estimate duration. Regardless of the technique you use, you must enter the estimates into Project at this stage in the planning process. Common techniques include but aren't limited to the following:

- Historical information
- Benchmarking
- Expert judgment
- Subject matter expert (SME) input
- Performance Evaluation and Review Technique (PERT)

These are self explanatory except for PERT, which is described in more detail later in this chapter. Using historical information, you base your estimates on previous project plans that are readily accessible and that have a high degree of similarity. This is why using templates can be an advantage to organizations: they provide an excellent starting point for estimates.

Benchmarks can also help. If you're working on a project patterned after a common methodology or approach, you may have access to established benchmarks, depending on the type of project or the industry. For example, on a drug development project, a benchmark from the last patient out of the final study to submitting your filing to the FDA may be three months. On a software development project, one iteration of development may be six weeks. These types of benchmarks may be developed internally and come from within your organization or be obtained externally from industry standards.

Entering Duration Estimates for a Project

Duration is based on working days and calendar options, as follows (default values):

> 1 day = 8 hours
>
> 1 week = 5 days = 40 hours
>
> 1 month = 20 days = 160 hours

You typically enter duration directly into the Duration column in Project at the task or milestone level and not at the phase or summary task level, because these are calculated fields that act as roll-ups for tasks indented or demoted below. However, Project 2010 supports top-down scheduling, which allows you to enter a duration estimate at the phase level and compare it to the details below, as discussed later in the chapter.

<hr>

🌐 **Real World Scenario**

Estimates Based on Benchmarks

Working at a client site, I was tasked to work with SMEs in the organization to develop a template for new drug-development initiatives. I was also asked to incorporate or map the estimates of five benchmark estimates for how long the project should take. This included the overall life cycle of the project, based on corporate expectations and the gold standard for the industry. Also included were a series of benchmarks around several internal processes such as the time from FDA approval to proceed with phase 1 study to first patient in.

After the benchmarks were incorporated into the template, the template became the de facto standard for project managers developing their initial plans. It was fine to deviate from the benchmark—managers just had to explain why they did so during the planning approval process. Project was ideally suited for this. In the end, the client obtained further benefits from continuing to improve the benchmarks within the template and improve on time to market, ultimately achieving faster first-profit dollars.

<hr>

You can enter duration into Project in minutes, hours, days, weeks, or months. I recommend trying to stick with the same unit of measure so it's more consistent when you're reviewing the plan. The default duration unit is days, which is a good starting point. However, this is just a guideline, and you're free to enter any unit you prefer.

As shown in Figure 6.1, follow these steps to enter duration in Project:

1. Select the cell in the Duration column of the first detail (not summary) task.

2. Enter the expected duration of the first task in the project.

3. Press Enter.

4. Continue to enter durations for all the detail tasks.

<hr>

New for Manual Scheduling

You can type words in the Duration column (or the Start or Finish column) if you have manual scheduling turned on. This allows you to enter descriptions such as **1 Week Assuming 100 Users** or **1 week After Delivery** and so on. Note that if you change from manual to automatic scheduling, the words will be replaced with calculated values.

<hr>

Automatic Scheduling: Bottom-Up Approach

When you have automatic scheduling turned on, Project treats duration estimates and the calculation of start and finish dates differently than it does for manual scheduling. As pointed out in Chapter 4, automatic scheduling uses Project's calculation engine to determine the start and end dates of tasks. This engine looks at six factors that affect your timeline:

- Project start date, covered in Chapter 4
- Calendars, covered in Chapter 4
- Duration estimates, covered in this chapter
- Dependencies (links), covered in Chapter 7
- Task constraints, covered in Chapter 7
- Resource assignments and task types, covered in Chapter 8

FIGURE 6.1 Entering duration estimates in Project

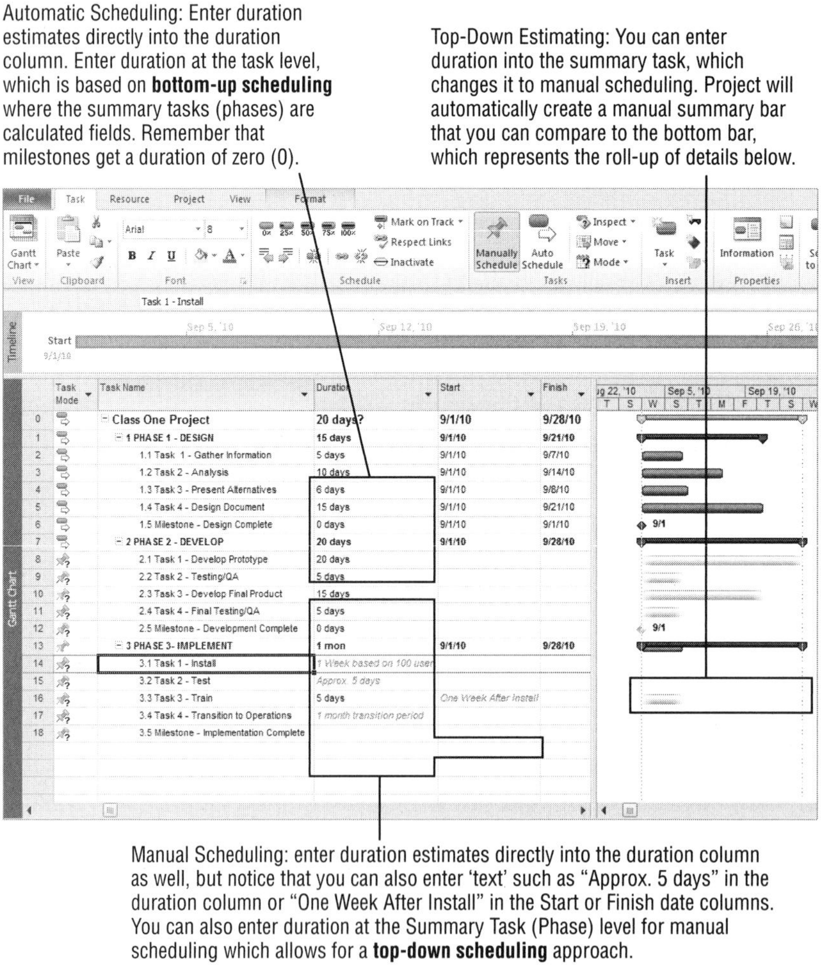
Automatic Scheduling: Enter duration estimates directly into the duration column. Enter duration at the task level, which is based on **bottom-up scheduling** where the summary tasks (phases) are calculated fields. Remember that milestones get a duration of zero (0).
Top-Down Estimating: You can enter duration into the summary task, which changes it to manual scheduling. Project will automatically create a manual summary bar that you can compare to the bottom bar, which represents the roll-up of details below.
Class One Project
1 PHASE 1 - DESIGN
1.1 Task 1 - Gather Information
1.2 Task 2 - Analysis
1.3 Task 3 - Present Alternatives
1.4 Task 4 - Design Document
1.5 Milestone - Design Complete
2 PHASE 2 - DEVELOP
2.1 Task 1 - Develop Prototype
2.2 Task 2 - Testing/QA
2.3 Task 3 - Develop Final Product
2.4 Task 4 - Final Testing/QA
2.5 Milestone - Development Complete
3 PHASE 3 - IMPLEMENT
3.1 Task 1 - Install
3.2 Task 2 - Test
3.3 Task 3 - Train
3.4 Task 4 - Transition to Operations
3.5 Milestone - Implementation Complete
Approx. 5 days
One Week After Install
1 month transition period
Manual Scheduling: enter duration estimates directly into the duration column as well, but notice that you can also enter 'text' such as "Approx. 5 days" in the duration column or "One Week After Install" in the Start or Finish date columns. You can also enter duration at the Summary Task (Phase) level for manual scheduling which allows for a **top-down scheduling** approach.

These factors are covered in detail in Chapters 4 through 8 and summarized and reviewed in Chapter 9. Project is set up to create automatic and dynamic schedules that are highly effective for you as a project manager. For example, if you need to change a resource assignment or duration estimate or task dependency, Project automatically calculates and displays these changes so you can easily view the impact of the change and make better decisions—you don't have to perform the calculations manually. As another example, suppose your project is delayed; by changing the start date, you cause the entire plan to be recalculated. If you need to pause work on a task or project, you can shift and reschedule the appropriate task, and the remaining project schedule is recalculated. Or maybe you want to see what happens to your plan if you add more resources or add more working time to your calendar. Project recalculates these types of changes automatically, putting you in a powerful position as a project manager.

Your goal should be to use automatic scheduling for the entire project or as much of the project as you can. Doing so lets you follow best practices around scheduling and get the most out of the tool. Another huge benefit of using automatic scheduling is the ability to view and analyze your critical path (see Chapter 7). In doing so, you also follow a bottom-up approach to planning. As pointed out in Figure 6.1, you enter duration estimates at the task and milestone level, whereas the Duration field at the summary task (phase) level is calculated based on the details below. As a result, you don't enter duration estimates at the summary level but rather at the task level, allowing Project to dynamically change the roll-up calculations for each summary level item all the way to the project level. This is ultimately what you want, because it's the most accurate approach to understanding big-picture items, which are driven by the details. As we progress through the rest of Part 2 of this book, you'll learn how to follow best practices that lead to more effective and efficient project schedules.

Manual Scheduling: Top-Down Approach

You can estimate duration using manual scheduling. This approach lets you start from a blank slate, with no predefined or precalculated values in the Duration, Start, or Finish fields. When you use manual scheduling, Project for the most part ignores its calculation engine and allows you to type whatever you want into the Duration column and Start and Finish dates, including descriptions or words as illustrated in Figure 6.1. Start and Finish dates are covered in more detail in Chapter 7, which deals with dependencies, constraints, and the critical path.

If you type descriptions into the Duration column, then when (or if) you switch to automatic scheduling, the descriptions will be replaced with duration values calculated by Project. For example, if you type **5 days based on 100 users**, and you switch to automatic scheduling for that task, Project will replace the text with the default *1d?* because it can't relate to the description. However, if you enter **1 wk** or **5 days**, Project can recognize this entry when you make a switch to automatic scheduling and convert it to a duration of 1 week or 5 days. This is also true for minutes, hours, and months. Project recognizes the following words and abbreviations automatically:

Minutes = mins

Hours = hrs

Days = days

Weeks = wks

Months = mons

You can also enter *elapsed days* (edays). Doing so allows you to enter duration into a plan in a way that takes into account both working and nonworking days. In other words, it ignores the calendar settings for nonworking time. For example, if you enter **5 edays**, then nonworking days such as weekends are included in the calculation of the Start and Finish dates; whereas if you enter **5 days**, Project calculates Finish to be later than it would be with edays if the task extends over nonworking times such as weekends.

Manual scheduling lets you take a top-down approach to scheduling. When you're planning at a high level, say at the summary level such as Phase 1-Design or Phase 2-Develop, you can enter the duration estimate directly into the Duration field: Project doesn't forcing Duration to be an automatically calculated field. After you enter duration estimates at the summary task level, Project automatically switches to the manually scheduled task mode. Don't panic—you can switch it back to automatic whenever you want.

One nice feature of the manually scheduled summary task is that you can add details below it, and Project creates two separate summary bars. As shown in Figure 6.2, the upper bar represents the manual estimate, and the lower bar represents the roll-up estimate of the details.

FIGURE 6.2 Top-down estimating

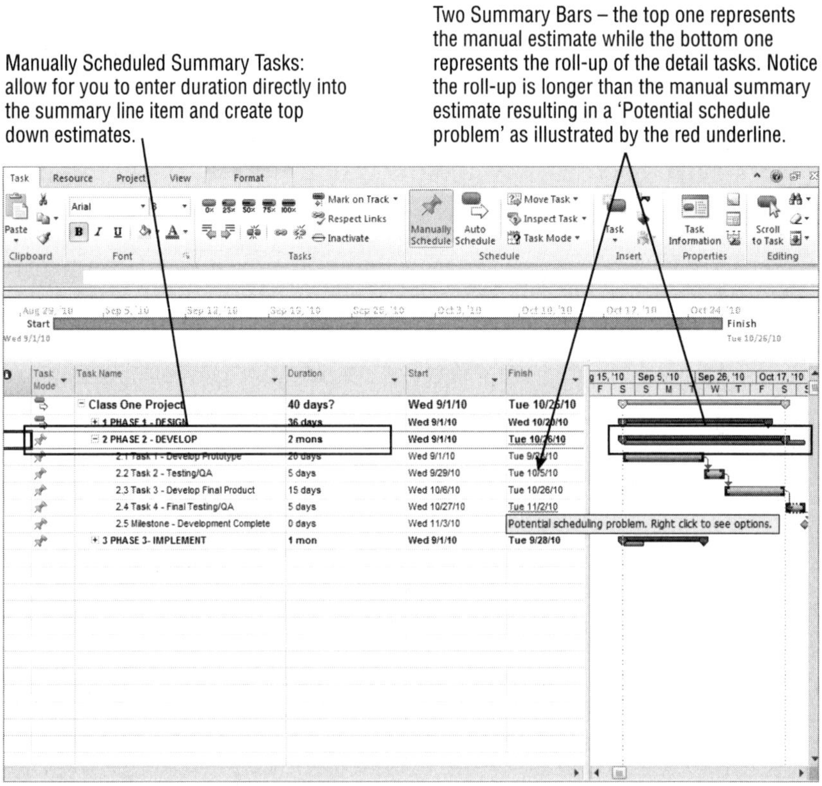

Notice that if the roll-up of the details is greater than or longer than the manually entered summary estimate, a red underline appears, which signals a potential scheduling problem. If you right-click the underline, one of the options is Fix in the Task Inspector. This Project 2010 feature identifies the controlling factors of tasks; if there are problems, it also provides suggestions for how to fix your schedule. See Figure 6.3.

FIGURE 6.3   Task Inspector

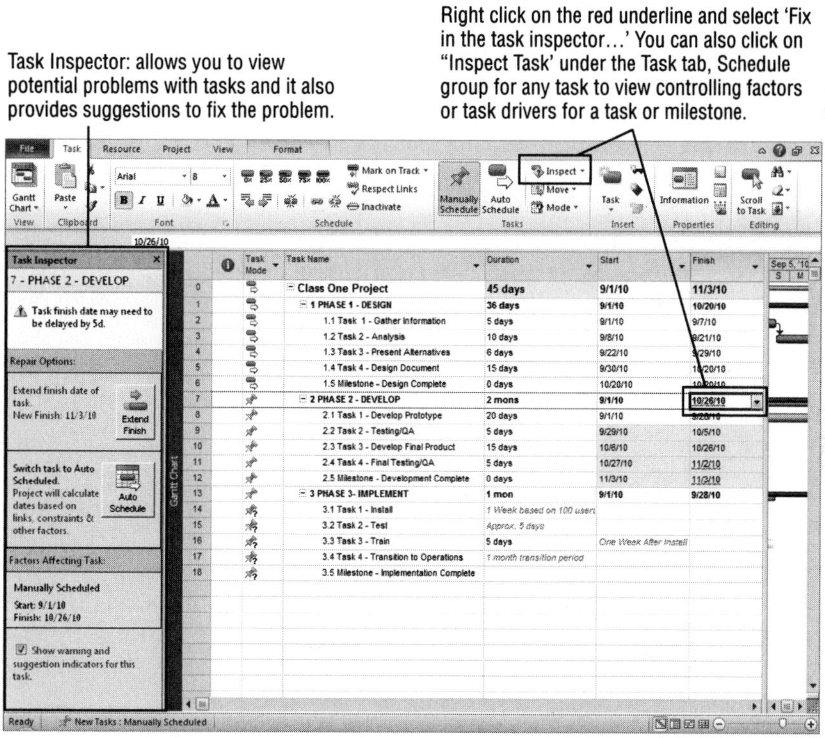

Right click on the red underline and select 'Fix in the task inspector...' You can also click on "Inspect Task" under the Task tab, Schedule group for any task to view controlling factors or task drivers for a task or milestone.

Task Inspector: allows you to view potential problems with tasks and it also provides suggestions to fix the problem.

Notice that the tasks in Figure 6.3 have dependencies linking them to each other to help establish a timeline. I cover this in the next chapter, which focuses on step 3 of the planning process: setting task dependencies. Using dependences here effectively illustrates how the detail tasks roll up for comparison to the manual summary bar.

Estimated Durations = ?

Notice that each task is scheduled to begin on the first day of the project. This is based on the start date of the project, which you're responsible for defining on the Project tab in the Project Information dialog box. Also notice that the default duration estimate is 1d? for each task if automatic scheduling is used; it's up to you to enter your estimate on top of this. If you're using manual scheduling, the Duration column remains blank.

The question mark stands for *estimated duration* in Project and can be used as an additional tool to help identify estimates that aren't yet finalized. You can also filter and report on estimated durations (see the section on filtering in Chapter 12, "Using Filters, Groups, and Sorts"). Estimated durations go away if you type over them. If you don't enter a new duration, then the estimated duration remains as the default. Estimated durations are also carried up to summary tasks; ultimately, the project summary task includes the question mark, which you may find useful or annoying. There is no reason to keep the estimated duration function switched on if you have no use for it, particularly if you want to hide the question mark. Figure 6.4 shows how to turn off the estimated duration feature by following these steps:

1. In the backstage, select Options.

2. Click the Schedule tab.

3. Deselect the Show that Scheduled Tasks Have Estimated Durations check box.

FIGURE 6.4   Turning off estimated durations

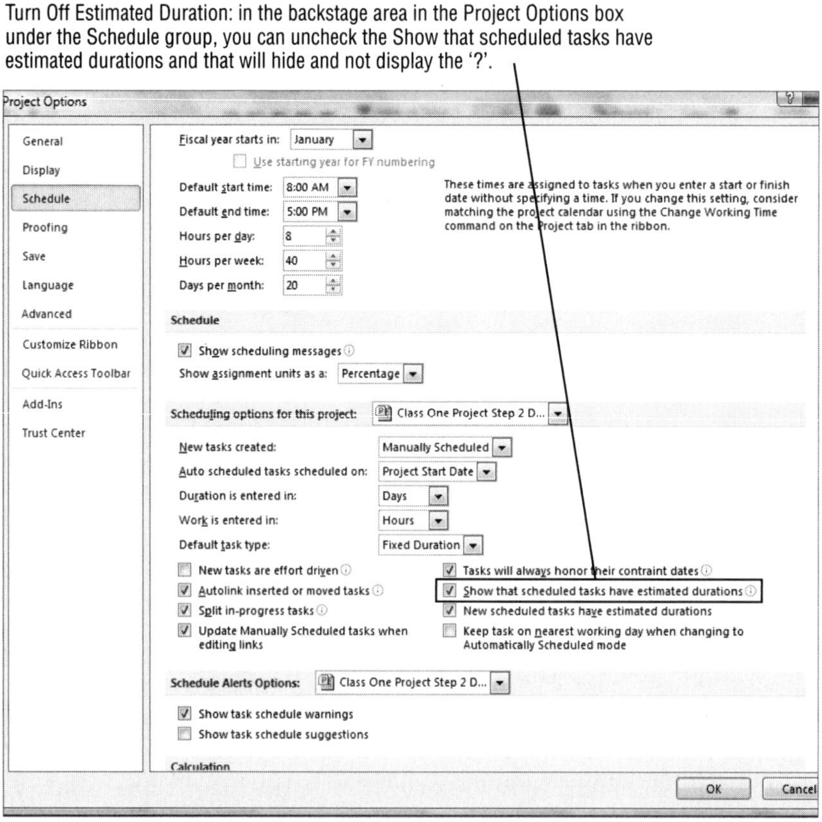

Turn Off Estimated Duration: in the backstage area in the Project Options box under the Schedule group, you can uncheck the Show that scheduled tasks have estimated durations and that will hide and not display the '?'.

In Project, there is usually more than one way to get things done. Over time, you'll learn to appreciate the value of being able to change your plan in a number of different ways depending on your preferences. This is certainly true for entering duration estimates. The simplest and most straightforward way to change duration is to enter it directly in the Duration column in the Gantt Chart view. As shown in Figure 6.5 you have many other options, such as entering duration in the split-screen view or by clicking and dragging the end of the task Gantt bar.

FIGURE 6.5 Other options for changing duration

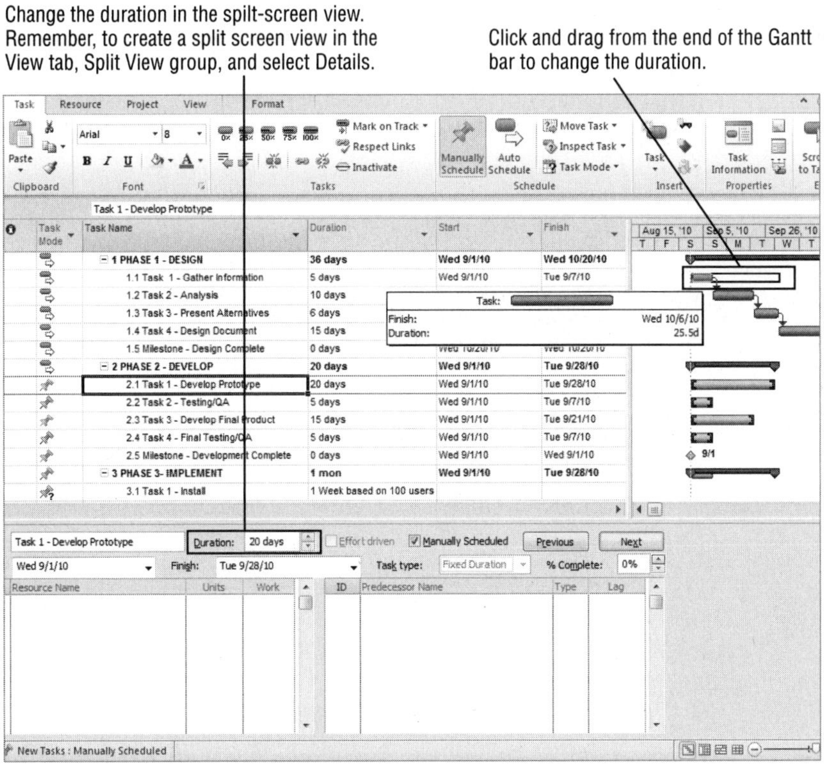

Change the duration in the spilt-screen view. Remember, to create a split screen view in the View tab, Split View group, and select Details.

Click and drag from the end of the Gantt bar to change the duration.

Using the Task Information Dialog Box

If you change the duration of a task in one view or dialog box, it changes in every other view as well. This is an appropriate time to introduce you to the Task Information dialog box. As discussed in Chapter 4, you can access and change information about the project in the Project Information dialog box; similarly you can access and change information about a task in the Task Information dialog box. The default Gantt Chart view consists of two main components: a table of information made up of specific data columns, and the chart or bar area that displays a graphical shape to represent the length of a task. The default table is the Entry table. It has specific data columns such as Task Name, Duration, Start, Finish, Predecessors, and Resources.

Every time you enter a task in the Task Name column, many data fields are automatically associated with that task. Some of these are user definable (covered in Chapter 11, "Using Tables and Custom Fields"), but the majority are maintained internally. You don't need to know all of these fields to be effective or successful with Project, but you'll need to know the primary ones covered in this book. The Task Information dialog box is a way to access much of this information.

You can access the Task Information dialog box by double-clicking a task or by going to Task tab ➢ Properties group and clicking Task Information. Figure 6.6 shows the Task Information dialog box.

FIGURE 6.6   Task Information dialog box

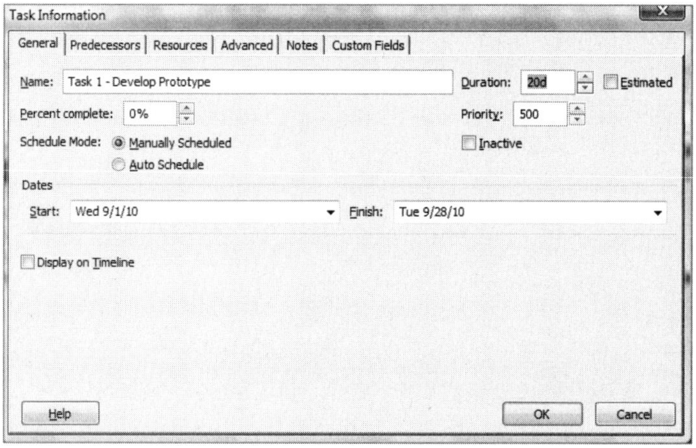

Estimating Work for a Project

As an alternative to estimating duration at this point in the planning process, you may choose to estimate work if you're following an effort-based or fixed-work scheduling approach. As discussed earlier in this chapter and in Chapter 4, work is different from duration. Work is all about effort put in by resources. Typically, work is calculated when resources are assigned to tasks, a topic covered in detail in Chapter 8. If you estimate duration first, then you don't have to estimate work at this time—this will be taken care of in step 4 of the planning process, when you assign resources (see Chapter 8).

The choice between work-based planning and duration-based planning is in large part governed by the type of work being done and the organization doing the estimating. For example, an IT organization that thinks in terms of the amount of work that needs to be done (effort) and lets the duration vary is an example of a fixed-work or fixed-units (with the Effort-driven option selected) task type. In other organizations and industries, including many IT shops I've worked with, it's more natural to estimate duration and let the work vary; this is a fixed-duration task type. If you choose to estimate work instead of duration before assigning resources, the tool calculates duration automatically, based on the number or percent allocation of resource assignments. This method is effective only if you're scheduling based on fixed work and want to take an effort-based scheduling approach. In this case, instead of entering duration in the Duration column, you can enter work in the Work column.

To enter work estimates in your plan before entering resources, you need to first add the Work column to the Entry table. As shown in Figure 6.7, you can do so by following these steps:

1. In the default Gantt chart Entry table, click the last column heading, Add New Column. You can also right-click any column heading in the table and select Insert Column.

   This opens the list of available columns to be added to the table.

2. In the list, find and select Work.

   You can type **w** to quick-pick from the list. You can also move the column by clicking and dragging the column heading to the left or right.

3. Enter work estimates directly in the Work column.

   The default unit for work estimates is hours. You can enter work in minutes, hours, days, weeks, or months. Work for milestones should be 0.

When you estimate work in this manner, the duration remains at the default of 1day? until you begin assigning resources or type a duration estimate directly into the Duration column to override the default. Resource assignments and their impact on work and duration are covered in greater detail in Chapter 8.

Also notice that you can't enter work into a summary line even if manual scheduling is turned on. Project doesn't support top-down estimating for work. The summary task for work is a calculated field based on the roll-up of the detail work below. After you begin assigning resources, the duration will be calculated based on the formula Work = Duration × Units. In this case, duration is calculated based on Duration = Work ÷ Units. For example, given a 40-hour work estimate, if you assign 1 person at 100%, the duration will be 5 days (Duration = 40 hours ÷ 1 = 40 hours or 5 days). Alternatively, on the same task, if you assign one person at 50%, the duration will be calculated as 10 days (Duration = 40 hours ÷ 0.5 = 80 hours or 10 days).

Program Evaluation and Review Technique

The Program (or Project) Evaluation and Review Technique (PERT) is a project-management technique designed to better estimate the task durations involved in completing a given project.

PERT is a duration-based estimating technique that uses three points (pessimistic, most likely, and optimistic) to determine the best estimate of duration on a task-by-task basis.

Project has some useful views and entry screens customized specifically for this scientific method of estimating.

FIGURE 6.7   Entering work estimates

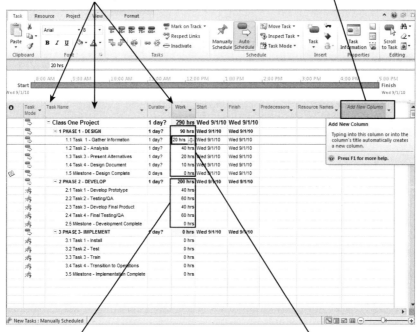

Note: you can also right click on any column heading and select **Insert Column** to add new columns to the left anywhere in a table.

Add New Column: Click on drop down list to select **Work** column or type directly into the column to quick pick from the list. Click and drag the column heading to the right or left to relocate it within the table.

Manual Scheduling: Enter work directly into the work column at the task level. You can not enter Work at the summary level even if you use manual. The duration will remain blank with manual scheduling on.

Automatic Scheduling: Enter work directly into the work column at the task level. You can not enter Work at the summary level even if you use manual scheduling. The duration estimate will default to 1day? until you assign resources or type over the duration estimate in the duration column.

What Is PERT?

I was introduced to PERT more than 15 years ago. I remember thinking, based on the name and the acronym, that it was going to be a very complex model for estimating that would ultimately provide little return for the time necessary to set it up. I was pleasantly surprised to find that it's a simple and straightforward technique that can add significant value in improving estimates and synthesizing varying points of views.

🌐 **Real World Scenario**

Estimating Work as an Alternative to Duration

An IT department's project management office (PMO) wanted to estimate work and have Project calculate the schedule based on resource availability and assignments. I worked with them to set up an enterprise project-management system. The project manager defined the generic resource needs (roles required) for each task and subsequently worked with the functional manager (the same as the resource manager in this case) of each group to substitute named resources. The manager not only provided the named resource but also reviewed availability and provided the percent allocation of that resource. This could range from 10% to 100%.

Based on the input from the functional manager, the project manager substituted the named resource for the generic resource and entered the units (% allocation). Project then automatically calculated the duration and end date for each task. The dependencies (task links) were already established; therefore, the results of the task assignments drove the milestones, phases, and overall project schedule. To tie all these concepts together, we'll discuss setting dependencies in Chapter 7 and assigning resources in Chapter 8.

PERT was developed primarily to enable and simplify the scheduling of large and complex projects. It's used to estimate and analyze the time needed to complete each task. It helps to incorporate the uncertainty of estimating by looking at the minimum time needed to complete a project in conjunction with the most likely and maximum time needed to complete a project. The model was invented by Booz Allen Hamilton, Inc. while the company was under contract to the United States Department of Defense (U.S. Navy) in the late 1950s.

The technique is based on applying weighted values of optimistic, pessimistic, and most likely time estimates for tasks. In the context of Project and this book, *time estimate* is synonymous with *duration estimate*. The following list describes each component of this technique:

Optimistic (O)   This is the minimum possible time or best-case scenario for accomplishing the task. This estimate assumes that things get done more quickly than normal.

Most Likely (M)   This estimate is based on things progressing as normal. In Project, this is referred to as *expected* time.

Pessimistic (P)   This is the maximum possible time or worst-case scenario for accomplishing the task. This estimate assumes that things take longer than normal and everything goes wrong.

When you've estimated these components, you can calculate the estimated time based on the following weighted-value formula:

PERT Estimate = (O + 4M + P) ÷ 6

This formula calculates the best estimate for the task based on the average with the assumption that the task would be repeated a number of times. The weighted value typically applied to the most likely parameter (M) is 4. However, it's possible to change the coefficients in Project, provided that they always add up to 6.

A simple example involves estimating the time it takes to drive to the airport to catch a flight. Suppose that on a good day, with no traffic or other issues to deal with, such as stopping for gas, and catching all the green lights, you can drive to the airport in 30 minutes; this represents your best-case scenario or optimistic estimate. However, if you have to leave during rush hour, or the traffic is bad due to an accident on the highway, it can take you 150 minutes; this represents the worst-case scenario or pessimistic estimate. On average, if everything is normal, the most likely estimate is 60 minutes. Applying PERT, you get the following result:

PERT Estimate = $(30 + (4 \times 60) + 150) \div 6 = 70$ minutes

When you use PERT, your duration estimates most often will be different than you'll get by estimating your most likely scenario. It takes into consideration best and worst case estimates, helping to integrate some of the uncertainties in your plan. It also provides a mechanism to synergize points of views from different stakeholders or SMEs into one estimate.

Summary

This chapter has focused on estimating duration, which is a key component of creating an effective project schedule. It also represents step 2 in the four-step planning process.

To estimate duration effectively, it's important to first be clear on the differences between duration and work. Duration represents the difference in time between the start and finish date of a task. Time is based on working days defined in the calendar, which defaults to 5-day (40-hour) work weeks, Monday to Friday. Think of duration as the difference between start and end dates, taking into account only working days. Elapsed time is the difference between start and end dates, inclusive of all dates.

Work represents the person-hours (effort or labor) that go into a task. This is associated with resource assignments, which are covered in Chapter 8. However, as an alternative for estimating duration in step 2, sometimes it may be appropriate to estimate work instead, particularly if you're scheduling using an effort-based approach. In this situation, duration will be automatically recalculated later in the process during step 4, when you allocate resources to the tasks.

I find that understanding the difference between work and duration is simple enough, but understanding how this applies in a duration-based approach versus an effort-based approach is usually difficult. A good question to ask yourself is, "What is really fixed? What am I more sure of—the length of time it will take to complete a task, or the amount of work it will take?" Here's another way to think about this: What do you want the system to calculate—how much work is required based on duration estimates and assigning resources, or how long a task will take based on work estimates and resource assignments? Keep in mind that this can be set on a task-by-task basis, but it's a good idea to adopt one overall approach as a standard or guideline.

Finally, I discussed PERT and how you can use it as an effective scheduling method. Project comes equipped with PERT analysis tools that allow for easy entry of PERT estimates and analysis of the results for pessimistic, most likely, and optimistic versions of your plan.

Hands-On Exercises

The following hands-on exercises are designed to test your understanding of the topics discussed in this chapter. We've provided files on the companion CD that will show you what your project file should look like as you perform these exercises.

EXERCISE 4

Estimating Duration

1. In the duration column, try entering in text such as `TBD` or `Approx. 2 Weeks.`

2. In the Task Mode column, change all tasks to Automatic Scheduling (notice the text is replaced with pre-formatted dates and duration).

3. In the Duration column, type in the following durations:

   PHASE I – DESIGN (do not enter duration at the phase/summary level)

       Task 1 – Gather Information: **5d**

       Task 2 – Analysis: **10d**

       Task 3 – Prepare/Present Options: **6d**

       Task 4 – Design/Document: **15d**

       Milestone – Design Complete: **0d**

   PHASE 2 – DEVELOP

       Task 1 – Develop Prototype: **20d**

       Task 2 – Testing/QA: **5d**

       Task 3 – Develop Final Product: **15d**

       Task 4 – Final Testing/QA: **10d**

       Milestone – Development Complete: **0d**

   PHASE 3 – IMPLEMENT

       Task 1 – Install: **5d**

       Task 2 – Test: **5d**

       Task 3 – Train: **10d**

       Task 4 – Support: **20d**

       Milestone – Implementation Complete: **0d**

4. Review the Gantt chart. What is the end date? Why?

5. On the Project tab, select Project Information, and click the Statistics button. Review the numbers again. Why is there no baseline data or no actual data? Why is there no cost data? Click the Close button.

6. Select Task 1 - Gather Information, and select Task tab Properties group Task Information (or double click on the task name directly in the task name column).

7. Change Duration to **15d**, and click the OK button.

8. Go to the Gantt bar, and place the cursor at the end of the bar for Task 1 – Gather Information. Click and drag the bar to change Duration back to 5d.

9. Change the Phase 1 – Design task mode to manual scheduling. Enter a duration of 30 days, and compare and analyze the summary bar for the manual and roll-up estimates in the Gantt bar area.

10. Change the task mode back to automatic. Analyze what happens to the Gantt bar areas. Your manual estimate of 30 days is recalculated based on the roll-up of the details.

Save the Class One Project file. Make sure you understand that you can change duration in many different areas. Also, make sure you understand the difference between entering duration at the phase/summary level (calculated for automatic scheduling vs. manual scheduling), at the detail task level (the final level of indentation), and for a milestone (duration equals 0).

Chapter

7

Setting Dependencies and the Critical Path

IN THIS CHAPTER, YOU'LL LEARN ABOUT THE FOLLOWING:

- ✓ Step 3 of the planning process: setting dependencies

- ✓ Managing different types of task relationships

- ✓ Understanding the impact of dependencies on manual vs. automatic scheduling

- ✓ Using task deadlines

- ✓ Working with task constraints

- ✓ Understanding and viewing the critical path

In this book, you're following a four-step process of setting up plans effectively in Project:

1. Enter the work breakdown structure.

2. Estimate duration (or work).

3. Set dependencies/task relationships.

4. Assign resources (and costs, if required).

This chapter focuses on step 3. This step is the key for setting up your timeline properly to define the task network and identify the critical path (concepts explored in this chapter). Mastering this step moves you from being an average scheduler with Project to being an excellent scheduler with Project. With this knowledge, you'll be able to take charge of managing your project's life cycle and quickly assessing the impact of change as it pertains to time. We'll also explore how to use constraints and deadlines and when it's most appropriate to apply them to your plan.

Setting Dependencies

Setting dependencies is a critical step in establishing your timeline. It's all about *networking* your tasks (determining how they're linked together) based on various types of relationships. Project calculates your timeline for you based on drivers such as the project start date, calendars, duration or work estimates, and dependencies, which you'll learn how to set in this chapter.

Understanding Dependencies

Before you start setting dependencies in Project, you should understand what dependencies are and the types of dependencies available in Project. It's also useful to explore the different types of scenarios you may encounter when setting dependencies.

In the context of this book, and in using Project, *setting task dependencies* means defining task relationships or links between tasks. This can also be referred to as *task networking*, which essentially means arranging tasks in a particular sequence. Dependencies, linkages, or relationships define the way tasks on a plan are scheduled relative to one another. For example, some tasks can be done in parallel, whereas others must be done sequentially (one after the other). In other scenarios, you may have tasks that overlap, such as one task starting when another task is half done. For example, if Writing and Editing are two tasks, the Editing task may start when the Writing task is half done. In Project, you can take advantage of using the *Lag field* to set up such relationships, as discussed later in this chapter. The following section describes the various types of task dependencies and the impact they have on the schedule.

Dependency Types

Project uses four main types of dependencies:

Finish-to-Start (FS)   This is the default relationship in Project. It defines the situation where one task has to finish before the next one can start. In other words, the second task (the successor) can't begin until the first one (the predecessor) is completed. This establishes a sequential relationship. For example, Printing Document won't start until Editing Document is finished.

Figure 7.1 illustrates this relationship. If the predecessor task (task 1) is delayed, the successor task (task 2) is automatically pushed out as well, and Project recalculates the start and finish dates accordingly.

FIGURE 7.1   Finish-to-start relationship

Finish-to-Finish (FF)   The completion of the successor task depends on the completion of its predecessor. In other words, both tasks end at the same time. Use an FF relationship when two tasks should finish simultaneously. For example, Printing Document can be finished when Prepare for Distribution is finished.

Figure 7.2 illustrates how an FF relationship is displayed in Project. In this type of situation, if the end of task 1 is delayed, it pulls the finish of task 2 along with it. Project automatically recalculates the start date of task 2 as well.

FIGURE 7.2   Finish-to-finish relationship

Start-to-Start (SS)   The start of the successor task depends on the start of its predecessor. In other words, the two tasks begin at the same time. Use an SS relationship when tasks should start simultaneously. For example, Distributing Document and Supporting End Users can start at the same time, after Printing Document is completed.

Figure 7.3 illustrates how an SS relationship is displayed in Project. In this situation, if the start of task 1 is delayed, then the start of task 2 is delayed as well, and Project automatically recalculates the start and finish dates.

Start-to-Finish (SF)   The finish of the successor task depends on the start of its predecessor. In other words, the first task begins after the second task ends. An SF relationship is seldom used but is included in Project so that all four relationships are available. You can use an SF relationship to create a backward type of scheduling scenario in which you want a task to complete when another task starts.

FIGURE 7.3   Start-to-start relationship

Figure 7.4 illustrates how this type of relationship is displayed in Project. If the start of task 1 is delayed, the finish of task 2 will move along with it, and Project automatically recalculates the start date as well.

FIGURE 7.4   Start-to-finish relationship

🌐 Real World Scenario

A Rare Example

I rarely use the SF relationship type. Once I was working on a manufacturing plan in which the materials had to be ordered one month ahead of the start of a manufacturing process to allow for procurement, shipping, and delivery. So, we had a task called Obtain Materials with a predecessor task of Begin Manufacturing set with a SF relationship. This way, if the start of Begin Manufacturing was delayed for any reason, the Obtain Materials start and finish date would move automatically to be one month prior.

Dependency Scenarios and Creating Networks

Consider the different types of scenarios that may occur during planning and creating your network of tasks. Three basic scenarios—sequential, concurrent, and overlapping dependencies—are illustrated here with both network diagram and Gantt chart examples:

Sequential Dependencies   This is the most straightforward of all the scenarios and is the default scenario in Project. Tasks happen one after the other in a sequential manner. In Project, you use the default link type, FS.

Consider the plan outlined in the network diagram in Figure 7.5, consisting of three tasks linked sequentially with a milestone at the end. In this example, if each task is two days long, then the total length of the project is six days. Task 1 is a predecessor to task 2, task 2 is a predecessor to task 3, and task 3 is a predecessor to the milestone. Each of these relationships is expressed as an FS dependency.

FIGURE 7.5   Sequential tasks

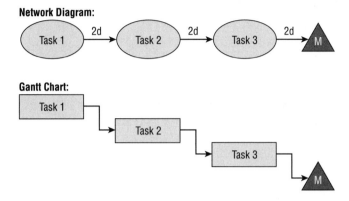

Network Diagram:

Gantt Chart:

Networking

You can think of setting dependencies between tasks as setting up your task network. When you network tasks, you attempt to define how tasks are interrelated, so you can better understand the sequence of events. Project allows you to establish task relationships in many different ways and many different views. After they're established, you can easily view how your tasks are interconnected by switching to the Network Diagram view, which gives you a glance at a logical representation of activities. I cover this and other views in Chapter 10, "Understanding Views."

Concurrent Dependencies   In this common scenario, tasks happen at the same time (concurrently). Unless you set a dependency between tasks, Project assumes everything can happen at the same time. As you enter tasks into Project, they're scheduled to begin at the same time—the project start date—until you set dependencies.

In Figure 7.6, task 1 and task 2 occur concurrently, but both must be finished before task 3 starts. In this situation, task 1 and task 2 are independent of each other. If each task takes two days, then the total length of the project is only four days (the more concurrent your tasks are, the shorter the project will be; the more sequential your tasks are, the longer the project will be). Task 1 is a predecessor to task 3, task 2 is a predecessor to task 3, and task 3 is a predecessor to the milestone. Each of these links is an FS dependency. There is no link between task 1 and task 2, but task 3 has two predecessors.

Overlapping Dependencies   Tasks may begin partway through another task. There are plenty of situations in which you'll have overlapping tasks, and in Project you can set them up using the Lag field. In Figure 7.7, task 2 starts halfway through task 1, and task 3 starts after task 2 is completed. If each of the tasks takes two days, the total duration of the project is five days.

FIGURE 7.6   Concurrent tasks

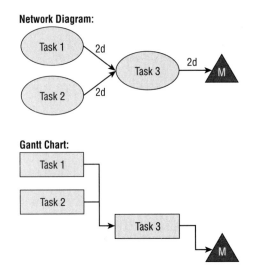

FIGURE 7.7   Overlapping tasks

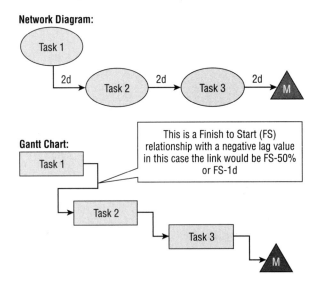

Task 1 is still a predecessor to task 2, using an FS relationship with a –1d lag (negative one-day lag) or a –50% lag, which establishes lead times between tasks. You can also create gaps between tasks by using positive lag. For example, if task 2 has to wait a week after task 1 is complete before it can start, you can put +5d in the Lag field (positive five-day lag). Perhaps you need to wait a week for cement or paint to dry before moving on to the next step.

Impact of User-Controlled (Manual) Scheduling on Dependencies

If you have manual scheduling turned on, Project may ignore its calculation engine and driving factors of your schedule, including the impact of predecessor or successor task relationships. This is an option that you can turn on or off even if you have the task mode set to manual scheduling. In other words, you can choose to respect the task links on manually scheduled tasks or not, without going to automatic scheduling. If you decide to respect the task links, then Project will recalculate the start and finish dates for those manual tasks based on the dependency you set. If you choose not to respect the tasks links, then Project will ignore the impact of any predecessor links.

You control the task mode for each task, milestone, and summary line, as discussed in Chapter 4, "Getting Started and Setting Up the Microsoft Project Environment." To change the default task mode for new tasks, follow these steps (see Figure 7.8):

1. On the Task tab, in the Tasks group, click the Task Mode command (drop-down list).

2. Select the default mode for new tasks. For user-controlled scheduling, select Manually Schedule.

FIGURE 7.8   Task mode for new tasks

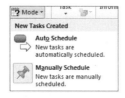

There are also option settings specifically for manually scheduled tasks. You can find these in the backstage by clicking the File tab and selecting options. One option in particular relates to how Project deals with task links with manually scheduled tasks: Update Manually Scheduled Tasks When Editing Links (see Figure 7.9). If this option is checked, then Project includes the impact of links when calculating the start and finish dates for tasks; these results also roll up to summary tasks. If this option is unchecked, then Project ignores the impact of task links on the calculation of start and finish dates. To find this option, follow these steps:

1. Go to the backstage by clicking the File tab.

2. Under the Project item, select Options.

3. Click the Schedule tab, and go to the Scheduling Options for This Project section.

4. Check or clear the Update Manually Scheduled Tasks When Editing Links option.

Figure 7.10 illustrates the result when Project ignores the impact of dependencies. In this case, I set the dependencies for the manual tasks in Phase 2—Develop. Notice that in the Predecessors column, the dependencies are underlined in red, a warning that reflects the fact that task links aren't being respected.

FIGURE 7.9   Options for manually scheduled tasks and dependencies

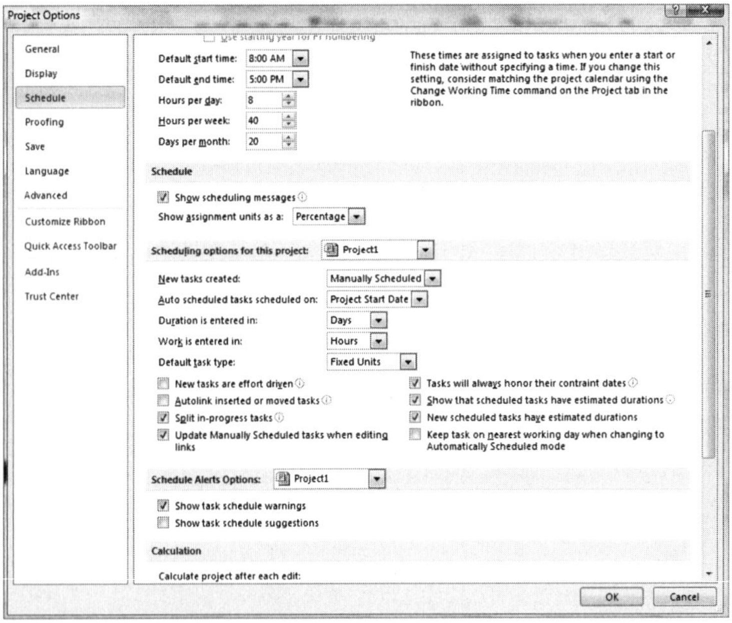

FIGURE 7.10   Ignoring the impact of task links

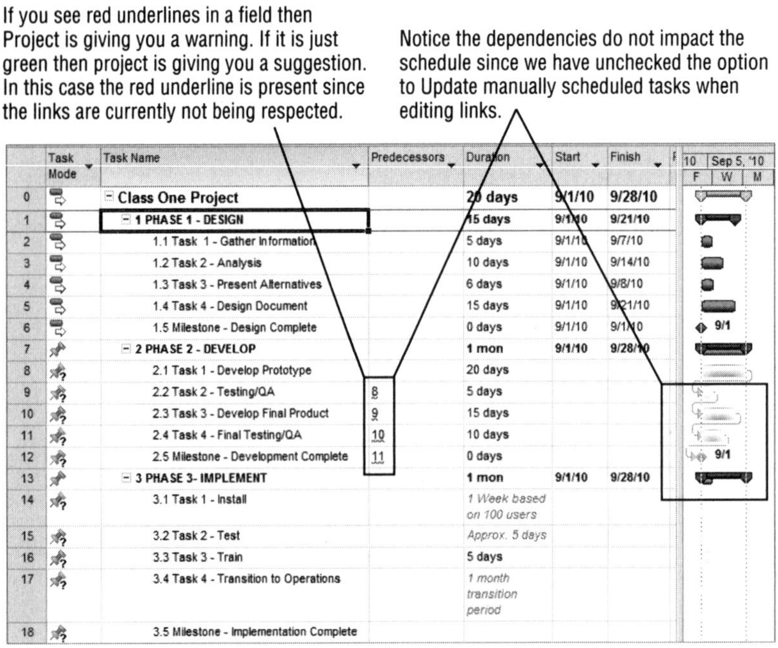

If you see red underlines in a field then Project is giving you a warning. If it is just green then project is giving you a suggestion. In this case the red underline is present since the links are currently not being respected.

Notice the dependencies do not impact the schedule since we have unchecked the option to Update manually scheduled tasks when editing links.

	Task Mode	Task Name	Predecessors	Duration	Start	Finish		10	Sep 5, '10
								F W	F W M
0		⊟ Class One Project		20 days	9/1/10	9/28/10			
1		⊟ 1 PHASE 1 - DESIGN		15 days	9/1/10	9/21/10			
2		1.1 Task 1 - Gather Information		5 days	9/1/10	9/7/10			
3		1.2 Task 2 - Analysis		10 days	9/1/10	9/14/10			
4		1.3 Task 3 - Present Alternatives		6 days	9/1/10	9/8/10			
5		1.4 Task 4 - Design Document		15 days	9/1/10	9/21/10			
6		1.5 Milestone - Design Complete		0 days	9/1/10	9/1/10		◆ 9/1	
7		⊟ 2 PHASE 2 - DEVELOP		1 mon	9/1/10	9/28/10			
8		2.1 Task 1 - Develop Prototype		20 days					
9		2.2 Task 2 - Testing/QA	8	5 days					
10		2.3 Task 3 - Develop Final Product	9	15 days					
11		2.4 Task 4 - Final Testing/QA	10	10 days					
12		2.5 Milestone - Development Complete	11	0 days				◆ 9/1	
13		⊟ 3 PHASE 3- IMPLEMENT		1 mon	9/1/10	9/28/10			
14		3.1 Task 1 - Install		*1 Week based on 100 users*					
15		3.2 Task 2 - Test		*Approx. 5 days*					
16		3.3 Task 3 - Train		5 days					
17		3.4 Task 4 - Transition to Operations		*1 month transition period*					
18		3.5 Milestone - Implementation Complete							

If you have the Update Manually Scheduled Tasks When Editing Links option checked (turned on), Project respects the links when you first set them. You can also make Project respect the links for a certain task or group of tasks; Project then incorporates those links into the calculation of start and finish dates. Figure 7.11 illustrates the impact of task links on your schedule. To make that choice, follow these steps:

1. Select the task or group of tasks for which you want Project to respect links.

2. Select Task tab ➢ Tasks group ➢ Respect Links.

3. Review the impact on the dates in the Start and Finish columns.

FIGURE 7.11   Respecting links for manually scheduled tasks

Select the group of tasks and click on Respect Links to allow Project to include the impact of task dependencies on the calculation of start and finish dates.

Notice the dependencies are now included in the calculation of start and finish dates. This will happen be default if you leave the options settings checked for "Update Manually Scheduled tasks" when updating links.

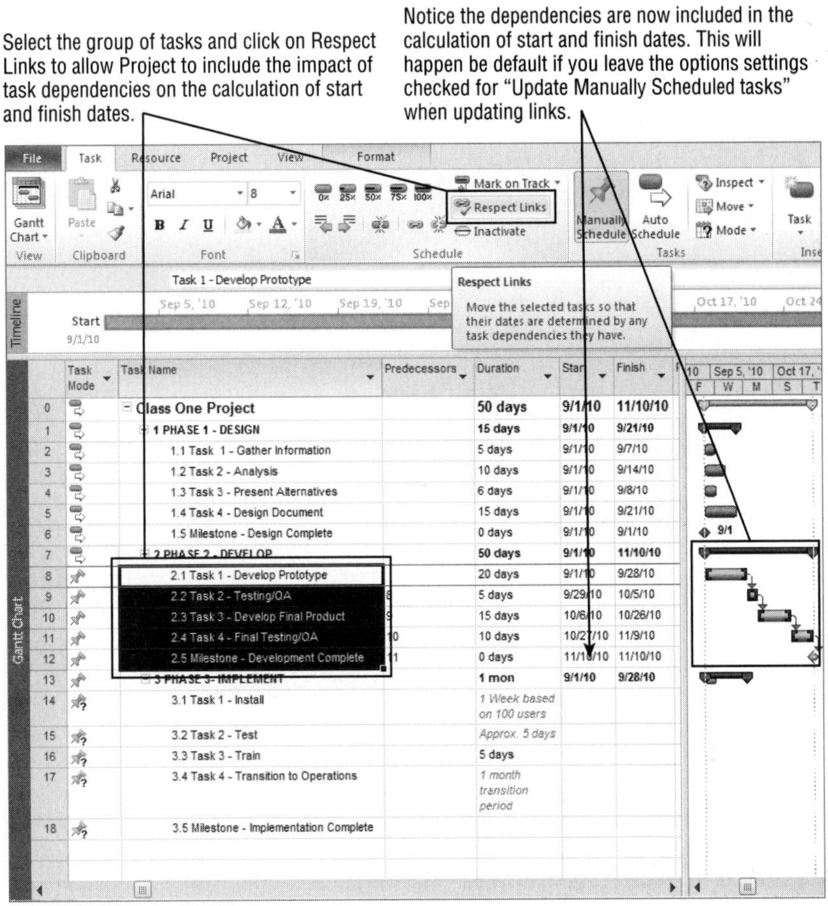

Dependencies and Top-Down Summary

In the past, Project's summary tasks were always roll-ups of its subtasks and as a result were calculated fields that you couldn't enter data into, as explained in Chapter 5 ("Creating and

Entering the Work Breakdown Structure"). Having top-down summary tasks enables planning scenarios where work items under a summary phase don't necessarily need to line up exactly with the top-down dates. Setting task dependencies affects the summary task; but if the summary task is set to manual scheduling, you have the option to enter your estimates directly at the summary level fields and compare them to the details below. This is shown in Figure 7.12, where you can see two roll-up bars. The lower bar is a reflection of the networked detailed tasks, and the upper bar represents the manual estimate.

FIGURE 7.12   Top-down summary tasks and dependencies

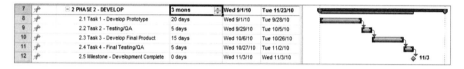

7		− 2 PHASE 2 - DEVELOP	3 mons	Wed 9/1/10	Tue 11/23/10	
8		2.1 Task 1 - Develop Prototype	20 days	Wed 9/1/10	Tue 9/28/10	
9		2.2 Task 2 - Testing/QA	5 days	Wed 9/29/10	Tue 10/5/10	
10		2.3 Task 3 - Develop Final Product	15 days	Wed 10/6/10	Tue 10/26/10	
11		2.4 Task 4 - Final Testing/QA	5 days	Wed 10/27/10	Tue 11/2/10	
12		2.5 Milestone - Development Complete	0 days	Wed 11/3/10	Wed 11/3/10	11/3

In Figure 7.12, the detail roll-up bar is blue given that it is coming in ahead of schedule of the manually entered estimate at the summary bar. If the detail roll-up bar extends past the manual summary bar, it will turn red and give you a red wavy line typically under the finish date of the tasks affected. You can right click on the red wavy line to take corrective action or ignore the problem.

This approach may be useful during initial planning, when you may start by capturing a set of high-level phases based on business needs and delivery timeframe. It may also be useful to compare your required timeframe with that of the detailed tasks as they're scheduled, based on duration estimates and task dependencies, as shown in Figure 7.12.

Inactive Tasks and Dependencies

After you create an initial plan, there may be scenarios where you want to see the impact on a schedule if the task were no longer included in the plan, but without actually removing it to test the scenario. Project Professional introduces a new feature—*inactive tasks*—to let you model such scenarios (this feature is only available in Project Pro). If a task is no longer part of the scope, or you just want to conduct a what-if scenario, you can cancel the task but keep it in the plan by deactivating it. The inactive task no longer affects the project's schedule, including any task dependencies associated with it. The task doesn't affect resource availability or how other tasks are scheduled. This feature is also useful during the execution and control stages of a project, when you're managing changes to the plan such as a change in scope that affects the WBS. This is covered in more detail in Chapter 16, "Updating and Tracking Status."

Although the net effect of deactivating a task is similar to deleting the task, the benefit of deactivating over deleting is that a record of the task and all of its properties remains with the project plan. If at some later point in the project cycle you want to reinclude the task in the plan, you can toggle it back to an active state. Figure 7.13 highlights the impact of a schedule including task dependencies when a task is made inactive.

FIGURE 7.13   Inactive task

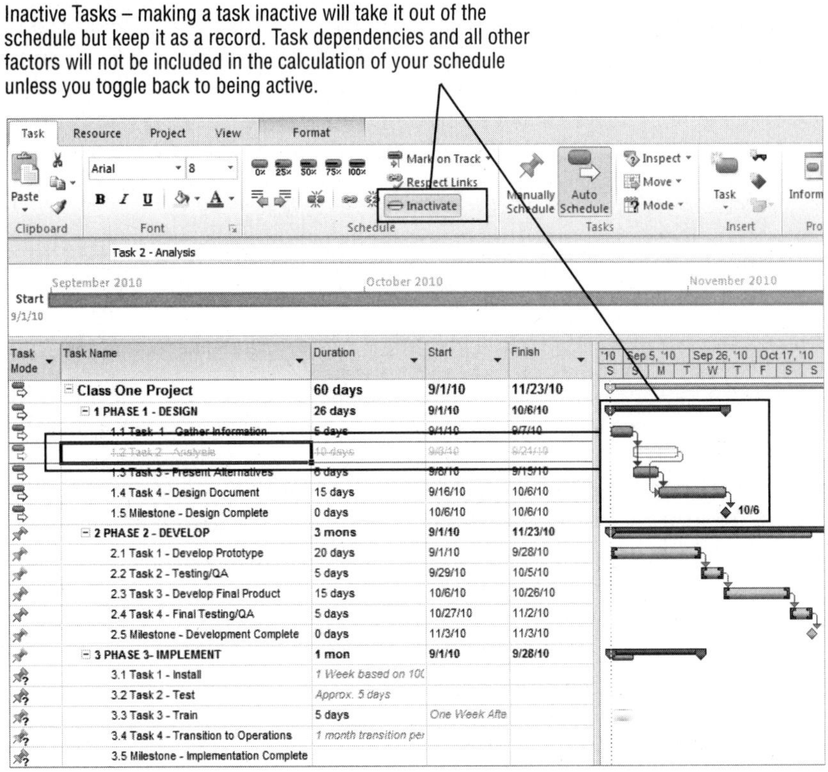

Inactive Tasks – making a task inactive will take it out of the schedule but keep it as a record. Task dependencies and all other factors will not be included in the calculation of your schedule unless you toggle back to being active.

To make a task inactive, follow these steps:

1. Select the task you want to make inactive.

2. Select Task tab ➤ Tasks group ➤ Inactivate option.

If you make a task inactive, it won't affect manually scheduled tasks. In Figure 7.13, Phase 1—Design is based on tasks that are auto-scheduled; you can see how deactivating a task affects the calculations on tasks that are linked to it.

Setting Dependencies in Project

One of the challenges that planners have when using Project is ensuring that all tasks are included in the network. A best practice and good guideline to follow is that every task should have a predecessor unless it's driven by the start date of the project, and every task should have a successor unless it's the last task or milestone in the project. In other words, all tasks and milestones should be networked. This may not always be possible, depending on the scenarios you're managing. If you're having difficulty finding a successor for a task or milestone, consider including a Project Complete milestone in your plan to link other tasks or milestones to.

Real World Scenario

Not All Tasks Have a Predecessor

The best practice around scheduling is to include all tasks in the network, which means every task should have a predecessor and a successor. If you don't add a predecessor, then you're assuming the task can be driven by the start date of the project, defined in Project Information. If a task doesn't have a successor, you're assuming that it's either the last thing in the project or it can be delayed without affecting anything else in the project, including the last task or milestone.

This isn't always the case. In many situations, there is no predecessor to link to. I once worked with a client to develop and launch a new video game. One line item was to receive a beta version of Sony's PlayStation, something the client had no control over; nor did the client have a project plan to link to. A different company had given the client the date they would receive the PlayStation. I had to enter the date manually and create a Start No Earlier constraint to schedule the task accordingly. (I discuss constraints in more detail later in this chapter.) Keep in mind that I was able to link other tasks and milestones to this event downstream in the schedule, but the driving factor for the start date wasn't a predecessor task; it was a constraint.

Using the Link Tool

The quickest and easiest way to set dependencies in Project is to use the Link tool. To do so, highlight two or more tasks, and click the Link tool; Project automatically sets up dependencies based on an FS, sequential relationship. See Figure 7.14.

Link Tool with User-Controlled, Manually Scheduled Tasks

If you use the Link tool for manually scheduled tasks, Project by default creates an FS, sequentially scheduled task relationship and turns on the Task tab ➤ Tasks group ➤ Respect Links option (see Figure 7.11). You're still free to move the manually scheduled tasks wherever you want, overriding the link even though it's present. You may see a red underline warning you that there is a problem; you can right-click it to take further action, such as respecting the link.

You can always choose Respect Links to reposition a task based on its dependencies. If you remove the dependencies using the Unlink tool after you set them for manual tasks, the tasks stay in place based on where the dependencies positioned them in the schedule. Project keeps them in place without the links because it automatically adds a constraint to the task. You can also change manually scheduled tasks to automatic; this includes the calculation of the links into the schedule.

FIGURE 7.14   Using the Link tool

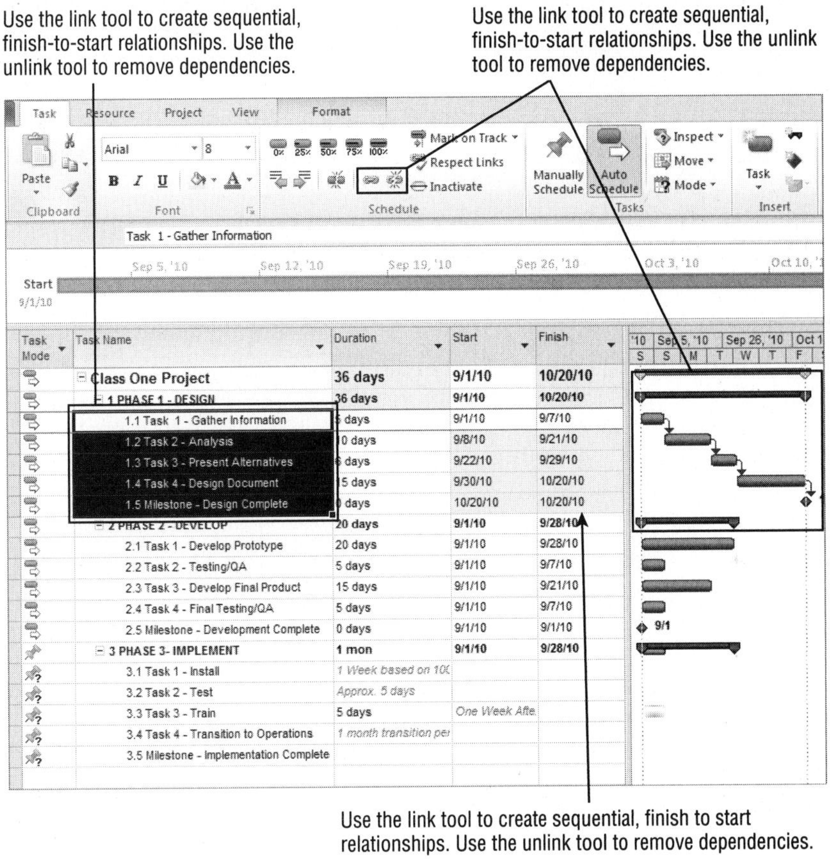

Use the link tool to create sequential, finish-to-start relationships. Use the unlink tool to remove dependencies.

Use the link tool to create sequential, finish-to-start relationships. Use the unlink tool to remove dependencies.

Use the link tool to create sequential, finish to start relationships. Use the unlink tool to remove dependencies.

Try to set dependencies at the task and milestone level and stay away from setting dependencies at the summary task or phase level. This way, you have a better chance of maintaining the integrity of the network and a better view of the critical path (discussed in detail later in this chapter). This approach also makes it easier to move tasks from one phase to another and avoid creating circular task relationships. If you decide to set links at the summary or phase level (for example, Phase 1—Design is a predecessor to Phase 2—Develop), you're limited to an FS or SS relationship. Summary tasks don't support FF or SF dependencies.

You can use the Unlink tool to remove dependencies that you don't want. You can also use multilevel undo to remove any dependency that you set and decide you don't want anymore.

Change Highlighting

The Change Highlighting feature lets you see the impact of changes throughout your plan. This helps you understand the effect of setting dependencies or any other change, so you can easily see if it affects a milestone, a phase, or overall project completion. Any cell that is changed is automatically highlighted in light blue.

In Figure 7.14, after setting the dependencies for the first phase, all the cells highlighted in light blue are the ones affected by the changes to the plan. This includes the finish dates for the phase and the project. This feature becomes even more useful during updating and tracking—for example, when a task is delayed and you want to visualize the impact of the delay throughout the plan.

Predecessor Column Approach

Another common way to establish dependencies is to type the ID number of the predecessor task directly into the Predecessors column. I call this the *talk-to-yourself* method of setting dependencies. Click the Predecessors cell of the task you want to set a predecessor link with, and ask yourself, "What is the predecessor to this task?" Then, enter the corresponding ID number from the ID column into the cell. If there is no predecessor for automatic scheduling, Project assumes you want the task to start at the project start date defined in the Project Information dialog box on the Project tab.

Figure 7.15 illustrates how this works in Project. If you use the Link tool described in the previous section, Project automatically enters the ID number into the Predecessors column for you.

FIGURE 7.15   Predecessors column

Corresponding ID number to the Predecessor column.

You can enter the ID number from the ID column of the predecessor task directly into the predecessor column. This will default to a finish to start (FS) type of link. You can also enter is lag values or SS, FF or SF for different scenarios as wll.

For multiple predecessors use a comma to separate the ID numbers.

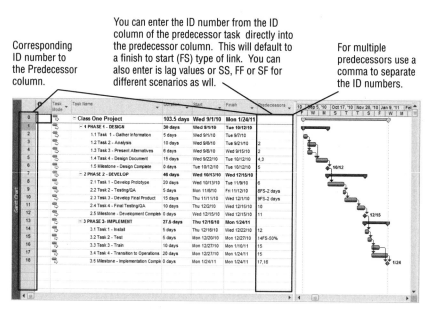

Split-Screen View with Details

If all your tasks are straightforward, with FS, sequential relationships, then you can probably get away with using the Link tool and the Predecessors column to set dependencies. However, life isn't always simple, and neither is network scheduling. Sometimes you need to either use different types of links, such as SS or FF, or create overlapping or lead-time scenarios using the Lag field. You can access all these dependency details by applying the split-screen view with details, which is a combination of the Gantt Chart view (or any other view) on top with the Task Form view on the bottom by default. There are two ways to open a split-screen view with details:

Method 1

1. Select View tab ➢ Split Screen group ➢ Details check box. You can have either Timeline or Details selected, but not both at the same time.

2. To the right of Details, from the drop-down list, select the view you want running at the bottom of the screen. The default is Task Form, which is used in the examples.

Method 2

1. Select Task tab ➢ Properties group ➢ Display Task Details button.

You can also click and drag from the bottom-right corner of the screen if the Timeline view isn't running. As discussed in Chapter 4, you can't have the Timeline view running with the project details.

With a split screen view established, you can modify the details of the task dependency information by selecting the dependency, type, or lag, as shown in Figure 7.16.

FIGURE 7.16   Split-screen view and dependencies

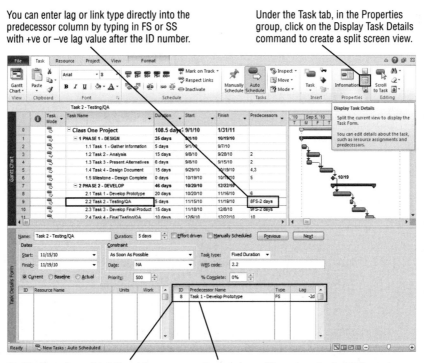

You can enter lag or link type directly into the predecessor column by typing in FS or SS with +ve or –ve lag value after the ID number.

Under the Task tab, in the Properties group, click on the Display Task Details command to create a split screen view.

Modify dependency details by adding predecessors, changing type, or lag.

Lag can be positive or negative to create overlap or lead times. You can also enter lag as days or %.

If you change any information in the bottom portion of the split-screen view (the task form), you must click the OK button for it to register and calculate.

Click-and-Drag Approach

The brave-at-heart with a steady hand can click and drag dependencies. Some professionals don't recommend this approach, but I think it's kind of neat. It's based on using the bar area of the Gantt view. You click the predecessor task, and drag and drop to the successor task. This can be hazardous to your plan because if you accidentally move the mouse or drop in the wrong place, you can end up moving tasks and inadvertently creating constraints.

Figure 7.17 illustrates how to set dependencies using the click-and-drag approach.

FIGURE 7.17   Click and drag to create dependencies.

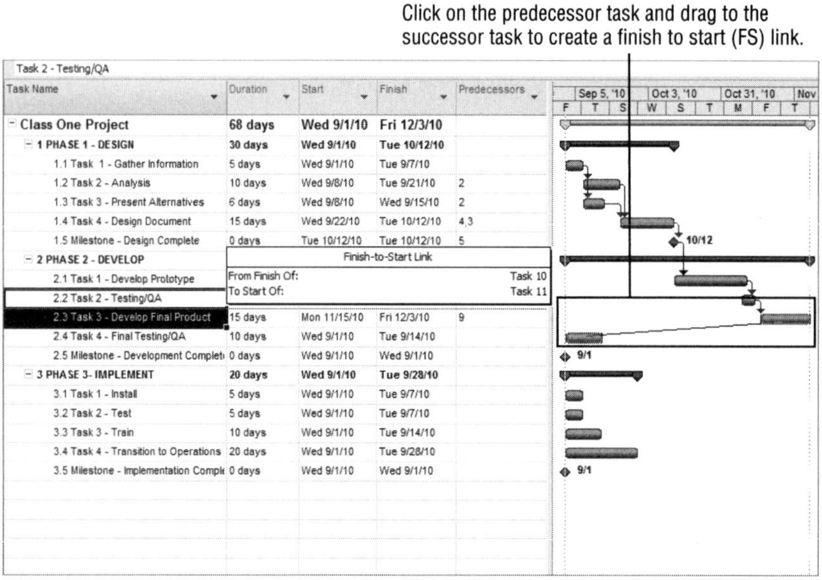

Task Information, Predecessor Tab Approach

Another way to set dependencies is to use the Task Information dialog box's Predecessors tab. As shown in Figure 7.18, follow these steps:

1. Choose Task tab ➢ Properties group ➢ Task Information, or double-click a task, to open the Task Information dialog box.

2. On the Predecessors tab, click the cell below Task Name.

3. From the drop-down list, select the predecessor task. You can also type in the ID number.

4. Under Type, select the appropriate link type (the default is FS).

5. Under Lag, enter lag if needed (the default is none).

6. Click OK.

FIGURE 7.18   Task Information dialog box, Predecessors tab

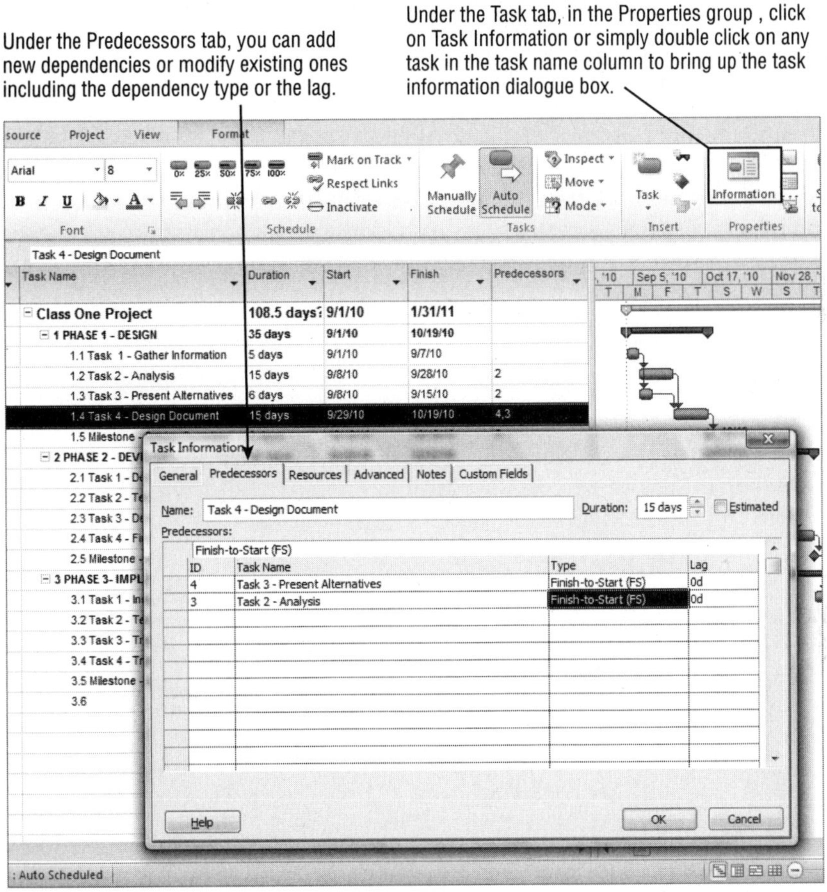

Under the Predecessors tab, you can add new dependencies or modify existing ones including the dependency type or the lag.

Under the Task tab, in the Properties group , click on Task Information or simply double click on any task in the task name column to bring up the task information dialogue box.

I prefer using a split-screen view to modify dependency details during the planning stage, because you don't have to open and close the dialog box as you move from one task to another. Anything to be more efficient and save a few clicks.

If you use the Lag field to account for delays between tasks, it can be hard for stakeholders to read or understand why the gap or lag is present. You may end up explaining more times than you care to, or even forget why you put the lag in the plan in the first place. A wise consultant once told me that it's better to replace lag with an actual task wherever it makes sense. For example, if you need five days for concrete to cure or paint to dry, include a task called Concrete Curing or Paint Drying; that way, the lag is more prominent and won't be removed by accident.

Leads and Lags in Project Management

You can use the Lag field in Project to add positive or negative numbers to create overlapping scenarios (lead times) or waiting periods (lag times) between tasks. *A Guide to the Project Management Body of Knowledge*, Fourth Edition (PMBOK), refers to the lead time as the overlapping scenario that allows for the acceleration of the successor activity. For example, perhaps you can begin editing a document halfway through writing it. This can be accomplished by setting an FS relationship with a –50% value in the Lag field. Or you can conversely create an SS relationship with a +50% lag to accomplish a similar result in the schedule.

PMBOK addresses the lag time as the networking scenario that creates a gap or delay in the start of a successor activity. For example, on a construction project, you may need to let the concrete cure for five days after it's poured, before starting the next task related to it. This can be accomplished by setting an FS relationship with a five-day lag in Project.

The key to understanding how to map your use of Project to PMBOK terminology is to remember that you use the Lag field to set both lead and lag times. FS with negative lag establishes lead times, and FS with positive lag establishes lag times. Figure 7.19 illustrates how each is presented in Project.

FIGURE 7.19 Leads and lags in Project

	Task Mode	Task Name	Duration	Start	Finish	Predecessors	Oct 17, '10	Oct 24, '10	Oct 31, '10	Nov 7, '10
1		– Lead Time Example	9 days	Tue 10/19/10	Fri 10/29/10					
2		Task 1	6 days	Tue 10/19/10	Tue 10/26/10					
3		Task 2	6 days	Fri 10/22/10	Fri 10/29/10	2FS-3 days				
4		– Lag Time Example	15 days	Tue 10/19/10	Mon 11/8/10					
5		Task 1	6 days	Tue 10/19/10	Tue 10/26/10					
6		Task 2	6 days	Mon 11/1/10	Mon 11/8/10	5FS+3 days				

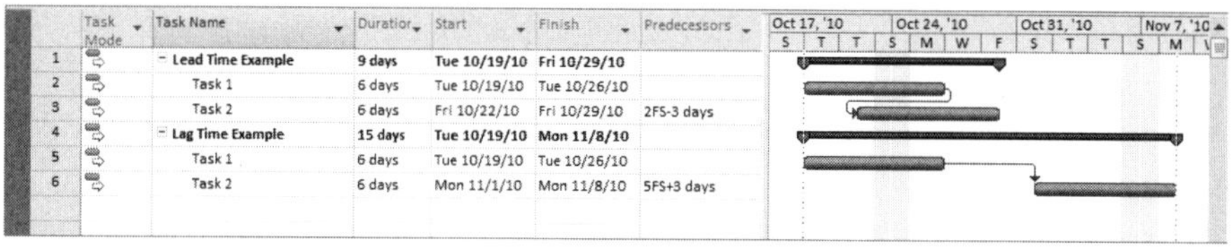

Using Constraints and Deadlines

This section explores the use of constraints and deadlines and how they affect your schedule and the calculation of start and finish dates.

Constraints

One of the most common difficulties in scheduling with Project is comprehending the impact of constraints, especially with user-controlled, manually based schedules. Project automatically adds constraints to tasks to hold them in place. This is the foundation of manually based scheduling, so it's important to understand constraints and how to add or remove them. The problem with constraints on manually scheduled tasks is that they limit your ability to use Project as an effective management tool. The initial outcome may look good, but a plan based on constraints requires manual updates and takes far more work to maintain.

Instead of allowing constraints to drive your schedule, you should focus on setting up a network of tasks with dependencies that determine when a task should start and finish. This lets Project use its calculation engine to drive the schedule, making it much more automatic and dynamic. However, task constraints can come in handy when you have a hard-coded date such as a tradeshow, regulated deadlines, contract constraints, and so on. Manual scheduling is also handy during the early stages of planning or when the details or estimates are fuzzy. When you're ready, though, automatic scheduling is far more efficient.

Project Standard defaults to As Soon As Possible for new tasks. The majority of your tasks should stay As Soon As Possible, with few exceptions. This way, when it comes time to make changes and do what-if scenarios, you can let Project recalculate each task's start and finish dates automatically. If your tasks are all constrained by specific dates, you'll be forced to manually review, analyze, and enter new dates for tasks affected by any changes. Task constraints may also have a significant impact on your critical path calculations, limiting your ability to manage the project life cycle. Constraints are useful tools, but they should be used wisely and with caution.

Constraints provide some flexibility in how tasks are scheduled. You can control start or finish dates that aren't controlled by the availability of a resource or by a predecessor. This often occurs when a task relies on a factor outside your plan or your scope of work. Constraints also let you impose time limits for such things as contract milestones, deliverables, and funding start dates.

Problems can occurs when project managers don't realize a constraint has been placed on a task and don't understand why a task is being scheduled at an unexpected date. The following is a list of constraints in Project that can be applied at the task or milestone level:

- *As Late As Possible (ALAP)*—Schedules the task as late as it can occur in the schedule without delaying subsequent tasks. Don't enter a constraint date with this constraint.
- *As Soon As Possible (ASAP)*—Schedules the task to begin as early as it can occur. This is the default constraint for tasks. Don't enter a constraint date with this constraint.
- *Finish No Earlier Than (FNET)*—Schedules the task to finish on or after the constraint date. Use it to ensure that a task doesn't finish before a certain date.
- *Finish No Later Than (FNLT)*—Schedules the task to finish on or before the constraint date. Use it to ensure that a task doesn't finish after a certain date.
- *Must Finish On (MFO)*—Schedules the task to finish on the constraint date. Sets the early, scheduled, and late finish dates to the date you type, and anchors the task in the schedule.
- *Must Start On (MSO)*—Schedules the task to start on the constraint date. Sets the early, scheduled, and late start dates to the date you type, and anchors the task in the schedule.
- *Start No Earlier Than (SNET)*—Schedules the task to start on or after the constraint date. Use it to ensure that a task doesn't start before a specified date.
- *Start No Later Than (SNLT)*—Schedules the task to start on or before the constraint date. Use it to ensure that a task doesn't start after a specified date.

The default constraint is As Soon As Possible. This is an unconstrained task that is free to be dynamically and automatically scheduled based on project start date, calendars, duration, dependencies, and resource assignments (see Chapter 9, "Understanding the Calculation Engine for Automatic Scheduling").

Most of the constraints are what I call *half constraints* or *soft constraints*: you can push them one way, either to the left or to the right, but not another. Consider the Start No Earlier Than constraint, which is the default constraint when you type the start date manually into the Start column. It means that no matter what, the task won't start earlier or be pushed to the left, but it can be pushed out to the right or start later. It can be pushed in only one direction.

Hard constraints occur when you use a Must Finish On or a Must Start On constraint. This means that, no matter what, that task or milestone isn't moving. These constraints override all other task drivers or controlling factors in Project, including dependencies, project start date, and calendars. When you use one of these hard constraints, it's automatically put on the critical path, whether it's in the network or not.

🌐 Real World Scenario

Use of Must Finish On Constraints

I was working with a Fortune 1000 company that required a formal plan and schedule for every major new product in development. One big date that was always tracked was the product-ready-for-launch date, which ultimately led to the first profit dollar realized. These dates were reviewed and agreed on by a steering committee, and permission was required in order to move them. The problem was that the project I was working on was very fluid, with ongoing changes and issues affecting the plan and schedules. We continually ran into scenarios where the launch date moved past before the steering committee approved a date change, which caused people to be concerned.

To solve this problem, we set the formally approved product-launch date with a Must Finish On date constraint but created a second milestone for the currently planned product launch. This allowed us to continually compare the dynamically scheduled milestone, which represented the current best estimate, with the anchored formally approved milestone. We used the formally approved milestone for roll-up reporting, and we used the current one to request changes to the schedule if needed.

Follow these steps to apply task constraints (see Figure 7.20):

1. Click Task tab ➤ Properties group ➤ Task Information (or double-click a selected task) to open the Task Information dialog box.

2. On the Advanced Tab, click the Constraint Type drop-down list, and select the appropriate constraint.

3. In the Constraint Date field, type or select the respective constraint date.

FIGURE 7.20   Setting constraints

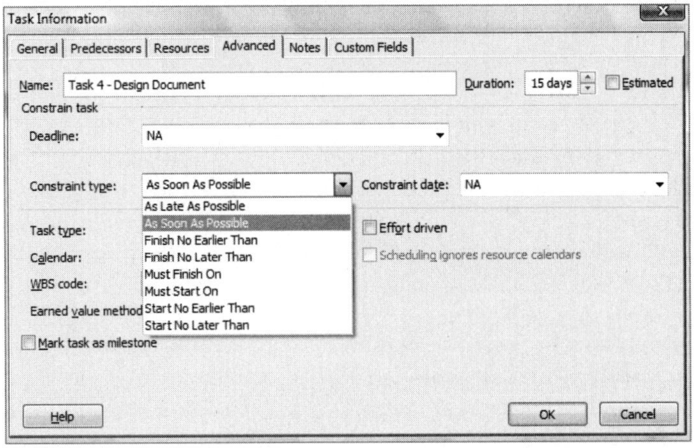

The Indicator column shows an indicator when a constraint other than As Soon As Possible is applied to a task. Figure 7.21 shows the indicator and the tooltip that appears when you hold your mouse over it.

FIGURE 7.21   Constraint indicators

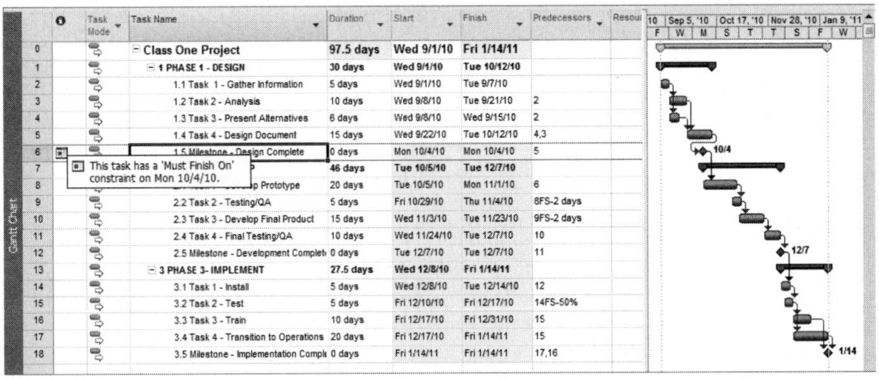

With a hard constraint (Must Finish On or Must Start On), the indicator is red instead of blue. Such constraints often result in scheduling conflicts. For example, in Figure 7.22, Design Document is linked to Design Completed, and Design Completed has a hardconstraint set. If Design Document takes longer than expected and finishes later than the constraint date on the milestone, Project automatically displays a schedule conflict message, as shown in the figure.

Technically, every task in Project has a constraint. If you create a task and don't specify a start or finish date, then Project assigns an As Soon As Possible constraint as the default for the task. If you enter a start date for a task, Project assigns a Start No Earlier Than constraint. If you enter a finish date for a task, Project assigns a Finish No Earlier Than constraint. The constraint must be assigned for the task to be scheduled at the date you specify. If you must assign a constraint to a task, Start No Earlier Than is probably the best choice, because it allows a task to be delayed forward in the schedule.

My guidance is to use constraints only when needed and as an exception rather than the rule. The majority of tasks should be free-flowing, with As Soon As Possible as the default. If you prefer to use manual scheduling techniques to establish your dates, be aware that constraints are most likely being established by Project and that when or if you switch to automatic scheduling, you may need to remove constraints by changing tasks back to As Soon As Possible.

Constraints Are Like Anchors

You can think about a constraint as being like throwing an anchor overboard to keep a boat in place on the water. Regardless of which way the wind blows or how the waves move, an anchor holds the boat in place, just like a constraint holds a task in place. Constraints override Project's automatic scheduling tools and should be used wisely and cautiously. I'm not saying you should never use them; but when you do, make sure you understand why you're doing so and the impact they have on your schedule.

Deadlines

The deadline feature is another tool you can use to manage important completion points in your plan. Deadlines are different from constraints in that a deadline acts as a comparator in which the task or milestone on which the deadline is set is still free to move based on dependencies and duration estimates. By using the Deadline field, you can set a target finish date for a particular task or milestone and watch the project plan to see if the planned finish date will fall before, on, or after the deadline date. I find this to be a very powerful feature to help manage deadlines and communicate more effectively to stakeholders why you will or won't meet a target finish date.

You can add deadline dates to any task except the project summary task, a summary task representing an inserted project, and the summary task of a recurring task series. To assign a deadline to a task, follow these steps:

1. Double-click the task to which you want to assign a deadline date. Doing so opens the Task Information dialog box.

2. Click the Advanced tab.

3. In the Deadline field, set a deadline date. Click OK.

When you assign a deadline date, a green down-arrow marker is set in the Gantt bar area so you can visually see how the deadline compares to your current estimate. If the task or milestone is pushed past the deadline date, a red indicator is displayed in the Indicator column. No indicator displays if a task finishes before the deadline. This provides you with a visible yet unobtrusive notification that the current scheduled finish is later than the planned deadline. Figure 7.23 shows how a deadline appears in a project plan if the milestone is late. The total slack for the milestone that has a deadline tells you how late or early you are compared to your deadline. I'll be covering how to change the look and feel of information in the Gantt chart area in more detail in Chapter 13, "Creating Custom Views, Formatting, and Reporting."

FIGURE 7.23   Deadline feature

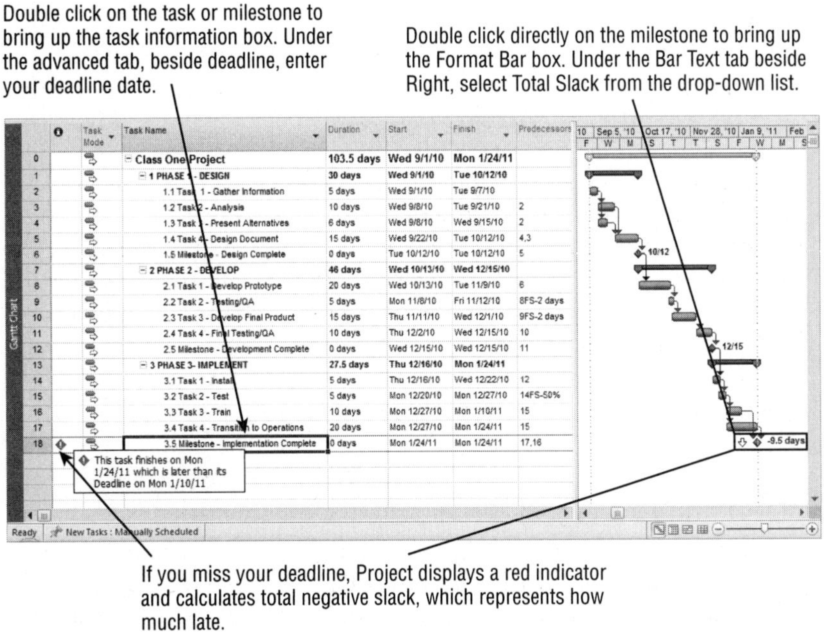

Double click on the task or milestone to bring up the task information box. Under the advanced tab, beside deadline, enter your deadline date.

Double click directly on the milestone to bring up the Format Bar box. Under the Bar Text tab beside Right, select Total Slack from the drop-down list.

This task finishes on Mon 1/24/11 which is later than its Deadline on Mon 1/10/11

If you miss your deadline, Project displays a red indicator and calculates total negative slack, which represents how much late.

Task Inspector

The Task Inspector is another useful planning and tracking feature in Project. This function allows you to determine the controlling factors driving the start of a task and view suggestions for corrective action if needed. Many times, these factors are obvious; but in a complex plan with many dependencies, custom calendars, and constraints, it may be difficult to tell what the controlling factor is for a task and what to do about it.

Figure 7.24 shows how the Task Inspector works in Project. To turn on the Task Inspector, follow these steps:

1. Select Task tab ➤ Schedule group ➤ Inspect Task. The Task Inspector pane appears on the left.

2. Click the X in the upper-right corner of the Task Inspector pane to close it.

FIGURE 7.24   Task Inspector

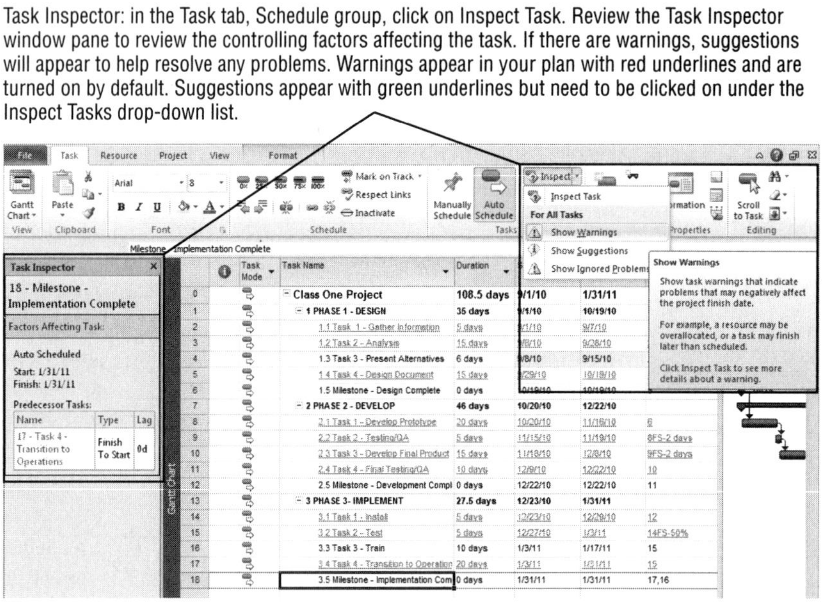

Task Inspector: in the Task tab, Schedule group, click on Inspect Task. Review the Task Inspector window pane to review the controlling factors affecting the task. If there are warnings, suggestions will appear to help resolve any problems. Warnings appear in your plan with red underlines and are turned on by default. Suggestions appear with green underlines but need to be clicked on under the Inspect Tasks drop-down list.

Understanding and Viewing the Critical Path

One of the key benefits of following automatic scheduling and the approach outlined in this book is the ability to identify and leverage the critical path. In this section, we'll explore what the critical path is, how it's calculated, and how you can use Project to be more effective as a project manager.

Real World Scenario

Shortening Your Project Life Cycle: Remove Constraints and Use Automatic Scheduling

Early in my career, I was sent to a client site to run a workshop to help a project team trim three months off a project plan for a new product launch. I was told that the plan was set up in Project and was ready to use. The client wouldn't show me the file until I was on site.

I arrived the day before the workshop and was shocked to find out that the entire plan, over 500 line items, was set with constraints and not dependencies. The project manager was new and didn't realize how Project worked and that changing the duration of one task didn't change the overall plan without an established network. To make matters worse, the team was distributed around the world, and people were flying in just for this meeting. We worked past midnight to establish the network and identify the critical path while removing the constraints—just in time to run a successful workshop.

Now, no matter what the situation is, I always ask to see work in progress or completed plans before making commitments like that.

What Is the Critical Path?

In any one-project network, one sequence of tasks fixes the duration of the project. Any slippage—failure to start a task on time or a task taking longer than estimated—causes the project to finish later than planned. This sequence is the *critical path*.

A critical path is the one in which

- The earliest and latest starts for tasks are the same
- The earliest and latest finishes for tasks are the same

The earliest start of any task is the duration of all related preceding tasks: they must be completed tasks. The earliest finish of any task is the earliest start plus the duration of the task.

The latest finish of any task is the duration of all related succeeding tasks: they can't commence until this task is completed. The latest start of any task is the latest finish minus the duration of the task.

Tasks that aren't on the critical path have *slack time*: flexible time in a schedule that lets tasks slip without causing schedule delays. The latest start minus the earliest start is the slack or *float*. Free slack is the amount of time you can delay a task before it affects the start of the first successor.

The critical path is the set of tasks in the plan for which there is no slack. Any slippage in a task on the critical path results in the project finishing beyond its target completion date.

Calculating the Critical Path

The critical path in Project is calculated using the critical path method: first calculating earliest start (ES), latest start (LS), earliest finish (EF), and latest finish (LF), and then calculating whether there is any difference. If there is a difference, then the task will have slack associated with it; if there isn't, then the task will have zero slack. In other words, the critical path in Project is calculated by looking at the slack of the various tasks in the plan in conjunction with task dependencies. The longest path through the plan represents those tasks with no slack ultimately defining the critical path. Any task with zero total slack means can't be delayed without pushing out the end date of the project and therefore is on the critical path. Project also uses the last task or milestone in the project plan as the basis of calculating the critical path.

Using deadlines also affects the calculation of the critical path. If you enter a deadline date before the end of the task's total slack, then total slack is recalculated by using the deadline date rather than the task's late finish. This can change the critical path.

Consider the network shown in Figure 7.25. Tasks are in circles, and the duration of each task is represented on top of the dependency lines.

FIGURE 7.25   Critical path network example

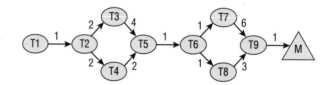

To do to a critical path analysis, you can begin by looking at task 3 (T3) and asking, "If everything is running on schedule, what is the earliest time T3 can start?" The ES for T3 is three days. Now ask, "Without delaying the end of the project, what is the latest time T3 can start?" The LS for T3 is also three days, because if it starts any later than that, it will push out T5 and delay the project.

Next, ask the same type of question for each of the finishes. If everything is running on schedule, what is the earliest time T3 will finish? The EF for task 3 is seven days (three days + four days). Without causing a delay in the end date of the project, the latest finish for T3 is seven days, because if it finishes any later, it will push out T5 and cause a delay in the end date of the project. There is no difference between the early and late starts and finishes; therefore, T3 has no slack and must be on the critical path.

You can repeat this line of questioning for each task, but the good news is that Project does this for you. The following table completes the analysis for T4, T7, and T8. These tasks are concurrent, with different durations, causing one of them not to be on the critical path:

TASK #	ES	LS	EF	LF	SLACK
3	3d	3d	7d	7d	0d
4	3d	5d	5d	7d	2d

TASK #	ES	LS	EF	LF	SLACK
7	9d	9d	15d	15d	0d
8	9d	12d	12d	15d	3d

ES = earliest start; LS = latest start; EF = earliest finish; LF = latest finish

T4 can be delayed up to two days without pushing out the end date, and T8 can be delayed up to three days. With this in mind, which tasks are on the critical path? They aren't limited to T3 and T7. You must consider the entire network, as shown in Figure 7.26. If any delay occurs along this path, the project will be delayed.

FIGURE 7.26   Identify the critical path.

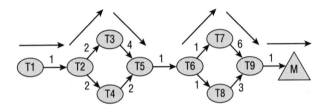

Using This to Your Advantage

Knowing your critical path is important because everyone is concerned with deadlines, time-to-market pressures, and understanding the controlling factors driving the completion of the project. The critical path highlights the tasks that ultimately drive your project life cycle; knowing this tells you what to focus on when you're trying to shorten your project timeline.

If you have many concurrent tasks and need to shorten your schedule, knowing which tasks are on the critical path also lets you better focus resources. In Figure 7.26, suppose you need to shave time off the plan. If you add resources to T4 or T8, you won't alter the end date of the project, because those tasks aren't on the critical path. All you'll do is increase the slack time.

If a task that isn't on the critical path is delayed long enough, it can become critical. For example, in Figure 7.26, if T4 is delayed by five days and ends up needing seven days, it will end up on the critical path, whereas T3 will fall off the critical path.

Viewing the Critical Path and Slack in Project

Let Project do the work for you; take advantage of the critical-path tools at your disposal. The default Gantt Chart view doesn't show the critical path, but you can turn it on.

The Gantt Chart view has a text area and a bar area. You need to format each one separately, so let's start with the text styles. Figure 7.27 shows the network from Figure 7.26 and a project plan that follows the first three steps in the planning process.

FIGURE 7.27   Formatting the critical path

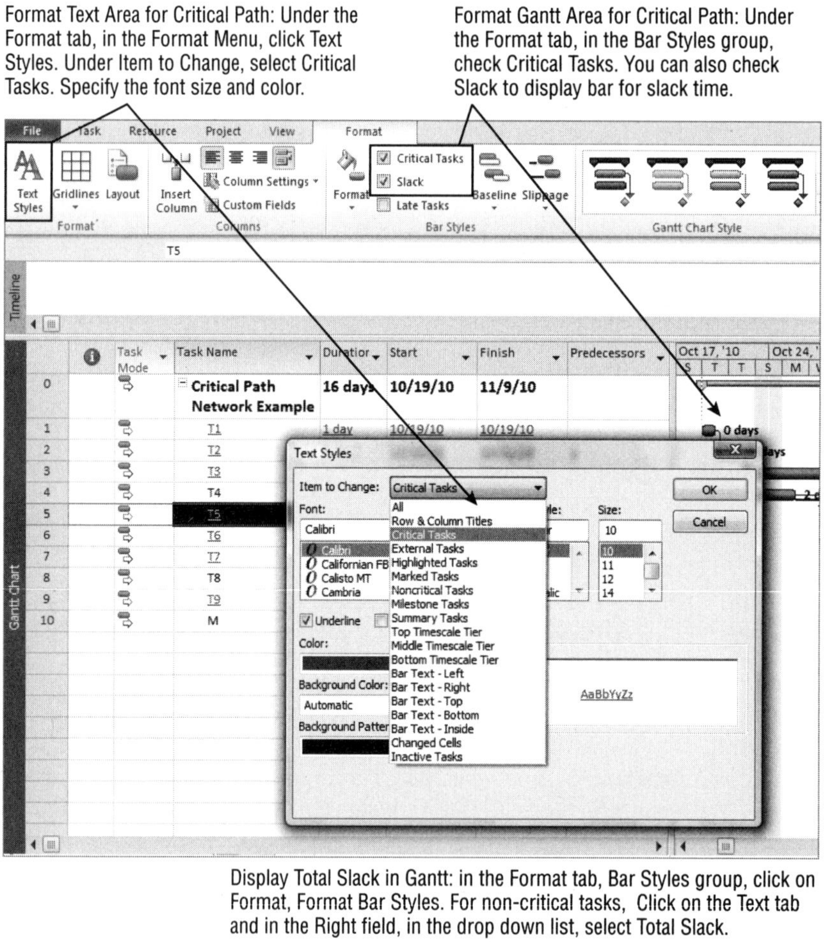

Format Text Area for Critical Path: Under the Format tab, in the Format Menu, click Text Styles. Under Item to Change, select Critical Tasks. Specify the font size and color.

Format Gantt Area for Critical Path: Under the Format tab, in the Bar Styles group, check Critical Tasks. You can also check Slack to display bar for slack time.

Display Total Slack in Gantt: in the Format tab, Bar Styles group, click on Format, Format Bar Styles. For non-critical tasks, Click on the Text tab and in the Right field, in the drop down list, select Total Slack.

You can format the text styles following these steps:

1. Select Format tab ➤ Format group ➤ Text Styles. The Text Styles dialog box opens.

2. From the Items to Change drop-down menu, select Critical Tasks. Notice that you can globally change other items as well.

3. From the Color list, choose Red. Click OK. You can also change the background color, font, bold, underline, and italics.

In Figure 7.27, I also formatted the bar styles to be red for the critical path and to display total slack to the right of the Gantt bars. You can do this by following these steps:

1. Choose Format tab ➤ Bar Styles group ➤ Critical Tasks. You can also click Slack to display slack bars.

2. Choose ➤ Bar Styles group ➤ Format ➤ Format Bar Styles.

3. Click the Text tab. From the Right drop-down menu, choose Total Slack.

4. Click OK.

Formatting is view-specific. As you move from one view to another, the formatting is different, based on either the defaults or the changes you've made. For example, if you format the Gantt chart to be red in this view, that formatting won't carry over into other views—if you switch to the Tracking Gantt view, it will have its own set of formats (see Chapter 9).

Figure 7.28 shows the Class One project example, formatted to show the critical path in the text area and the bar area. I decided to display the total slack not in the Gantt bar area but rather as a column in the text area. You can always add the total slack as a column in the text area or beside the Gantt bars. To add a column, use the Add Column feature at the end of the table.

FIGURE 7.28   Critical path display in the Class One Project example

---

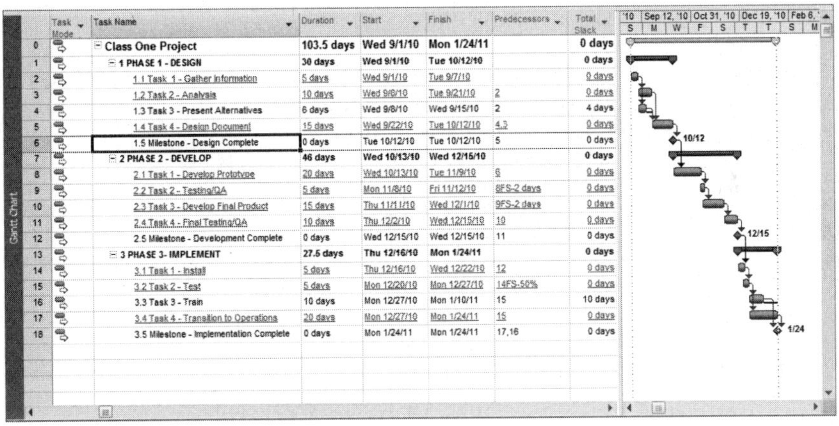

🌐 **Real World Scenario**

Shortening the Project Life Cycle

Working with a large organization, I was asked to help shorten the life cycle for new product development projects. We started by following the steps in this book to create a solid template. Then, we gathered the subject matter experts for a facilitated workshop. We walked through the plan in Project with the critical path highlighted in red.

Working with the team, we were able to focus on critical-path items and think of ways to accelerate tasks or make them overlap or more concurrent. With the input from the team and the use of the tool, we were able to shave two months from their current process. While this was going on, the critical path changed frequently; but Project made it easy to identify the critical path and continue to improve the project life cycle.

Summary

In this chapter, you learned about the importance of setting up a network for your plan by establishing dependencies between tasks and milestones. Best practice is to set dependencies at the task and milestone level and try to avoid setting links at the phase or summary task unless you have a compelling reason to do so. It's better to have key milestones at the end of each phase that you can use to link the start of tasks in subsequent phases. Also, to ensure that you have a free-flowing and dynamic schedule, minimize your use of constraints on tasks; constraints are created by default if you type a date directly into the Start or Finish column or if you apply manual scheduling techniques.

If you use manual scheduling early in the planning process, think about switching to automatic scheduling at some point, after the details become clearer. This will allow for more efficient scheduling when it comes to managing changes and controlling your project life cycle. This means you may need to change task constraints that were placed automatically by Project back to As Soon As Possible.

When you've finished setting up dependencies, you can view the project's critical path, which is the path that drives the end date of the last task or milestone in your plan. Knowing the critical path gives you an effective means of controlling the project life cycle and focusing resources when you need to compress the schedule.

You can also use the deadline feature to establish target-completion dates that don't directly affect your schedule but provide a powerful means of tracking your plan.

By completing the first three steps of the planning process—entering the WBS, estimating duration, and setting dependencies—you've created an effective schedule to track scope and time (two of the three components of the triple constraint). In the next chapter, you'll move on to step 4 in the planning process: assigning resources and costs to your plan.

Hands-On Exercises

The following hands-on exercises are designed to test your understanding of the topics discussed in this chapter. We've provided files on the companion CD that will show you what your project file should look like as you perform these exercises.

EXERCISE 5

Setting Dependencies

Using the network diagrams shown, create the following task relationships in Class One Project:

- Circles represent the tasks in each phase, and triangles are milestones.

- The milestone at the end of each phase drives the start of the first task of the next phase.

- Lines in phase 2 and phase 3 with boxes on top represent lag time to create overlap between tasks.

Phase 1:

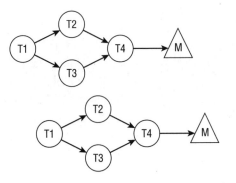

Phase 1:

EXERCISE 5 *(continued)*

Phase 2:

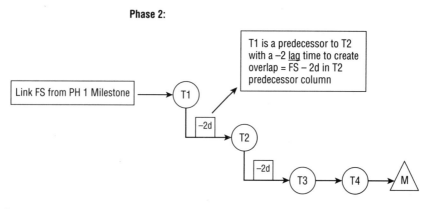

Phase 2:

T1 is a predecessor to T2 with a −2 lag time to create overlap = FS − 2d in T2 predecessor column

Link FS from PH 1 Milestone → T1

−2d

T2

−2d

T3 → T4 → M

Phase 3:

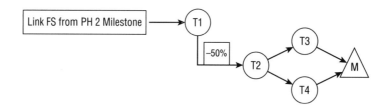

Phase 3:

Link FS from PH 2 Milestone → T1

−50%

T2

T3

T4

M

Save the Class One Project file.

Make sure you understand the ways tasks are related and how to model that relationship in Project using linking and lead/lag.

EXERCISE 6

Critical Path

In the following network diagram, tasks are represented in circles and duration is in days found on top of or below the arrows:

EXERCISE 6 *(continued)*

Exercise 6: Critical Path

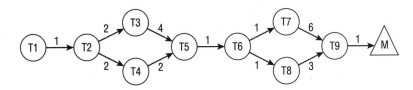

TASK #	ES	LS	EF	LF	SLACK/FLOAT
T3	3d	3d	7d	7d	0d
T4	3d	5d	5d	7d	2d
T7					
T8					

ES = earliest start; LS = latest start; EF = earliest finish; LF = latest finish

1. Complete the table for T7 and T8.
2. Circle the critical path.
3. Think of at least two key reasons why it's important to know your project's critical path.

You can't identify the critical path if you don't take the time to set your dependencies. After your dependencies are set, your ability to use the plan as a management tool will increase significantly. Please make sure you understand why!

EXERCISE 7

Critical Path, Continued

1. Create a new project. In the backstage area, select New.
2. In the Task pane, click Blank Project.
3. In the backstage, select Save as, and name the project **Class Two Project**.
4. Choose Project tab ➤ Project Information, and set the start date as one month from today. Click OK.

5. Enter the project plan represented by the network diagram in Exercise 6.

6. Choose Format tab ➤ Format group ➤ Text Styles ➤ Item to Change ➤ Critical Tasks. Choose the color Red, and click OK.

7. Select Format tab ➤ Bar Styles group ➤ Critical Tasks.

Save the Class Two Project file.

 Make sure you understand the ways that tasks are related and how to model that relationship in Project using a.) linking and b.) lead/lag. Start and finish dates may vary from the examples on this CD or book depending on when your project start date is set and where the holiday settings impact the calendar.

Chapter

8

Assigning Resources and Costs

IN THIS CHAPTER, YOU'LL LEARN ABOUT THE FOLLOWING:

- ✓ Step 4 of the planning process: assigning resources and costs

- ✓ Setting up a resource pool

- ✓ Defining resources to use in a project plan

- ✓ Assigning resources to tasks

- ✓ Evaluating the impact of resource assignments on the schedule

- ✓ Assigning costs and managing project budgets

This chapter covers how to share resources across projects and analyze your resources from a demand versus capacity standpoint. You'll learn how to make better decisions and take corrective action related to resource utilization, taking advantage of powerful and easy-to-use resource-management tools. This chapter also discusses resource leveling, so you can decide whether this functionality is right for you and your plan.

Setting Up Your Resource Pool

A *resource* is any type of entity that you need to accomplish a task in your plan. A resource can be a person (named or generic), equipment, or material, and may include expense items such as travel. When you assign resources in Project, you think of the type of resource you need and its quantity, availability, and cost. You don't have to include costs or rates if you don't need to track them.

When you're assigning resources to tasks in your project plan, first take the time to create a standard resource pool that can be sourced for your project plan or shared with other project plans. Many people make the mistake of typing names directly into Project's Resource Name column, unaware that those names are automatically added to the resource pool. This almost always results in duplicate or inaccurate resource names being added to your plans.

For example, you may enter **Peter Smith** for a task or one project, and someone else may enter **Pete Smith** for another project or another task, resulting in having two separate and distinct resources populated in the resource pool. Even a single character typed by accident in the Resource Name column is automatically added to the resource pool; you can delete it from the Resource Name column, but it still lives in the resource pool. Although it may be tempting to go the Entry table and start typing names, it's best practice to define your resources first in the Resource Sheet view. When the resources are defined, Project lets you draw from that pool to assign resources to tasks. In this manner, you can select resources from a predefined list and not type them directly into the Resource Name field.

Using the Resource Sheet View

The best place to build a resource pool is the Resource Sheet view. As discussed in Chapter 4, "Getting Started and Setting Up the Microsoft Project Environment," there are two basic types of views in Project: one set for tasks and another set for resources. Project makes it easy to navigate from task-related activities to resource-related activities by selecting either the Task tab or the Resource tab. Task views and resource views have unique fields, tables, filters, and groups; these are covered in more detail in Part 3, "Communicating and Reporting Essentials."

Sharing Resources and EPM

When it comes to sharing resources across multiple projects or even across departments, it's a good idea to start to think about using an Enterprise Project Management (EPM) solution, as discussed in Chapter 3, "Enterprise Project Management and Other Key Considerations." Although you can share resource-pool files using Project 2010 in a desktop environment, it's limited in scope, access, size, and reporting. If you require more than just sharing among a small group of resources and a few projects, it's time to consider Microsoft Project Server 2010.

In a split-screen view, it's fine to mix and match resource views with task views. For example, you can have the Timeline view running above the Resource Sheet view.

To launch the Resource Sheet view (see Figure 8.1), follow these instructions:

1. Go to Resource tab ➤ View group.

2. From the Team Planner drop-down list, select Resource Sheet.

FIGURE 8.1   Applying the Resource Sheet view

Resource Sheet view: under the Resource tab, in the View group, click on the drop-down list by Team Planner and select Resource Sheet.

You can also find the Resource Sheet view in the View Slider at the bottom of your screen. This will allow you to quickly change back and forth from the Gantt chart view to the Resource Sheet view.

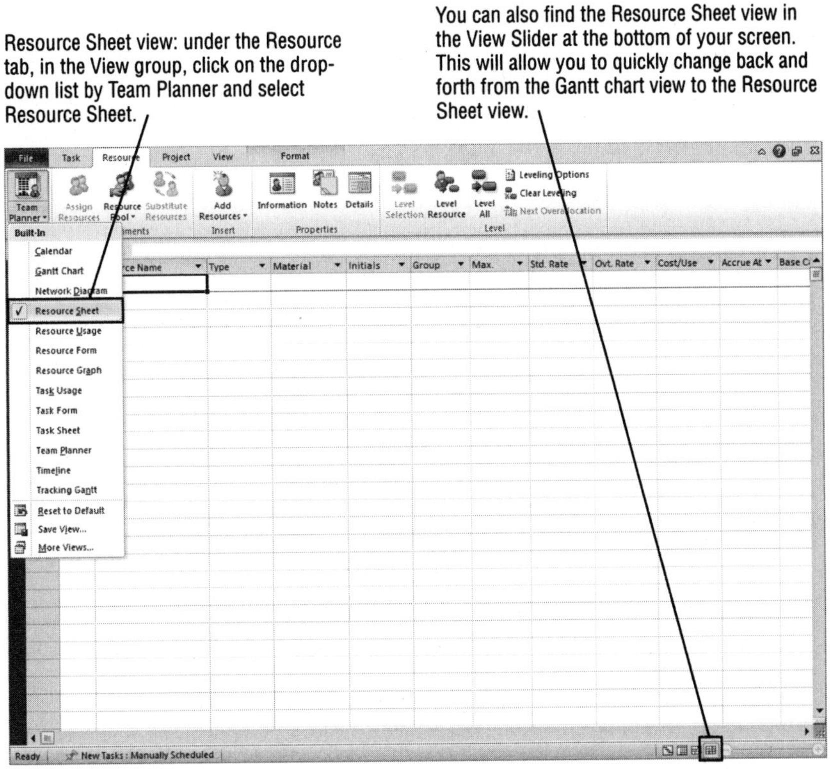

You can also find the Resource Sheet view in the view slider in the lower-right corner of your screen. This lets you quickly move from one view to another without using tabs.

Like the default Gantt Chart view, the Resource Sheet view starts with a default table called Entry. You can confirm this by looking on the View tab in the Data group. Click the Tables drop-down list, and ensure that Entry is checked. Chapter 11, "Using Tables and Custom Fields," explains in detail how to change tables and create custom tables with custom fields.

Resource Types

Before you begin entering resources into the resource sheet, think about what types of resources you want to track. Standardize your approach, whether for just one project or many projects across a group or department. This includes defining standard conventions for named resources, such as first and last name or first initial and last name. Be consistent, to avoid duplicate resource entries such as David Blair, Dave Blair, and D. Blair, which would be indentified as separate and unique resources.

You may also decide to use generic resource names, such as Engineer, Analyst, Electrician, Project Manager, and Statistician, to represent resource utilization. These may be used as placeholders, to be replaced by named resources down the road or to capture demand for that resource skill. You may also decide to set up pools of resources for particular roles, such as Engineers or Project Managers, where the generic name becomes plural and you define avail-ability to be more than one person or unit.

You can optionally flag resources as generic; doing so lets you filter, group, or search by generic resources. This is important if you're using Project Professional and connect to Project Server to access enterprise resources. It's also useful if you need to replace generic resources with named resources. To formally make a resource generic, double-click it to bring up the Resource Information dialog box, and check the Generic box (Figure 8.2).

FIGURE 8.2   Making resources generic

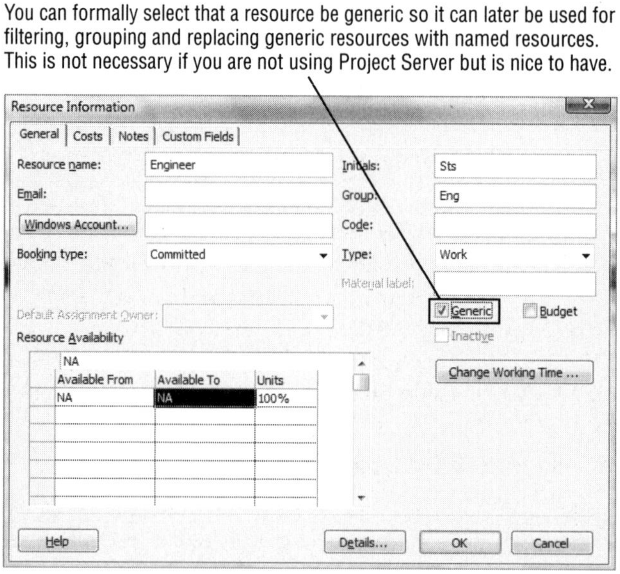

You can formally select that a resource be generic so it can later be used for filtering, grouping and replacing generic resources with named resources. This is not necessary if you are not using Project Server but is nice to have.

┌───┐

🌐 **Real World Scenario**

Using Generic Resources to Capture FTE Requirements

I worked with a planning department that wanted to use Project to capture full-time equivalents (FTEs) for various groups across their major programs. The first wave of success was defined by understanding this requirement across departments by role and not named resources. This meant setting up a resource pool using generic resources and sharing them across projects. When each project was populated with resource assignments, I was able to create custom views to look at resource demand versus capacity by role and by department over time. The tricky part wasn't setting the tools up to do this but getting accurate assignment estimates from each of the stakeholders.

└───┘

You may also need to track nonhuman resources such as materials, machinery, and equipment. Project offers the following resource types:

Work   Resources are people (named or generic) and sometimes equipment whose utilization is based on time as a measure for work and limited by availability associated with a calendar. Including equipment in this category lets you track bottlenecks that can occur if a piece of equipment or a facility (such as a paint shop or bulldozer) is over-allocated or unavailable. These resources may also have associated standard and overtime rates, such as hourly wages, to help track costs.

Material   Resources are more like supplies based on units that you want to track. One way to think about them is as unit costs. For example, you may need to buy 100 training manuals for the task called Conduct Training, or you may need to acquire 100 additional software licenses for the task called Install Software, or you may need to purchase 1,000 tons of steel for the Structural Steel task. These types of resources also have a material label you can assign, such as Manual, License, or Ton. When you assign the type of resource to tasks, you can enter information such as 100 licenses or 1000 tons or 100 manuals. You can also include a cost per unit: $100 per license, $400 per ton, $50 per manual, and so on. Certain fields, such as Max Units, Overtime Rates, and Calendars, aren't available for this type of resource, because they don't apply.

Cost   Resources can be used to track cost items that aren't associated with duration or work. Sometimes you may want to add costs to tasks—such as travel or other types of expenses that you want to associate with a resource name for reporting and budgeting purposes—but don't want their assignment to impact the schedule. When you create cost resources, certain fields (such as Max Units, Std. and Ovt.Rates, and Calendars) aren't available, because they don't apply. Costs are assigned when you associate this type of resource with a task.

Adding Resources to the Resource Pool

Adding resources to the resource pool is best done in the Resource Sheet view. Type the name of the resource directly in the Resource Names field, and press Enter. Repeat this process for each resource, whether it's a named resource, a generic resource, or another type of resource. You can either enter all the resources first and complete the other details later or enter the details one at a time. I prefer to enter all the resources first and fill in the rest of the information afterward.

You may also want to use resource pools built in other applications. Project 2010 has some enhanced copy and paste features that let you paste in data from other applications.

You can also add resources from Active Directory or your address book (see Figure 8.3). Follow these steps:

FIGURE 8.3   Adding resources from Active Directory or address book

1. Go to Resource tab ➢ Insert group.
2. From the Add Resources drop-down list, select Active Directory or Address Book.
3. Select the resource you want to add to the resource pool.

Repeat this for each resource you want to add.

If you're connected to Project Server 2010, you'll notice the option Build Team from Enterprise on the Add Resources drop-down list, as shown in Figure 8.3. This allows you to select resources from an enterprise resource pool instead of building a resource pool from scratch. If you have Project Professional and aren't connected to Project Server, then this option is grayed out, as shown in the figure.

Figure 8.4 illustrates various types of resources that can be added to a resource pool, with their associated characteristics.

Max Units

The Max Units field is the value that Project uses to determine whether you've over-allocated or under-allocated a particular resource. The default value for a typical work resource is 100%, which represents 1 unit or 1 person full time. The available time is based on the base calendar associated with the resource:

- 100% represents 8 hours per day.
- 80% represents 6.4 hours per day.
- 50% represents 4 hours per day.

These values assume the base calendar is set to a standard of eight working hours per day. The value in the Max Units field is also used as the default assignment value when resources are assigned to a task, unless it's greater than 100%, as is the case for a pool of resources. For example, if you have four electricians to draw from, you may want to define the Max Units as 400%, representing four people in that generic pool; but when you assign that resource to a task, Project reverts back to a 100% default assignment.

If you want to view resources in terms of FTE values, you can switch the display from % to decimal. For example, you may want to see 1 instead of 100% or 4 instead of 400%, and so on. To do this, go to the backstage, and click Options. On the Schedule tab, in the Schedule group area, change Show Assignment Units from Percentage to Decimal. This is a global setting that affects how all resource units are displayed, not just one.

FIGURE 8.4   Adding resources in the resource sheet

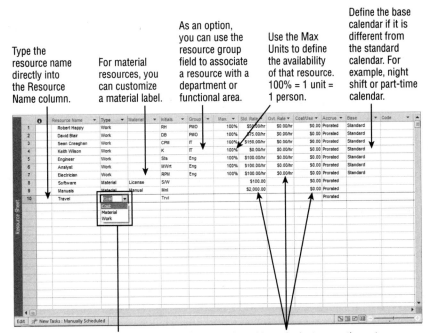

Type the resource name directly into the Resource Name column.

For material resources, you can customize a material label.

As an option, you can use the resource group field to associate a resource with a department or functional area.

Use the Max Units to define the availability of that resource. 100% = 1 unit = 1 person.

Define the base calendar if it is different from the standard calendar. For example, night shift or part-time calendar.

Choose the resource type to be work, material, or cost.

You can also add standard rates, overtime rates, or cost/use values to help track costs for your resources

You're free to modify each resource unit value on a task-by-task assignment basis. For example, sometimes you may want to allocate a resource 50% to a task or even 10% to a task. Project calculates duration or work based on the task type selected, using the following formula:

Work = Duration × Units

Project uses the Max Units value to determine whether you've created a resource conflict by over-allocating that resource. Project won't stop you from over-allocating a resource; it will just show you that you've done it. It's up to you to determine what action, if any, to take to resolve the conflict. For more details, see "Analyzing Resource Usage and Resource Leveling" later in this chapter.

🌐 Real World Scenario

Max Units and Non-Project Working Time

One IT organization I consulted with set Max Units for each resource to 80%, to account for non-project time or administrative time. The company was trying to reflect the fact that approximately 20% of each person's time was used for administrative time or non-project working time. Although this was a general estimate across all resources, it struck a nice balance; the company didn't have to spend a lot of time tracking administrative tasks but accounted for them in allocating a resource's time across projects, to help determine whether the resource was being over-utilized.

This meant that every time a resource was assigned to a task, the default unit assignment was 80% or 6.4 hours per day to work on project-related activities. Anything over that was considered over-allocation and a resource conflict, giving the organization a simple way to account for other work activities outside of any project. There are more precise methods to account for administrative time, but they usually involve creating timesheets for administrative tasks or setting up administrative tasks within a designated project plan to which each resource is then assigned.

You can also establish availability profiles over time, as shown in Figure 8.5. Some situations may require Max Units to fluctuate based on a resource's availability because you either lose a resource for a time or don't have full access to that resource. If you need to create availability profiles over time, follow these steps:

1. Double-click the resource to open the Resource Information dialog box.

2. Go to General tab ➢ Resource Availability area ➢ Available From, and enter the date when the availability changes.

3. In the Available To column, enter the date when the availability changes back or shifts again.

4. Repeat this process for each date range where the availability shifts.

FIGURE 8.5   Resource availability profiles

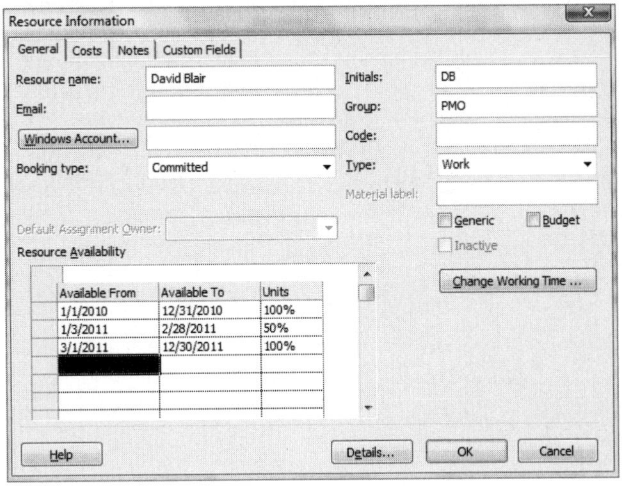

If you establish availability profiles, Project takes them into consideration when you assign resources to tasks, to determine their available work hours and whether the resources have been over- or under-allocated.

Resource Group and Initials

You can use the Resource Initials field to abbreviate the resource name. This may come in handy if you have more than one resource assigned to a task and you want to display the resources associated with the task without taking up a lot of screen real estate. I'll cover this in more detail when I discuss customizing and formatting tables and the bar area in Part 3.

I find the Resource Group field useful. I recommend using it to identify which department or functional area a resource belongs to so you can generate more effective views and reports. For example, you can group resources by department and see how many hours or peak units are required for the entire group over any time period: hours, days, months, quarters, and so on. I cover this functionality in more detail in Chapter 12, "Using Filters, Groups, and Sorts."

Standard Rates, Overtime Rates, and Cost per Use

To manage and track costs on a project, you can set up *standard rates* for work resources or material resources. For work resources, you typically put in an hourly rate for that person or the generic role you've defined. You don't have to assign a standard rate if you don't need or want to. Many people I work with assign resources to track demand and capacity and don't have the requirement to track costs; many groups don't even have access to such information.

When defining the standard rate for a person or generic role, you can enter the rate on a daily, weekly, monthly, or annual basis. If you need to, you can enter the cost on a per-minute basis. The default standard rate in Project is on an hourly basis. To change this, type **d** for day, **w** for week, and so on. If you type **m** for month, the rate may default to minutes—you need to type **mo** for months.

Defining standard rates for material resources is a matter of typing the amount without the unit; Project automatically associates it with the material label you put in the Material column. So, if you enter $100 for software, and the material label is **license**, the cost is $100 per license. There is no overtime rate for material resources.

You can specify separate *overtime rates* that apply to *overtime hours*. Overtime hours are treated differently from regular hours and need to be added to a task in a separate Overtime Work field. These hours use the overtime rate that you define in this field.

You can also enter rates in the Per Use Cost field. This field is used for a one-time cost or lump-sum cost that is added to the total cost every time you assign that resource, regardless of the number of hours or units you assign. For example, if you need to rent a piece of equipment such as a bulldozer, there may be a delivery charge of $500 plus the hourly rate. Or maybe you're using equipment that has a set-up fee regardless of how long you need it. You can use the Per Use Cost field to capture those types of charges, and you can do so with or without having any values in the standard rate fields.

Just as with availability profiles, you can also build cost-rate profiles for standard rates, overtime rates, and cost-per-use fees. For example, if a resource's hourly rate changes over the life of a project, you can reflect that by defining the cost profile over various date ranges. To change the cost-rate profile, follow these steps (see Figure 8.6):

1. Double-click the resource name you want to change, to open the Resource Information dialog box.

2. Go to Costs tab ➤ Effective Date, and enter the date the rate will change.

3. Enter the new hourly rate in the Standard Rate column. You can also enter a new overtime rate or per use cost. If you enter a percentage such as **10%**, Project calculates the new hourly rate based on the percentage you enter added to the previous rate (entering **–10%** decreases the rate instead of increasing it).

FIGURE 8.6 Cost rate profiles

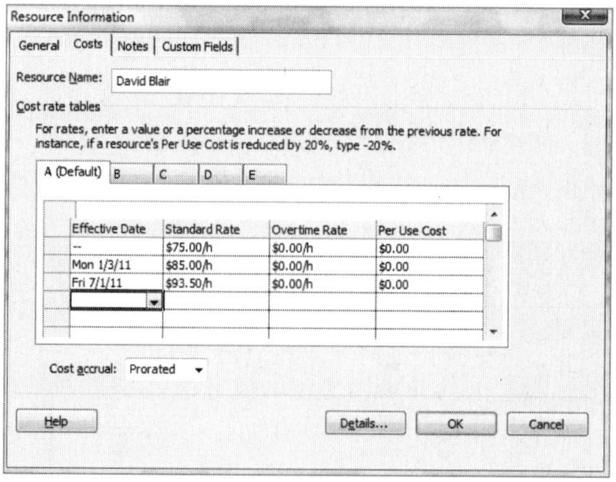

In Figure 8.6, for the third rate I entered **10%** directly into the Standard Rate field in the cost table. Project calculated the new rate automatically to be $93.50 per hour, which is 10% more than $85 per hour.

Changing Working Time for Resources

Chapter 4 covered the topic of creating and applying calendars at the project, task, or resource level. Now you'll put those concepts to work. Recall that before you apply calendars to a project, task, or resource, you must first create one or modify an existing one. Select Project tab ➢ Properties group ➢ Change Working Time. For example, if you have part-time resources or shift workers, you create the calendar first; subsequently, in the resource sheet, you apply that calendar under the base calendar field.

Every time you add a new work resource to the resource pool, a calendar is automatically established for that resource based on the standard calendar. If you change the base calendar, you may still want to add the personal time off (PTO) or vacation for individual resources as exceptions to their calendar.

If you create a custom organizational or company calendar that captures organization-wide holidays like Independence Day and Thanksgiving and select this calendar at the project level in the Project Information dialog box, you should use this as the base calendar for each resource. Even if you need to create new calendars to reflect varying working times for shifts or Monday–Thursday type calendars, start with the base organizational calendar if you've created one, because it includes holidays that apply to everyone.

Add PTO or vacation time at the resource level or for that particular resource calendar without changing the base calendar or the project-level calendar. For example, the organization may have one day off for Thanksgiving, but a resource may take off that entire week for vacation. To reflect that in the working time for that resource and have Project take it into account when it's calculating the start and finish date of scheduled tasks, you can change the working time for that resource. Follow these steps (see Figure 8.7):

1. Double-click the resource to open the Resource Information dialog box.

2. Click Change Working Time to open the calendar for that specific resource.

3. Enter exceptions for that resource to reflect personal time off, and click OK.

Budget Resources

The Budget Resources feature allows you to set either cost or work budget amounts at the project summary level by first defining budget resources and then assigning them to the project summary task.

When you identify a resource as a budget resource, it can only be assigned to the project summary task. You use budget resources at the project level to reflect the planned budget for the entire project and then later compare them to the amounts being generated by the work and costs you schedule.

FIGURE 8.7 Adding vacation time or PTO for individual resources

For PTO or vacation time you can add in exceptions for the each individual resource calendars by clicking on Change Working Time in the Resource Information box.

If you have customized the base calendar to reflect organization wide holidays they will automatically show up for each resource calendar.

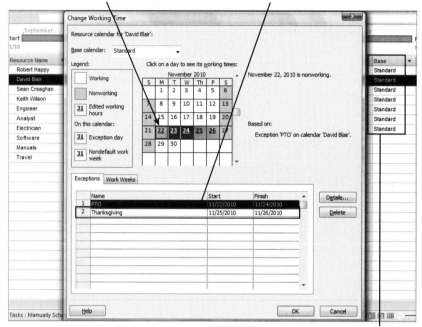

Change Base Calendar to reflect various groups of working times such as part-time calendar, shift work, short week and so on. Try and match base calendars with calendar applied at project level unless they have different holidays and or working times.

To make a resource a budget resource, follow these steps:

1. Double-click a resource in the resource sheet to open the Resource Information dialog box.

2. Select the Budget check box, and click OK.

Sharing Resources across Projects

It's possible to create a resource pool and share it among a group of projects without using Project Server. Before I show you how to do this in Project, there are some key things to keep in mind. First, you need to understand that you're dealing with an MPP file, which is a standalone, single-user file that can only be opened as read-write by one person at a time. Project isn't designed to be a multiuser system; for that capability, you may need to consider using Project Server as a solution.

To share resources across projects using Project (rather than Project Server), create a project, preferably without tasks, with a group of resources listed. Save the file, and then point to it from other projects, using the Share Resource function, as shown in Figure 8.8. For example, you can build your team in the Resource Sheet view and save it as a file named *<department>*ResourcePool.mpp (for example, ITResourcePool.mpp or MarketingResourcePool.mpp).

FIGURE 8.8   Sharing resources

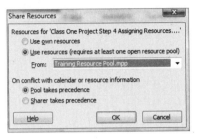

In the example for Figure 8.8, I created a file called Training Resource Pool.mpp. Using the Class One Project file, I pointed to it as follows:

1. Ensure that both the resource pool file and the sharer file are open at the same time.

2. Select Resource tab ➢ Assignments group ➢ Resource Pool ➢ Share Resources.

3. From the From drop-down list, select the resource pool file whose resources you want to share.

4. Click OK.

You now have access to the resources in the resource pool file and can assign them to tasks.

When you save the file while sharing resources, the next time you open it, you're presented with a message asking to open the resource pool, as shown in Figure 8.9. This allows you to determine whether you want to see the resource assignments across other sharer files.

At any time, you can switch back to using your own resources by going back to the Resource Pool function and selecting Use Own Resources. Doing so stops the sharing of resources from the resource pool and removes assignments in your plan from the resource pool if they're shared with other projects.

FIGURE 8.9   Open Resource Pool Information dialog

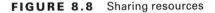

Assigning Resources and Costs

After you've built a resource pool, it's now time to assign the resources to your tasks. In this section, you'll learn how to assign resources to tasks in the most efficient manner possible. I'll also cover more complex topics such as understanding the details associated with each resource assignment and how work, duration, and units are calculated based on task type. And I'll cover the new Team Planner feature (available only in the Project Professional version), which takes resource planning and management to a new level.

It's best practice to assign resources at the task level to capture work and have them roll up to summary tasks and ultimately the project summary. You have a choice in Project to assign resources at the summary task or phase level, but you should generally avoid doing so, especially if you have the same resources assigned at the task level: this will duplicate the calculation of the work and costs. However, there may be a scenario in which you want to assign a resource across an entire phase or summary to reflect level-of-effort assignments. For example, you may have a project manager who generally spends 10% of their time over the lifespan of a phase such as design or develop. You can assign the project manager to the phase and make the units 10%, and Project will calculate the work based on the duration of the phase. But remember that you don't control the duration: it's a roll-up of the details, unless you're using user-controlled, top-down scheduling, covered in Chapter 6, "Estimating and Entering Duration or Work." As a guideline, you should focus on resource assignments at the task level.

Using the Resource Names Column

Now that the resources have been defined in the resource sheet, you can assign them directly from the Resource Names column in the Gantt Chart view. To assign a resource to a task, follow these steps (see Figure 8.10):

1. In the task row where you want to assign resources, go to the Resource Names column and click the corresponding field.

2. In the drop-down list, check the resource or resources (multi-select) you want to assign to the task. The drop-down list is blank if you haven't created a resource pool in the resource sheet or shared resources with another project file.

3. Press Enter.

If you assign resources using this method, be aware that Project is doing more calculations in the background. Regardless of whether you plan to track work hours and resource utilization, Project calculates the work automatically based on the following formula:

Work = Duration × Units

If you assign resources from the Resource Names column, Project assumes 1 unit or 100% allocation of that resource unless Max Units is set to less than 100% in the resource sheet. If the default units are set at 100%, the calculation of work is straightforward, based on whatever is in your duration estimate. For example, if the task has a duration of 10 days, then the work is as follows:

Work = 10d × 100% = 80 hours (based on 8-hour working days from the calendar hours/day)

FIGURE 8.10   Assigning resources using the Resource Names column

You can click on one or more resources allowing you to multi-select assignments. You can also uncheck resources to an assign them.

Task Name	Duration	Start	Finish	Predecessors	Resource Names
⊟ **Class One Project**	**103.5 days**	**Wed 9/1/10**	**Mon 1/24/11**		
⊟ PHASE 1 - DESIGN	**30 days**	**Wed 9/1/10**	**Tue 10/12/10**		
Task 1 - Gather Information	5 days	Wed 9/1/10	Tue 9/7/10		David Blair,Robert Hap
Task 2 - Analysis	10 days	Wed 9/8/10	Tue 9/21/10	2	☐ Analyst
Task 3 - Present Alternatives	6 days	Wed 9/8/10	Wed 9/15/10	2	☑ David Blair
Task 4 - Design Document	15 days	Wed 9/22/10	Tue 10/12/10	4,3	☐ Electrician
Milestone - Design Complete	0 days	Tue 10/12/10	Tue 10/12/10	5	☐ Engineer
⊟ PHASE 2 - DEVELOP	**46 days**	**Wed 10/13/10**	**Wed 12/15/10**		☐ Keith Wilson
Task 1 - Develop Prototype	20 days	Wed 10/13/10	Tue 11/9/10	6	☐ Manuals
Task 2 - Testing/QA	5 days	Mon 11/8/10	Fri 11/12/10	8FS-2 days	☑ Robert Happy
Task 3 - Develop Final Product	15 days	Thu 11/11/10	Wed 12/1/10	9FS-2 days	☐ Sean Creaghan
Task 4 - Final Testing/QA	10 days	Thu 12/2/10	Wed 12/15/10	10	☐ Software
Milestone - Development Complete	0 days	Wed 12/15/10	Wed 12/15/10	11	☐ Travel
⊟ PHASE 3- IMPLEMENT	**27.5 days**	**Thu 12/16/10**	**Mon 1/24/11**		
Task 1 - Install	5 days	Thu 12/16/10	Wed 12/22/10	12	
Task 2 - Test	5 days	Mon 12/20/10	Mon 12/27/10	14FS-50%	
Task 3 - Train	10 days	Mon 12/27/10	Mon 1/10/11	15	
Task 4 - Transition to Operations	20 days	Mon 12/27/10	Mon 1/24/11	15	
Milestone - Implementation Complete	0 days	Mon 1/24/11	Mon 1/24/11	17,16	

This is easy to manage if you have one resource assigned to a task at 100% every time, but that is rarely the case.

> **NOTE**   It's also possible to assign resources to manually scheduled tasks. Project calculates work based on the scheduling formula, with one exception: you can't change task types. Project calculates work as if it were a fixed-duration task type.

Split-Screen View and Details

One effective way to review the details of resource assignments is to use the split-screen view. Choose Task tab ➤ Properties group ➤ Display Task Details, or View tab ➤ Split View group ➤ Details box.

When you have the split-screen view with details running, you can see how Project calculates work, units, and duration based on the task type you've selected. In the example shown in Figure 8.11, the task type is Fixed Duration and the default Max Units is 100%, from the resource sheet.

FIGURE 8.11   Reviewing assignment details

Review the resource assignment details in the split screen view. Project defaults to 100% unit assignment and will calculate work based on the scheduling formula: Work = Duration × Units

You can modify the task type in this view to impact how Project calculates your schedule based on the scheduling formula. You can also combine effort driven scheduling with fixed duration or fixed units to keep the work fixed in conjunction with duration or units. Fixed work by default is effort driven.

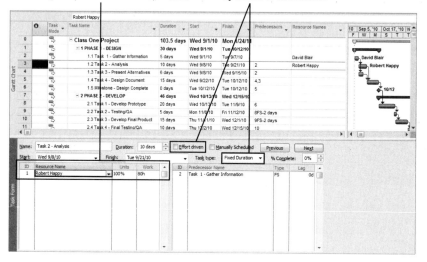

Because I selected Robert Happy from the Resource Names column, Project defaulted to 100% assignment and calculated work to be 80 hours based on the scheduling formula.

Fixed-Duration Scheduling

Fixed-duration scheduling is based on the idea that your duration estimates will remain constant regardless of how many resources you assign to a task. Therefore, either work or units is recalculated based on your assignments. If you assign one resource from the resource column, Project defaults to 100% unit assignment and calculates work accordingly. If you assign two resources, Project defaults to 100% unit assignment for each resource and calculates work accordingly, keeping duration fixed. In this case, the work continues to increase or decrease depending on how many resources you assign.

Consider the example of attending a conference that is 10 days long. If one person attends, then your organization spends 80 hours of work and the duration is 10 days. If 2 people go, then your organization spends 160 hours of work and the duration remains 10 days. If 10 people go, that's 800 hours of work, and the duration remains fixed at 10 days. If one person attends for 50% of their time, meaning you enter 50% into the units field, that equates to 40 hours of work, but the duration remains fixed at 10 days.

That is the benefit of fixed duration: it stays the same and doesn't change the start- and finish-date calculations as you vary your resource assignment levels. Consider the example shown in Figure 8.12. I've added the Work column to the table by using the Add Column function at the end of the table, as explained in Chapter 6. This lets me keep an eye on both duration and total work estimates as I modify resource assignments. When I add the second resource to the task, notice that the duration remains fixed and the work increases.

FIGURE 8.12   Fixed-duration scheduling

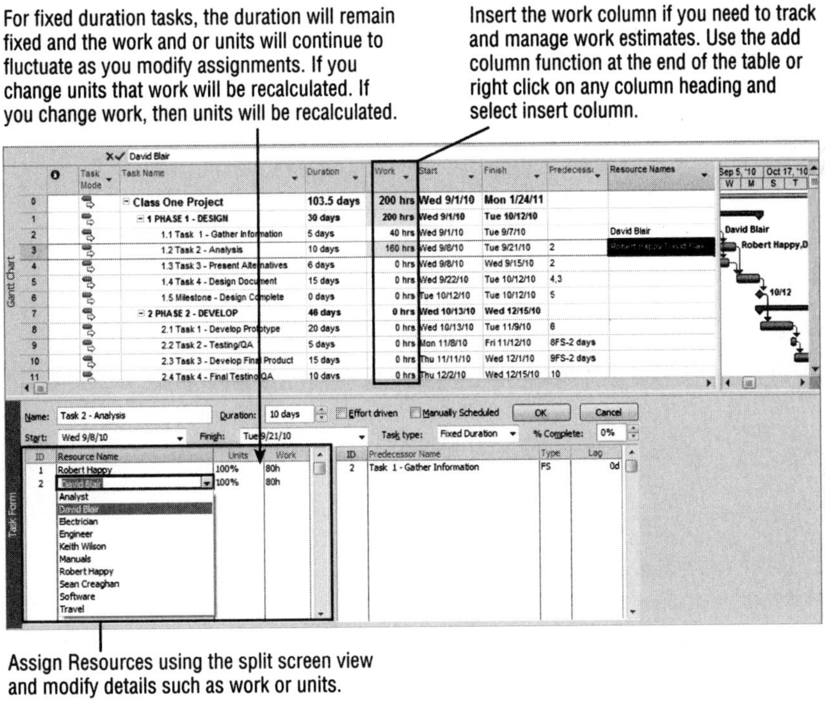

For fixed duration tasks, the duration will remain fixed and the work and or units will continue to fluctuate as you modify assignments. If you change units that work will be recalculated. If you change work, then units will be recalculated.

Insert the work column if you need to track and manage work estimates. Use the add column function at the end of the table or right click on any column heading and select insert column.

Assign Resources using the split screen view and modify details such as work or units.

You can modify the assignment details by changing the units to recalculate the work. Maybe I want David to spend 10% of his time on this task. If I change the units to 10%, Project recalculates the work to be 8 hours (10% of 10 days) for David, all the while keeping the duration fixed.

> **NOTE** In Project 2010, unlike previous versions, the calculation engine for units is slightly different in that the assignment units are no longer automatically modified to be greater or less than the default value of 100%. For example, if you change work on a fixed duration task, the assignment units will not be modified from the original entry. Instead, Project utilizes the Peak Units field to reflect any variation in units over time.

If you change the duration of a fixed-duration task, you must ask yourself whether you want the work to increase along with the duration. If the answer is no, and you want to keep the work unchanged, then you may want to select Effort Driven and choose Fixed Duration for the Task Type. This lets you keep the total work fixed as you manually change your duration estimates. You can use the smart tags to help you with this decision-making, as shown in Figure 8.13.

FIGURE 8.13   Using the smart tags for better decision-making

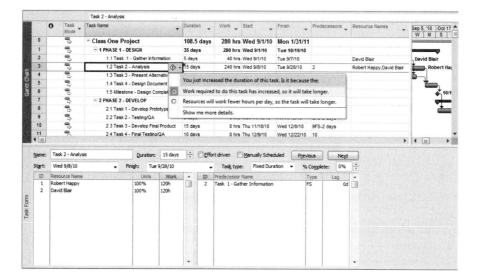

If you increase duration with resources already assigned to tasks, Project recalculates the work unless you tell it not to by looking at the smart tag and choosing Resources Will Work Fewer Hours Per Day. If you make that selection, Project automatically checks Effort Driven, assuming you want to keep the work fixed when you change duration of a fixed-duration task.

Fixed-Work (Effort-Driven) Scheduling

Fixed-work scheduling is the purest form of effort-driven scheduling in Project. When you select this as your scheduling approach, Project grays out the Effort Driven option, because that is synonymous with fixed work. When you choose an effort-driven approach to scheduling, you're letting Project know that you want the work estimate to remain fixed and duration to be calculated or recalculated as you change resource assignments. As you assign more resources, the duration decreases and thus adjusts your finish date for that task; if you assign fewer resources, the duration increases.

With Fixed Work as the Task Type, if you adjust duration, units remain the same but the peak units amount will adjust to reconcile the formula, which is new behavior in Project 2010 as all previous versions had the primary assignments units field change; and if you adjust units, then duration changes for each resource assignment. If you adjust the work estimate, then the duration is recalculated. Keep in mind that Project is a scheduling tool, and it goes after duration first in a non-fixed-duration task type. Figure 8.14 shows what happens when you assign more resources to a fixed-work task. In this example, Task 1—Gather Information had fixed work of 40 hours, with David assigned 100% of his time. The 40 hours is now the fixed component of the scheduling formula, and as I add or change resource assignments, Project keeps that portion fixed and distributes the work among the new and existing resources accordingly.

FIGURE 8.14   Fixed-work assignments

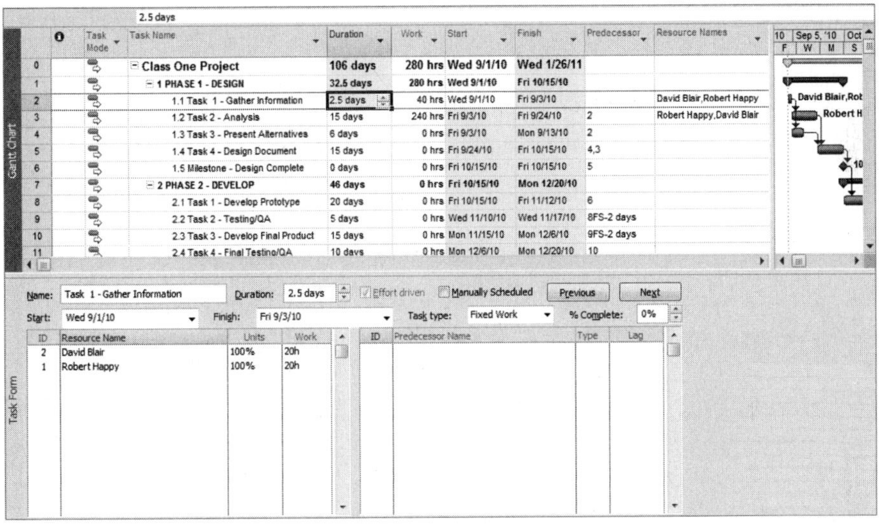

The fixed total work remained at 40 hours. But adding the second resource cut the duration in half and distributed the work equally between the two resources at 20 hours each.

> **TIP**
>
> You can enter fixed-work estimates directly in the Work column if you add it to the table, as discussed in Chapter 6. If you take this approach, then as you assign resources, Project calculates duration based on the resource allocations. If you don't enter a work estimate prior to assigning resources, then your first set of resource assignments drives the work estimate based on the scheduling formula. After the first resource assignment is made and the initial work is calculated, that value becomes the fixed-work component.

Fixed Units with Effort-Driven Turned On

The default Task Type setting for Project is Fixed Units with Effort Driven enabled. This behaves much like an effort-driven task, in that as you assign more resources, duration gets shorter; and as you assign fewer resources, duration grows longer. The key difference between this setting and fixed work is that under this scenario, if you change the duration of a task, Project changes work because the units are fixed. If you have fixed work and you adjust the duration, then peak units are changed (see Table 8.1). Keep in mind that in

Project 2010, the new calculation approach is based on keeping the assignment units field to reflect what you manually enter or the initial default assignment of 100% unless you change it manually. The peak units field will reflect the variation in units over time.

TABLE 8.1   Recalculation Matrix

If the Task Type Is...	And You Change...	Then Project Recalculates...
Fixed Duration	Duration	Work
	Units	Work
	Work	Peak Units
Fixed Units	Duration	Work
	Units	Duration
	Work	Duration
Fixed Work	Duration	Peak Units
	Units	Duration
	Work	Duration

Try testing various task-type scenarios by setting up each task type in a test plan and then assigning resources. Make changes to the units, work, and duration to make sure you understand the impact each change will have on your schedule. Try adding the assignment units field and peak units field to the table to see the impact on these fields as you modify work for a fixed duration task or modify duration for a fixed work task. Adding fields to tables is covered in detail in Chapter 11, "Using Tables and Custom Fields." Doing so will help you make the right choice in the overall approach you take for managing projects going forward.

There isn't a one-size-fits-all recommendation for selecting a task-type approach. Your choice depends on how you want Project to calculate your schedule in the planning stage and recalculate scheduling during execution when you make changes. If your projects are driven more by duration and dates, then consider starting from a fixed-duration approach; if they're driven more by work and resource availability, then perhaps an effort-driven approach such as Fixed Work or Fixed Units with Effort Driven enabled is more appropriate. You can vary your Task Type selection from one task to another.

For summary tasks, you don't have a choice: they're calculated by rolling up information from below. Project sets the summary tasks as fixed duration; if you choose to assign resources at the summary task level, the calculation of work is based on fixed-duration scheduling.

Assign Resources Function

One of the most efficient tools for assigning resources to tasks is the Assign Resources function. This is a floating dialog box that can remain open as you move from one task to another, making multiple assignments to multiple tasks at the same time. It also makes it easy to replace existing resource assignments with new ones or make bulk assignments.

To use the Assign Resources function, refer to Figure 8.15, and follow these steps:

1. Click Resource tab ➤ Assignments group ➤ Assign Resources to open the Assign Resources dialog box.

2. With the Assign Resources dialog box open, click the tasks for which you want to assign resources. Hold down Ctrl and click to select multiple tasks.

3. In the Assign Resources dialog box, click the resource or resources you want to assign to the selected tasks. Hold down Ctrl and click to select multiple resources.

4. Click the Assign button. You can enter units before clicking Assign if you want something different than the default 100%.

5. Repeat this process as many times as necessary without closing the Assign Resources dialog box.

Sometimes you may want to replace existing resource assignments: for example, if a resource is replaced on your project with another person, or if you assigned a generic resource as a placeholder for a named resource and you've determined who the named resource is. To use the Replace function, follow steps 1 through 3; then, in step 4, click Replace instead of Assign. You can apply the same approach to removing resources as well. Refer to Figure 8.15.

In the Assign Resources dialog box, you can click the Graph button for a selected resource to view their existing work assignments and availability in a graphical manner.

Task Information

Another way to assign resources is through the Task Information dialog box discussed in Chapter 6. To open the Task Information dialog box, double-click any task in the Task Name column. On the Resource tab, shown in Figure 8.16, you can pick from a drop-down list which resources you want to assign or change the units for. The one item you can't change from here is the work hours or work estimates. You also must close the dialog box to move on to the next task and open it again for each new task assignment. I find it more efficient to use the split-screen view or the Assign Resources dialog box.

FIGURE 8.15 Assign Resources function

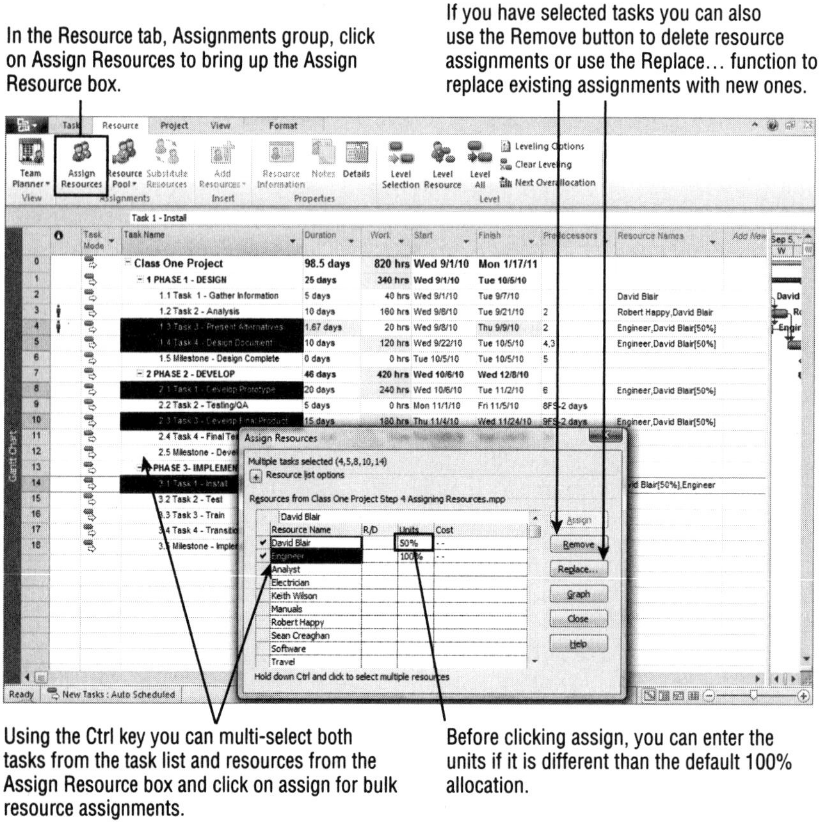
In the Resource tab, Assignments group, click on Assign Resources to bring up the Assign Resource box.
If you have selected tasks you can also use the Remove button to delete resource assignments or use the Replace… function to replace existing assignments with new ones.
Assign Resources
Multiple tasks selected (4,5,8,10,14)
Resources from Class One Project Step 4 Assigning Resources.mpp
Assign
Remove
Replace...
Graph
Close
Help
Hold down Ctrl and click to select multiple resources
Using the Ctrl key you can multi-select both tasks from the task list and resources from the Assign Resource box and click on assign for bulk resource assignments.
Before clicking assign, you can enter the units if it is different than the default 100% allocation.

FIGURE 8.16 Assigning resources with the Task Information dialog box

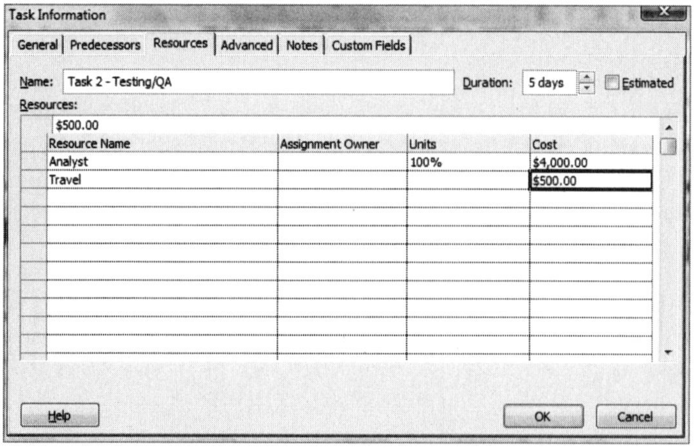
Task Information
General
Predecessors
Resources
Advanced
Notes
Custom Fields
Name: Task 2 - Testing/QA
Duration: 5 days
Estimated
Resources:
$500.00
Resource Name
Assignment Owner
Units
Cost
Analyst
100%
$4,000.00
Travel
$500.00
Help
OK
Cancel

🌐 Real World Scenario

Using the Replace Generic Resources Function with Named Resources

A client I worked with had developed some project templates that not only included a good WBS with duration estimates and dependencies but also included generic resource assignments. This made it easy for project managers to go through the planning cycle for creating new plans. Each step in the planning process consisted of modifying steps instead of entering or creating steps. Step 1—Enter WBS was replaced with Modify WBS. Step 2—Estimate Duration was replaced with Modify Duration Estimates. Step 3—Set Dependencies was replaced with Modify Dependencies. Finally, Step 4—Assign Resources was replaced with Replace Generic Resources with Named Resources.

To apply Step 4, the project managers were taught how to use the Assign Resources dialog box to quickly make bulk resource replacements. In this manner, project managers became extremely efficient at creating meaningful project schedules with fully loaded resource assignments. Although it took more time up front to add the generic resource assignments into the templates, the savings in time reaped by the project managers was significant.

When you assign resources and click OK, Project calculates the work and associated costs automatically. Another nice thing about the Assign Resources dialog box is the ability to assign a cost resource such as Travel and immediately type in the associated cost. For work resources, cost is calculated automatically.

Team Planner (Project Professional Only)

Project Professional includes the Team Planner view.

> The features of Project Professional that don't ship with Project Standard are as follows:

- Team Planner
- SharePoint List Synchronization
- Active and Inactive Task feature
- Project Server Collaboration features (not covered in this book)

The Team Planner is a resource-scheduling view that allows you to interact with your task and resource assignments in a way that wasn't possible in Project versions earlier than Project 2010. In this view, you can see at a glance what your project team members are working on and easily move tasks from one person to another by clicking and dragging, as shown in

Figure 8.17. You can also view unassigned work and click and drag those tasks to appropriate team members. Furthermore, you can view over-allocations for team members and shift those assignments around using the click-and-drag method.

FIGURE 8.17   Team Planner view

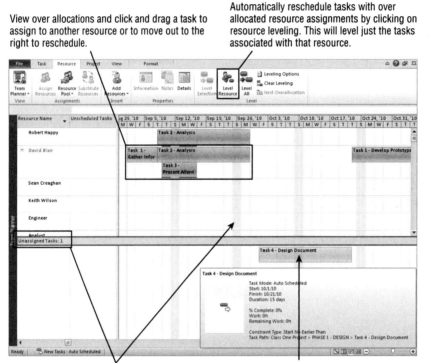

You can open the Team Planner view by any of these methods:

- Select Resource tab ➢ View group ➢ Team Planner.

- From the view finder at lower-right on the screen, click the Team Planner button.

- Select Task tab ➢ View group ➢ Gantt Chart drop-down list ➢ Team Planner.

In the Team Planner view, you can view the tasks beside each team member with the appropriate timeline display. This allows you to quickly identify over-allocation or under-allocation for resources. For example, in Figure 8.17, two tasks are assigned to David for the same time period. In the Team Planner view, you can solve this problem by clicking and dragging one of the tasks to another resource or out into the future. You can even have Project reschedule it for you automatically by using the Level Resource function (see the next section) for that specific resource.

If you move a task by clicking and dragging it to change assignments, Project keeps the network intact if you keep the task in the same time frame (move it up or down without moving it to the left or right on the timeline). Clicking and dragging to the left or right changes the start date for that task; Project automatically creates a Start No Earlier Than constraint on that task even if it has a link.

If you manage resources and need to pay close attention to resource utilization, you'll appreciate this view. I've never found it easier to move assignments from one task to another and deal with conflicts and availability than I have with the Team Planner view.

Analyzing Resource Usage and Resource Leveling

After you've assigned team members to tasks, you can use various views and tools to view resources and make any necessary adjustments. This section will discuss how to use views to analyze resource assignments and then will cover the concepts and tools associated with resource leveling. You can access all of these views via Resource tab ➤ View group ➤ Team Planner drop-down list or via View tab ➤ Resource Views group.

Analyzing Resource Utilization

When you assign resources to tasks, you may want to analyze the results, looking for over-allocations, under-allocations, and problem areas and then taking corrective action.

Resource Sheet

One of the first places you can review and analyze resources is the Resource Sheet view. Although you may not review the actual task assignments in the resource sheet, you can quickly see which resources have been over-allocated, because they're highlighted in red. You can also add columns such as Work and Cost to see the total cost of each resource and how much work they have been allocated, as shown in Figure 8.18.

To add columns to the resource sheet, follow these steps:

1. Click a column title to highlight the entire column. The new column will be entered directly to the right of the column you select.

2. Right-click the column title, and select Insert Column.

3. From the drop-down list, choose the column you want to add. You can start typing the column name for quick picking.

Repeat for each new column you want to add, such as Work or Cost.

FIGURE 8.18   Analyzing resources in Resource Sheet view

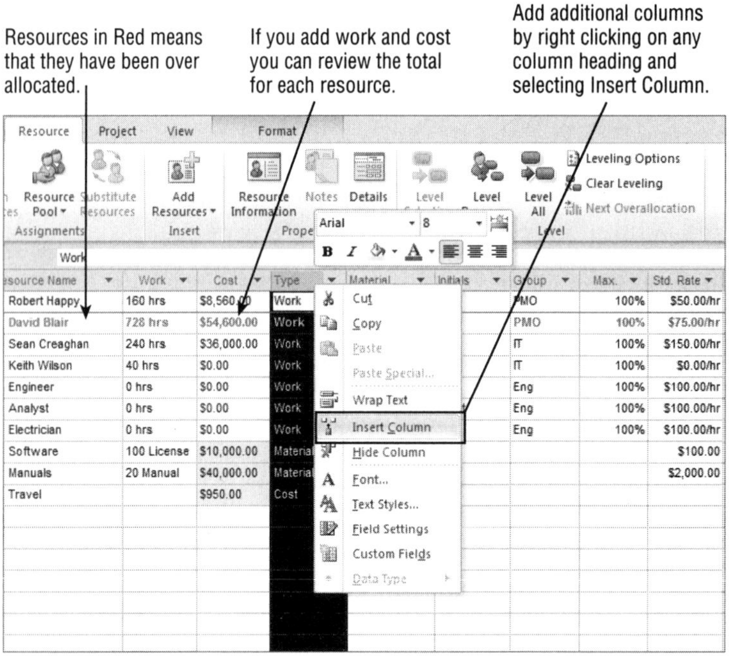

Resources in Red means that they have been over allocated.

If you add work and cost you can review the total for each resource.

Add additional columns by right clicking on any column heading and selecting Insert Column.

Resource Usage

The Resource Usage view helps you analyze resource work across all tasks. Usage views are referred to as *time-phased views* because they present the data in a cross-tab format over time. In Figure 8.19, you can see how work, cost, and units are allocated across a desired time scale by day, week, month, quarter, or year. You can change the time scale by using the view slider at lower right.

Resource Graphs in Conjunction with the Gantt Chart

To see resource allocation levels in a more graphical manner, you can choose the Resource Graph from the view list. Remember that Max Units is the limit Project uses to determine whether the graph bars are red, as shown in Figure 8.20. You can scroll along the bottom part of the view to change graphs for each resource. You can also change the time scale, just as in other views, by using the view slider at lower right.

Task Usage

Task usage is another time-phased view; but instead of viewing by resource first then task details, you look at the data by task first and then resource details. As in the Resource Usage view, you can change the timescale or add detail columns such as Cost, as shown in Figure 8.21.

FIGURE 8.19   Resource Usage view

Right click anywhere
under details to insert
more fields such as cost.

Review the details of
over-allocated resources
to determine what tasks
are causing the conflicts.

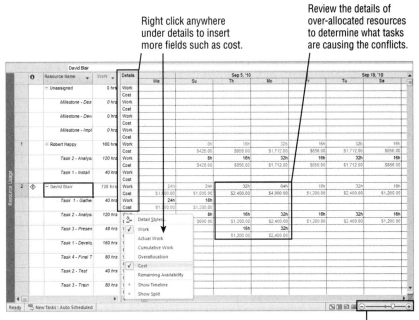

Change the time scale by selecting
– or + from the view slider.

FIGURE 8.20   Resource graphs

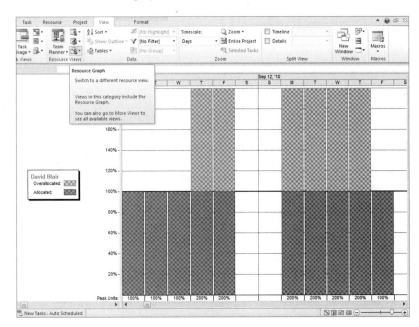

FIGURE 8.21   Task Usage view

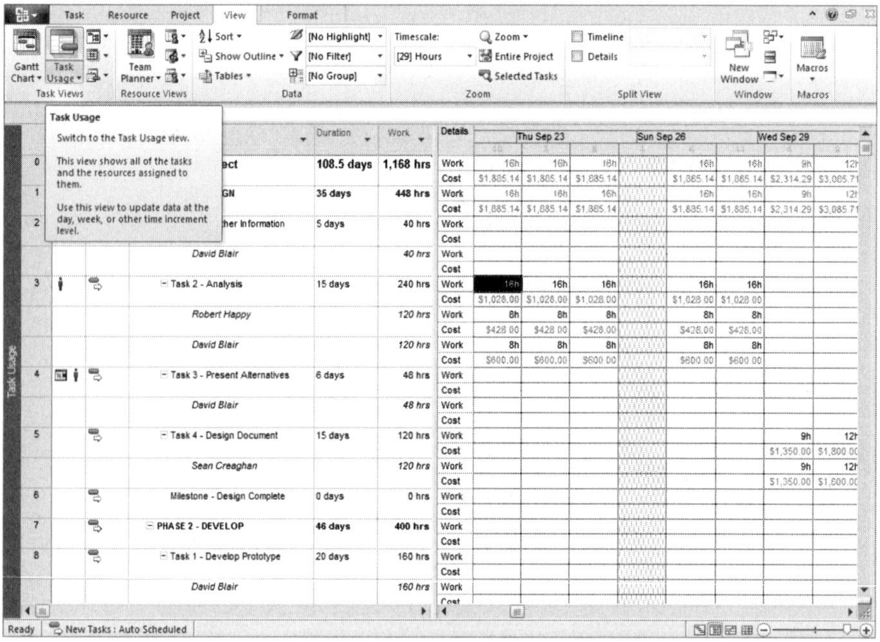

In this view, the project summary lets you analyze work and cost distribution across the entire project. You can change the time scale to quarters, for example, to see how much the project costs you in each quarter. You can analyze the data by phase or down to the task level to see where the work and costs are coming from based on each resource assignment.

Resource Leveling

Resource leveling is a scheduling technique based on resolving resource over-allocations or conflict by scheduling tasks based on resource availability. The idea is to push over-allocations below the Max Units line for each resource, which results in tasks being rescheduled. An example of an over-allocated resource is having one person assigned to 2 tasks in the same day at 100%, with work totaling 16 hours. This is 100% over-allocation for that one-day period, based on availability of 8 hours per day.

Although Project has automatic leveling tools, you may want to consider taking a manual approach. You can analyze resource conflicts and take corrective action by replacing the over-allocated resource with an available resource or rescheduling the task. As discussed earlier in this chapter, the Team Planner view is an excellent place to conduct this kind of approach to resolving resource over-allocations.

Important Factors in Leveling

When using leveling in Project, be aware of the following factors that are taken into account during the rescheduling of tasks with over-allocated resources:

Priority   Tasks with higher priority are scheduled before lower-priority tasks.

Constraints   Tasks without constraints are delayed before tasks with constraints.

Predecessor Links   Predecessors are taken into account.

Total Slack   Tasks with higher slack are delayed first.

Start Date   Earlier start dates are done before later start dates.

You can control priorities for tasks by opening the Task Information dialog box and setting the Priority value, as shown in Figure 8.22.

FIGURE 8.22   Setting priorities for tasks

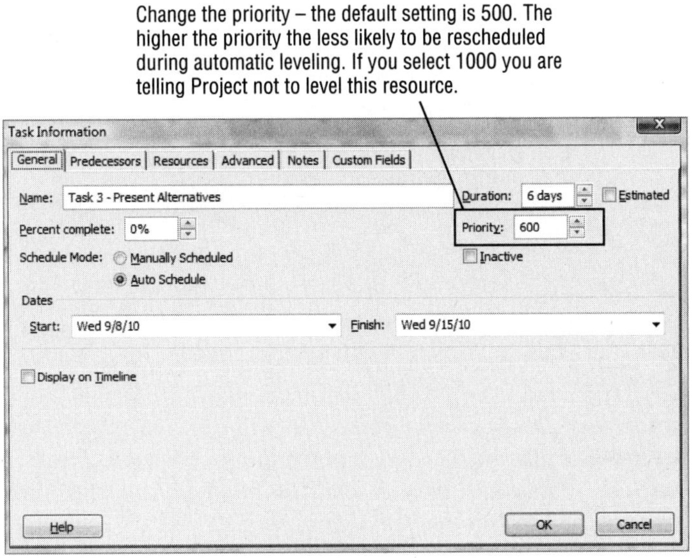

Change the priority – the default setting is 500. The higher the priority the less likely to be rescheduled during automatic leveling. If you select 1000 you are telling Project not to level this resource.

To set a priority for a task, follow these steps:

1. Double-click the task to open the Task Information dialog box.

2. On the General tab, in the Priority field, enter a number between 1 and 1000. The default is 500. The higher the number, the higher the priority; 1000 means the task won't be leveled.

The Priority setting is only used in calculations if you turn on the automatic leveling function, as described in the next section. There are also leveling options that you can change depending on your needs, as shown in Figure 8.23. To access leveling options, choose Resource tab ➢ Level group ➢ Leveling Options; review the options, and select the appropriate settings.

FIGURE 8.23   Leveling options

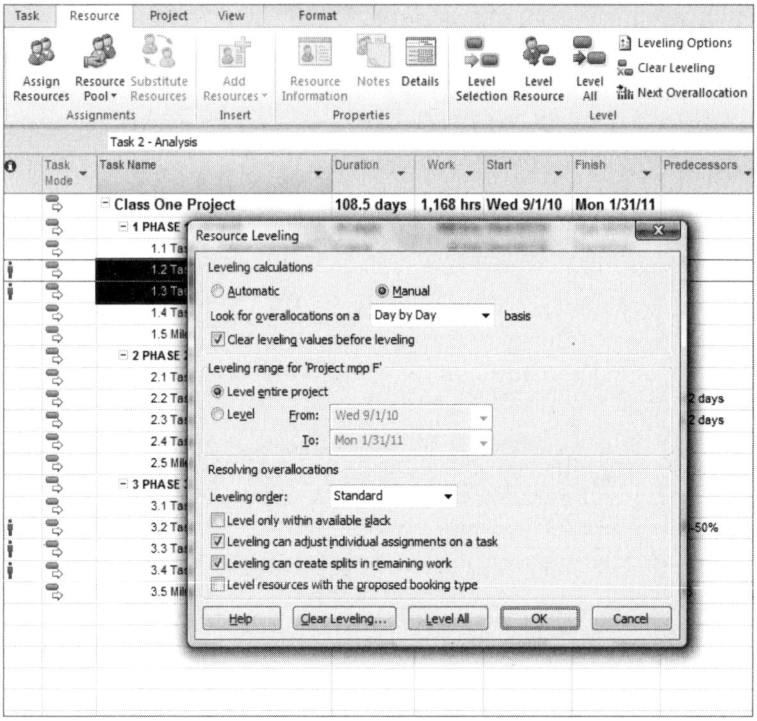

You can select options such as Leveling Only Within Available Slack or choose a specific date range. You can also change the leveling over-allocation periods from Day by Day to Hour by Hour or Week by Week, and so on, to only level within that time frame. Day by Day is the recommended approach. In addition, you can change the leveling order from Standard to Priority, Standard. Standard takes into consideration priority, constraints, predecessor links, total slack, and start date. If you want priority to always be considered over other factors, then switch to Priority, Standard. You can also select Level Now to level across the project or Clear Leveling to remove automatic leveling factors.

Leveling All

You can take three approaches for automatic leveling: you can level across the entire project, on a task-by-task basis, or on a resource-by-resource basis.

Leveling across a project is fairly straightforward by using the Resource Leveling dialog box and selecting Level Now. Or, select Resource tab ➢ Level group ➢ Level All, as shown in Figure 8.24. Select Clear Leveling to remove leveling calculations if you don't like the resulting schedule.

The highlighted tasks in the schedule shown in Figure 8.24 have been affected by selecting Level All. If you want to better view the impact of leveling on your schedule, you can also run the Leveling Gantt view, as shown in Figure 8.25. In this view, the pre-leveled Gantt chart is represented by green bars, and the leveled Gantt chart is represented by blue bars. The Leveling Delay column displays the number of elapsed days (edays) a task is delayed by leveling; edays equals the total number of days including both working and nonworking days. To access the Leveling Gantt view, select View tab ➤ Task Views group ➤ Gantt Chart drop-down list. Select More Views, click Leveling Gantt, and click Apply. To return to the regular Gantt chart, select Gantt Chart from the Gantt Chart drop-down list.

FIGURE 8.24   Schedule after leveling all

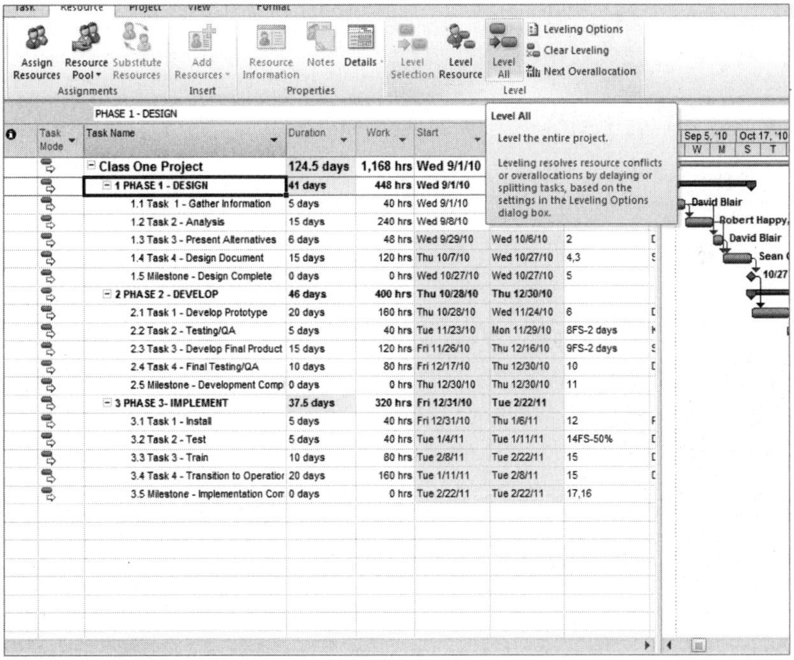

Leveling by Resource

You can use the Team Planner to level tasks by resource. You can also level by resource across the project. To do so, select Resource tab ➤ Level group ➤ Level Resource. In the Level Resource dialog box, click the resource you want to level, and click Level Now. Figure 8.26 displays the resource graph before David Blair is leveled. The red bar represents over-allocation above the 100% Max Units line.

When leveling is turned on, all the red is pushed below the Max Units line, resulting in rescheduled tasks and (usually) delay in the project. The result removes the red over-allocated portions of your schedule.

FIGURE 8.25 Viewing the effect in the Leveling Gantt view

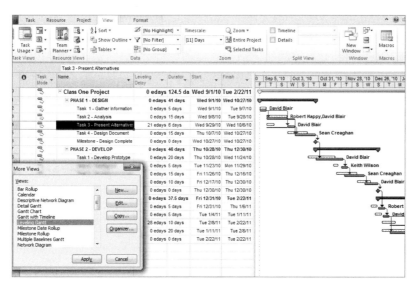

FIGURE 8.26 Leveling by resource with the Resource Graph view

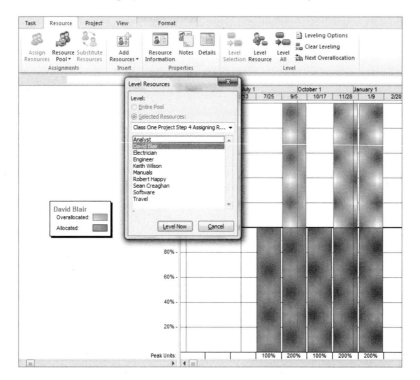

Leveling by Task

You can also level by task, focusing only on a selected region of your project. To take advantage of this function, highlight the tasks you want to level by selecting the rows in sequence or by holding down the Ctrl key to multi-select tasks. Then, select Resource tab ➢ Level group ➢ Level Selection.

A red stick man figure appears in the Indicator column if you've over-allocated a resource on a task. You can right-click this figure and choose the Reschedule to Available Date option to reschedule the selected task to the next available time for that resource, as shown in Figure 8.27.

FIGURE 8.27   Rescheduling to available date

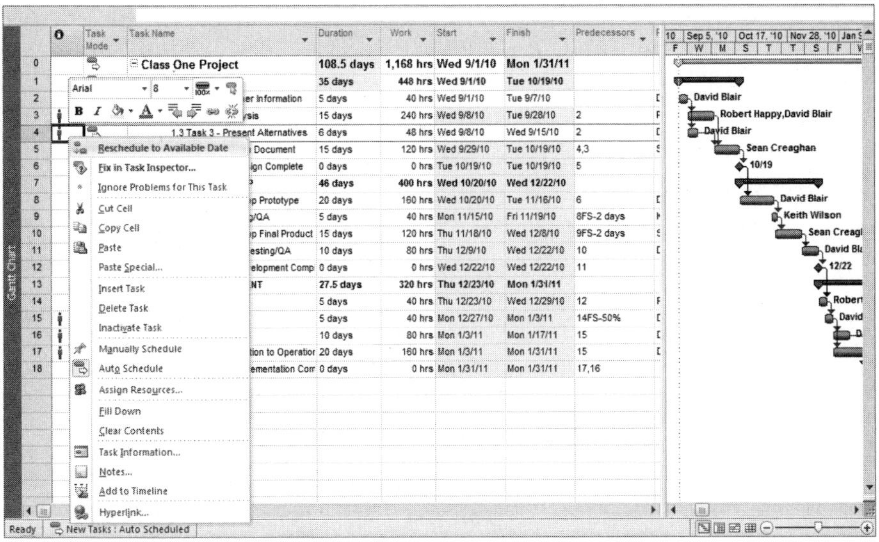

This option allows you to focus on the immediate task affected by the resource conflict without leveling the entire project or the entire resource. You can always select Clear Leveling at any time to remove automatic leveling calculations.

Summary

This chapter covered the concepts and techniques associated with the last step in the four-step planning process: assigning resources and costs. Sometimes you'll want to assign resources without costs, and that is fine. Before assigning resources to tasks, you need to create a resource pool consisting of the people, equipment, and other types of resources you need to accomplish the tasks in your plan. This is typically done in the resource sheet, but it's also possible to share resources from another project plan that already has a resource pool.

When the resource pool is ready, you can assign resources to tasks in a variety of different ways. You can use the Assign Resources function to quickly and easily assign multiple resources to multiple tasks, including replacing existing resource assignments. Depending on the Task Type you've selected (Fixed Duration, Fixed Work, or Fixed Units), Project calculates your schedule differently.

After you've assigned your resources, you can analyze allocation levels in the Task Usage or Resource Usage view. If you choose, you can use various leveling techniques to reschedule tasks with over-allocated resources. In Project, you can level one task at a time by right-clicking the red stick man in the Indicator column; or, use the Team Planner view to level one resource at a time.

Hands-On Exercises

The following hands-on exercises are designed to test your understanding of the topics discussed in this chapter. We've provided files on the companion CD that will show you what your project file should look like as you perform these exercises.

EXERCISE 8

Assigning Resources

1. In Class One Project change views: Select View tab ➤ Resource Views group ➤ Resource Sheet.

2. Create a resource pool in the resource sheet with cost rates (if applicable), using fictitious or real names and generic names.

3. Individually, assign resources to the entire project. Try all the different methods: split screen, Assign Resources function, and Resource Names column. Remember, resource assignments are made at the detail task level, not the summary task level. Also, milestones, by definition, don't generally have work-related resource assignments.

4. Use the Team Planner view to move tasks around to change assignments (Project Professional only).

5. Try over-allocating a resource by assigning the same resource to two concurrent tasks, such as Analysis and Present Alternative.

6. Choose Resource tab ➤ View group ➤ Resource Usage View. Notice the data available in this view. Why are there tasks under the resource Unassigned?

7. Try using the resource-leveling tools in the Resource tab ➤ Level group, to level for the entire project, for one resource, and for selected tasks. Don't forget to clear leveling when you're done.

8. Zoom in and out on the timescale. Expand and collapse the Resource Names. How might this view be useful when you're communicating about resource usage (over-allocation) on your project?

9. Right-click Details in the timescale area. Select another setting from the menu that appears, such as Cost. What happens to the information in the timescale? Reset the information back to Work.

10. Select Task tab ➤ View group Task Usage View. Toggle back and forth between this view and the Resource Usage View. What do you notice about the differences in how the information is structured between these two views?

Save the Class One Project file.

EXERCISE 8 *(continued)*

There are many ways to assign resources in Project. Make sure you're familiar with at least two different ways to assign resources. Be sure you understand that a resource pool is necessary in order to assign resources to tasks (Project adds resources automatically if they don't explicitly exist in the resource pool). Make sure you understand that Project views are either task-centric or resource-centric and how you can use these views to analyze and communicate effectively about your project. Also, be sure you understand that the scheduling formula ($w = d \times u$) only comes into play as resources are assigned.

Chapter

9

Understanding the Calculation Engine for Automatic Scheduling

---

IN THIS CHAPTER, YOU'LL LEARN ABOUT THE FOLLOWING:

✓ Understanding six drivers that drive the calculation of time

✓ Understanding four drivers that drive the calculation of cost

✓ Understanding the impact from switching from manual to automatic scheduling

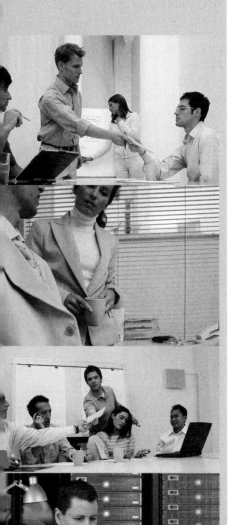

The ability to develop plans with either user-controlled manual scheduling or automatic scheduling simplifies planning with Project. However, it's important to understand the calculation drivers that determine your schedule from both a time perspective and a cost perspective, particularly when you're using automatic scheduling. We've touched on all of these factors in previous chapters, but this chapter presents and summarizes them in one place to help you make more effective use of the tool and do more effective troubleshooting.

Sometimes you'll find yourself asking why a task starts on a particular date or costs so much. You may want to change dates or costs; and to do this effectively, you need to know about the tools summarized in this chapter. Also, as you mature in your planning process and scheduling techniques, you'll need to switch from manual scheduling to automatic. Comprehending these factors will improve your efficiency with Project.

Six Factors that Drive the Calculation of Time (Dates and Duration) for Automatic Scheduling

Knowing the driving factors that have an impact on your start and finish dates will take you a long way toward optimizing your plans so they reflect the reality of your situation and your customer requirements. This section describes the six key factors that drive the calculation of time (dates and duration) in Project:

- Project start date
- Calendars
- Task constraints and deadlines
- Task durations
- Task dependencies
- Resource assignments and task types

Project Start Date

Project start dates are covered in Chapter 4, "Getting Started and Setting Up the Microsoft Project Environment." Project initially determines when your project will start or finish based on what is defined in the project Start Date or Finish Date field located in the Project Information dialog box shown in Figure 9.1. When you start a new project, the default is to apply the current date (today's date) as the start of the project. However, it's important to define this date yourself to reflect the plan you're creating.

FIGURE 9.1   Setting the project start date

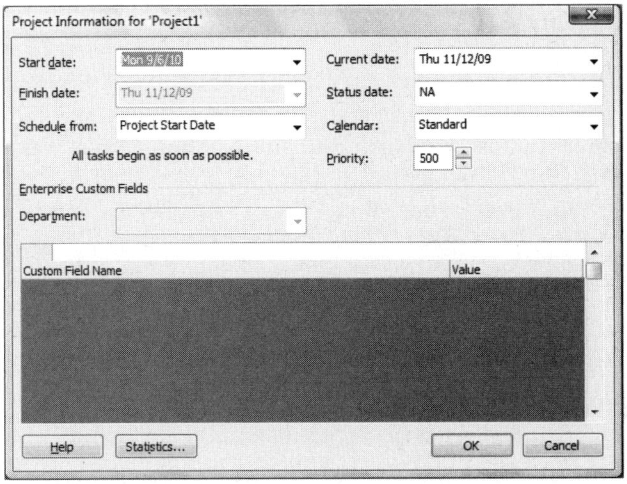

You can always change the project start date to do what-if scenarios that involve delaying or moving up the start of a project. Setting this date is not only a critical step in your project plan but also a powerful tool that you can use to recalculate your entire plan if necessary and then easily communicate with your various project stakeholders.

To define your project start date, follow these steps:

1. Go to Project tab ➢ Properties group, and click Project Information.

2. In the Start Date box, type or select the project start date.

3. Click OK.

You can also choose to schedule from the project end date and apply a backward scheduling technique. This may be useful for initial planning based on a deadline or target end date you've been given. However, I recommend that you change to forward scheduling (scheduling from the project start) prior to implementation so that any delays will result in the schedule being pushed to the right (later) instead of to the left (earlier).

At any time, you can shift your plan to start earlier or later using the Move Project dialog box, as shown in Figure 9.2:

1. Go to Project tab ➢ Schedule group, and click Move Project.

2. In the New Project Start Date field, type or select the new project start date.

3. Click OK.

FIGURE 9.2   Move Project dialog box

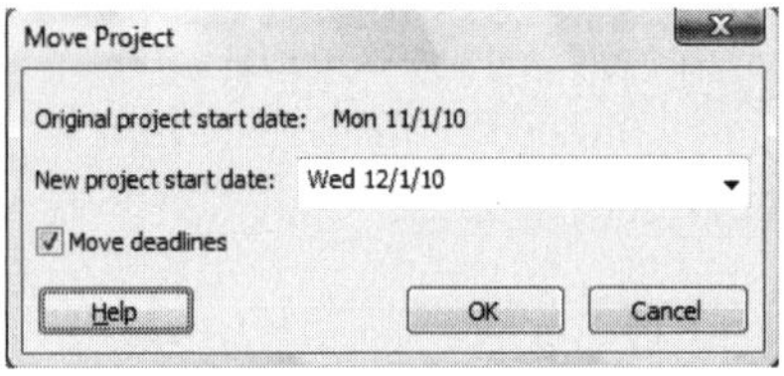

If you're using any constraints or deadlines, Project recalculates them relative to the amount of time you move your project start date. For example, if you delay the start of your project by one week, all of your constraints and deadlines also move out one week. You can clear the Move Deadlines check box if you don't want them to move accordingly. To learn more about constraints and deadlines, refer to Chapter 7, "Setting Dependencies and the Critical Path."

This feature may be particularly useful if you're starting a project from a template with predefined tasks, duration estimates, and dependencies. The first thing you can do after you open the project template is change the start date by using the Move Project dialog box. Then, modify the remaining details to match the unique needs of your project, following the four-step planning process outlined in Chapter 5 ("Creating and Entering the Work Breakdown Structure") through Chapter 8 ("Assigning Resources and Costs").

Calendars

Another important factor in the calculation of your start and end dates is the application of calendars (covered in detail in Chapter 4). Calendars can be defined in three different areas as follows:

- Project level (affects the calculation of the entire project)
- Task level (affects the calculation of just that task)
- Resource level (affects the calculation of tasks to which that resource has been assigned)

Before you can apply custom calendars at any of these levels, you must create them by selecting Project tab ➤ Properties group ➤ Change Working Time.

Applying Calendars at the Project Level

You can select and apply the project-level calendar in the Project tab ➤ Properties group ➤ Project Information dialog box. You can also use project calendars to simulate what-if scenarios based on different working times. For example, if you're on a tight schedule and you want your staff to work on Saturdays, you can set up a new calendar and apply it to the project to see the affect the change will have on the timeline.

Applying Calendars at the Task Level

You can apply calendars at the task level (see Figure 9.3) in the Task Information dialog box. Often, specific tasks warrant a different calendar, but you don't want it to affect the calculation of the entire project. You can access this via Task tab ➤ Properties group ➤ Task Information dialog box or by double-clicking a task.

FIGURE 9.3   Applying calendars at the task level

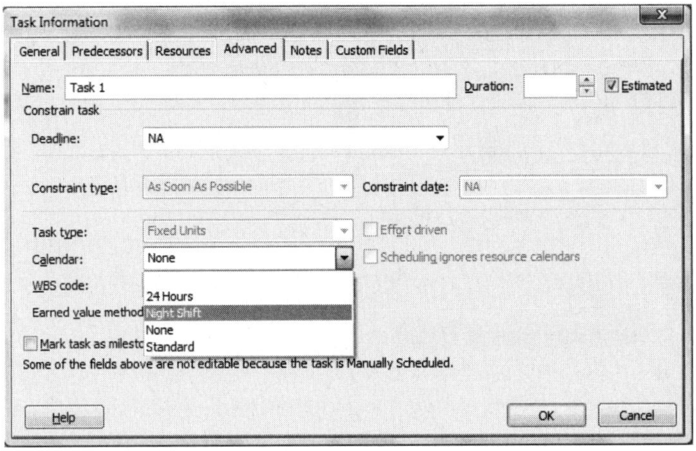

Applying Calendars at the Resource Level

After you've defined a resource in the resource pool as discussed in Chapter 8, you can apply different base calendars and also change the resources' working time to reflect personal time off. You can do this by accessing the Change Working Time dialog box shown in Figure 9.4 via Resource tab ➤ Properties group or double-clicking a resource name in the resource sheet and clicking the Change Working Time button. For this to work, you must have the Resource Sheet view displayed and a resource selected.

You can select a different base calendar or modify the working times for that specific resource. This is usually done to reflect personal time off, such as personal vacation days. When the resource is applied to a task, Project takes the nonworking days into consideration when assigning work, thus affecting the calculation of start and finish dates. Keep in mind that this applies only to auto-scheduled tasks.

Task Constraints and Deadlines

If you're using an auto-scheduled approach to scheduling, one of the commonest mistakes is to type dates directly into the Start and Finish Date fields. Doing so sets up a schedule based on task constraints and seriously limits your ability to use Project as an effective automated scheduling tool. Although this approach may be fine for manual scheduling, it isn't the best practice for auto-scheduling.

Instead of using constraints to drive your schedule, you should focus on setting up a network of tasks, with dependencies driving when a task should start in conjunction with these other tools. However, task constraints can come in handy when you have a hard date such as a trade show, regulated deadlines, contract constraints, and so on.

FIGURE 9.4   Applying calendars at the resource level

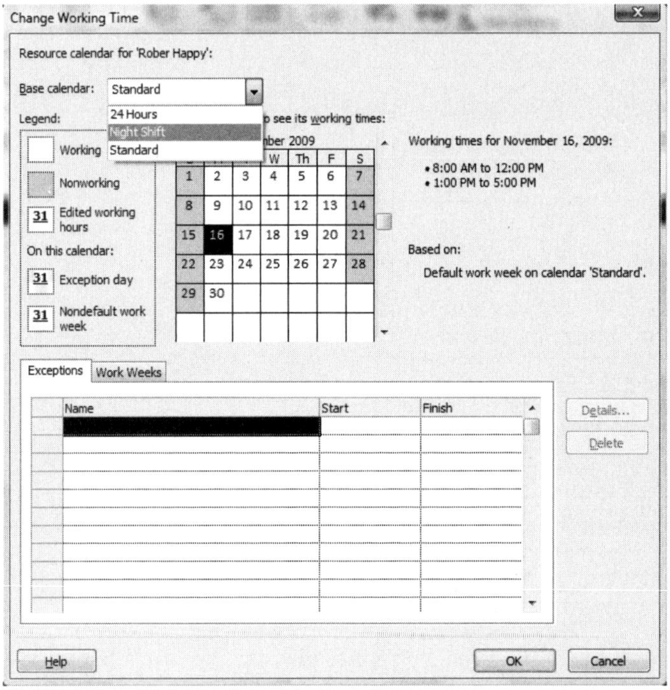

Change Working Time

Resource calendar for 'Rober Happy':

Base calendar: Standard

24 Hours					
Night Shift					
Standard					

Working times for November 16, 2009:

- 8:00 AM to 12:00 PM
- 1:00 PM to 5:00 PM

Legend:

☐ Working

☐ Nonworking

31 Edited working hours

On this calendar:

31 Exception day

31 Nondefault work week

to see its working times:

ber 2009

		W	Th	F	S
1	2	3	4	5	6	7
8	9	10	11	12	13	14
15	16	17	18	19	20	21
22	23	24	25	26	27	28
29	30					

Based on:

Default work week on calendar 'Standard'.

Exceptions | Work Weeks

Name	Start	Finish

Details...

Delete

Help   OK   Cancel

> **NOTE** If at some point you switch from manual scheduling to automatic scheduling, and no links have been established, Project automatically adds constraints to your schedule to hold the manual dates in place.

Project defaults to As Soon As Possible for new tasks. You should try to have the majority of your tasks stay As Soon As Possible. This way, when you need to make changes and do what-if scenarios, you can let the tool recalculate each task's start and finish dates automatically. If all your tasks are constrained, you may have to enter the new dates manually for tasks that are affected by changes. Task constraints may also have a significant impact on your critical-path calculations, limiting your ability to manage the project life cycle. (See Chapter 7.) Constraints are useful tools but should be used wisely and with caution.

To apply task constraints, use the following steps (see Figure 9.5):

1. Click Task tab ➤ Properties group ➤ Task Information (or double-click a selected task).

2. Select the Advanced Tab, click the Constraint Type drop down list, and select the appropriate constraint.

3. In the Constraint Date field, type or select the appropriate constraint date.

FIGURE 9.5   Changing task constraints

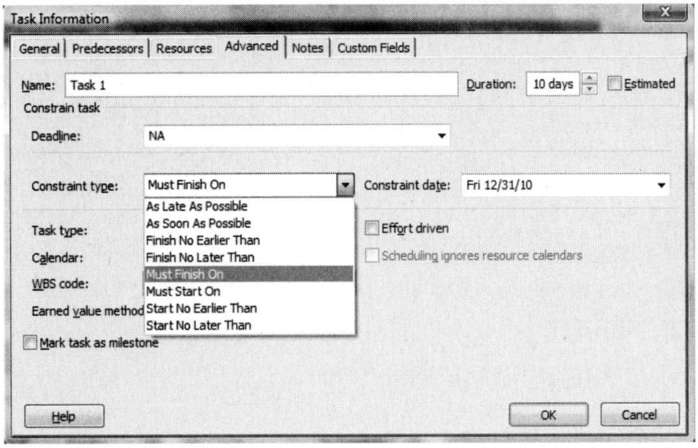

Any constraint with Earlier Than or Later Than in its description can move or be pushed around one way but not another. For example, Start No Earlier Than can be pushed to the right (later) but not to the left (earlier). I refer to these as *half constraints*.

Must Start On and Must Finish On are *full constraints* that can't be pushed to the right or to the left. These constraints are automatically placed on your critical path—for better or for worse. This can be an interesting approach to forcing something onto the critical path, but Project doesn't calculate based on the constraint's position in the network.

You can also apply task deadlines to help manage project and task finish dates. Selecting a deadline in the Task Information dialog box in Project Standard doesn't constrain the task and anchor it in place but rather recalculates the task and compares it to the deadline. Task deadlines also affect the critical-path calculation. Deadline dates can affect the total slack for tasks; if you enter a deadline date that's before the end of the task's total slack, then total slack is recalculated by using the deadline date rather than the task's late finish date. The task becomes critical if the total slack reaches zero.

Depending on which constraint you select, it may override other calculation tools such as project calendars and task dependencies. The Must Start On and Must Finish On constraints are the two strongest; they anchor the task in place, even on a nonworking day.

You can use a Must Finish On constraint to help manage project end dates and allow Project to calculate whether you're going to be late or early by displaying total slack. Project calculates negative slack for you and calculates how many days the project is past the constraint. A scheduling conflict message appears first; but after allowing the scheduling conflict, Project calculates negative slack—how many days past your finish date you are—by displaying negative values.

Task Durations

Estimating task durations obviously has an impact on the calculation of start and finish dates. You can enter task durations directly into the Duration field in any table or dialog box that has the field displayed.

Remember that duration is based on working days as defined in the project calendar. For example, 1 day = 8 hours, 5 days = 1 week, and 20 days = 1 month. If you want to enter 1 month in the Duration field, and you type in **30 days**, then duration is calculated as 6 weeks. Make sure that if you enter days, you make the correct conversions. To review these conversion factors, as shown in Figure 9.6, follow these steps:

1. Click the File tab to access the backstage , and click Options.

2. Click Schedule.

3. Review the scheduling options for this project.

FIGURE 9.6   Scheduling options

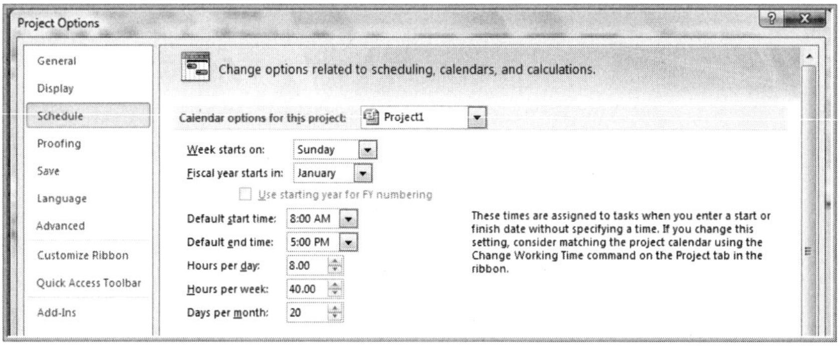

Be careful not to change these settings without considering the project calendar settings and working times. For example, if you decide to make 10 hours per day your conversion factor, then your existing 1-day estimates will change to 0.8 days. And if you enter 1 day into your duration estimate, Project will calculate the finish date to be the next day, because the calendar only allows for 8 working hours by default unless you change the working time to match the hours per day.

Task Dependencies

One of the most critical steps in scheduling is to establish a network for your tasks by setting task dependencies. Chapter 7 covers this in detail. This step in scheduling makes the difference between a plan that can be used as an effective automated schedule and a plan that can be used only for manually scheduling. After the dependencies are set and the network is established, you can easily identify the critical path and understand the driving factors to the project end date. You can also easily make changes to one task and immediately see the impact it will have on the rest of the plan.

There are many ways to set dependencies in Project. Chapter 7 discusses the following techniques:

- Using the Link tool
- Using the split-screen approach
- Using the Predecessors column approach
- Using the click-and-drag approach

For automatic scheduling, the challenge is to ensure that all tasks are in the network. Although this is sometimes a difficult goal to achieve, a best practice is to have a predecessor for each task, unless it's driven by the start date of the project; and to have a successor for each task, unless it's the last task or milestone in the project. Consider including a project-complete milestone in your plan to link other tasks or milestones.

Resource Assignments and Task Types

One major contributor to the calculation of start and finish dates is the manner in which planners assign resources to tasks and set the corresponding task types. This is covered in Chapter 8.

First, you must understand that three variables are calculated each time a resource is assigned to a task. These variables are tied together by the formula Work = Duration × Units, keeping in mind that duration is based on calendar hours/per day which defaults to 8 hours per day. If you change a variable, then one of the other two variables is recalculated, depending on what task type you select for that task. New in Project 2010 however, as discussed in Chapter 8, the units field, which is referred to as assignment units in Project, remains unchanged unless you manually change it. Project 2010 actually recalculates the Peak Units field instead if there are fluctuations to work assignments over time.

Selecting the task type is based on the scheduling technique you want applied to that task or project. Scheduling uses two main approaches: duration-based and effort-based. Duration-based scheduling is generally applied to tasks that are driven by dates and deadlines that won't be affected by the number of resources assigned. An example is a trade show: no matter how many resources you assign to the trade show task, the duration will always be the same.

 It's better to set the default task type before entering tasks; otherwise, you'll have to rework the plan and change each task type setting after your tasks are entered. Changing the default task type afterward will affect only new tasks, not existing tasks. You can set the default task type in the backstage's Options area; refer to Chapter 4 for more details.

Effort-based (work-driven) tasks are ones for which the duration is recalculated based on the number of resources assigned. The more resources assigned to a task, the less time is calculated in the Duration field. The opposite is also true: as you assign fewer resources, duration increases. The so-called *stuffing envelopes* approach can apply to a variety of tasks. To set the task default to recalculate duration based on resource assignments, select Fixed

Work (by default, the Effort-Driven attribute is checked for each task), or select Fixed Units with Effort-Driven selected. Remember, you can always change this setting on a task-by-task basis in the Task Information dialog box.

> **NOTE**   Project has smart tags that guide you through changes in task durations, work, and assignment units. These smart tags correspond to the appropriate task type and relate to the formula Work = Duration × Units. A series of choices is presented, allowing you to select the calculation behavior you desire; the appropriate values are changed accordingly.
>
> Project Standard also offers resource leveling, which affects the calculation of start and finish dates. Resource leveling affects your schedule only if resource assignments cause over-allocation based on resource availability. You must knowingly activate this feature for it to affect the schedule.

🌐 Real World Scenario

Troubleshooting and Calculation Mode

I've worked with many students and clients who couldn't figure out why a date was scheduled the way it was in Project. Using the six factors described in this section, you can troubleshoot 99 percent of such problems.

I recently had this list on hand while looking at a plan. I went through each item, trying to determine why Project wasn't taking the task dependencies into consideration. My first thought was a constraint, but there was none. After going through the list, I decided to check the Calculation Mode settings. Sure enough, the plan was set to manual calculation.

The Calculation Mode override setting is in the backstage in the Options area, under Schedule. You can turn the schedule mode for auto-schedule tasks from automatic to manual; then, as you make changes to any of the six factors discussed in this section, they won't be calculated unless you click Project tab ➢ Schedule group ➢ Calculate Project button.

Four Factors that Affect the Calculation of Cost

This section outlines four important factors that affect the calculation of the Cost field in Project. It will give you the techniques you need to optimize the cost in a project plan in Project Standard.

These factors are the primary components that affect how total cost is calculated into the main Cost field:

- Standard and overtime rates
- Cost per use
- Fixed cost
- Resource assignments (work, material, and cost resources)

Mastering these calculation tools gives you a framework to develop and maintain cost plans effectively, gives you the necessary tools for troubleshooting, and eliminates the majority of problems you may encounter when optimizing your plan for cost.

Standard and Overtime Rates

Project bases much of its cost calculation on the standard rate applied to each resource in the resource pool you create. It also gives you the option to have a separate overtime rate in case you want to assign overtime hours for a task and calculate those hours applying a separate cost rate. You can find the Standard Rate field in resource views. (Project Standard has two basic types of views: one for tasks and one for resources. When making modifications to a resource, such as the standard rate, you need to open a resource view; see Chapter 8.)

The standard rate is multiplied by how many hours (or minutes, days, weeks, months, or years) a resource has been assigned to a task. For example, if a programmer costs $100 per hour and is assigned to work 10 hours on one task, the cost is $1,000. This cost is included in the roll-up calculation of the summary task and total project cost.

The same method works for material resources. When you set up a material resource in a resource pool, you give it a standard rate that can be applied to the number of material units you assign to a task. For example, computer software may have a standard rate of $100 per license. If you assign 1,000 licenses (units) to a task, the cost is calculated to be $100,000. When you set up material resources, you define the unit manually in the Material Label field, whether it's per license, per gallon, per desktop, per manual, and so on.

To change the standard or overtime rates for a resource, follow these steps:

1. Select ➤ Resource tab ➤ View group ➤ Team Planner drop-down list ➤ select Resource Sheet.
2. Type the name of the resource in the Resource Name column.
3. In the Type drop-down list, click Resource or Material.
4. For material resources, select Material Label, and enter the name of the label.
5. Select Standard Rate, and enter the rate per minute, hour, day, week, month, or year (for material resources, no unit is needed).
6. If applicable, select Overtime Rate, and enter the rate.

Project also allows you to use generic resources as well as named resources. For example, if you want to track programmers, you can enter the title or skill into the Resource Name column, open the Resource Information dialog box, and check the Generic option. You can assign standard and overtime rates to generic resources as well capture their respective costs for planning purposes even if they may eventually be replaced by named resources.

Cost Per Use

The Cost/Use field is available in the resource sheet. It acts like a lump-sum cost for a resource: every time you assign that resource to a task, the cost per use is applied, calculated into the Cost field, and added to the total project cost. You can combine cost per use and standard rates. For example, if you have a large setup cost for a piece of equipment and you also pay by the hour, you can use both for the same resource. The cost per use is added regardless of how many hours you assign that resource.

To modify the Cost/Use field as shown in Figure 9.7, follow these steps:

1. In Resource Sheet view, click the Cost/Use field for the resource you wish to change.

2. Enter the appropriate cost-per-use amount.

FIGURE 9.7 Cost/Use field

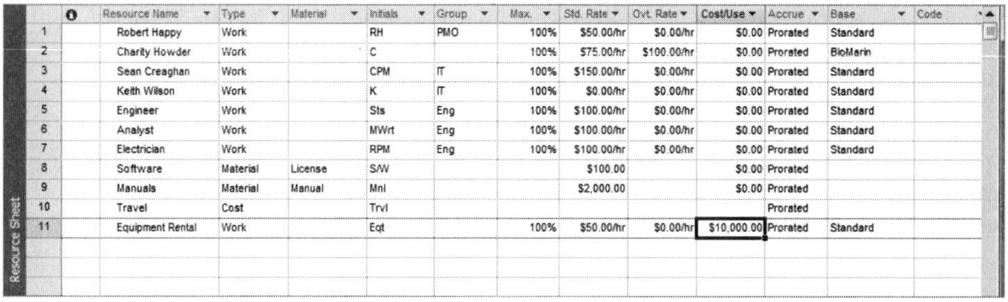

	ⓘ	Resource Name	Type	Material	Initials	Group	Max.	Std. Rate	Ovt. Rate	Cost/Use	Accrue	Base	Code
1		Robert Happy	Work		RH	PMO	100%	$50.00/hr	$0.00/hr	$0.00	Prorated	Standard	
2		Charity Howder	Work		C		100%	$75.00/hr	$100.00/hr	$0.00	Prorated	BioMarin	
3		Sean Creaghan	Work		CPM	IT	100%	$150.00/hr	$0.00/hr	$0.00	Prorated	Standard	
4		Keith Wilson	Work		K	IT	100%	$0.00/hr	$0.00/hr	$0.00	Prorated	Standard	
5		Engineer	Work		Sts	Eng	100%	$100.00/hr	$0.00/hr	$0.00	Prorated	Standard	
6		Analyst	Work		MWrt	Eng	100%	$100.00/hr	$0.00/hr	$0.00	Prorated	Standard	
7		Electrician	Work		RPM	Eng	100%	$100.00/hr	$0.00/hr	$0.00	Prorated	Standard	
8		Software	Material	License	S/W			$100.00		$0.00	Prorated		
9		Manuals	Material	Manual	Mnl			$2,000.00		$0.00	Prorated		
10		Travel	Cost		Trvl						Prorated		
11		Equipment Rental	Work		Eqt		100%	$50.00/hr	$0.00/hr	$10,000.00	Prorated	Standard	

In the example in Figure 9.7, every time the resource Equipment Rental is assigned to a task, $10,000 will be added to the cost of that task regardless of hours or duration associated with it.

Fixed Cost

Another way to affect the calculation of cost for a task and therefore the project is to take advantage of the Fixed Cost field. This field lets you assign costs at the task level, summary level, or project level without having to assign resources. It can be a great option if you're looking to load up costs at the task level or summary task level without having to use a resource pool. These costs are part of the total cost calculation in the Cost field. You can manually add costs into the Fixed Cost column at the summary level, which contributes to the overall total cost but doesn't roll up the detail task's fixed costs. This is true only for the Fixed Cost column.

To add a fixed cost, run a table that has the field displayed as a column, or add it to an existing table, as shown in Figure 9.8. It's a good idea to place the Fixed Cost column next to the Cost column so you can easily review the impact when you make changes. Follow these steps:

1. In the Entry table (the default table), click the Add Column heading.

2. In the drop-down list of fields, scroll down or enter **c**; click Cost to add it to the table.

3. Repeat steps 1 and 2 for Fixed Cost.

4. Enter a cost value to the task or summary task in the Fixed Cost field.

5. Observe the calculation in both the Fixed Cost and Cost fields.

FIGURE 9.8   Adding fixed cost to your plan

	Task Name	Duration	Work	Start	Finish	Predeces:	Resource Names	Cost	Fixed Cost	Add New
0	− Class One Project	108.5 days	1,168 hrs	Wed 9/1/10	Mon 1/31/11			$200,110.00	$0.00	
1	− PHASE 1 - DESIGN	35 days	448 hrs	Wed 9/1/10	Tue 10/19/10			$34,420.00	$0.00	
2	Task 1 - Gather Information	5 days	0 hrs	Wed 9/1/10	Tue 9/7/10			$0.00	$0.00	
3	Task 2 - Analysis	15 days	120 hrs	Wed 9/8/10	Tue 9/28/10	2	Robert Happy	$6,420.00	$0.00	
4	Task 3 - Present Alternatives	6 days	0 hrs	Thu 9/9/10	Thu 9/16/10	2		$0.00	$0.00	
5	Task 4 - Design Document	15 days	120 hrs	Wed 9/29/10	Tue 10/19/10	4,3	Sean Creaghan	$18,000.00	$0.00	
6	Milestone - Design Complete	0 days	0 hrs	Tue 10/19/10	Tue 10/19/10	5		$10,000.00	$10,000.00	
7	− PHASE 2 - DEVELOP	46 days	400 hrs	Wed 10/20/10	Wed 12/22/10			$38,000.00	$0.00	
8	Task 1 - Develop Prototype	20 days	0 hrs	Wed 10/20/10	Tue 11/16/10	6		$0.00	$0.00	
9	Task 2 - Testing/QA	5 days	40 hrs	Mon 11/15/10	Fri 11/19/10	8FS-2 days	Keith Wilson	$0.00	$0.00	
10	Task 3 - Develop Final Product	15 days	120 hrs	Thu 11/18/10	Wed 12/8/10	9FS-2 days	Sean Creaghan	$18,000.00	$0.00	
11	Task 4 - Final Testing/QA	10 days	0 hrs	Thu 12/9/10	Wed 12/22/10	10		$0.00	$0.00	
12	Milestone - Development Complete	0 days	0 hrs	Wed 12/22/10	Wed 12/22/10	11		$20,000.00	$20,000.00	
13	− PHASE 3 - IMPLEMENT	27.5 days	320 hrs	Thu 12/23/10	Mon 1/31/11			$73,090.00	$0.00	
14	Task 1 - Install	5 days	40 hrs	Thu 12/23/10	Wed 12/29/10	12	Robert Happy,Softw	$12,140.00	$0.00	
15	Task 2 - Test	5 days	0 hrs	Mon 12/27/10	Mon 1/3/11	14FS-50%		$0.00	$0.00	
16	Task 3 - Train	10 days	0 hrs	Mon 1/3/11	Mon 1/17/11	15	Manuals[20 Manual]	$40,000.00	$0.00	
17	Task 4 - Transition to Operations	20 days	0 hrs	Mon 1/3/11	Mon 1/31/11	15	Travel[$950.00]	$950.00	$0.00	
18	Milestone - Implementation Complete	0 days	0 hrs	Mon 1/31/11	Mon 1/31/11	17,16		$20,000.00	$20,000.00	

To clear a fixed cost value, you need to enter a zero in the Fixed Cost field.

Fixed cost totals don't roll up in the Fixed Cost column but do roll up in the regular Cost column; this gives you the flexibility to enter costs at summary task levels. You can also use this technique to create milestone payment plans by adding costs to milestones in a plan, particularly when you need to hire and pay vendors or outsource certain components of work packages without tracking their respective work hours.

Resource Assignment Level

One of the other biggest contributors to costs in Project comes from resource assignments. However, this is true only if the resources you've created in the resource pool have a value in the Standard/Overtime Rate or Cost/Use field. Otherwise, assigning resources doesn't affect the cost calculation. It's fine to not put values into the rate fields if you're only interested in tracking hours or responsibility for each task.

As discussed in Chapter 8, Project bases its calculation of work on the three-variable formula Work = Duration × Units. These variables behave differently depending on the type of scheduling methodology you're applying, through your task-type selection of Fixed Duration, Fixed Work, or Fixed Units, with Effort-Driven turned on or off for each selection.

As you assign resources to tasks, Project defaults to 100% unit allocation and therefore bases the work calculation on whatever is in the Duration field (see Chapter 8). As the work-hour assignment increases or decreases, so does the cost.

Try to assign resources at the detail task level and let the summary tasks total the hours and costs for you. Summary tasks have a default fixed-duration task type that you can't change; therefore, work and cost are calculated from the total duration driven by the detail tasks. The duration of the summary task continues to change as the details change and therefore automatically recalculates the work and costs.

It's a good idea to add Work and Cost to your table using the Add Column approach as described earlier in this chapter. I usually put Work and Cost beside the Resource Name column, as shown in Figure 9.09.

FIGURE 9.9 Tracking work and cost together

	❶	Task Mode	Task Name	Duration	Start	Finish	Predeces:	Resource Names	Work	Cost
1			− PHASE 1 - DESIGN	35 days	Wed 9/1/10	Tue 10/19/10			448 hrs	$24,420.00
2			Task 1 - Gather Information	5 days	Wed 9/1/10	Tue 9/7/10			0 hrs	$0.00
3			Task 2 - Analysis	15 days	Wed 9/8/10	Tue 9/28/10	2	Robert Happy	120 hrs	$6,420.00
4			Task 3 - Present Alternatives	6 days	Thu 9/9/10	Thu 9/16/10	2		0 hrs	$0.00
5			Task 4 - Design Document	15 days	Wed 9/29/10	Tue 10/19/10	4,3	Sean Creaghan	120 hrs	$18,000.00
6			Milestone - Design Complete	0 days	Tue 10/19/10	Tue 10/19/10	5		0 hrs	$0.00
7			− PHASE 2 - DEVELOP	46 days	Wed 10/20/10	Wed 12/22/10			400 hrs	$18,000.00
8			Task 1 - Develop Prototype	20 days	Wed 10/20/10	Tue 11/16/10	6		0 hrs	$0.00
9			Task 2 - Testing/QA	5 days	Mon 11/15/10	Fri 11/19/10	8FS-2 days	Keith Wilson	40 hrs	$0.00
10			Task 3 - Develop Final Product	15 days	Thu 11/18/10	Wed 12/8/10	9FS-2 days	Sean Creaghan	120 hrs	$18,000.00
11			Task 4 - Final Testing/QA	10 days	Thu 12/9/10	Wed 12/22/10	10		0 hrs	$0.00
12			Milestone - Development Complete	0 days	Wed 12/22/10	Wed 12/22/10	11		0 hrs	$0.00
13			− PHASE 3 - IMPLEMENT	27.5 days	Thu 12/23/10	Mon 1/31/11			320 hrs	$56,090.00
14			Task 1 - Install	5 days	Thu 12/23/10	Wed 12/29/10	12	Robert Happy,Softv	40 hrs	$12,140.00
15			Task 2 - Test	5 days	Mon 12/27/10	Mon 1/3/11	14FS-50%	Charity Howder ⌄	40 hrs	$3,000.00
16			Task 3 - Train	10 days	Mon 1/3/11	Mon 1/17/11	15	Manuals[20 Manual]	0 hrs	$40,000.00
17			Task 4 - Transition to Operations	20 days	Mon 1/3/11	Mon 1/31/11	15	Travel[$950.00]	0 hrs	$950.00
18			Milestone - Implementation Complete	0 days	Mon 1/31/11	Mon 1/31/11	17,16		0 hrs	$0.00

NOTE The process of assigning resources may include using the cost-type resource. This is a good option if you want to assign cost to a task without having the cost recalculated by the scheduling formula. For example, you may want to include travel costs by typing in the cost amount at the time of the assignment, without adding units or work. When you add a cost-type resource to the resource sheet, you don't have the option to assign a standard rate, because it's a lump-sum cost.

Figure 9.10 shows how you can enter a cost-type resource at the time of the assignment. In the Task Information dialog box, enter the Cost value associated with the assignment. No units or work hours are associated with a cost resource, but it's included in the total cost of the task and project.

FIGURE 9.10   Entering costs for cost-type resource

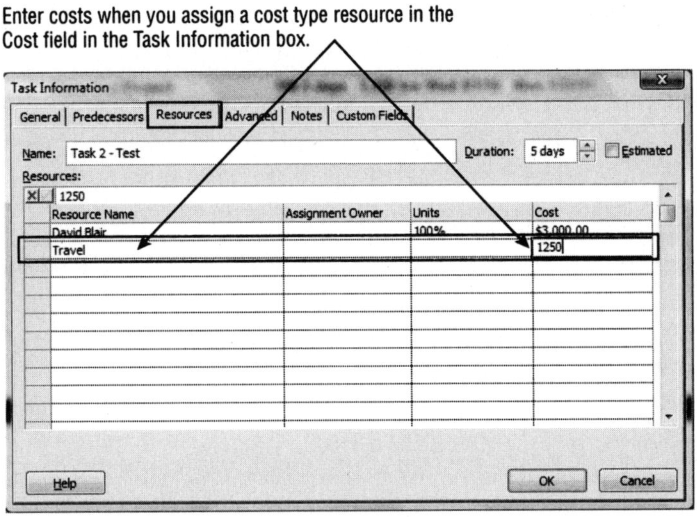

Enter costs when you assign a cost type resource in the
Cost field in the Task Information box.

Switching from Manual Scheduling to Automatic Scheduling

As you progress in your planning process and mature with your planning techniques, you may find it useful to switch from manual scheduling to automatic scheduling. When you do, it's important to understand the impact this has on your schedule both at the task level and at the summary level.

Task Level

Usually, when you apply manual scheduling at the task level, you enter estimates directly into the Duration column or the Start Date and Finish Date columns. You most likely haven't set dependencies at this time, although it's possible to set dependencies with manual tasks, as discussed in Chapter 7. If you have no dependencies and make the switch from manual scheduling to automatic scheduling, Project automatically fills in the duration and dates based on existing information and takes into consideration all the key factors that affect your schedule (discussed earlier in this chapter).

Given the absence of dependencies, Project automatically places a constraint on your tasks to hold the dates in place. To switch a task from manual to automatic, follow these steps:

1.   Highlight the task or series of tasks you want to change.

2. Select Task tab ➤ Schedule group ➤ Auto Schedule.

3. Review the impact this has on your schedule.

Figure 9.11 shows a manually based schedule before switching the tasks to automatic. In this scenario, the summary task is already set to automatic. Some of the tasks have real dates, and others have words typed into the Duration, Start, and Finish fields.

FIGURE 9.11   Example: before switching to auto-schedule

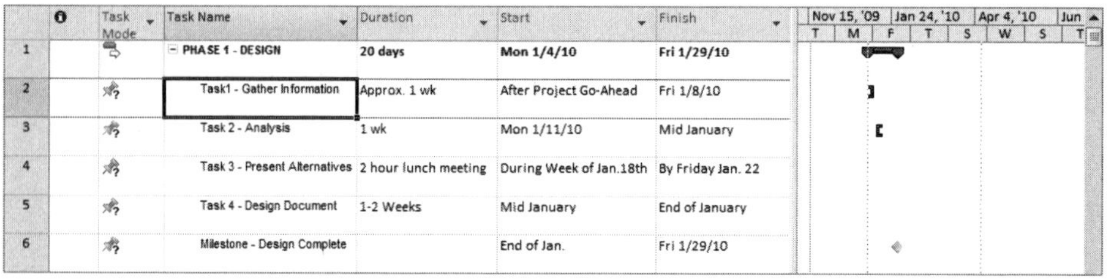

After you switch, Project kicks into gear the calculation engine and the factors covered in this chapter. For tasks without dependencies or that have no identifiable date in the Start, Finish, or Duration field, data are auto-scheduled based on the project start date. If tasks have dates or duration, they're incorporated into the schedule and have constraints placed on them to hold them in the appropriate place in the timeline, as shown in Figure 9.12.

FIGURE 9.12   After switching to auto-schedule

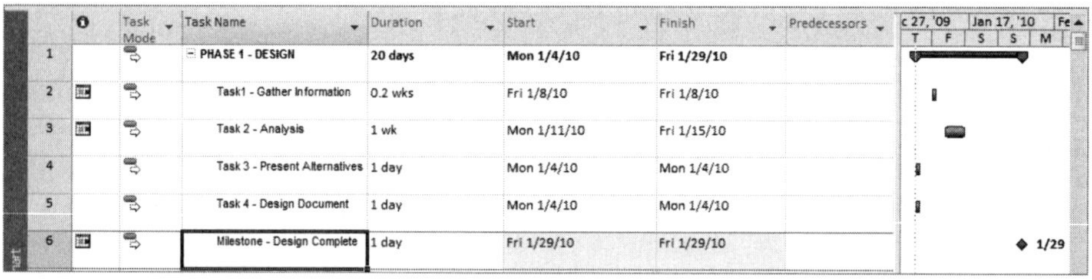

Following best practices for scheduling, you may have to go back and set dependencies or modify the schedule using the techniques I've covered, applying the four-step process for creating plans effectively. If you've set dependencies in conjunction with manually scheduled tasks, Project takes this into consideration when you switch to automatic to calculate your start and finish dates. If you haven't set dependencies, and constraints are automatically applied, the best approach is to establish task dependencies, remove the constraints, and let Project calculate your schedule for you accordingly, as shown in Figure 9.13.

Summary-Level Impact

When switching from manual to automatic scheduling, you need to be aware of the impact this has on your summary-level tasks. Two types of scenarios may unfold. First, you may choose to change both the detail tasks and the summary-level tasks to all be automatic at the same time. In fact, you may already have your summary tasks as automatic and the detail tasks manual, because this is the default setting for Project. In this scenario, Project replaces all existing data, including manually entered data, with calculated data at the summary level, as shown in Figure 9.14.

FIGURE 9.13   Removing constraints

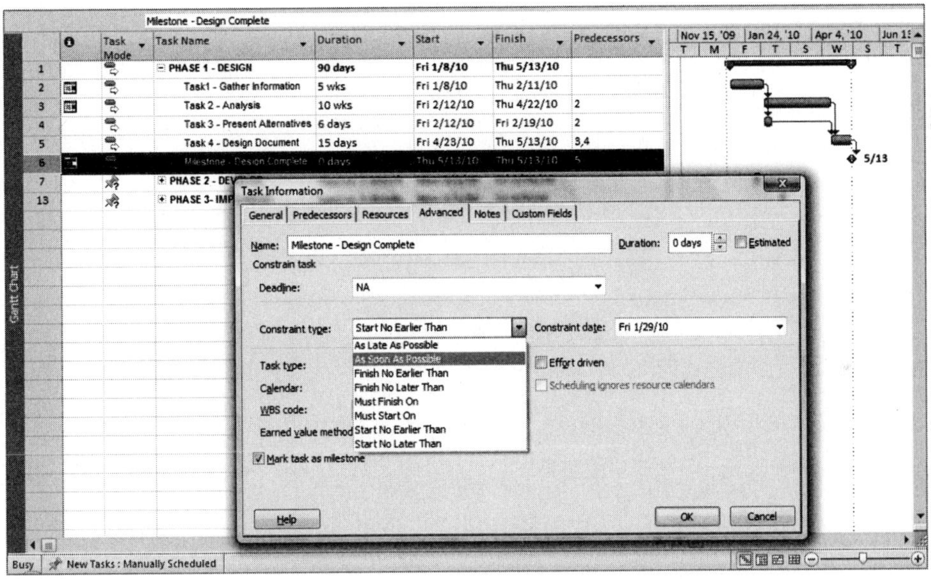

FIGURE 9.14   Impact on summary tasks

Tasks that have text such as "Approx. 6 Months" will be replaced with calculated data. The duration, start and finish dates at the summary level will be based on the calculated roll-up data from the detail tasks from within that summary. In this example Phase 2-Develop was switch to auto and the manually entered text data was replaced with calculated data. You can see that Phase 3- Implement is still manually scheduled and can still contain text based, non-calculated data.

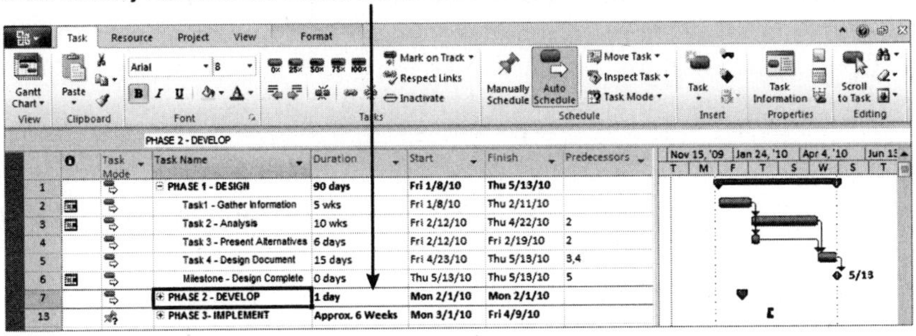

You may also choose to have your detail tasks become automatic while keeping your summary task manual. This gives you an option to conduct a top-down scheduling scenario, as discussed in Chapter 6, "Estimating and Entering Duration or Work." You can have the details automatically scheduled and compare them to your desired summary result. For example, you may want Phase 1—Design to take one month; as you schedule the details, you can see how they compare to your needs, as shown in Figure 9.15.

FIGURE 9.15   Keeping the summary manual with automatic detail tasks

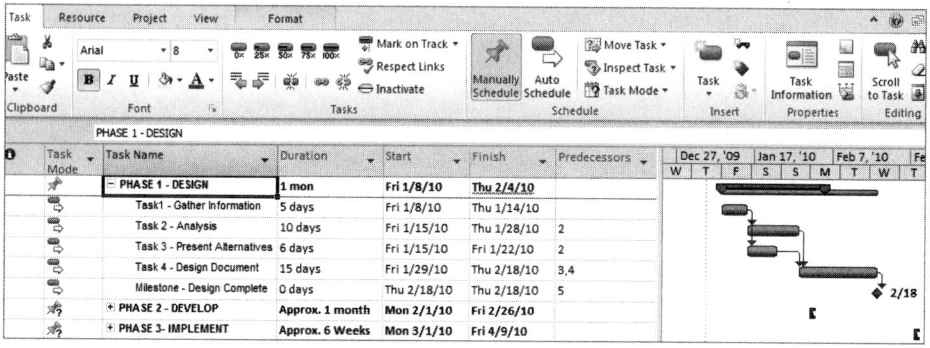

In this scenario, two bars are shown at the summary bar level. The top bar, which is black, represents the manually entered summary data. The bottom bar, which is burgundy red, represents the roll-up calculated data from the detail tasks that belong to that phase. In Figure 9.15, the detail tasks' roll-up bar extends past the manually entered summary bar, telling you that you most likely won't meet your manually entered estimate of one month.

You can use the Task Inspector to help resolve schedule problems that arise as you modify your plan. Project automatically displays a red squiggly line if a potential problem occurs. In Figure 9.16, you can see the red squiggly line under the finish date at the summary level. This highlights that a problem exists. You can right-click the red underline and choose to change to auto-schedule or fix the issue in the Task Inspector, which provides more options. You can also decide to ignore the problems associated with this task, in which case Project removes the red underline.

If you choose the Fix in Task Inspector option, you're presented with various repair options, such as Extend Finish Date of Task and Switch Task to Auto Scheduled, as shown in Figure 9.17. After you make your choice, you can review the impact of the change on your plan. The Task Inspector also displays the controlling factors affecting the task and any problems that exist.

In addition to right-clicking the red squiggly line to run the Task Inspector, you can follow these steps to turn it on:

1. Go to Task tab ➤ Tasks group.

2. Click Inspect.

FIGURE 9.16   Schedule problems and the red underline

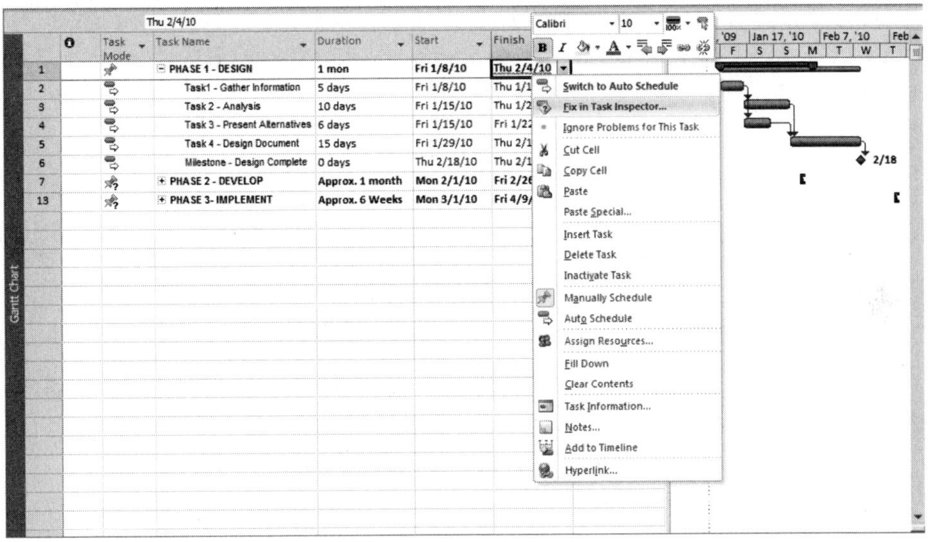

FIGURE 9.17   Task Inspector

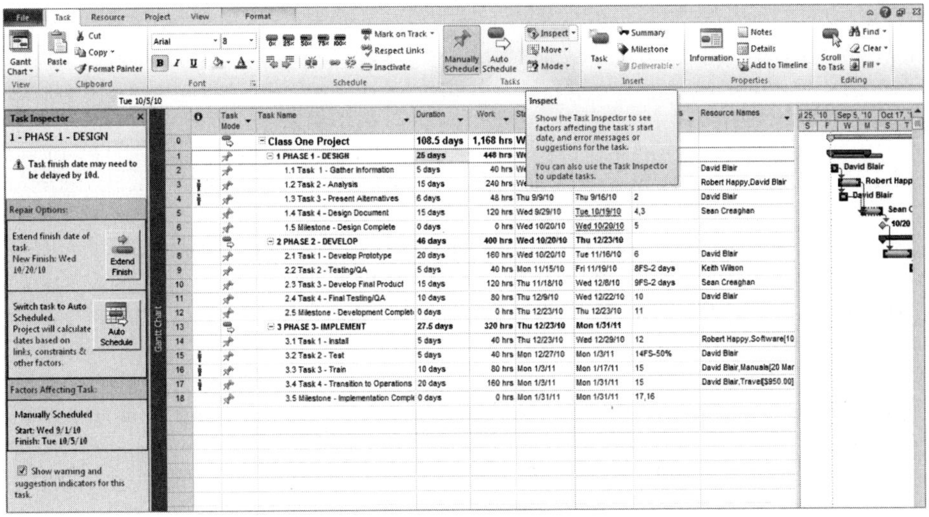

Summary

This chapter has summarized the six key factors that affect the calculation of start and finish dates in your schedule. You need to know these if you want to apply automatic scheduling techniques and follow best practices. These factors are as follows:

- *Project start date*—Defined in the Project Information dialog box.

- *Calendars*—Created with Change Working Time. You can apply them at the project, task, or resource level.

- *Task constraints and deadlines*—Use carefully and with compelling reasons. Most of your tasks should be As Soon As Possible for automatic scheduling.

- *Task durations*—Displayed in working days: 1 d = 8 hours; 5 d = 1 week; 20 d = 1 month.

- *Task dependencies*—Set up at the task and milestone level. If a task doesn't have a predecessor (or constraint), then it's driven by the start date of the project, unless it has been resource-leveled.

- *Resource assignments and task types*—Scheduling formula: Work = Duration × Units. Project calculates your schedule as you assign resources based on the task type you've chosen—Fixed Duration, Fixed Work, Fixed Units—and whether you have Effort-Driven combined with Fixed Units or Fixed Duration.

The chapter also summarized the four key factors you should know if you're interested in tracking costs:

- *Standard and overtime rates*—Can be applied to both work and material resources. As you assign work hours or material units, cost goes up or down and is summarized up to the project total.

- *Cost per use*—A lump-sum cost that is added to the cost calculation every time you assign that resource to a task.

- *Fixed cost*—A non-resource-related cost that can be added at the summary, task, or milestone level and that is included in the Cost field calculation.

- *Resource assignments (work, material, and cost resources)*—Affect costs, assuming resources have standard rates applied. If you assign a cost resource, the cost is added at the time of assignment.

You also learned about the impact of switching from manual scheduling to automatic scheduling. Often, when you switch, you end up with constraints that you need to deal with, such as Start No Earlier Than. It's best practice to establish dependencies and remove constraints whenever possible and let Project dynamically calculate the start and finish dates.

In addition, you learned that if you enter text into the Duration, Start Date, or Finish Date field, such as "Approx. 1 month" or "1 Week Before Delivery," this text is replaced with an automatically calculated date when you change to automatic scheduling.

Hands-On Exercises

The following hands-on exercises are designed to test your understanding of the topics discussed in this chapter. We've provided files on the companion CD that will show you what your project file should look like as you perform these exercises.

EXERCISE 9

Key Drivers for Time and Cost Calculations in the Project for Auto Scheduling

1. List the six key factors that impact the calculation of time in Project:

    1.

    2.

    3.

    4.

    5.

    6.

    In Project, adjust each of these factors and observe the impact it has on your schedule.

2. List the four key factors that impact the calculation of cost in Class One Project:

    1.

    2.

    3.

    4.

    In Class One Project, adjust the standard rate of a resource you've assigned to a task. Try adding the Cost/Use value for a resource. Add the Cost field and Fixed Cost field to your plan. Add a fixed cost to one of your tasks, review the impact, and then replace the fixed cost with zero dollars to remove it.

3. Change a task from manual to automatic or from automatic to manual, and review the impact of the change on your schedule.

4. Change a summary task from manual to automatic or from automatic to manual. Review the impact of the change on your schedule.

5. Keep your summary task manual, and change all the detail tasks to automatic. Type in a duration at the summary level, and compare it to the roll-up of the detail tasks. Do not save changes.

Communicating and Reporting Essentials

PART

III

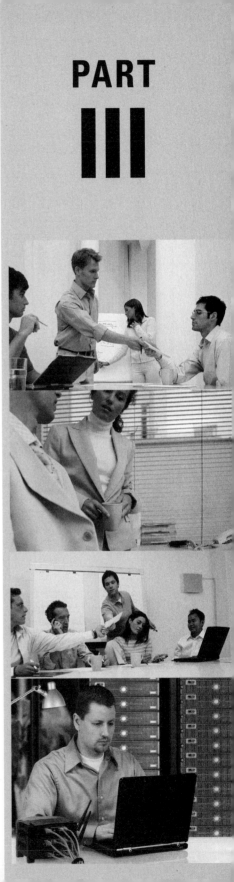

Part III covers how to use Project to create effective communications and reports for the various stakeholders you need to work with throughout a typical project. You may need to share project information before the project starts and you begin tracking status. Tracking and updating are covered the last section of the book. You can skip to Part IV, "Tracking Essentials," and come back to Part III if you have an immediate need to do so.

THIS PART FOCUSES ON THE FOLLOWING:

- ✓ **Understanding and changing views**

- ✓ **Using and creating custom tables and fields**

- ✓ **Using and creating custom filters and groups**

- ✓ **Creating and modifying global text styles and bar styles**

- ✓ **Creating custom stakeholder views and using the Organizer to share views between projects**

- ✓ **Creating master consolidated plans**

This part will help you become proficient at creating meaningful reports and sharing project information with team members, functional managers, executives, end users, vendors, various departments, and external agencies.

Chapter

10

Understanding Views

IN THIS CHAPTER, YOU'LL LEARN ABOUT THE FOLLOWING:

✓ Understanding major view components

✓ Using task views and resource views

✓ Moving around key views

You should feel comfortable moving around different views and not remain stuck in the Gantt Chart view. Project has much more to offer; the more familiar you become with the various views, the more effective you'll be at managing your projects.

Understanding Major View Components

You can think of a view as how you look at information. In each view, you can control what you see. For example, the default view in Project is the Gantt Chart view with the Timeline view on top. These are two separate and distinct views with their own default settings in terms of what you see. The Gantt chart consists of a table (text area) and a timescale (bar area) that are customizable. The same is true for the rest of the views. Project serves up information in these views with default data, but you're free to change everything. As we move through the next four chapters, you'll learn how to do this in detail; but first, you need to understand the main components of a typical view.

Referring to Figure 10.1, you can see that a view may consist of many parts.

FIGURE 10.1   Understanding view-specific components

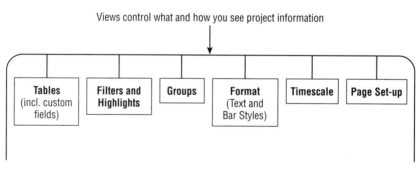

As you move from one view to another the above items are **view specific** and will change depending on how you have set up the view.

Each component is view-specific. You can customize views in the following ways:

- As you change from one view to another, you can have another table open, displaying a different set of fields, including custom fields. This is covered in detail in Chapter 11, "Using Tables and Custom Fields."

- You can have a different filter or group running, as discussed in Chapter 12, "Using Filters, Groups, and Sorts."

- You can have differently formatted bar styles and text styles with different colors and fonts, as covered in Chapter 13, "Creating Custom Views, Formatting, and Reporting."

- You can change the timescale and define page-setup settings to use specific headers and footers that apply only to a specific view.

- You can combine these options to create custom views, as discussed in Chapter 13, " Creating Custom Views, Formatting and Reporting."

As you move from view to view, you see different components with different formats. For example, if you format your critical path to be red and underlined in one view, those changes don't automatically apply to another view.

The default Gantt Chart view (see Figure 10.2) comes with the default Entry table, applied with no filters or groups running.

FIGURE 10.2   Default settings for the default view

Clicking on Timeline activates the Timeline view and associated commands. Clicking on Gantt Chart activates the Gantt Chart view and associated commands. Commands may be different as you switch from one view to another.

You can click and drag along the line at the end of the Timeline view to fit the entire Gantt bar into current time scale area below.

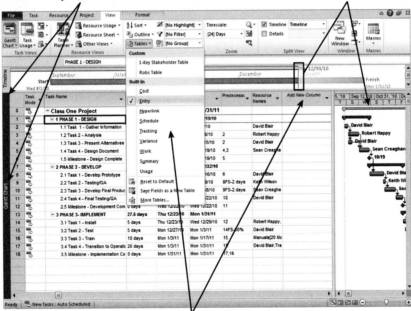

The default table is the entry table but you can easily switch tables or add new columns to an existing table.

Click the timeline portion of the screen to activate the commands associated with that particular view; commands may change or be grayed out as you move from one view to another. You can turn off the Timeline view by deselecting View tab ➤ Split View group ➤ Timeline. Doing so eliminates the combination view.

View-specific tools are on the Format tab. Different tools and commands are available for each view, to reformat the look and feel of what you see on the screen. Depending on which view you're in, Project displays the appropriate format tool set above the Format tab. Chapter 13 covers formatting in more detail.

Data Group

You can find the Data group on the View tab. The Data group (see Figure 10.3) contains powerful tools that help you manage the communication of project information. As you switch from one view to another, notice that a Data group is associated with other views, although some commands may be grayed out, depending on the view you're in. You can generally apply tools such as filters, groups, sorts, and highlights.

FIGURE 10.3   Data group

Tables

Different views may have different tables applied to them, each with a different set of columns. For example, if you're in the Tracking Gantt view, you may want to run the Variance table to better analyze planned versus actual information. You can select columns from either the standard field list or a customized list. You can also customize or create new tables (see Chapter 11).

As shown in Figure 10.4, you can change tables by selecting View tab ➤ Data group ➤ Tables drop-down list ➤ new table. The default table is Entry.

Filters and Highlights

Filters and highlights are based on the same concept of applying different conditions to focus on specific set of tasks. Filtering removes tasks from the view that don't meet the condition you've specified, and highlights keep the other tasks in view but highlight the tasks that meet the specific condition you've applied.

For example, you may want to filter on milestones, as shown in Figure 10.5, to generate a Milestones view to report from. To do this in the Data group, click the drop-down list next to the Filter button (it says [No Filter]) and select Milestone.

FIGURE 10.4 Changing tables

FIGURE 10.5 Applying a filter

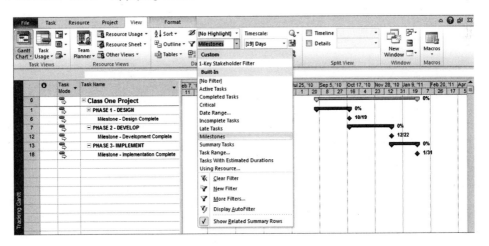

As I noted in Chapter 4, "Getting Started and Setting Up the Microsoft Project Environment," when you were introduced to the ribbon, commands and functions may appear slightly different depending on your screen resolution setting. For many of the screen shots in this book I have the resolution set to 1024 by 768 pixels which will change how the commands appear. For example, in Figure 10.5 there is no label for 'Filter' beside the filter command but you may very well see the word 'Filter' on your screen based on your screen resolution settings.

Highlights behave in a similar fashion: you select from the same list of conditions in the Data group, but this time you choose the condition from the Highlight drop-down list. In Figure 10.6, notices that milestones are highlighted in blue, while the rest of the tasks remain in view. You can change the color of the highlights from blue to other colors (see Chapter 13).

FIGURE 10.6   Applying highlights

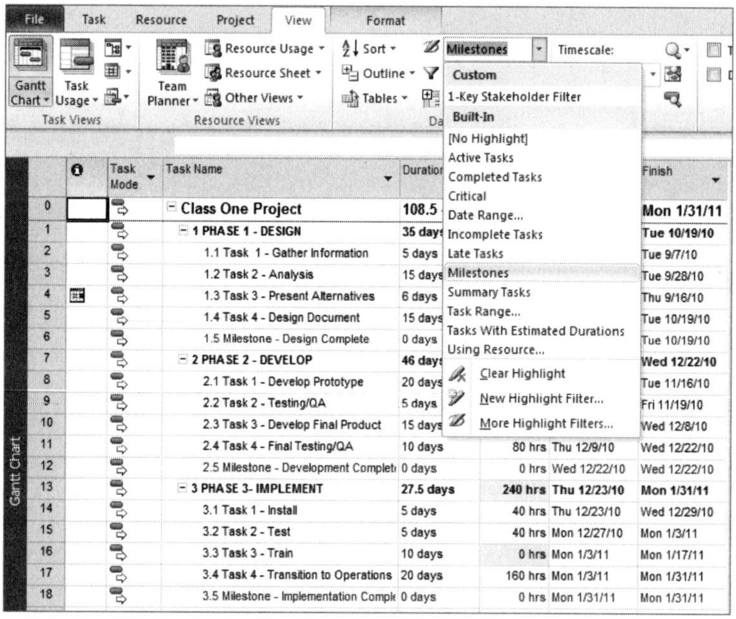

To clear a filter or a highlight, select [No Filter] or [No Highlight], respectively. Sometimes you may forget you have a filter running and wonder what happened to some of your tasks. They're still there—they just don't show because of the filter. Project lets you know in the lower-right corner of your screen that a filter or highlight is applied.

Groups

Grouping is another useful analytical and communication tool to help slice and dice project information. It's similar to filtering in that you apply a specific condition. But instead of eliminating tasks that don't meet the condition from the view, grouping reorganizes tasks based on the condition criteria. Figure 10.7 shows a group being applied in the Gantt Chart view based on milestones, to create a quick and easy milestone-type report. To apply a group, click the drop-down list next to the Group button (it says [No Group]), and select the desired condition, such as Milestones.

FIGURE 10.7   Applying groups

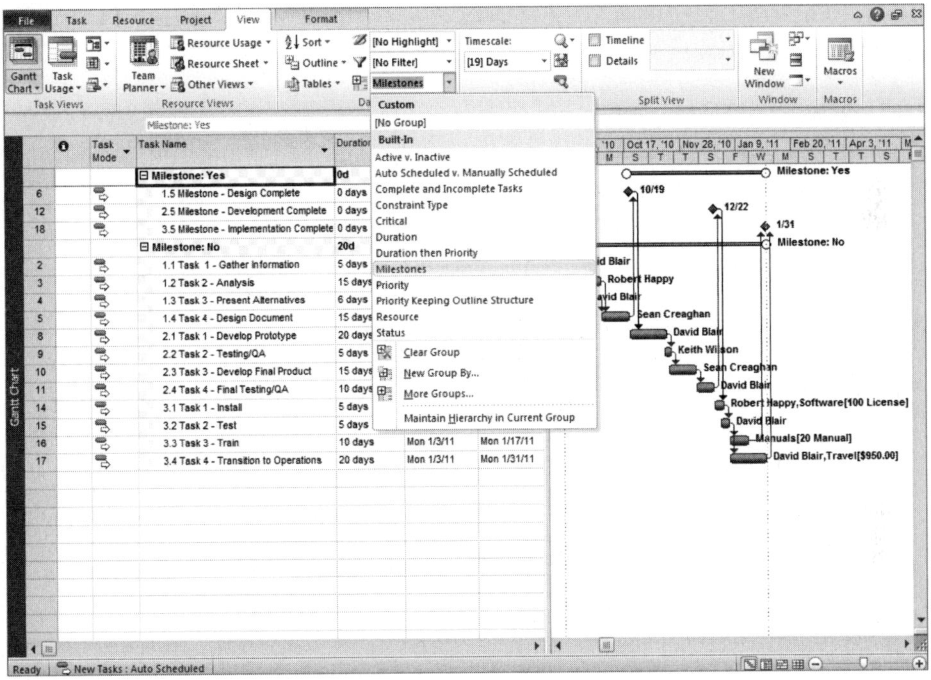

You can apply groups in both task-type views and resource-type views; they aren't limited to the default Gantt chart. To clear a group, select Clear Group or [No Group] from the Group drop-down list.

Sorts

The default sort is based on ID number. You can choose to sort your data some other way. For example, you can sort by start date or finish date, as shown in Figure 10.8, or click Sort By to create custom multiple-sort conditions.

FIGURE 10.8   Applying sorts

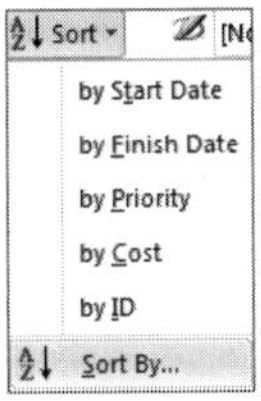

Auto Sorts, Filters, and Groups

Project 2010 lets you quickly apply automatic filters, sorts, and groups by clicking the drop-down arrow beside a column heading. For example, as shown in Figure 10.9, you can click the drop-down arrow beside Start and then select Sort, Group By, or Filters based on the unique characteristic of that field. You can also apply filters by checking or clearing specific criteria.

FIGURE 10.9   Auto sort, group, and filter

Click on the drop-down arrow beside any column heading to apply a Sort, Group or Filter related specifically to that column.

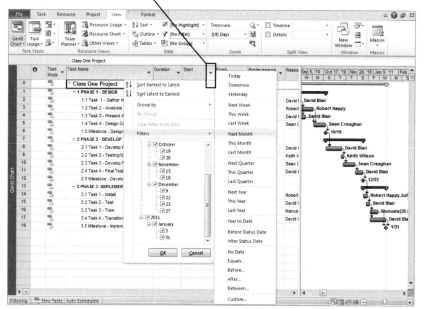

Other View Commands

Project makes it even easier to modify view settings with functionality found in the zoom group, split view group and the window group.

Zoom Group

Use the zoom commands in the View tab ➤ Zoom group to change the timescale. You can view the entire project or a series of selected tasks, or you can change the timescale tier from days to weeks to months.

For example, as shown in Figure 10.10, you can highlight or select a series of tasks and then, in the Zoom group, click Zoom Selected Tasks.

FIGURE 10.10   Zooming selected tasks

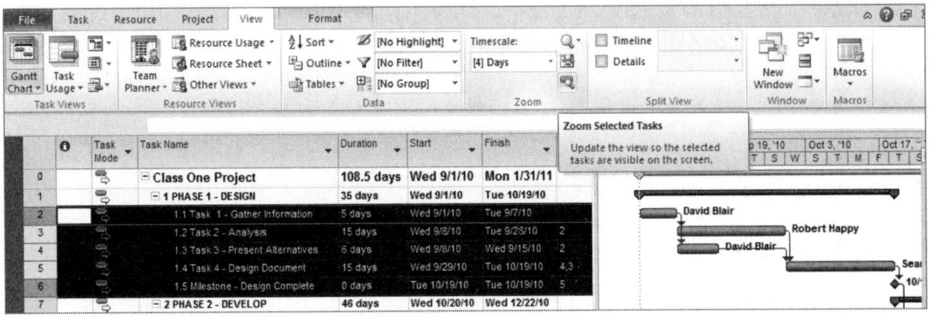

Split View Group

Project allows you to have more than one view running at a time to create a combination view (see Chapter 4). The default is to have the Timeline view running on top of the Gantt Chart view, but you can change that in the View tab ➤ Split View group. You can turn the timeline on or off by checking or clearing the Timeline check box.

You can also create a split-screen view the project details in the bottom half, as shown in Figure 10.11. You can't have three views running at the same time, so when you click Details, the Timeline view is automatically deselected; and when you click Timeline, the Details view is automatically deselected. To create a split-screen view with details, follow these steps:

1. Select View tab ➤ Split View group ➤ Details. The Task Form view appears in the bottom.

2. To change the Task Form details, right-click anywhere in the Task Form view and select another view option. The default is to display resources and successors.

3. To change the bottom view from Task Form view, click the Details Task Form drop-down list in the Split View group.

Window Group

You can use the Window group if you need to display more than one project at a time. Select the Arrange All command, as shown in Figure 10.12.

Task Views

As noted earlier in this chapter, Project offers two basic types of view: one is based on task information as the prime data source, and the other is based on resource information as the prime data source. You can apply different tables, filters, and groups in both types of view, but they will have different fields (columns) to select from. This section provides an overview of each of the main task views. The following chapters take deeper dives into how to customize the look and feel of each major component.

FIGURE 10.11 Creating split-screen views

Click on Details to create a split screen view. Change the default Task Form view by clicking on the drop down list beside Task Form and selecting another type of View.

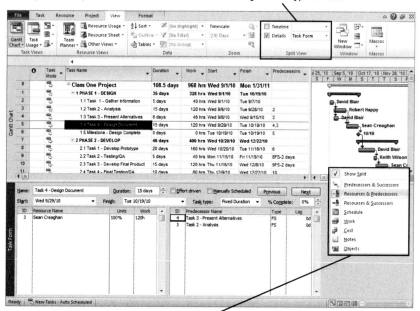

Right Click in the bottom view (Task Form) and change the default detailed information form Resources and Predecessors to another desired selection.

FIGURE 10.12 Viewing more than one project with Arrange All

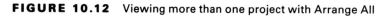

Accessing Other Views from the Gantt Chart

From the default Gantt Chart view, you can access other views in many ways (see Figure 10.13).

FIGURE 10.13   Changing views

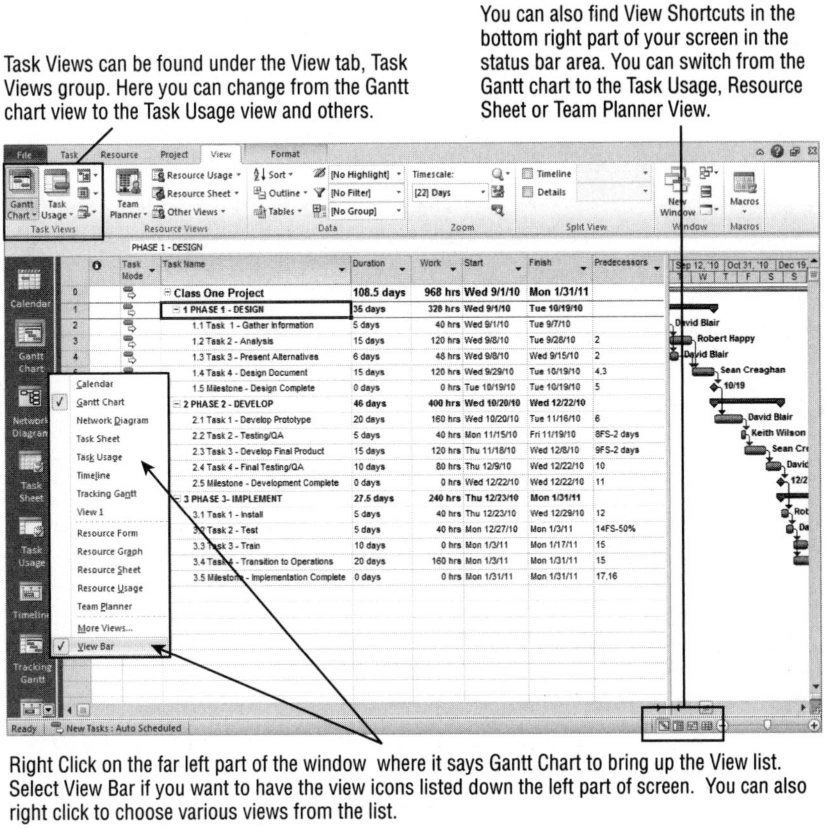

Task Views can be found under the View tab, Task Views group. Here you can change from the Gantt chart view to the Task Usage view and others.

You can also find View Shortcuts in the bottom right part of your screen in the status bar area. You can switch from the Gantt chart to the Task Usage, Resource Sheet or Team Planner View.

Right Click on the far left part of the window where it says Gantt Chart to bring up the View list. Select View Bar if you want to have the view icons listed down the left part of screen. You can also right click to choose various views from the list.

You can also change views in Task tab ➤ Views group. If you click the drop-down list under the Gantt Chart button, you see a list of all the main views.

As you can see, there are many ways in Project to switch from one view to another. I like to have the View bar running, as shown in Figure 10.13. To activate the View bar, follow these steps:

1. In the Gantt Chart view, right-click Gantt Chart at far left.

2. In the View list, select View Bar.

Some people don't like the View bar, because it takes up real estate on the screen and they feel that they have many other quick and easy ways to access views. I prefer the icons. You can always right-click the left side of the screen to select from the View list in any view.

Project offers additional views that don't appear on any drop-down list or view shortcuts. At the bottom of most of the drop-down lists for views is the More Views option; selecting it opens the More Views dialog, as shown in Figure 10.14.

FIGURE 10.14 More Views dialog

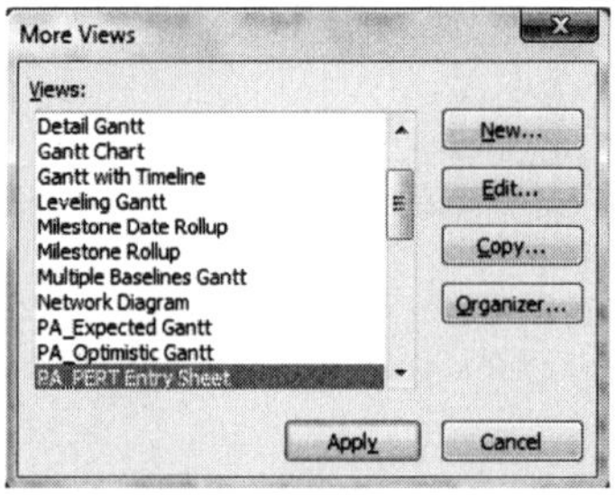

You can also create custom views (see Chapter 13, "Creating Custom Views, Formatting, and Reporting").

Timeline View

Project 2010 includes a Timeline view that provides a concise overview of the entire project. You can format the Timeline view to include rolled-up milestones, tasks, and decision points. After you format it, you can include it in presentations, emails, and other applications.

The timeline is displayed above other views by default. You can zero in on the timeline and display it by itself without the Gantt chart as follows:

1. Go to the Task tab ⮞ View group.
2. Click the drop-down list under the Gantt Chart button.
3. Click Timeline. The timeline is displayed. Click the Gantt Chart button to return to the Gantt Chart view.

You can easily add milestones and tasks to the Timeline view. Doing so is useful for creating meaningful reports and communications. As shown in Figure 10.15, you can add key milestones (or tasks) as follows:

1. While in the Gantt Chart view, select the milestone you want to add.
2. Right-click the milestone (or task).
3. From the context menu that opens, select Add to Timeline.

After you've added milestones (or tasks) to the timeline, you can format them. Formatting is covered in depth in Chapter 13, but I'll provide a quick overview here. Activate the Timeline view either by selecting it as described earlier or by clicking the timeline portion of the screen if you have it running above the Gantt chart. To format the milestones as shown in Figure 10.16, follow these steps:

1. In the Timeline view, select the Format tab. Remember, each view has its own format commands.

2. Click the milestone you want to format.

3. In the Font group, select an appropriate fill color for the milestone shape.

4. In the Font group, select an appropriate font for the text associated with the milestone.

5. Create a callout for tasks by clicking the task that has been added to the timeline and selecting Display as Callout from the Current Selection group.

FIGURE 10.15   Adding milestones (or tasks) to the Timeline view

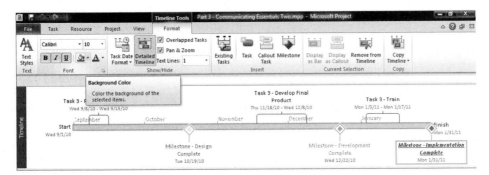

FIGURE 10.16   Formatting the timeline

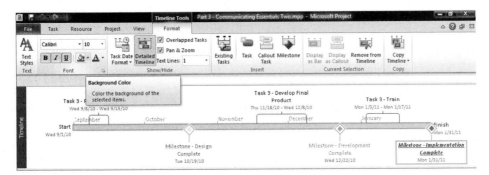

When you've formatted your timeline, you can send it in an email or place it in a presentation. Make sure you have the Timeline view active, and follow these steps:

1. Select Format tab ➢ Copy group ➢ Copy Timeline button.

2. From the drop-down list (as shown in Figure 10.17), click For E-mail, For Presentation, or Full Size.

FIGURE 10.17   Copying the timeline

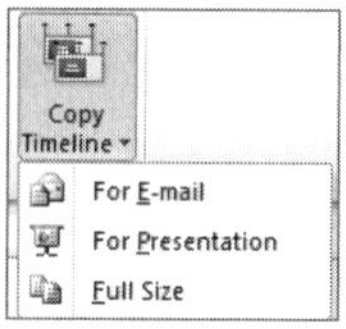

3. Go to the chosen application, and paste from the clipboard. You can continue to format the timeline using the features of the target application.

This technique works great for applications like PowerPoint or Outlook and is a communication tool that you'll find incredibly useful.

Task-Usage Views

Task Usage views are like cross-tab reports. They display data like work or costs across a specific timescale (by hour, day, week, month, and quarter). The Task Usage view provides a breakdown over time of how resources are being utilized based on the tasks they're assigned to.

Figure 10.18 shows an example with the timescale in quarters. You can quickly see how hours and costs are spread across the tasks and by what resources.

The default in Project is to show assigned work hours as the cross-tab data; but in the example in the figure, I added costs too. To add cost, follow these steps:

1. Select View tab ➢ Task Views group ➢ Task Usage view.

2. Click Format tab ➢ Details group ➢ Add Details button.

3. In the Detail Styles box, in the Available Fields list, click Cost.

4. Click the Show button, and then click OK, as shown in Figure 10.19.

You can also right-click in the time phase area directly under the details colum where it says 'work' and choose which details you want to include.

You can change the timescale by clicking the plus or minus symbol in the zoom slider at lower right.

In addition, you can edit assignments and work hours for each resource directly in the timescale area. This can be useful if you have to get into exact details of when a resource will work on a task. In Figure 10.20, I've modified Sean's work for the week, based on the hours he'll work each day.

FIGURE 10.18   Task Usage view

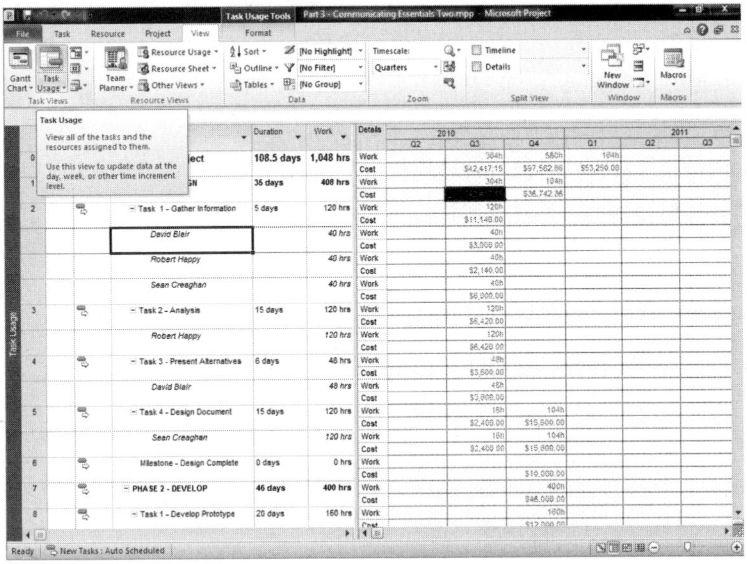

FIGURE 10.19   Adding details like cost to the Task Usage view

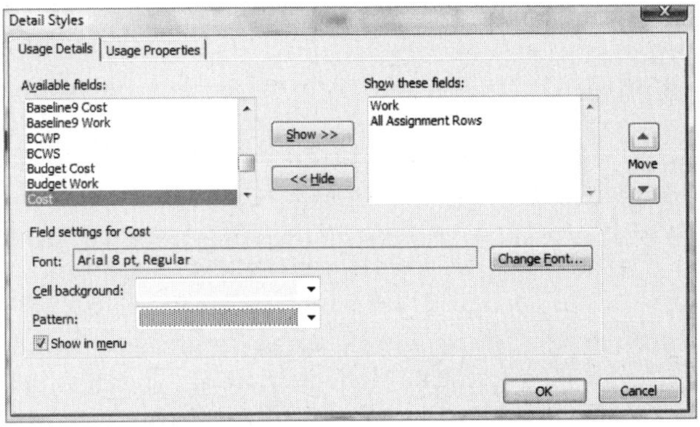

FIGURE 10.20   Modifying work assignments in the Task Usage view

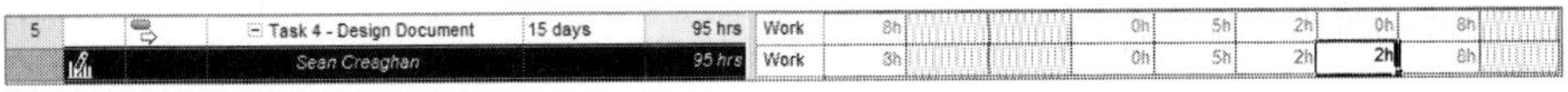

Notice that on some days, I assigned zero hours of work for this resource. A new symbol shows up in the Indicator column; it highlights the fact that the resource assignment has been contoured. Resource assignments are covered in detail in Chapter 8, "Assigning Resources and Costs"; but the Task Usage view is an excellent view to modify assignment details if you need to.

You can also have Project contour the assignments in this view. Figure 10.21 shows Project's many predefined contoured options. You can choose an automatic contour option by double-clicking the resource in the Task Usage view.

FIGURE 10.21  Resource contour options

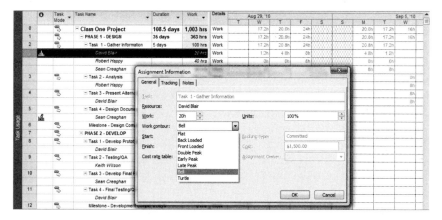

In this example, I've chosen to contour the work for David using a bell shape. The hours are automatically distributed for that specific task assignment, with fewer hours allocated up front, more hours in the middle, and time tapering off until the end, simulating the bell contour.

Network Diagram

Networking tasks means setting dependencies and defining task relationships in terms of links. You can look at dependencies and establish links in the network diagram. You've already been exposed to a basic network diagram in Chapter 7, "Setting Dependencies and the Critical Path."

In the network diagram, Project displays tasks as boxes with lines between them representing links or dependencies. The network diagram provides an excellent view of how a project tasks flow from beginning to end. In Figure 10.22, you can see how Phase 1 of the project flows. To launch the network diagram, follow these steps:

1. Go to the View tab ➢ Task Views group.

2. Click the Network Diagram button. You don't have to select the drop-down list to activate it.

You can scroll to the left and to the right to see how tasks flow. You can also collapse and expand phase-level boxes just as you do in the Gantt chart, by clicking the plus or minus button at the top of each summary box.

FIGURE 10.22   Network Diagram view

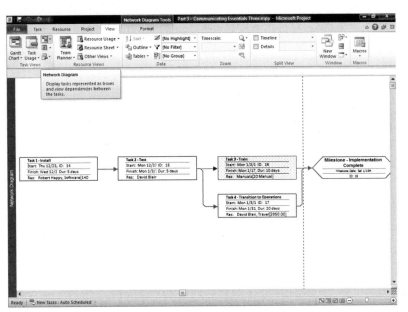

Collapse and Zoom

You can format the network diagram using the Format tab. For example, you may want to see more boxes on screen at one time. You can do this by selecting the Collapse Boxes command in conjunction with using the zoom slider as shown in Figure 10.23. Follow these steps:

1.   Select Format tab ➢ Display group ➢ Collapse Boxes button.

2.   At lower right, use the zoom slider's minus button to shrink the network to an appropriate size (you can use the plus button to increase the size).

Collapsing a box hides the box's detailed information, shrinks the box, and displays the ID number of the task.

FIGURE 10.23   Collapse boxes and zoom

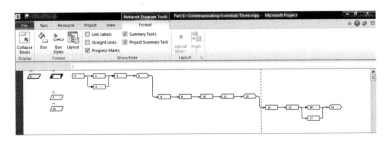

Modifying the Layout

You can also modify the layout of the network diagram to change its look and feel. For example, as shown in Figure 10.24, you can change things like layout mode, box layout, link style, link color, and diagram options. One interesting option changes the layout mode from automatic to manual. This allows you to manually click and drag a box and place it wherever you desire in the network diagram, even if a dependency is associated with it.

FIGURE 10.24   Network diagram layout options

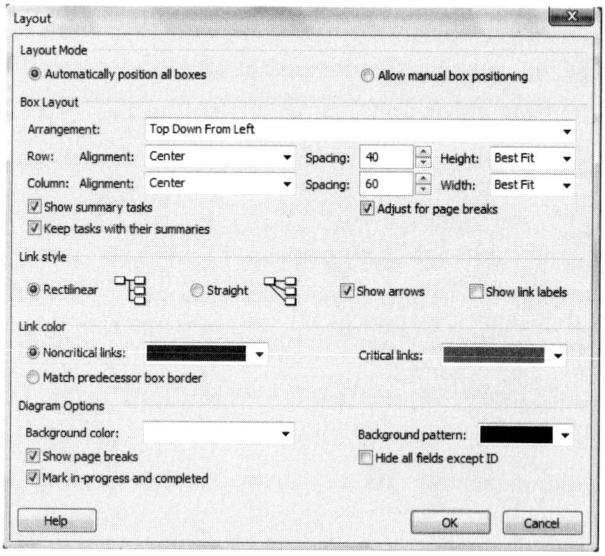

Setting Links and Inserting tasks

The network diagram is a visual place to set dependencies between tasks. After you've entered phases, tasks, and milestones, you can link tasks by clicking and dragging between the boxes, as shown in Figure 10.25.

If you make changes to tasks that affect the data or scheduling, those changes are reflected in all the other views, including the Gantt chart.

Calendar View

In the Calendar view, task information is displayed in a traditional calendar format, displaying the tasks across the days. As shown in Figure 10.26, you can view the calendar by month, by week, or by a custom date range that you set. To run the Calendar view, follow these steps:

1. In the View tab, go to the Task Views group.

2. Click the Calendar button to activate the Calendar view.

FIGURE 10.25   Setting dependencies and inserting new tasks

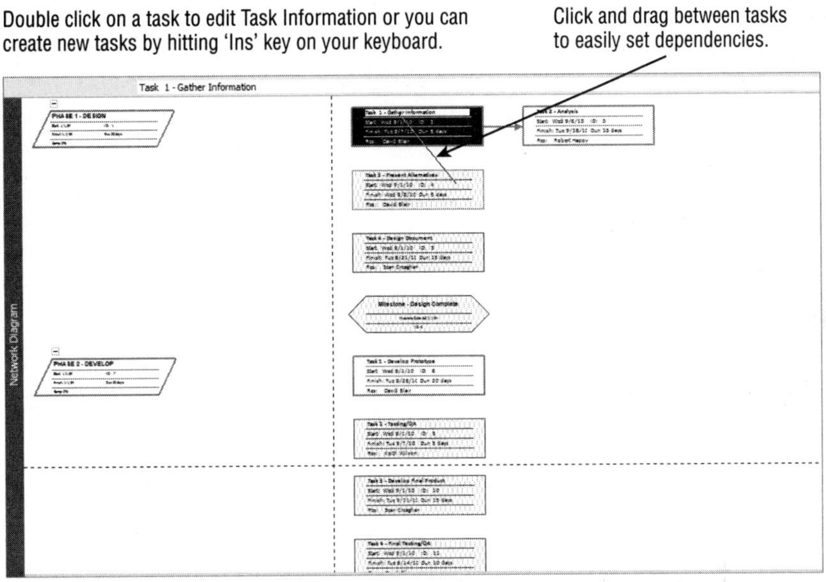

Double click on a task to edit Task Information or you can
create new tasks by hitting 'Ins' key on your keyboard.

Click and drag between tasks
to easily set dependencies.

FIGURE 10.26   Calendar view

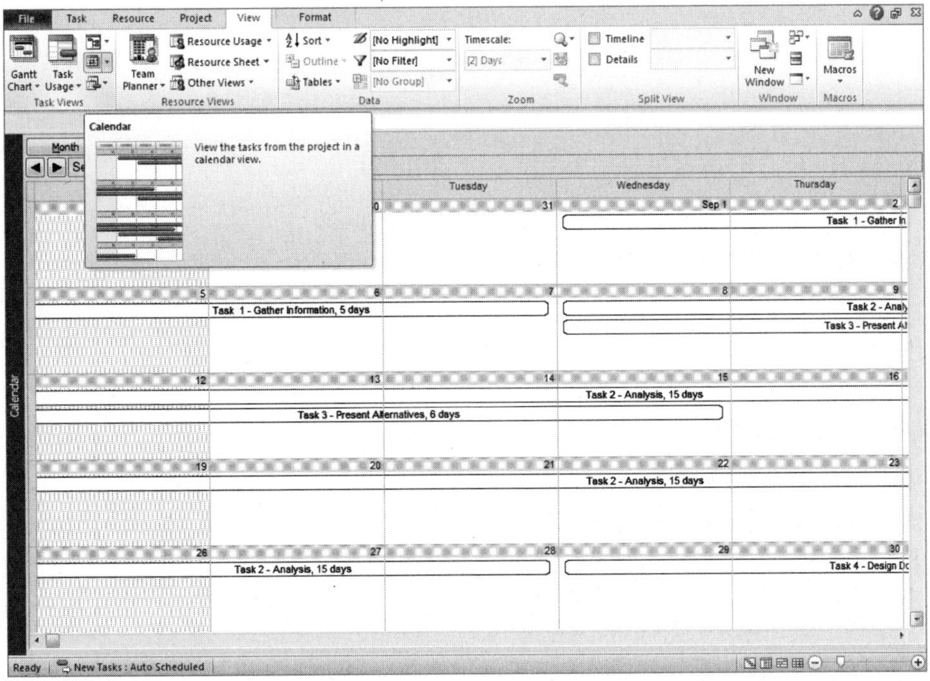

You can select a day and review the tasks for that day in a list, as shown in Figure 10.27. To see the list of tasks for a day in the Calendar view, follow these steps:

1. In the Calendar view, click the day you want to review.

2. Select Format tab ➤ Show/Hide group ➤ Task List button.

From the task list, you can double-click a task to review the details in the Task Information dialog box.

FIGURE 10.27   Reviewing the task list for a day

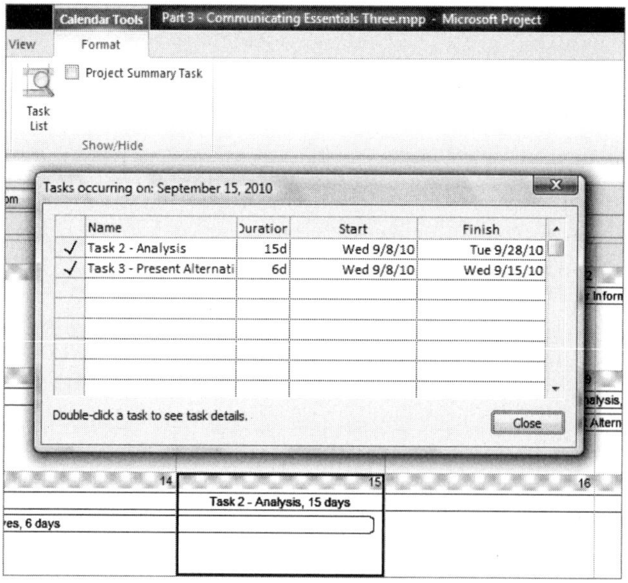

Resource Views

This section covers the main views that have resource information as their primary data focus. You can apply different tables, filters, and groups in resource views; but they're based on resource-specific fields (columns), which are different from task fields. The views covered in this section are as follows:

- Team planner
- Resource sheet
- Resource usage
- Resource form
- Resource graph

Team Planner View (Project Professional)

This view (discussed in Chapter 8) helps you assign resources to tasks and manage resource assignments effectively.

Traditionally, project planners have been tied to the process of assigning resources to tasks; but Team Planner view lets you analyze your resource allocations and assign tasks to resources. As shown in Figure 10.28, you can click and drag tasks up to the appropriate and available resource. You can even drop the task in the appropriate time slot, thus changing the start and finish dates of the task.

FIGURE 10.28   Clicking and dragging to assign tasks to resources

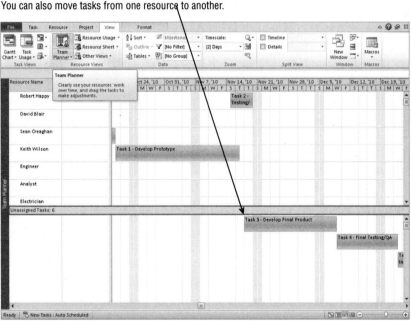

As discussed in Chapter 8, you can apply leveling for one resource at a time very effectively in the Team Planner view. In Chapter 14, "Creating Master Schedules with Inserted Projects," I cover how to apply these techniques across multiple projects.

Resource Sheet View

The Resource Sheet view is essential for resource planning. You can apply various filters, groups, and tables for more effective communication. For example, you may want to add new columns to display total work hours and costs for each resource, and then group by department to analyze how many hours and dollars you're spending across each department.

As shown in Figure 10.29, adding new columns is easy with the Add New Column option. Follow these steps:

1. Click View tab ➤ Resource Views group ➤ Resource Sheet button to activate the Resource Sheet view.

2. Scroll to the right of the table, and click Add New Column.

3. From the drop-down list, select Work; or enter **wo** to quick-pick from the list.

4. Repeat step 3 for Cost.

5. Click and drag the Work column heading to the left of Resource Name (or anywhere you prefer).

6. Repeat for the Cost column.

FIGURE 10.29   Inserting columns into the resource sheet

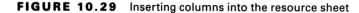

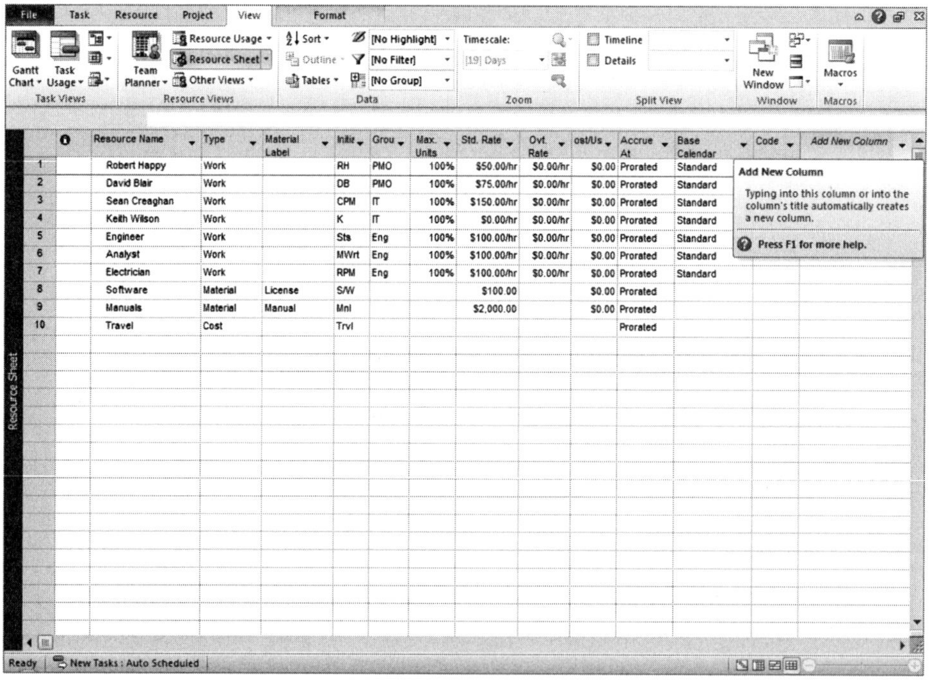

After adding the column you want to analyze, you can group by department using the Group function, as shown in Figure 10.30. Follow these steps:

1. In the Resource Sheet view, select the View tab.

2. In the Data Group, select Resource Group from the [No Group] drop-down list.

3. To clear the group, repeat the process but select [No Group].

FIGURE 10.30   Applying groups to resource sheets

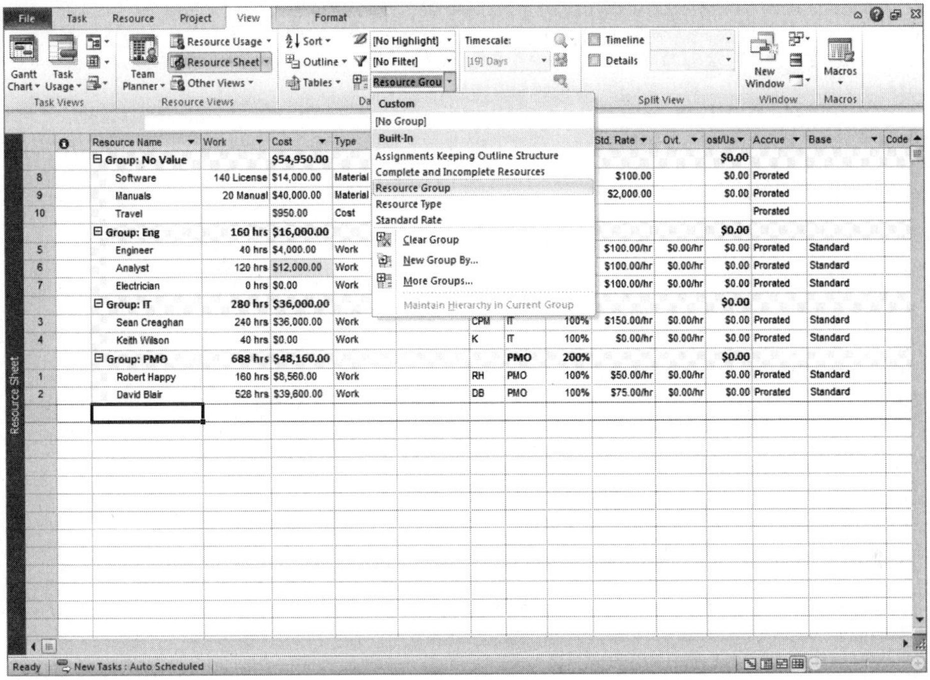

For the example in Figure 10.30, I filled the Group field in the resource sheet with department names for each resource. You can create a new custom field for this type of activity (see Chapter 11). I like to use the Group field to identify departments or groups within a department because Project has predefined filters and groups based on this field.

Resource Usage View

The Resource Usage view is similar to the Task Usage view: it's a cross-tab, time-phased type of view, but in this case the primary data driver is the resource name. The Resource Usage view lists the resource name first followed by each task assigned to that resource, versus the Task Usage view, which lists tasks first with associated resource assignments. The Resource Usage view is more useful for analyzing individual resource assignments. Chapter 14 covers how to review resource assignments across multiple projects.

As shown in Figure 10.31, you can view and analyze resource assignments in the Resource Usage view. Follow these steps:

1. Go to the View tab ➤ Resource Views group.

2. Click Resource Usage.

In Figure 10.31, you can see that David has been over-allocated: an exclamation symbol appears to the left of his name (and is colored red on the screen). The time-phased portion of the view shows where the over-allocations are occurring; you can see where to take corrective action such as resource leveling (see Chapter 8), reassigning that task to another person, or rescheduling the task manually. If you have Project Professional, you can manage this type of planning in the Team Planner view, which lets you click and drag tasks from one resource to another.

FIGURE 10.31 Resource Usage view

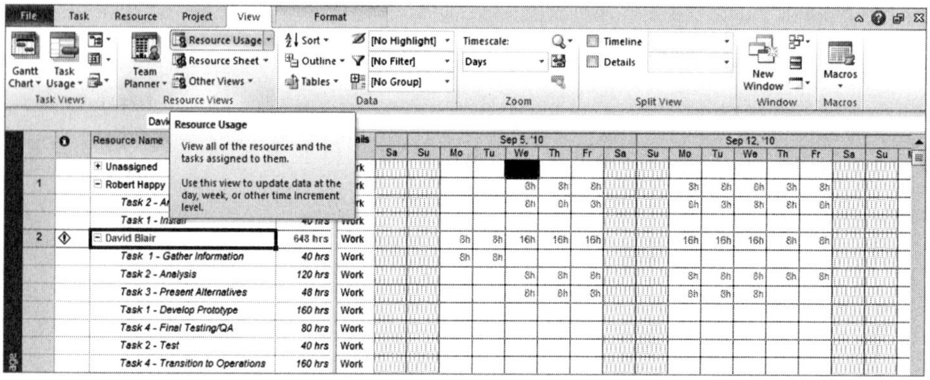

In the Resource Usage view, you can edit how hours are distributed directly in each time-phased cell, just as you can in the Task Usage view. In Figure 10.32, David's assignments are modified on a day-by-day basis to resolve the over-allocations.

FIGURE 10.32 Modifying a resource's work distribution

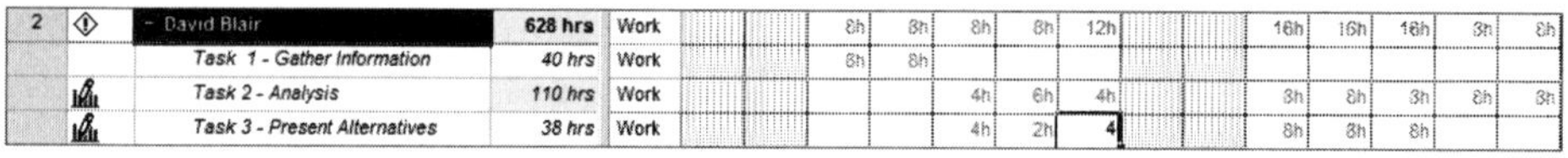

Resource Form

As with the Gantt chart, you can create split-screen views in resource views. But in a resource view, instead of bringing up the task form, Project brings up the Resource Form. The Resource Form provides details about each resource and which tasks have been assigned to it, as shown in Figure 10.33. To access the Resource Form in a split-screen view, follow these steps:

1. Turn on the Resource Sheet view (View tab ➤ Resource Views group ➤ Resource Sheet).

2. Select View tab ➤ Split View ➤ Details.

To run the Resource Form view by itself, follow these steps:

1. On the View tab, in the Resource Views group, click the Other Views drop-down list.

2. Select Resource Form. If you already have a split-screen view running, you may want to clear the Details check box in the Split View group.

FIGURE 10.33   Resource Form view

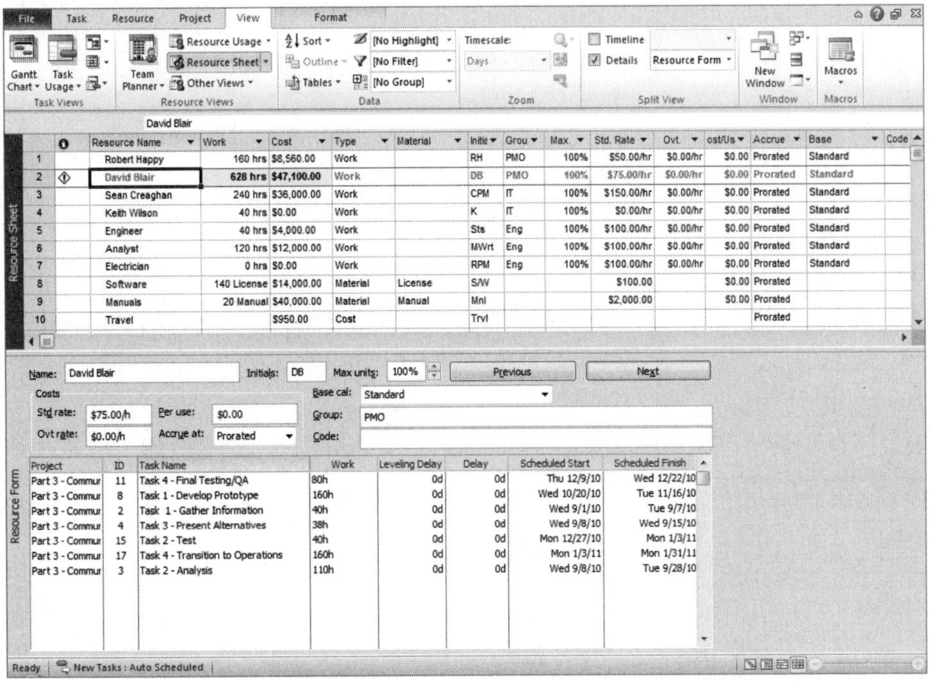

Resource Graph

The Resource Graph view lets you look at how a resource has been allocated over time in comparison to its Max Units line. Max Units, as discussed in Chapter 8, is the line Project uses to determine if a resource has been over-allocated. If it has been, Project turns the resource and over-allocated assignments red. Typically, a resource's Max Units value is 100%, representing 1 unit or 1 person.

Running the Resource Graph in conjunction with the Resource Form as a combination view lets you analyze where over-allocations are taking place in a more visual manner, as shown in Figure 10.34. Follow these steps:

1. Select View tab ➤ Resource Views group ➤ Other Views drop-down list ➤ Resource Graph.

2. In the Split View group, select the Details check box.

3. Use the scroll bar at lower left in the Resource Graph view to change from one resource to another.

FIGURE 10.34 Resource Graph view

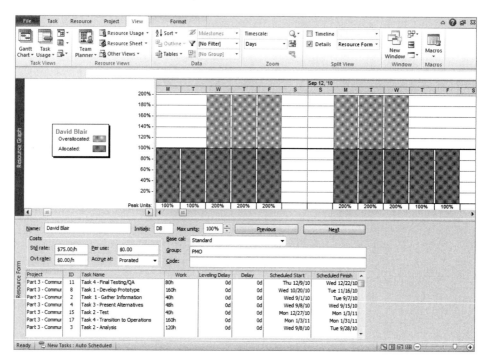

Summary

In this chapter, you learned about the primary views in Project that you can use to better manage projects and communicate project information. Communicating projects in different ways to different stakeholders largely depends on the types of views you use as the basis of your reporting.

There are two basic types of views: one for tasks and one for resources. Each view has its own set of formatting tools on the Format tab, and these commands and functions change as you move from one view to another. While in each view, you can apply different tables, filters, groups, sorts, and custom fields, as covered in more detail in Chapters 11 through 14. In Chapter 14, you'll learn how to create custom views tailored toward your specific communication needs.

Hands-On Exercises

The following hands-on exercises are designed to test your understanding of the topics discussed in this chapter. We've provided files on the companion CD that will show you what your project file should look like as you perform these exercises.

EXERCISE 10

Applying Different Views

1. On the View tab, in the Task Views area:

   a. Click each of the task views.

   b. In the Split View group, select and deselect Details.

2. On the View tab, in the Resource Views area:

   a. Click each of the resource views.

   b. In the Split View group, select and deselect Details.

3. At lower right on screen, in the status bar, click the four view shortcuts.

4. While in the Gantt Chart view, right-click Gantt Chart at far left to bring up the View list.

5. Select View Bar.

6. Repeat to unselect View Bar.

Chapter

11

Using Tables and Custom Fields

IN THIS CHAPTER, YOU'LL LEARN ABOUT THE FOLLOWING:

✓ Creating custom fields

✓ Using formulas and graphical indicators

✓ Using and creating custom tables

Chapter 10 discussed using various views in Project to control how you look at project information. In this chapter, you'll learn about how to control what you see in each view by customizing both fields and tables. An important aspect of each view is determining what fields and columns are displayed to help meet your communication and reporting needs.

Creating Custom Fields

Project lets you customize fields for more effective project planning, tracking, and reporting. Each field can be applied in various views such as tables, filters, groups, and sorts. Figure 11.1 illustrates the types of fields you can customize. You can access the Custom Fields dialog box in most of the task views, such as the Gantt Chart and Task Usage views, and most of the resource views, such as the Resource Sheet and Resource Usage views. Follow these steps:

1. Go to Format tab ➤ Column group.
2. Click the Custom Fields button. This may not be available in all views, such as the Team Planner view and the Network Diagram view.

As you can see in Figure 11.1, you can customize a variety of different types of fields, for both task views and resource views. Table 11.1 lists the field types with the number of fields available for each type. The same number of fields are available for resource views and assignment views as well.

TABLE 11.1   Available Custom Fields

Field Type	Number of Fields per View Type	Data Type
Cost	10	Formatted in $
Date	10	Formatted using date from option settings
Start	10	Formatted using date from option settings
Finish	10	Formatted using date from option settings

TABLE 11.1   Available Custom Fields *(continued)*

Field Type	Number of Fields per View Type	Data Type
Flag	20	Yes or No
Number	20	Unformatted numbers
Text	30	Unformatted text
Outline codes	20	Formatted from outline data in hierarchical structure

FIGURE 11.1   Custom Fields dialog box

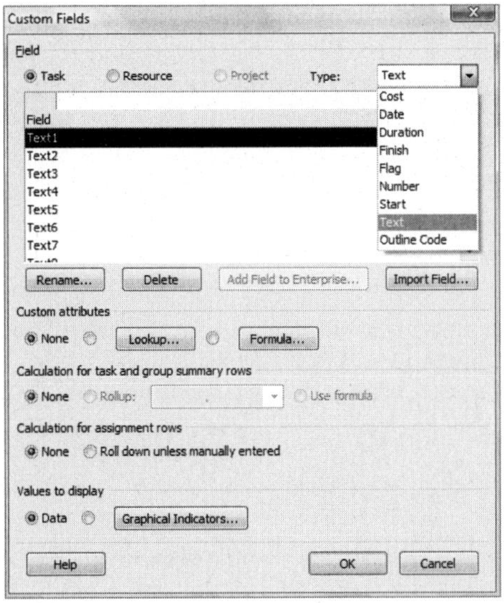

The text fields and number fields offer the greatest flexibility due to their unformatted structure. That's why there are more of them to customize. Flag fields are next, with the rest following.

Custom Text Fields

Custom text fields are versatile. You can rename a field, such as changing Text1 to Comments, or you can make fields more complex with lookup tables, formulas, and graphical indicators.

Renaming a Field

If you want to use a text field for a specific purpose across the project in tables, filters, groups, or sorts, you can rename it without adding formulas or lookup tables. The example in Figure 11.2 renames Text1 to Comments. It can then be used in a custom table to create a column where you can freely enter comments about a specific task.

FIGURE 11.2   Renaming a custom field

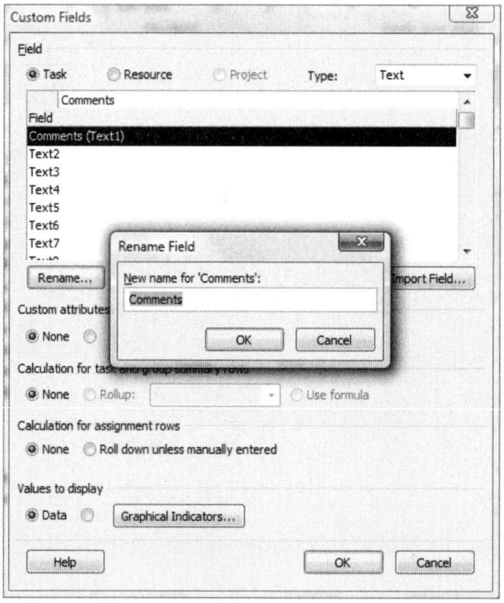

Follow these steps to rename a field:

1.   In the Gantt Chart view, go to Format tab ➤ Columns group, and click Custom Fields.

2.   In the Custom Fields dialog box, under Field, be sure Task is selected (it should be by default).

3.   In the Type drop-down list, select Text.

4.   Click Text1 in the Field list (or click any other text field you want to change).

5.   Click the Rename button below the Field list.

6.   In the Rename Field dialog box, enter the custom name for this field, and click OK (in this example, enter **Comments**).

7.   Click OK again.

The customized text field is now ready to be inserted into any task-view table or used for filtering, grouping, or sorting. You can even place the field in the bar area to the left, right, top, bottom, or inside of a Gantt bar. This is covered in more detail in Chapter 13, "Creating Custom Views, Formatting and Reporting." Later in this chapter, I discuss how to insert these types of fields into a custom table.

Creating a Lookup Table

Each field may also have a lookup table, displayed as a drop-down list associated with the custom field, which allows users to select from that custom list. Let's create a lookup table for a custom field to capture Task Finish Status (see Figure 11.3).

Follow these steps to create a lookup table:

1. Rename Text2 field to **Task Finish Status**, following steps 1–7 in the section "Renaming a Field."

2. Under Custom Attributes in the Custom Fields dialog box, click the Lookup button.

3. In the Edit Lookup Table dialog box, under Value, enter the first item to be included in the drop-down list—for example, **On Time**—and press Enter.

4. Repeat step 3 for additional items: for example, **At Risk** and **Late**.

5. Optionally, enter a description for each value in the list. For example, the description for On Time is **Going According to Plan**.

6. Select a value as the default by selecting Use a Value from the Table as the Default Entry for the Field check box and clicking the Set Default button.

7. Review other options, such as display order and data entry options.

8. Click Close, and then click OK.

FIGURE 11.3 Creating a custom lookup table

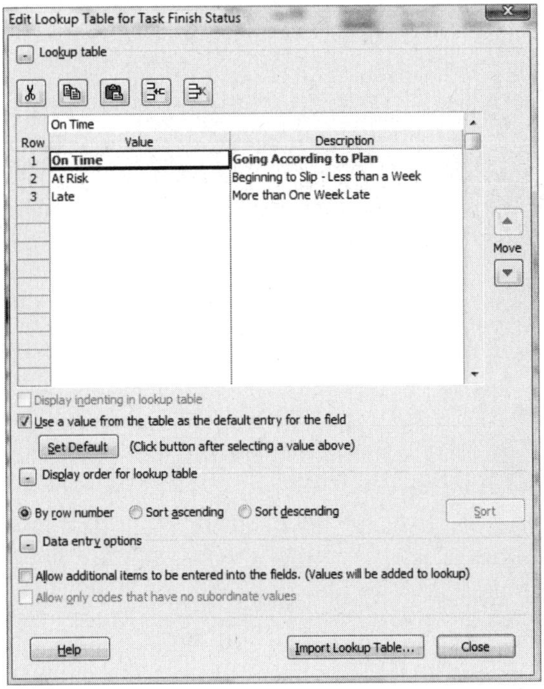

The example shown in Figure 11.3 assigns On Time as the default value to be entered into the field automatically, which is why it's bold and blue in Project. When you add the field to a table, On Time will display by default. If you don't choose a default, the field will appear blank until you select a value from the drop-down list.

Applying a Graphical Indicator

After you've created a lookup table, you can associate a graphical indicator with each value instead of a word. When the value is selected, a graphical image will appear, such as a red light, yellow light, or green light. There are many graphical indicators to choose from. Note that you can associate graphical indicators with both lookup table values and formula values (discussed in the next section). If you attach a graphical indicator to a lookup table, it's more manually driven; applying graphical indicators to a formula is automatically driven. In other words, if you use a lookup table, you select the value from a drop-down list which represents the graphical indicator. You control it via your selection. If the graphical indicator is associated with a formula, then it will change automatically based on the value driven from the formula, which means you do not have to select anything after it has been set-up.

The example shown in Figure 11.4 attaches graphical indicators to the lookup table you created for the Task Finish Status field. To apply graphical indicators to values in a custom field with a lookup table, follow these steps:

1. Rename a custom field as described in the section "Renaming a Field."

2. Create a custom lookup table as described in the previous section, "Creating a Lookup Table."

3. In the Custom Fields dialog box, under Values to Display, click the Graphical Indicators button.

4. In the Graphical Indicators dialog box, in the first empty field below Test for "Task Finish Status," click the drop-down list.

5. Select Equals.

6. In the Value(s) field, enter **On Time**.

7. In the Image field, click the drop-down list, and select an appropriate indicator. In this case, choose a green light.

8. Repeat steps 4 through 7 for **At Risk** and **Late**.

9. In the Indicator Criteria For area, you can optionally define graphical indicators for summary rows and project summary rows.

10. Click OK, and click OK again.

Take the time to review the Image drop-down list to see options for indicators. If you scroll to the bottom, you'll see a different version of the green, yellow, and red lights with happy and not-so-happy faces.

FIGURE 11.4   Applying graphical indicators

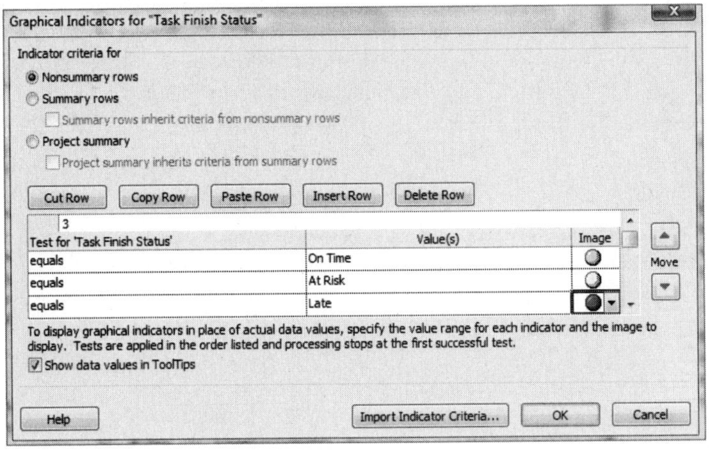

Real World Scenario

Automatic vs. Manual Indicators

Recently, working with a client on a large IT project, we created an automatic graphical indicator that displayed a green light if a task was on time or early, a yellow light if it was up to one week late, and a red light if it was more than one week late. This formula was based on setting baselines.

After a few iterations, the project managers were fine with the red light; but if the red light was acceptable over time, or if a plan was in place to fix the problem, the project managers wanted the option to change the indicator. In this case, we created a custom field called PM Perception, which allowed them to manually override or complement the automatic indicator with a green light beside it.

Over the years, I've noticed that if the green light indicator is always manually driven by the project manager, there is a tendency to have more green lights even if some should be red.

Creating a Formula

You can also create a formula for a custom field. Formulas can range from very simple to incredibly complex. I've used formulas to determine cost or schedule overruns. I've used complex formulas to create indicators for task-finish status and budget status. And I've used simple formulas to create indicators for things like finish status. Maybe you want to add a burdening rate to your costs and include that in your cost total; you can multiply cost by 15% and add the result to the total cost.

Project lets you apply formulas in many ways. The following example is a simple formula using finish variance and a graphical indicator to create a custom Stoplight field. As shown in Figure 11.5, you can select various fields and functions to be included in formulas.

To create a custom field using a formula, follow these steps:

FIGURE 11.5   Creating a custom formula

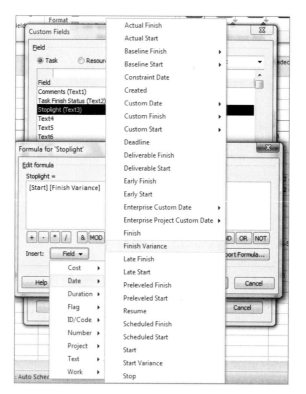

Rename Field

1. In the Gantt Chart view, go to Format tab ➤ Columns group, and click Custom Fields.
2. In the Custom Fields dialog box, under Field, be sure Task is selected (it should be by default).
3. In the Type drop-down list, select Text.
4. Click Text3 in the Field list (or any other text field you want to change).
5. Click the Rename button below the Field list.
6. In the Rename Field dialog box, enter the custom name for this field, and click OK. In this example, enter **Stoplight**.

Add Formula

1. Under Custom Attributes in the Custom Fields dialog box, click the Formula button.

2. In the Formula dialog box, beside Insert, click the Field drop-down list.

3. Scroll to Date, and select Finish Variance from the list.

4. Click OK.

Apply Graphical Indicators

1. Under Values to Display in the Custom Fields dialog box, click the Graphical Indicators button.

2. In the Graphical Indicators dialog box, in the first empty field below Test for "Stoplight," click the drop-down list.

3. Select "is less than or equal to."

4. In the Value(s) field, enter 0 (zero).

5. In the Image field, click the drop-down list, and select an appropriate indicator. In this case, choose a green light.

6. In the next empty field below Test for "Stoplight," click the drop-down list, and select "is greater than."

7. In the Value(s) field, enter 0 (zero).

8. In the Image field, click the drop-down list, and choose a red light.

9. Click OK, and click OK again.

When you insert this column into a table, it has green light indicators unless the finish variance is greater than 0, in which case the indicator automatically turns red. In this example, the indicator is either green or red, with no yellow or other indicator options. You can build in various other indicators based on different test values or values from formulas and add them in the graphical indicator value fields.

Figure 11.6 is an example of a much more complex formula that is designed to turn on a graphical indicator based on the following criteria:

- Green = On time or early

- Yellow = Delayed up to two days

- Red = Delayed past two days

- Dash = No baseline set

- Checkmark = Completed

This formula was created by my long-time colleague David Blair, who creates custom fields such as this in response to client requests. This formula is on the attached CD as a Project file, Formula Task Finish Status for 2010.mpp.

Figure 11.7 shows how the graphical indicators are set up. The values in the graphical indicators are associated with the values in the formula, and the duration values are calculated in minutes. That is where the value of 960 comes from: there are 480 working minutes in 1 day (8 hours × 60 minutes), and you multiply that by 2 to get the total for 2 days.

FIGURE 11.6 Complex formula for finish status

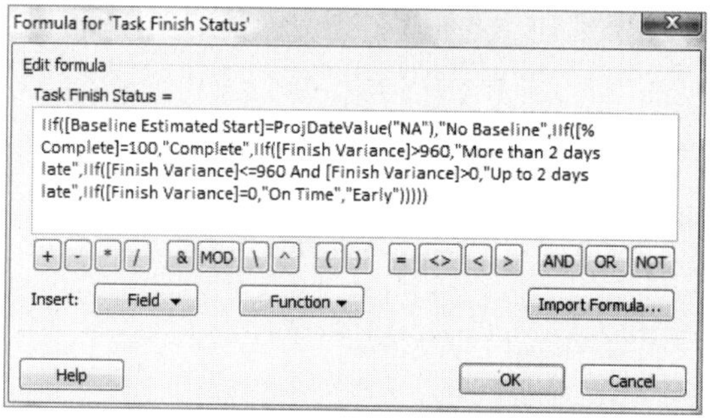

FIGURE 11.7 Task Finish Status graphical indicators

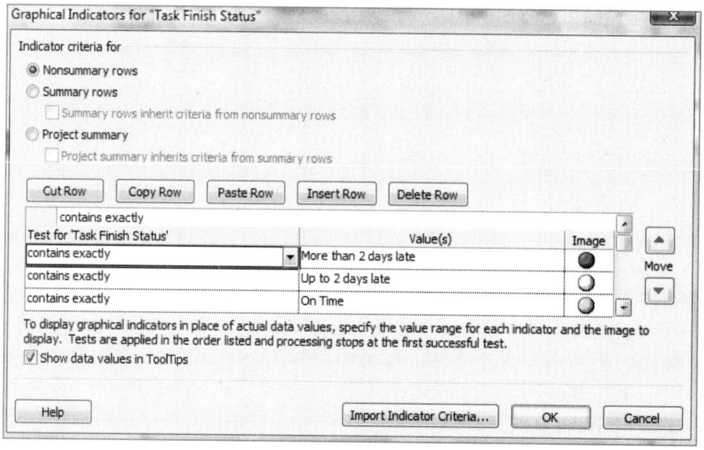

Figure 11.8 shows the final result in Project when the Task Finish Status indicator is included in the table.

I included an indicator for Early because some clients I've worked with prefer to have a different color indicator if a task is coming in early. One client used a blue stoplight.

FIGURE 11.8 Task Finish Status example

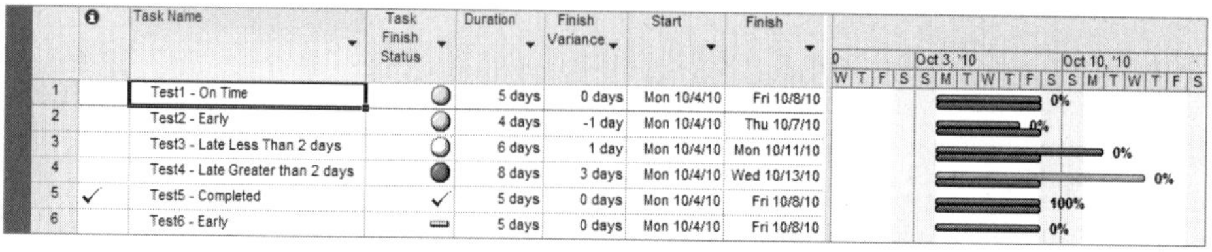

⊕ Real World Scenario

Graphical Indicator Example: Tasks that Need Updating

I worked with a client that typically held project-review meetings weekly for a strategic project to launch a new product. The project plan was complex, and the current version (in Project) was projected on a screen. Part of the meeting was spent reviewing current updates and changes to the schedule; but after the first meeting, the client was having trouble identifying tasks that weren't updated but needed to be.

The client wanted a visual way to flag tasks that didn't receive any updates if they were past due and were forgotten or needed attention. One of my company team members made a custom field called Needs Updating, which was a combination of a formula and graphical indicator designed to literally place a red flag beside any task that was left off the current status update but not done—in other words, tasks from the past that hadn't been updated yet.

Over time, all the project managers began to rely on that field to help them quickly identify which tasks needed updating, so they could prepare for project-review meetings. I continue to use that field in every significant project I work on.

If you use a formula, you must also determine how you want the task or group summary rows to behave with regard to the formula. You can select None, use a roll-up, or apply the formula you've created. You can find this setting in the middle of the Custom Fields dialog box (see Figure 11.1).

Other Custom Fields

Other custom fields are available, as follows.

Custom Flags

You may find it useful to use flag fields to help filter out a specific set of milestones or tasks that otherwise don't meet any predefined condition. Flag fields automatically create a yes/no choice or Boolean condition to allow only one of two options. For example, quite often I create dashboard-type views that are based on only four or five key milestones (not all the milestones) for each project, which can be rolled up and formatted for one project or across multiple projects. I create four or five flag fields that represent whether a particular milestone type should be included in the roll-up.

Other examples include filtering tasks by a specific functional area if they don't match the filter for resource assignments or resource group. You can flag those tasks and create a custom filter that only displays those tasks. I cover filtering with flags and other fields in

Chapter 12, "Using Filters, Groups, and Sorts"; but sometimes you need to create the custom fields first.

To customize a flag field (see Figure 11.9), follow these steps:

FIGURE 11.9   Custom flag fields

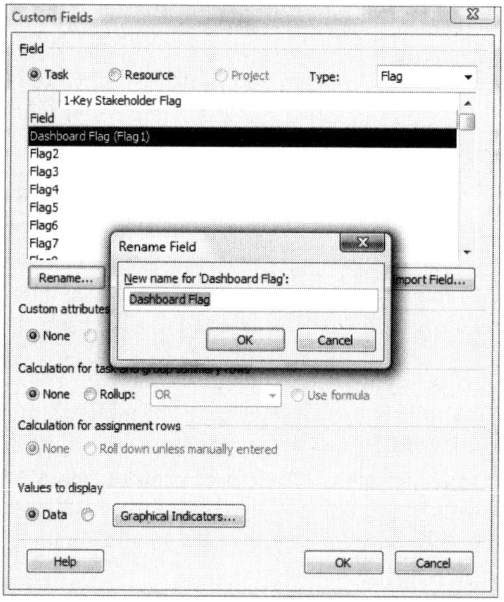

1. In the Gantt Chart view, go to Format tab ➤ Columns group, and click Custom Fields.
2. In the Custom Fields dialog box, under Field, be sure Task is selected (it should be by default).
3. In the Type drop-down list, select Flag.
4. Click Flag1 in the Field list (or any other flag field you want to change).
5. Click the Rename button below the Field list.
6. In the Rename Field box, enter the custom name for this field, and click OK. In the example, enter **Dashboard**.

You can add graphical indicators to flag fields by adding an image for Yes and an image for No. I've used this approach to call out a series of tasks with a graphical indicator—for example, to identify tasks that may have an external dependency to another project before setting up cross-project links.

Remaining Field Types

You can develop custom number fields the same way as custom text fields, with lookup tables or formulas, and combine them with graphical indicators. Custom outline fields are slightly different in that they can contain a hierarchy structure, such as for an organizational structure.

Custom dates and duration fields are self-explanatory; they allow you to have various start and finish dates if you want to use them for alternative schedules within one plan.

Finally, you can use custom cost fields to create different cost versions or to enter cost data manually regardless of the resources assigned. If you use custom cost fields, they aren't included in the calculation for the core cost field used to calculate total costs.

Using Tables and Creating Custom Tables

Project comes equipped with many useful predefined tables for planning and tracking project information. It is worthwhile to explore these tables to see if they can meet some of your immediate needs. You can also create as many custom tables to support more precisely your planning, tracking, and reporting needs. In this section you will learn how to use existing tables and create new custom ones.

Using Existing Tables

As discussed in Chapter 10, "Understanding Views," tables are an essential part of views. If you think of a view as how you look at project information, you can think of tables as the information you see in that view. Project comes equipped with many predefined tables for both task views and resource views, each consisting of a set of columns that displays project data based on the type of field.

It's worthwhile to take the time to explore the various tables that are available for you to use and to understand how to control the settings for each column and even add columns on the fly.

Task View Tables

Many task-centric views are available in Project, and most of them come with a variety of built-in tables. A *table* is a set of columns driven by the fields you want to display, which can be either off the shelf or customized. You can modify existing tables or create new ones. This section focuses on how to change tables depending on the type of view you're in.

The default table in the Gantt Chart view is the Entry table. It focuses on key fields you can use to enter project information when building plans. It may not be the best table to use for communicating to stakeholders; therefore, it's important to understand how to change tables and how to create custom tables.

To change tables in a task view like the Gantt chart, follow these steps (see Figure 11.10):

1. Select View tab ➢ Data group ➢ Tables drop-down list ➢ a table such as Tracking.

2. Repeat for each built-in table.

3. To return to the default, select Entry.

The table list is divided into two main parts: one for custom tables and one for built-in tables. This helps you differentiate between the tables that come with Project and tables you've developed.

FIGURE 11.10 Changing tables

At the bottom of the list, you can reset the table to default, view more prebuilt tables, or save a current table under a custom name that you may have modified. If you select More Tables from the bottom of the Tables list, you see an even longer list of built-in tables that doesn't display in the initial menu (see Figure 11.11). You can find other tables for things such as earned value, which is covered in Chapter 17, "Variance Analysis and Taking Corrective Action." You can review this list and create new tables from the More Tables dialog box (See "Creating Custom Tables" later in this chapter).

FIGURE 11.11 The More Tables dialog box

Figure 11.12 shows the Tracking table, which is useful for recording actuals.

Figure 11.13 shows the Variance table, which comes in handy when you set a baseline and want to look for start or finish variances (covered in detail in Chapter 16, "Updating and Tracking Status").

Figure 11.14 shows more details about Work, a table to use if you need to more closely track work hours for each task and resource.

As you can see, built-in tables may be useful for more effective planning, tracking, or reporting. Take the time to review the existing tables before you start creating new ones.

FIGURE 11.12   Tracking table

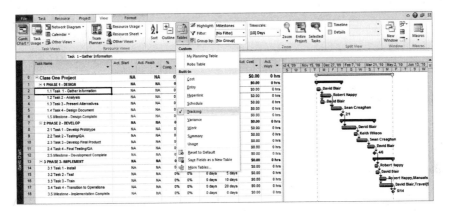

FIGURE 11.13   Variance table

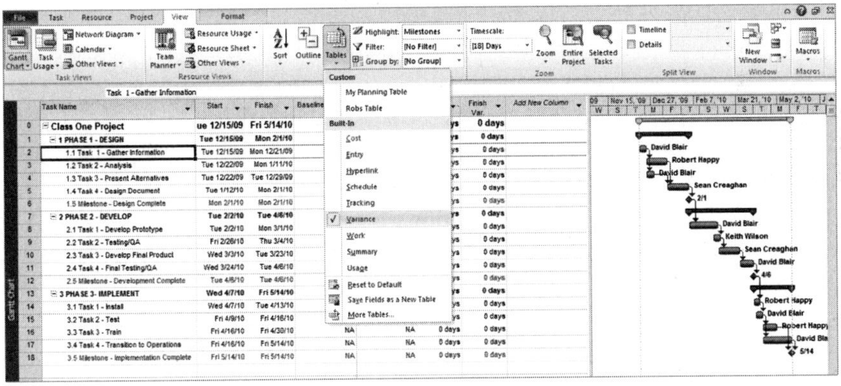

FIGURE 11.14   Work table

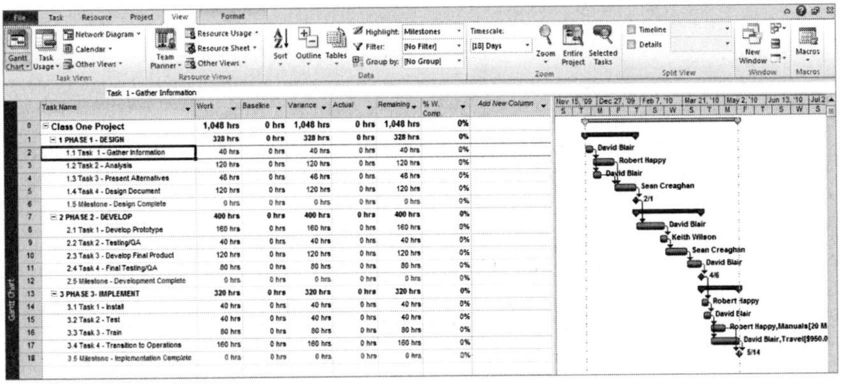

You can apply these tables in various views as well. For example, Figure 11.15 shows the same Work table, but this time in the Task Usage view. This can provide excellent insight into how resource work has been distributed over time on each task.

FIGURE 11.15   Work table in the Task Usage view

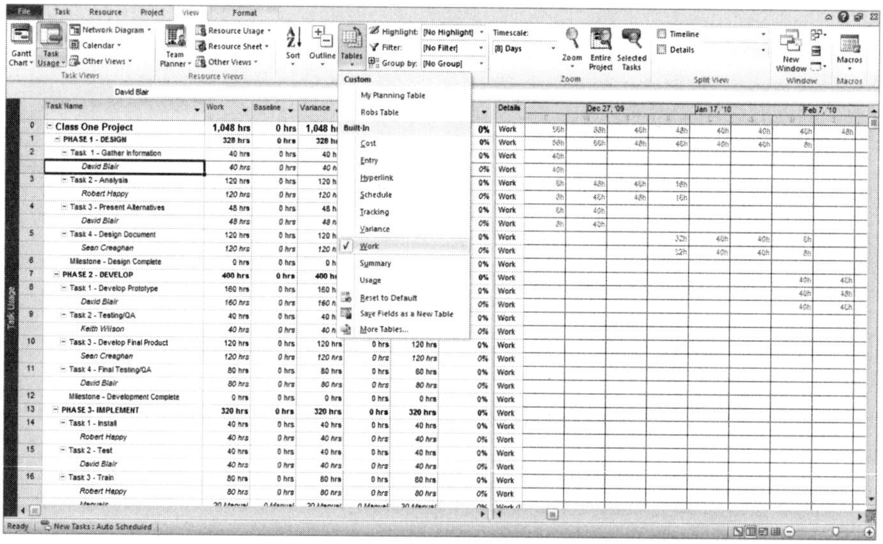

Tables don't work with views where they don't make sense. For example, the Calendar view, Network Diagram view, and Timeline view aren't based on tables, so no tables apply to these views.

Resource View Tables

There are also many built-in tables for resource views. To change tables in a resource view such as the Resource Sheet (see Figure 11.16), follow these steps:

1. Select View tab ➤ Resource Views group ➤ Resource Sheet.
2. Select View tab ➤ Data group ➤ Tables drop-down list ➤ a table such as Cost.
3. Repeat for each built-in table.
4. To return to the default, select Entry.

The table is composed of columns (fields), as task tables are, except the list of fields to select as columns isn't identical. Task tables have task fields, and resource tables have resource fields.

Figure 11.17 is an example of the Work table applied in the Resource Sheet view.

Figure 11.18 is an example of the Cost table applied in a Resource Usage view. To change to Task Usage view, click the Task Usage button in the View tab ➤ Resource Views group.

FIGURE 11.16   Changing tables in a resource view

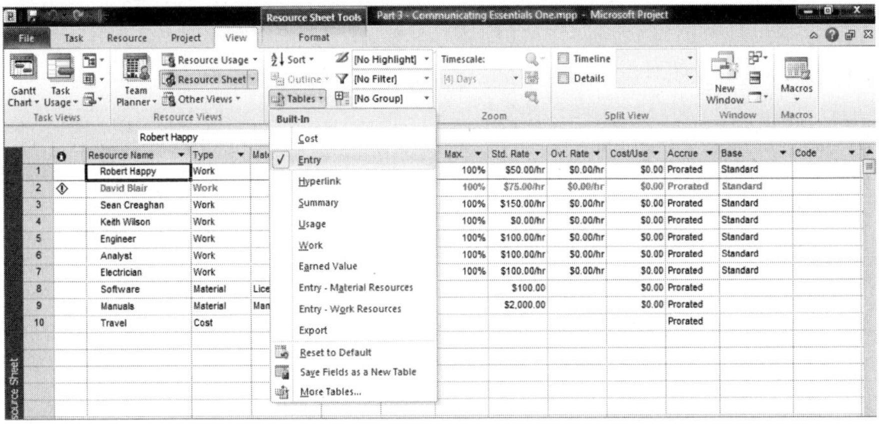

FIGURE 11.17   Work table in the Resource Sheet

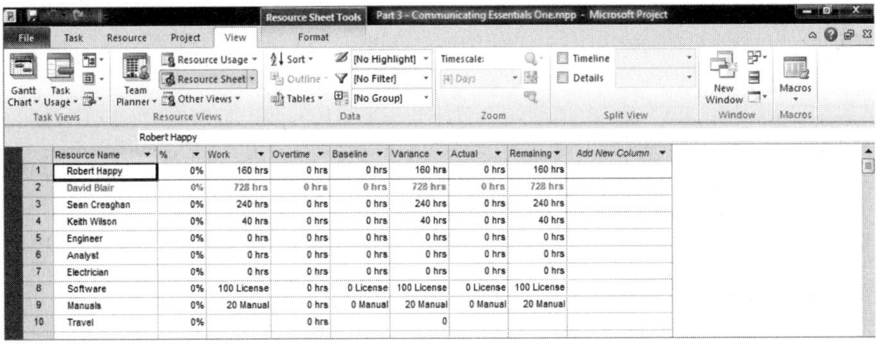

The Resource Usage view in Figure 11.18 not only displays work in the timescale (time-phased) portion of the view but also shows cost. To add cost, right-click in the Details area of the view (or anywhere in the left part of the screen, under the timescale), and select Cost in the list that appears.

Tables don't apply to all resource views. For example, the Team Planner view, the Resource Graph, and the Resource Form don't work with tables, because they're constructed with different components.

Creating Custom Tables

Project makes it easy to create custom tables whether you are modifying existing tables or creating new ones from scratch.

FIGURE 11.18   Cost table in the Resource Usage view

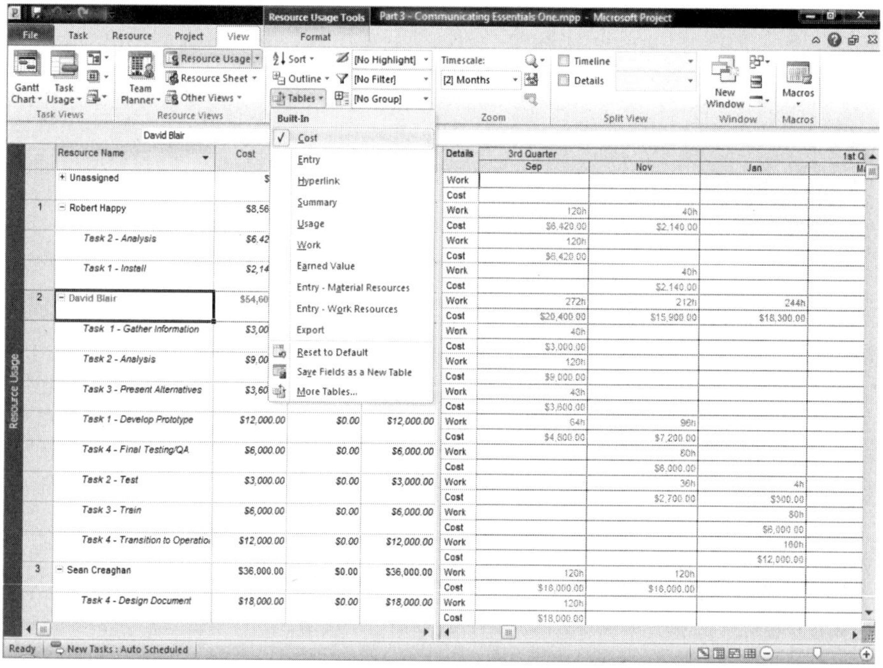

Adding Columns to Existing Tables

You can add columns to existing tables on the fly with the Add Columns feature. At the end of every table is an extra column named Add New Column; it allows you to quickly add as many new columns as you want to any table.

As shown in Figure 11.19, you can turn this feature on or off by following these steps:

1.   Go to Format tab ➢ Columns group.

2.   From the Column Settings drop-down list, select or deselect Display Add New Column.

By default, this option is selected; and Add New Column appears at the end (to the right) of every table in both task and resource views. To add new columns using this feature, as shown in Figure 11.20, follow these steps:

1.   In the Gantt Chart view (or any view with a table), find Add New Column at the end of the table.

2.   Click the drop-down arrow to the right of the column name.

3.   Either scroll down the list to select a field or type in the first few letters of the field name to make a quick pick.

4.   Click the column heading, and drag and drop the column at your desired location.

FIGURE 11.19   Displaying Add New Column

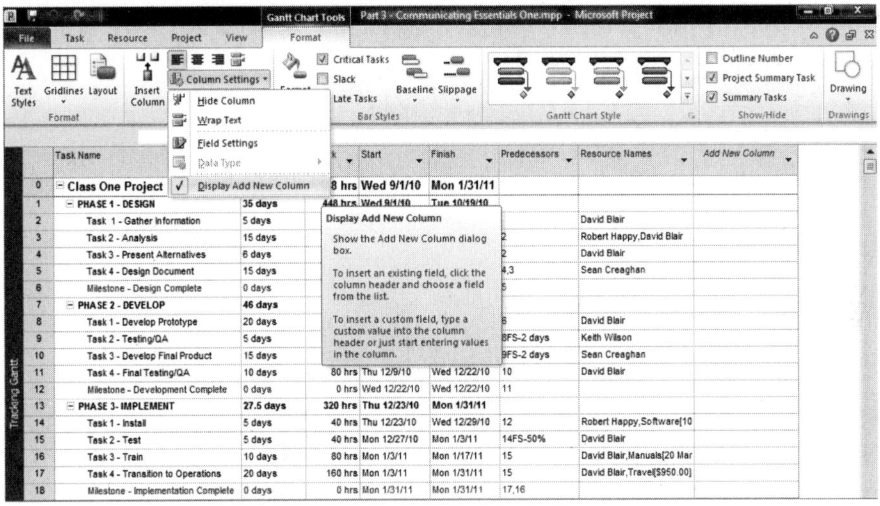

FIGURE 11.20   Adding a new column

Click on the drop-down arrow beside Add New
Column. You can either scroll down the list or start
typing the first letters of the field for a quick pick.

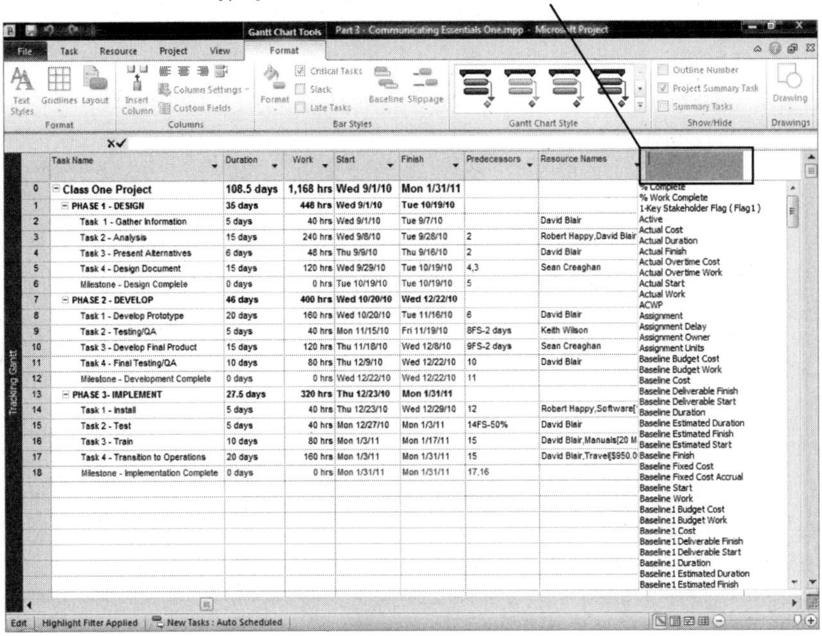

If you start typing data into a blank field under the column heading, Project automatically adds a new custom-formatted column based on the type of data you enter (see Figure 11.21). For example, if you enter **On Time**, a new text field is added automatically; if you enter **$1000**, a new cost field is added automatically.

FIGURE 11.21   Auto-creating new custom fields

As you type in data in a blank field under "Add New Column", Project will automatically select a custom column format based on the type of data you enter.

Column Settings

After you've added columns to your table, you can modify the column settings. You can click and drag columns to reposition them in the table, and you can also control other settings.

You can change column settings such as Wrap Text for any column heading in your table. In the example in Figure 11.22, I added a new text field automatically by typing text data directly into an empty field under Add New Column, as illustrated in Figure 11.21. To allow for text wrapping, follow these steps:

1. Click the cell or column you want to format.

2. Select Format tab ➢ Columns group ➢ Column Setting drop-down list ➢ Wrap Text.

Figure 11.23 shows the table with wrapped text turned on. You can also right-click the cell or column and select Wrap Text from the context menu. Directly above the Column Settings button in the Columns group, you can align data and click the shortcut button for Wrap Text.

You can customize the title of any column at any time using the Column Settings. In the example shown in Figure 11.24, I've customized the title of the new text field to Comments. Follow these steps:

1. Click the column heading you want to customize.

2. Select Format tab ➢ Columns group ➢ Column Settings ➢ Field Settings.

4. In the Field Settings dialog box, in the Title field, enter the custom name for this field in this table. Note: the custom title applies to this table only.

5. Click OK.

FIGURE 11.22   Column settings and wrapping text

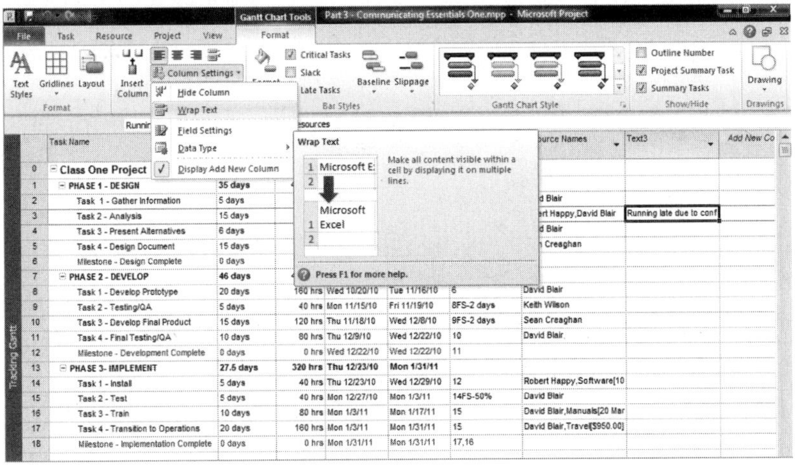

FIGURE 11.23   Wrapped text applied

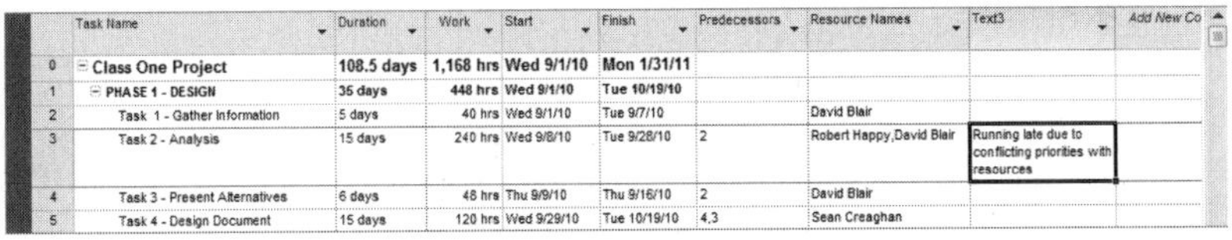

FIGURE 11.24   Creating a custom title

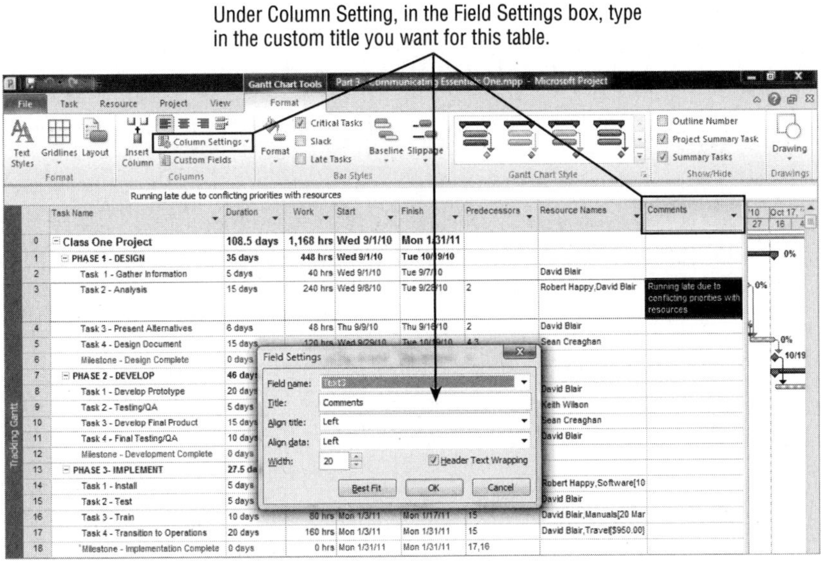

Under Column Setting, in the Field Settings box, type
in the custom title you want for this table.

> If you customize the name of a field in this manner, it retains the custom title for this table only. If you apply the same field in another table, it will revert back to its original name. To permanently change the name of the field, you must rename it in the Custom Fields area, as described earlier in this chapter.

Saving Tables You've Modified

If you've modified a table in any way, such as adding new columns, you may want to save it with a new name to make a custom table. That way, it won't be mixed in with the built-in tables. After you've saved a table, it shows up under the Custom section of the Tables list. Follow these steps to save the custom table (see Figure 11.25):

1. Select View tab ➢ Data group ➢ Tables drop-down list ➢ Save Fields as a New Table.

2. In the Save Table dialog box, you can select either Update Current Table or Save As New Table. In this case, select Save As New Table.

3. In the Name field, enter a new custom name for the table. In this example, name it **Comments**.

4. Click OK. The table is added to the Tables drop-down list under Custom.

FIGURE 11.25 Creating a custom table on the fly

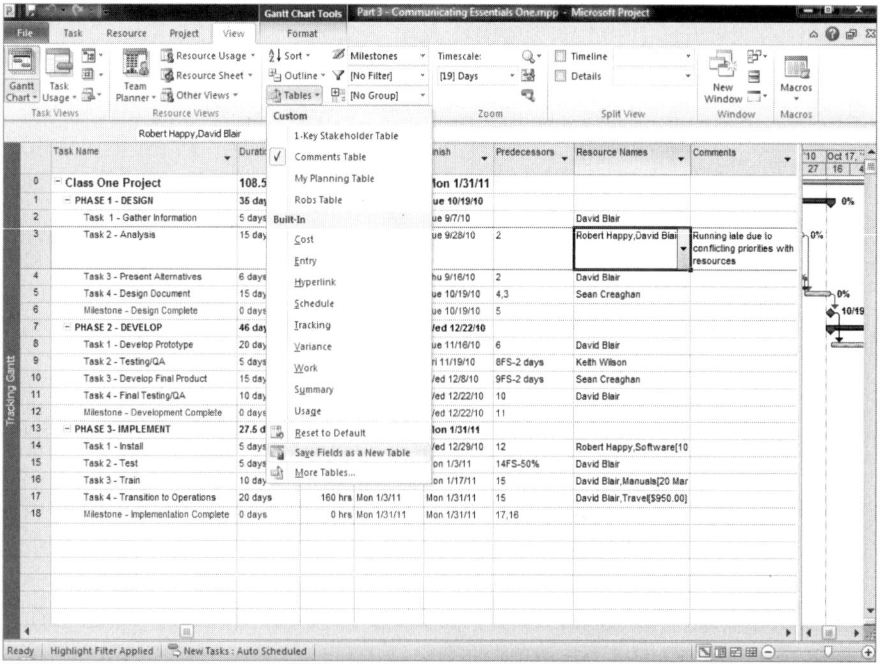

Creating a custom table isn't the same as creating a custom view. A table is only one component of a view and can be applied in many different views. A view is a compilation of components such as tables, filters, groups, sorts, and specific formats. See Chapter 13, "Creating Custom Views, Formatting, and Reporting."

Creating a New Table from Scratch

In addition to the built-in tables that ship with Project, you may need to create your own tables to meet your communication and management needs. You can modify existing tables, or you can create tables from scratch. If you need to add custom fields with graphical indicators or formulas, you must create them before you can incorporate them in a custom table.

I've found three basic tables to be useful over the years to meet various client needs: one for planning, one for tracking, and one for communicating to stakeholders.

Let's first look at planning. Project comes equipped with the default Entry table, which is very useful for planning. It's called the Entry table because it's good for entering project data. However, it may not satisfy all your needs in terms of how you plan. For example, if you need to plan for resource assignments and work hours, perhaps you should consider adding Work to the table. Maybe you need to track costs as well. If that is the case, consider adding a Cost column, too. If you plan to create a dashboard view that displays a filtered set of tasks based on four or five milestones or events, you may need to add those custom flag fields so you can display Yes beside those tasks for reporting purposes. Perhaps you need to add a custom Comments field. And so on.

To create a custom table from scratch, such as the one illustrated in Figure 11.26, follow these steps:

1. In the Gantt Chart view, select View tab ➤ Data group ➤ Tables ➤ More Tables. Note: For resource tables, start from a resource view.

2. In the More Tables dialog box, select New (or Copy to start from an existing table).

3. In the Name field, enter the custom name for the table. In this example, use **My Planning Table**.

4. In the upper-right corner, select Show in Menu, so you'll see the table in the menu of tables when you want to choose it.

5. Under Field Name, click the first blank space, and select the drop-down list.

6. Select the column you want to insert. Start with the ID column, because this lets you always know the ID number of the task, regardless of the table.

7. Under Field Name, click the blank space below that column, and repeat for each additional field you want to add to the table.

8. Click Apply to see the new table in the view.

The new table appears in the drop-down list when you select the Tables command again, in the Custom section.

FIGURE 11.26   Creating a new table

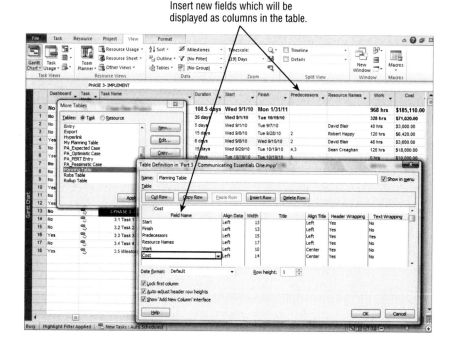

I also often create a custom tracking table to help incorporate the key fields used to match how my clients monitor and control their project. Figure 11.27 is an example of a custom tracking table. I usually start from a copy of the Variance table, because it has a lot of the main ingredients built in. You can add fields like **% Complete** or **Task Finish Status**, which is a custom-built field.

FIGURE 11.27   Custom tracking table

	% Complete	Task Name	Task Finish Status	Start	Duration	Finish	Baseline Start	Baseline Finish	Finish Var.
0	0%	⊟ Class One Project		Wed 9/1/10	108.5 day	Mon 1/31/11	NA	NA	0 days
1	0%	⊟ PHASE 1 - DESIGN		Wed 9/1/10	35 days	Tue 10/19/10	NA	NA	0 days
2	0%	Task 1 - Gather Information	◯	Wed 9/1/10	5 days	Tue 9/7/10	NA	NA	0 days
3	0%	Task 2 - Analysis	◯	Wed 9/8/10	15 days	Tue 9/28/10	NA	NA	0 days
4	0%	Task 3 - Present Alternatives	◯	Wed 9/8/10	6 days	Wed 9/15/10	NA	NA	0 days
5	0%	Task 4 - Design Document	◯	Wed 9/29/10	15 days	Tue 10/19/10	NA	NA	0 days
6	0%	Milestone - Design Complete	◯	Tue 10/19/10	0 days	Tue 10/19/10	NA	NA	0 days
7	0%	⊟ PHASE 2 - DEVELOP		Wed 10/20/10	46 days	Wed 12/22/10	NA	NA	0 days
8	0%	Task 1 - Develop Prototype	◯	Wed 10/20/10	20 days	Tue 11/16/10	NA	NA	0 days
9	0%	Task 2 - Testing/QA	◯	Mon 11/15/10	5 days	Fri 11/19/10	NA	NA	0 days
10	0%	Task 3 - Develop Final Product	◯	Thu 11/18/10	15 days	Wed 12/8/10	NA	NA	0 days
11	0%	Task 4 - Final Testing/QA	◯	Thu 12/9/10	10 days	Wed 12/22/10	NA	NA	0 days
12	0%	Milestone - Development Complete	◯	Wed 12/22/10	0 days	Wed 12/22/10	NA	NA	0 days
13	0%	⊟ PHASE 3- IMPLEMENT		Thu 12/23/10	27.5 days	Mon 1/31/11	NA	NA	0 days
14	0%	Task 1 - Install	◯	Thu 12/23/10	5 days	Wed 12/29/10	NA	NA	0 days
15	0%	Task 2 - Test	◯	Mon 12/27/10	5 days	Mon 1/3/11	NA	NA	0 days
16	0%	Task 3 - Train	◯	Mon 1/3/11	10 days	Mon 1/17/11	NA	NA	0 days
17	0%	Task 4 - Transition to Operations	◯	Mon 1/3/11	20 days	Mon 1/31/11	NA	NA	0 days
18	0%	Milestone - Implementation Complete	◯	Mon 1/31/11	0 days	Mon 1/31/11	NA	NA	0 days

To help differentiate custom tables, I often use a prefix such as *My* or a three-letter acronym that describes the organization that is using the custom table. This helps keep the custom tables better organized in the list of tables. You can use the same strategy for custom fields, filters, groups, and views.

Another table I often create is one for a dashboard view. This is usually based on a custom table along with a custom filter that displays a subset of the important tasks and milestones. A dashboard table may contain limited information such as task name, finish status, finish date, and comments. Figure 11.28 shows a dashboard table as part of a view based on applying a custom filter (discussed in Chapter 12).

FIGURE 11.28   Dashboard table example

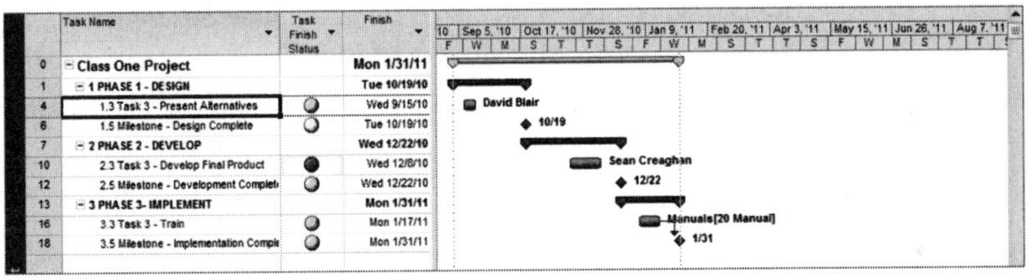

Summary

In this chapter, you learned about creating custom fields and tables. These are key ingredients when you're creating effective views for planning, tracking, and communicating project information.

I covered how to create custom fields with either custom lookup tables or custom formulas, both of which can have associated graphical indicators. These can be effective tools for communicating project information to various stakeholders. Fields are the core components that make up tables, which belong to various views. Before you can create custom tables and views, you need to first understand how to create custom fields if they're needed. There are many types of custom fields to choose from, some formatted (such as date fields) and some unformatted (such as text fields). There are also fields specifically designed for tasks or specifically designed for resources or assignments.

After you create custom fields, you can add them to tables. Tables can be based on built-in fields or can display any custom fields you create. Project comes equipped with many different built-in tables, both for task views and resource views. However, you'll often need to create custom tables. You can do this on the fly by modifying existing tables, or you can create new tables from scratch.

Tables are a main building block for views. Think of views as how you look at project information; then you can think of tables as what you're looking at within that view. Another important component of views is filters, which I cover in the next chapter.

Hands-On Exercises

The following hands-on exercises are designed to test your understanding of the topics discussed in this chapter. We've provided files on the companion CD that will show you what your project file should look like as you perform these exercises.

EXERCISE 11

Creating a Custom Field

Rename the Field

1. In the Gantt Chart view, select Format tab ➤ Columns group ➤ Custom Columns.

2. In the Custom Fields dialog box, under Field, be sure Task is selected.

3. From the Type drop-down list, select Text.

4. Click Text3 in the Field list (or any other text field you want to change).

5. Click the Rename button below the Field list.

6. In the Rename Field dialog box, enter the custom name for this field, and click OK. In this exercise, enter **Stoplight**.

Add a Formula

1. Under Custom Attributes in the Custom Fields dialog box, click the Formula button.

2. In the Formula dialog box, beside Insert, click the Fields drop-down list.

3. Scroll to Date, and select Finish Variance from the list.

4. Click OK.

Apply Graphical Indicators

1. Under Values to Display in the Custom Fields dialog box, click the Graphical Indicators button.

2. In the Graphical Indicators dialog box, in the first empty field below Test for "Stoplight," click the drop-down list.

3. Select "is less than or equal to."

4. In the Value(s) field, enter **0** (zero).

5. In the Image field, click the drop-down list, and select an appropriate indicator. In this case, choose a green light.

6. In the next empty field below Test for "Stoplight," click the drop-down list, and select "is greater than."

7. In the Value(s) field, enter **0** (zero).

8. In the Image field, click the drop-down list, and choose a red light.

9. Click OK, and click OK again.

EXERCISE 12

Creating a Custom Table

1. In Class One Project, select View tab ➤ Data group ➤ Tables ➤ More Tables.

2. In the More Tables dialog box, click the Copy button to make a copy of the Entry table.

3. Name the table **My Planning Table**, and select the Show in Menu option.

4. Add/Modify the following field names: ID, Name, Stoplight, Start, Duration, Finish, and Cost. Customize the title in the Name field to **Activity**. Note: You can delete or insert a row by selecting a row and clicking Delete or Insert Row. The Stoplight field is a custom field created in the previous exercise.

5. Click the OK button, and click Apply.

6. Select View tab ➤ Data group ➤ Tables. Your new table has been added to the list under Custom. You can also right-click the upper-left square in the current table and then select from the drop-down list.

7. Change the values in the Stoplight field to see the various indicators.

Chapter

12

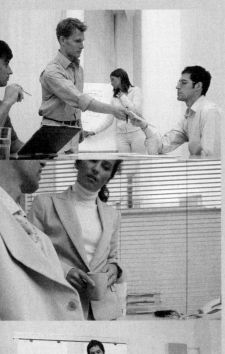

Using Filters, Groups, and Sorts

IN THIS CHAPTER, YOU'LL LEARN ABOUT THE FOLLOWING:

✓ Using filters and highlights

✓ Creating custom filters

✓ Working with groups

✓ Creating custom groups

✓ Using sorts

✓ Understanding auto-filtering groups and sorts

Chapter 10 covered using various views in Project to control how you look at project information. Chapter 11 discussed creating custom fields and tables to control what you see in each view. In this chapter, you'll learn about how to control what you see even further by using filtering, grouping, and sorting.

All of these functions help you achieve more effective communications and analysis of project information. These tools also help tailor what you report to your stakeholders, depending on their needs. For example, senior management or the project customer may only be interested in a few specific milestones; so, you can create a filter that reports just those milestones. Maybe you have a functional or resource manager who is interested in seeing only the tasks their group is responsible for; so, you group your tasks by resource or by department.

Using Filters and Highlights

This section discusses using predefined filters and highlights, which allow you to zero in on specific subsets of data for more effective communication and reporting. Although Project comes equipped with many predefined filters, you can also create your own. This section also covers how to create custom filters.

Using Predefined Filters

Project comes with predefined filters you can use as is. Filtering works by displaying only a set of line items (phases, tasks, milestones) based on a specific criterion or condition. When the specified condition is applied, Project presents those items that satisfy the condition in the view in which you apply the filter. For example, as shown in Figure 12.1, if you want to view milestones only, you can apply the Milestones filter, which is based on the condition of the Milestone field being equal to Yes. To apply the Milestones filter, follow these steps:

1. In the Gantt Chart view, go to View tab ➤ the Data group.
2. Beside the Filter button, click the drop-down list that says [No Filter].
3. From the drop-down list, select Milestones.

To clear a filter, you can select Clear Filter or [No Filter] from the same filter list. At lower left in the window, in the status bar area, Project displays Filter Applied if you're running a filter.

FIGURE 12.1   Applying a Milestones filter

To apply a filter, click on the drop-down list beside the Filter Button [No Filter] under the View tab, in the Data group. Project will also show in the Status Bar whether a filter is applied or not.

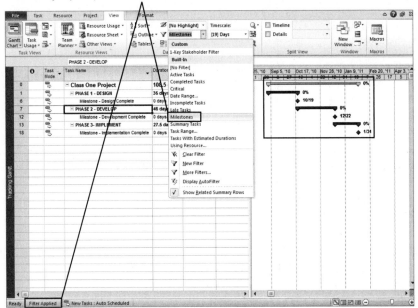

Many useful filters appear in this list, such as the Using Resource filter. In Figure 12.2, I've filtered by all the tasks David Blair is working on so I can meet with him to review his workload on this project. When you apply the Using Resource filter, you're prompted to select a resource from the resource pool list.

The Date Range filter lets you focus on tasks over a specific period. For example, if you're getting ready for a project-review meeting and you want to review the tasks that are coming up for the next week or month, you can run the Date Range filter. When you apply this filter, you're prompted for the following two items:

- Show tasks that start or finish after

- And before

Figure 12.3 is an example of a Date Range filter that displays only tasks for the month of October.

Project shows the most commonly used filters in the initial drop-down list, but you can access additional predefined filters, as shown in Figure 12.4. Follow these steps:

1. Select Task tab ➤ Data group ➤ Filter button drop-down list ➤ More Filters.

2. In the More Filters dialog box, scroll down to review and select other filters.

3. Click Apply.

FIGURE 12.2   Applying the Using Resource filter

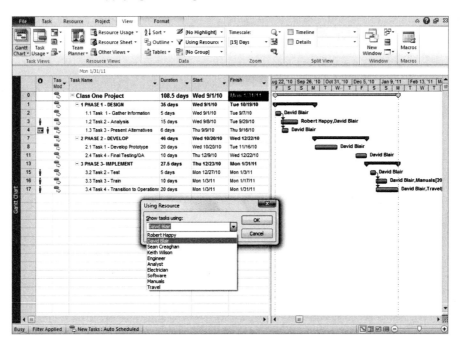

FIGURE 12.3   Applying the Date Range filter

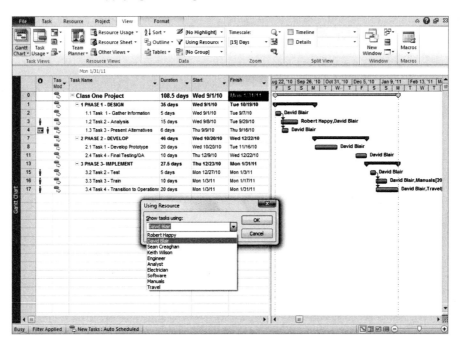

FIGURE 12.4   More Filters dialog box

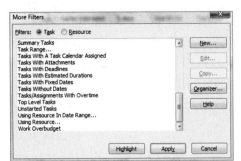

The next section discusses how to create custom filters. Take some time to review the predefined filters, because they come in handy when you need to communicate in various ways to project stakeholders.

Using Highlights

Highlights are similar to filters in that they use the same criteria and conditions to focus on a specific subset of data. However, instead of removing line items from the project plan that don't match a condition, highlighting keeps all the line items in view and highlights the items that meet the condition.

For example, you may want to highlight milestones or the tasks that a specific resource is working on. To do so, you use the highlight function, as shown in Figure 12.5. In this example, I've highlighted the milestones by following these steps:

1.   Go to Task tab ➤ Data group, and click the Highlight drop-down list.

2.   Select Milestones.

FIGURE 12.5   Applying milestone highlights

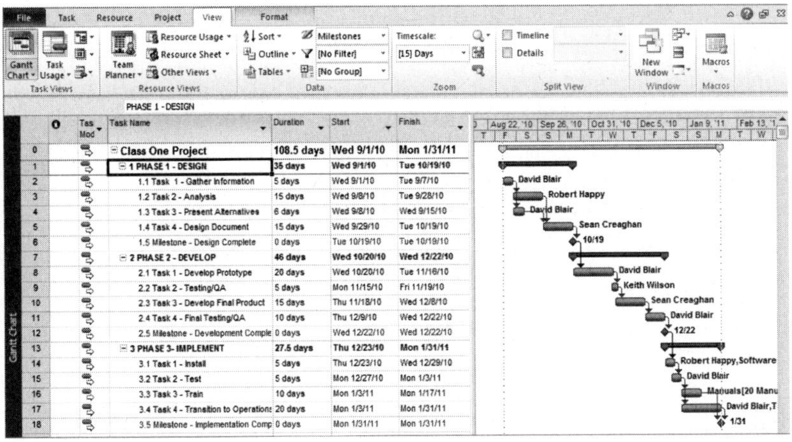

The default color for highlighted tasks is blue. You can change the font characteristics of highlights by modifying the text styles which will also be covered in more detail in Chapter 13, "Creating Custom Views, Formatting, and Reporting." As shown in Figure 12.6, to change the font or color of the highlights, follow these steps:

1. Go to Format tab ➢ Format group, and click the Text Styles button.

2. In the Text Styles dialog box, from the Item to Change drop-down list, select Highlighted Tasks.

3. Select the appropriate characteristics. You can apply different fonts, styles, sizes, and colors as desired.

FIGURE 12.6   Changing text styles for highlighted tasks

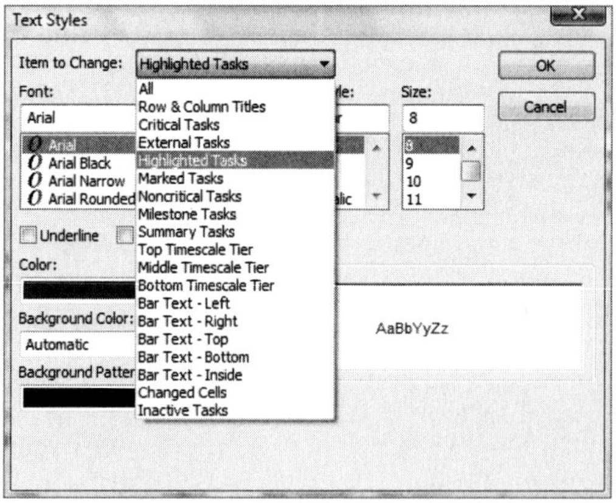

Creating Custom Filters

Although Project comes with many filter options, sometimes you may need to create and customize your own filters. Filters are based on conditions that meet some criteria defined by existing fields, including custom fields.

For example, if a stakeholder only needs to see a few milestones and tasks, you can create a filter for that need. If no field exists, you can create a custom field, such as a flag field that you can subsequently use in a filter. Creating a custom field is covered in Chapter 11, "Using Tables and Custom Fields."

To create a custom filter, as shown in Figure 12.7, follow these steps:

1. Select View tab ➢ Data group ➢ Filter drop-down list ➢ More Filters.

2. In the More Filters box, click New.

3. In the Filter Definition dialog box, in the Name field, enter the custom name for your filter. In this example, use **Key Stakeholder Filter**.

4. Select the Show in Menu check box if you want the filter to be displayed in the drop-down list.

5. Under Field Name, click the first blank space, and click the drop-down list. Select the field you want to filter with. In this example, choose the custom field Key Stakeholder Flag.

6. Under Test, select the appropriate test. In this case, choose Equals.

7. Under Value, select the appropriate value. In this case, choose Yes (you can also type in a value).

8. Select the Show Related Summary Rows check box if you want the parent tasks to be displayed as well.

9. Click Save.

10. Click Apply (if you want to run the filter).

FIGURE 12.7 Creating a custom filter

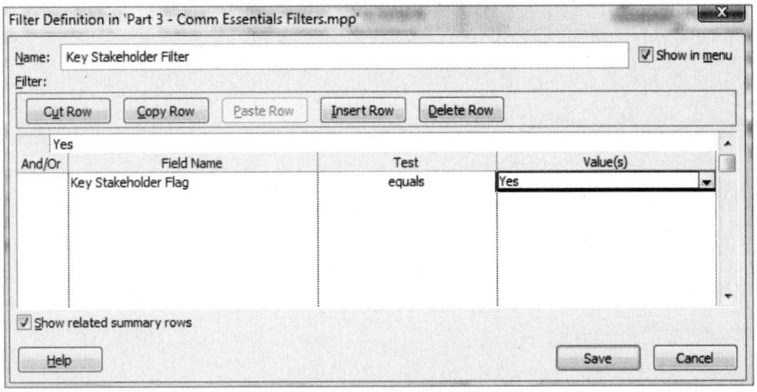

Because this filter example is based on a custom flag field, it has tasks to display only if Yes appears in the custom flag field, as discussed in Chapter 11 and illustrated in Figure 12.8.

FIGURE 12.8 Applying custom filters

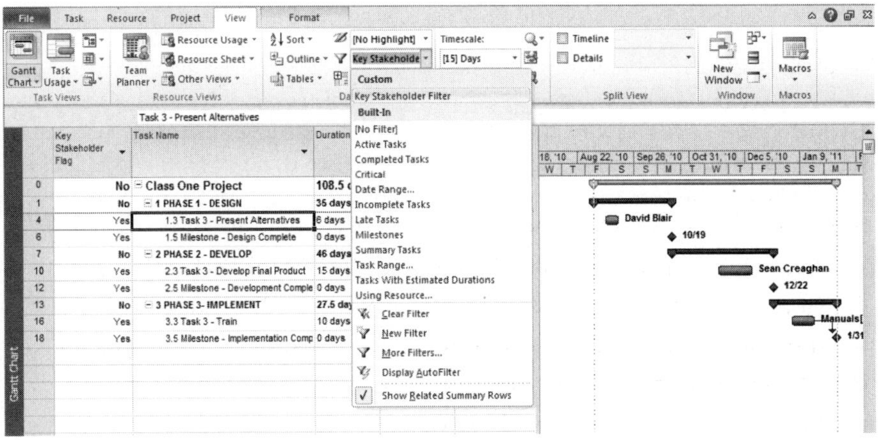

In the figure, I added the custom column to the table shown in Chapter 11. You can see that tasks with Yes in the Key Stakeholder Flag field are included in the filter. But the summary tasks that have No in the field are also included. Why? Because when I created the filter, I selected Show Related Summary Rows.

To clear a filter, select Clear Filter or [No Filter] from the drop-down Filter list.

NOTE Project automatically separates custom filters from built-in filters in the drop-down list. This makes it easy for you to decipher which filters you created and which filters come with Project.

Review the built-in filters to see how they're constructed, because filters can be complex. The previous example is simple, but you can use And/Or functions to build more complex filters. Figure 12.9 shows how the Date Range filter was built.

To edit an existing filter, you can follow these steps:

1. Select View tab ➤ Data group ➤ Filter drop-down list ➤ More Filters.

2. In the More Filters dialog box, click Edit.

3. In the Filter Definition dialog box, edit or review the filter properties.

FIGURE 12.9 Date Range filter construction

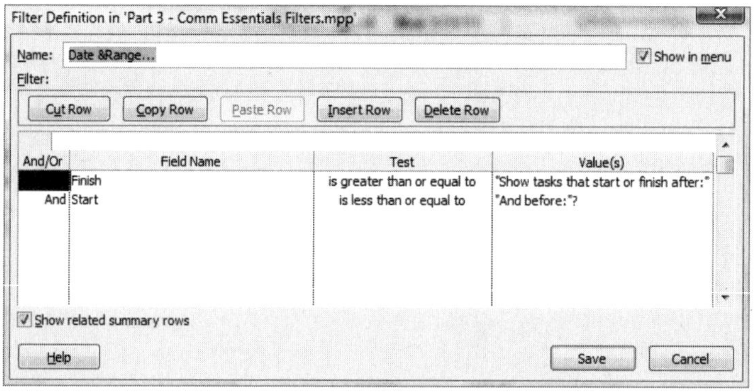

Filter Definition in 'Part 3 - Comm Essentials Filters.mpp'			
Name: Date &Range...			☑ Show in menu
Filter:			
Cut Row	Copy Row	Paste Row	Insert Row	Delete Row

And/Or	Field Name	Test	Value(s)	
	Finish	is greater than or equal to	"Show tasks that start or finish after:"	
And	Start	is less than or equal to	"And before:"?	

☑ Show related summary rows

Help | Save | Cancel

You can also create a new custom filter by starting from an existing filter. For example, if you want to create a custom filter that displays only specific tasks based on a date range, you can start from the Date Range filter and add the filter portion to it, as shown in Figure 12.10. Follow these steps to start from an existing filter:

1. Select View tab ➤ Data group ➤ Filter drop-down list ➤ More Filters.

2. In the More Filters dialog box, click Copy.

3. In the Filter Definition dialog box, add the new criteria. In this example, add the Key Stakeholder Flag field.

FIGURE 12.10   Copying from an existing filter to create a new one

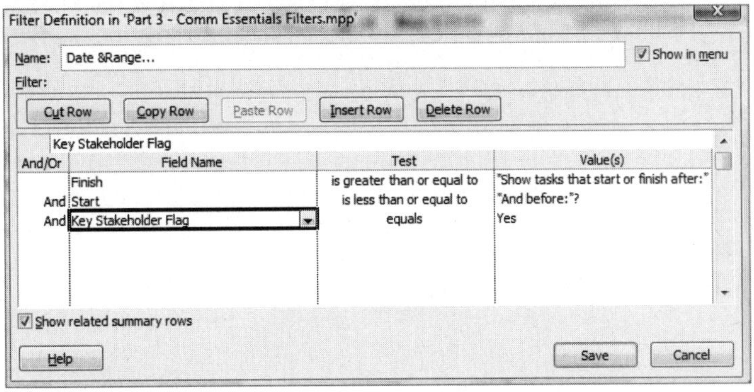

Using an AND statement narrows your filter, and using an OR statement expands your filter criteria. For example, if you create a filter that shows tasks that have David AND Robert assigned, the result may be very few tasks or none at all. However, if you create the condition based on David OR Robert, then the result will include many more tasks; the filter will select all tasks to which David is assigned, all tasks to which Robert is assigned, and all tasks to which both are assigned.

Using Groups

This section explains how to use built-in groups and create custom groups. Groups can be applied on both task and resource views. They provide an effective way to communicate and analyze project information.

Built-in Groups

As with filters, Project comes with many built-in groups that you can use right out of the box. Grouping is similar to filtering in that it uses the same types of criteria and conditions, but instead of eliminating tasks that don't meet the conditions, like filtering does, it reorganizes the tasks based on the conditions. For example, in Figure 12.11, grouping by milestone instead of filtering by milestone leaves the non-milestone line items in view; it just reorganizes the line items based on the grouping criteria.

To run a group, follow these steps:

1.   Go to View tab ➤ Data group, and click the [No Group] drop-down list.

2.   From the list, select Milestones.

I often group by Critical to help focus on critical tasks more effectively when I need to bring my end date in to the left. This is useful when you're meeting with project team members to crash or fast-track your schedule. To run the Critical group, as shown in Figure 12.12, follow these steps:

1. Go to View tab ≻ Data group, and click the [No Group] drop-down list.
2. From the list, select Critical.

FIGURE 12.11   Grouping by milestone

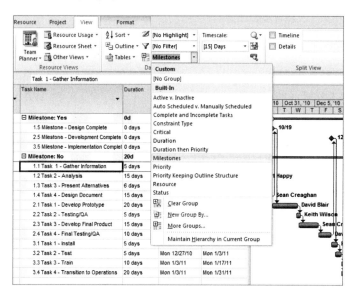

FIGURE 12.12   Grouping by Critical

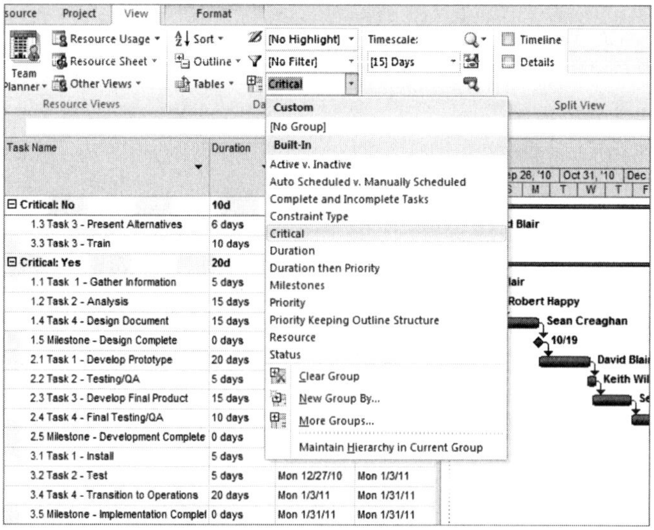

Clients often need to manage resource workloads more effectively, and grouping can play a significant role. You can run groups in either task views or resource views. The scenario in Figure 12.13 uses the Gantt chart, which is a task view, to group by resource; this shows how tasks are distributed among your project team. To apply the Resource group, follow these steps:

1. Go to View tab ➤ Data group, and click the [No Group] drop-down list.

2. From the list, select Resource.

FIGURE 12.13 Grouping by resource

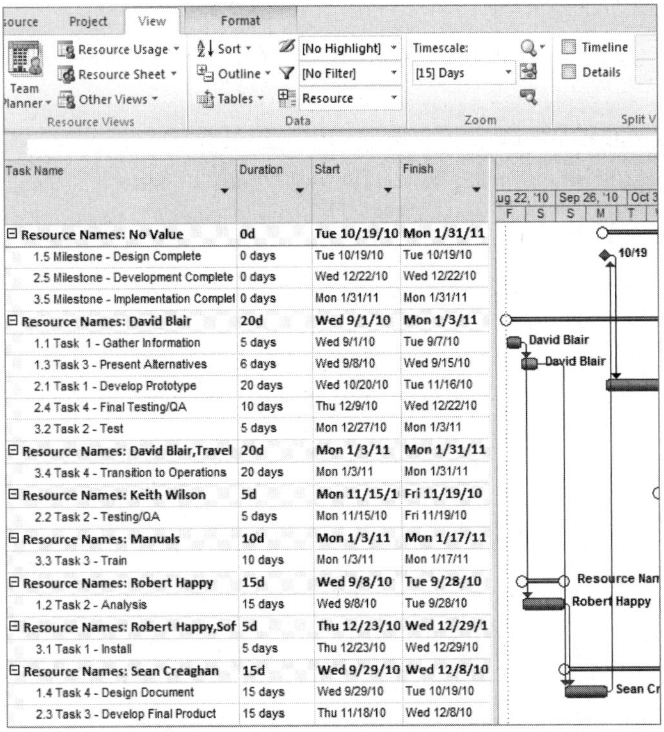

Groups can also be applied in resource views. You can use the Group field in the Resource Sheet view, as shown in Figure 12.14. This example gives each resource a group that reflects which department they work in. To add departments for each resource in the Resource Sheet view, follow these steps:

1. Go to View tab ➤ Resource Views group, and click Resource Sheet.

2. In the Group column, add the appropriate department name for each resource in your resource pool.

FIGURE 12.14   Using the Group field

Resource Name	Work	Cost	Type	Material	Initials	Group
Robert Happy	160 hrs	$8,560.00	Work		RH	PMO
David Blair	528 hrs	$39,600.00	Work		DB	PMO
Sean Creaghan	240 hrs	$36,000.00	Work		CPM	IT
Keith Wilson	40 hrs	$0.00	Work		K	IT
Engineer	0 hrs	$0.00	Work		Sts	Eng
Analyst	0 hrs	$0.00	Work		MWrt	Eng
Electrician	0 hrs	$0.00	Work		RPM	Eng
Software	100 License	$10,000.00	Material	License	S/W	Materials
Manuals	20 Manual	$40,000.00	Material	Manual	Mnl	Materials
Travel		$950.00	Cost		Trvl	Expenses

For example, David Blair belongs to the PMO group and Sean Creaghan belongs to the IT group. You can now group by department to communicate and report hours and cost at the department level. As shown in Figure 12.15, you can create this type of group by following these steps:

1. In the Resource Sheet view, go to View tab ➤ Data group, and click the [No Group] drop-down list.

2. From the list, select Resource Group.

FIGURE 12.15   Applying the Resource Group in the resource sheet

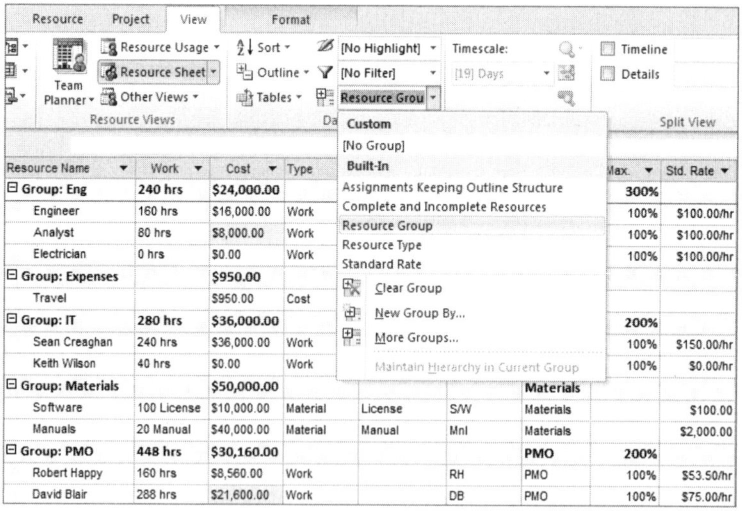

I've added two columns to the resource sheet to display work and cost (adding columns is covered in Chapter 11). This allows you to see both the total hours and total costs for each department.

You can apply the same group in the Resource Usage view for even more in-depth analysis of where hours and costs are going over time (see Figure 12.16). To do this, follow these steps:

1. Go to View tab ➢ Resource Views group, and click Resource Usage.
2. Go to View tab ➢ Data group, and click the [No Group] drop-down list.
3. From the list, select Resource Group.

FIGURE 12.16 Applying the Resource Group in the Resource Usage view

Resource Name	Work	Cost	Details	4th Quarter Nov	Dec
⊞ Group: Eng	240 hrs	$24,000.00	Work	96h	80h
			Cost	$9,600.00	$8,000.00
			Peak Units	100%	100%
⊞ Group: Expenses		$950.00	Work		
			Cost		
			Peak Units		
⊞ Group: IT	280 hrs	$36,000.00	Work	112h	48h
			Cost	$10,800.00	$7,200.00
			Peak Units	200%	100%
⊞ Group: Materials		$50,000.00	Work		
			Cost		$10,000.00
			Peak Units		
⊟ Group: PMO	448 hrs	$30,160.00	Work		76h
			Cost		$4,840.00
			Peak Units		200%
⊟ Robert Happy	160 hrs	$8,560.00	Work		40h
			Cost		$2,140.00
			Peak Units		100%
Task 2 - Analysis	120 hrs	$6,420.00	Work		
			Cost		
			Peak Units		
Task 1 - Install	40 hrs	$2,140.00	Work		40h
			Cost		$2,140.00
			Peak Units		100%
⊟ David Blair	288 hrs	$21,600.00	Work		36h
			Cost		$2,700.00
			Peak Units		100%
Task 1 - Gather Information	40 hrs	$3,000.00	Work		
			Cost		
			Peak Units		

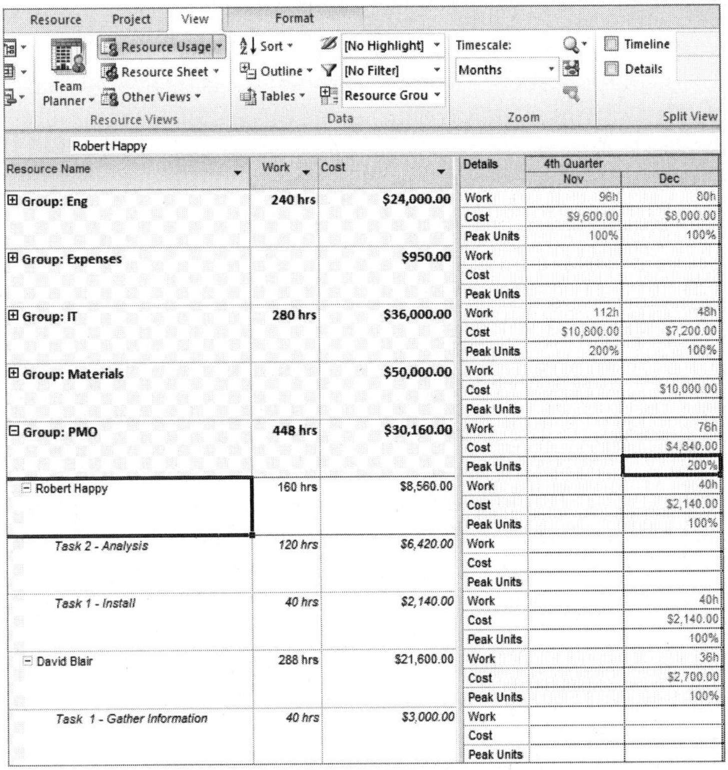

I've added the Cost column at right and also added costs and peak units in the time-phased portion of the view (see Chapter 11 for instructions). You can change the timescale using the zoom commands on the View tab or the zoom slider at lower-right in the window. In this example, the timescale is set at quarters and months, which lets you see how each department is spending hours and costs by quarter and by month. Adding the peak units under Details also allows you to analyze how many people you need during each time period. For example, 200 percent indicates that two resources are required during the peak work for that time period.

🌐 Real World Scenario

FTE by Resource Group

I worked with a client that wanted to know how many full-time equivalents (FTEs) were required to manage their specific project workload. Using the Resource Usage view and the Resource Group function, I created the view and communicated the information the way they wanted by combining peak units with the details.

There was one catch: they wanted to see this information across projects, not just for one project. Without having Project Server installed—an ideal solution for this type of reporting—I was able to replicate the view by creating a master consolidated plan and sharing the resource pool across projects. Setting up master plans is covered in Chapter 14, "Creating Master Schedules with Inserted Projects."

Custom Groups

Just as you can create custom tables and filters, you can also create custom groups. Groupings follow the same principle as filters: they're based on specific criteria defined by fields you select. You can base a group on fields that come predefined with Project or fields that you've customized.

Your selection of tables, groups, and filters depends on whether you're in a task view or a resource view. For example, in the Gantt Chart view (task type); the Critical group is listed but not the Resource Group. On the other hand, in the Resource Sheet view, you won't see the Critical group, but you will see the Resource Group.

You can create custom groups to apply in either a task or a resource view. For example, you can organize your tasks by department in the Gantt Chart view. Because there isn't a predefined group for this purpose, you can create a new group using the Resource Group field, as shown in Figure 12.17. Follow these steps:

1. In the Gantt Chart view, select View tab ➢ the Data group ➢ [No Group] drop-down list ➢ More Groups.

2. In the More Groups dialog box, click New.

3. Name the new group. In this example, name it **By Department**.

4. Select Show in Menu.

5. Under Field Name, beside Group By, select Resource Group from the drop-down list.

6. Click Save, and then click Apply.

You can apply the same approach you used for custom fields you've created (Chapter 11). For example, you can create a custom group for the custom Key Stakeholder Flag field to flag specific tasks. Follow the previous set of steps, but instead of choosing Resource Group as the field name, select Key Stakeholder Flag (see Figure 12.18).

FIGURE 12.17   Creating a custom group

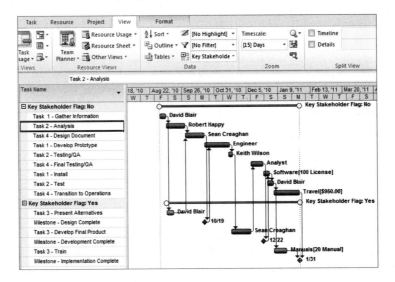

FIGURE 12.18   Custom group for Key Stakeholder Flag field

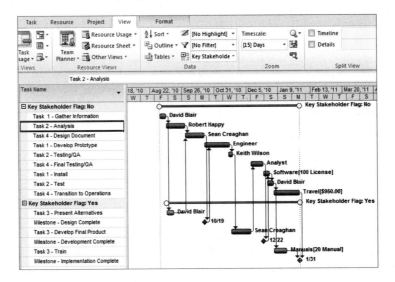

Using Sorts and Auto-filters

You can use the sort function to better communicate and report project information. Project also makes it easy to filter, group, and sort by taking advantage of the auto-filter function.

Sorts

Sorts act similarly to sort functions in other applications such as Excel. In Project, by default, line items are organized and sorted by ID number (the numbers at far left in the Gantt Chart view in the Entry table). The ID numbers are another field; every line item, whether it's a summary, task, or milestone, has its own ID number.

You can change the sort by using the sort function for other criteria. For example, you can sort by start date or finish date to see a cascading left-to-right view of your tasks.

As with filters and groups, Project comes equipped with predefined sorts. As shown in Figure 12.19, you can access the sort function by following these steps:

1. Go to View tab ≻ Data group, and click Sort.

2. From the drop-down list, choose the desired sort criteria. Note that the default sort is based on ID number.

FIGURE 12.19   Applying sorts

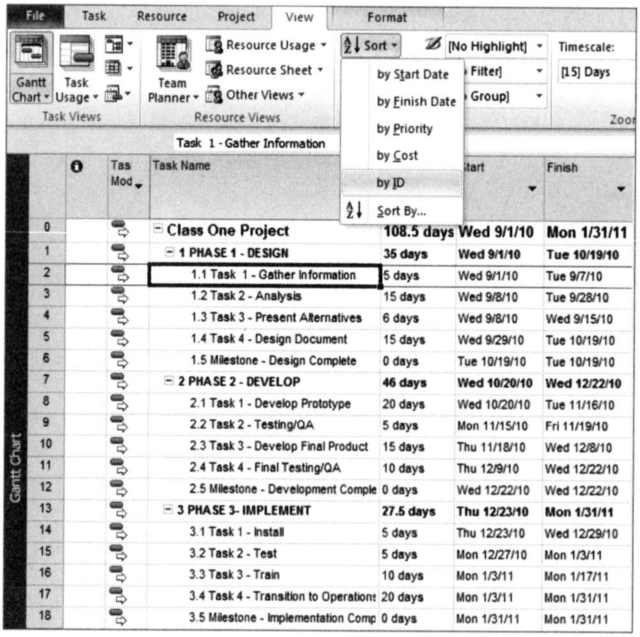

To undo a sort or revert to the original sort, you must apply the By ID sort. You can also create a custom sort, as shown in Figure 12.20, by following these steps:

1. Select View tab ➤ Data group ➤ Sort drop-down list ➤ Sort By.

2. In the Sort dialog box, from the Sort By drop-down list, select the field you want to sort by.

   If you wish, you can add up to two more sorts using the Then By options.

3. Choose Ascending or Descending.

4. Optionally, you can permanently renumber the tasks based on the order that results from the sort.

5. Click Sort.

FIGURE 12.20   Creating a custom sort

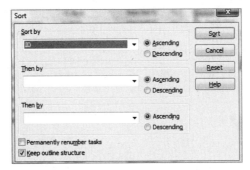

Auto-Filters

The auto-filter tool is activated by default for each column in each table you have running in a specific view. This function is indicated in the column headings by the appearance of a drop-down arrow. Every column has its own drop-down arrow, giving you access to the auto-filter for that column in each table.

Although this function is based on the auto-filter command, as shown in Figure 12.21, you can also run sorts and groups. This is a practical way to get at information in the way you want. It may replace the need to use group, sort, and filter commands directly.

The example shown in Figure 12.21 uses the auto-filter to create a view that displays only the tasks in the coming month (October). To create this view, follow these steps:

1. In the Start column, click the drop-down arrow to open the auto-filter list.

2. Under Filters, deselect the months you don't want to include. In this case, only select the October options.

   Alternatively, click Filters ➤ Next Month.

3. Click OK.

4. To remove the filter, select Clear Filter from Start from the same drop-down list.

FIGURE 12.21 Applying a custom auto-filter

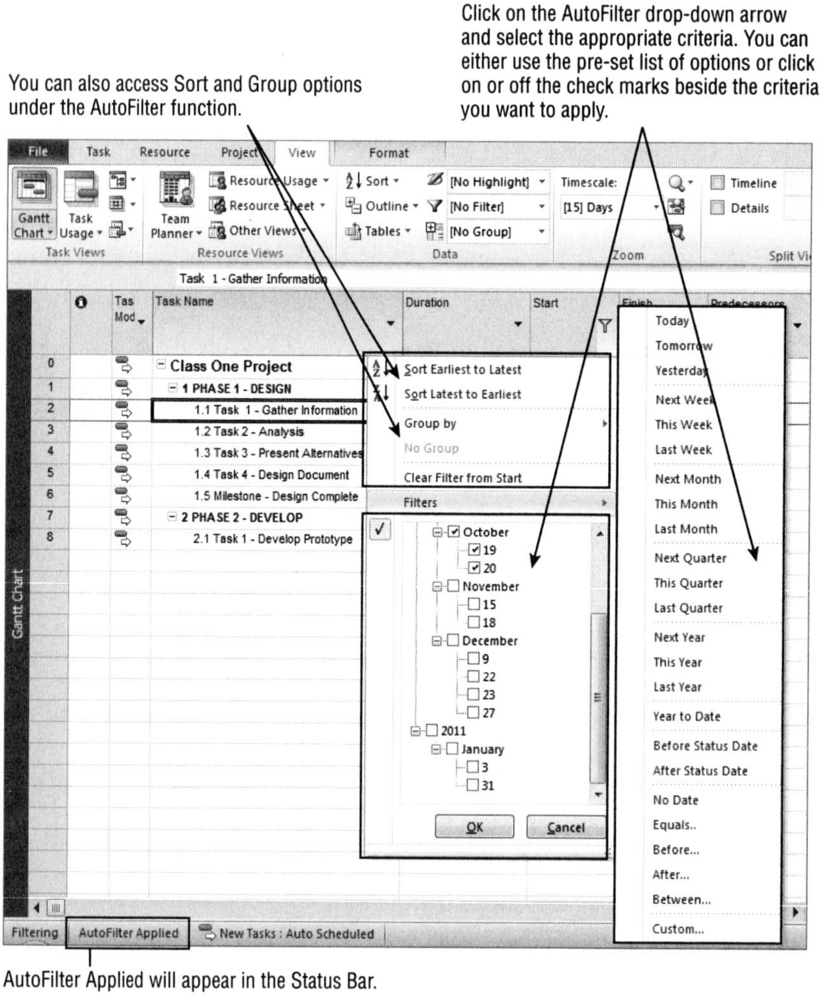

You can also access Sort and Group options under the AutoFilter function.

Click on the AutoFilter drop-down arrow and select the appropriate criteria. You can either use the pre-set list of options or click on or off the check marks beside the criteria you want to apply.

AutoFilter Applied will appear in the Status Bar.

This example is useful for team meetings when you need to review upcoming activities for the next period. You'll also find this useful with other columns, such as resource names, finish dates, and costs, and even to find specific tasks in the Task Name column.

Although the default is to have the auto-filter drop-down arrow appear in each column heading in each table, you can turn it off. To turn off the auto-filter, follow these steps:

1. Go to View tab ➤ Data group, and click the [No Filter] drop-down list.

2. From the list, select Display AutoFilter to turn off (or on) the auto-filter function.

Summary

In this chapter, you learned about the importance of applying built-in filters, highlights, groups, and sorts, or creating custom ones, to meet your unique needs. These are key ingredients for displaying project information in an effective manner, resulting in better communications and analysis.

You learned that Project comes equipped with useful built-in options that can be applied right out of the box. However, you also have the flexibility to create custom filters, group, and sorts, so that you can tailor your communications in a more meaningful way. After they're created, filters and groups appear in the Custom section of the menu lists and can be reused at any time.

You also learned about the auto-filter tool. It lets you quickly apply filters as well as groups and sorts from the same drop-down list.

Hands-On Exercises

The following hands-on exercises are designed to test your understanding of the topics discussed in this chapter. We've provided files on the companion CD that will show you what your project file should look like as you perform these exercises.

EXERCISE 13

Applying Filters, Groups, and Highlights

1. Go to View tab ➤ Data group, click the [No Filter] drop-down list, and review the built-in filter options.

2. Select various filters, such as Milestones, Critical, and Using Resource. Review the tasks that remain on the screen. Notice the Filter Applied message in the status bar at lower left.

3. Clear the filter by selecting [No Filter] or Clear Filter from the drop-down list.

4. Repeat these steps, but this time use highlights. Notice that highlights use the same conditions as filters. To clear highlights, select [No Highlights] or Clear Highlights from the drop-down list.

5. Repeat these steps with groups. Notice that the groups list is different than that for filters. To clear groups, select [No Group] or Clear Group from the drop-down list.

EXERCISE 14

Applying Sorts and Auto-Filters

1. Click the drop-down arrow in the Start column, and select various auto-filter options from the menu that appears.

2. Clear the filter by selecting Clear Filter from Start from the drop-down menu.

3. Click the drop-down arrow in the Finish column. How might you use the auto-filter tool to quickly produce an ad hoc, filtered report?

4. Try using the sort or group function in the auto-filter drop-down list for any of the column headings. Remember, you can clear a group from the same list after it has been applied.

5. Select View tab ➤ Data group ➤ Sort By ➤ Start Date.

6. Sort by ID to return to original schedule organization.

EXERCISE 15

Creating a Custom Filter

1. Working with the Class One Project, select View tab ➤ Data group ➤ [No Filter] drop-down list ➤ More Filters.

2. In the More Filters dialog box, click the New button. Name the filter Long Tasks, and select the Show in Menu option.

3. Under Field Name, select Duration. Under Test, choose Greater Than. Under Value, enter **10d**. Click OK.

4. Click the Apply button.

5. Clear the filter by selecting [No Filter] or Clear Filter from the drop-down list. Notice that your filter has been added to the custom list.

6. Save the Class One Project file.

The ability to create custom tables and filters gives you an incredible amount of power to adapt information to the audience with which you need to communicate. Take the time to explore the wide variety of prebuilt views, tables, and filters in Project 2010.

Chapter

13

Creating Custom Views, Formatting, and Reporting

IN THIS CHAPTER, YOU'LL LEARN ABOUT THE FOLLOWING:

- ✓ Creating custom views
- ✓ Using text styles
- ✓ Using bar styles
- ✓ Formatting the Timeline view
- ✓ Swapping project elements
- ✓ Sharing and sending project information

In Chapter 10, "Understanding Views," you learned how to change or apply various built-in views that come with Project. Chapters 11, "Using Tables and Custom Fields" and Chapter 12, "Using Filters, Groups, and Sorts," covered the key components that make up views, such as custom fields, tables, filters, groups, highlights, and sorts. In this chapter, you'll learn how to create custom views using either built-in components or custom components.

You'll also learn about formatting options that are view-specific. For example, you can change the font of milestones to green in one view and a different color in another view.

Last, you'll learn how to share components between projects, using the Organizer to configure the global.mpt file, which controls the defaults that launch when you start Project or create a new project. You can easily swap items such as custom fields, tables, filters, and more in the Organizer tool. You can also share project information with other applications, including synchronizing with SharePoint 2010.

Creating Custom Views

In this section, you'll learn about creating custom views. Chapter 10 covered task views and resource views and how to switch from one view to another. You also learned that a view is composed of specific parts such as tables, filters, groups, highlights, and formatted text and bars, which are covered later in this chapter. In creating custom views, you can set up all these components in the manner that best suits your needs for planning, tracking, and communicating.

Key Elements of a View

Project comes with predefined views that may be sufficient for your needs. However, setting up custom views often makes for more effective use of the tool. Before you learn about customizing new views, it's important to understand the primary elements that make up a view.

Figure 13.1 shows the core components of a view. This example is the view definition for the default Gantt Chart view. To access the View Definition dialog box, follow these steps:

1. In the Gantt Chart view, go to View tab ➤ Task Views group. Note: For resource views, go to the Resource Views group.

2. From the drop-down list beside any of the View buttons, select More Views.

3. In the Views list; highlight the View you want to edit.

4. Click Edit.

5. Review the core components in the View Definition dialog box. To exit the dialog box without making changes, click Cancel, and click Cancel again.

FIGURE 13.1 View Definition dialog box

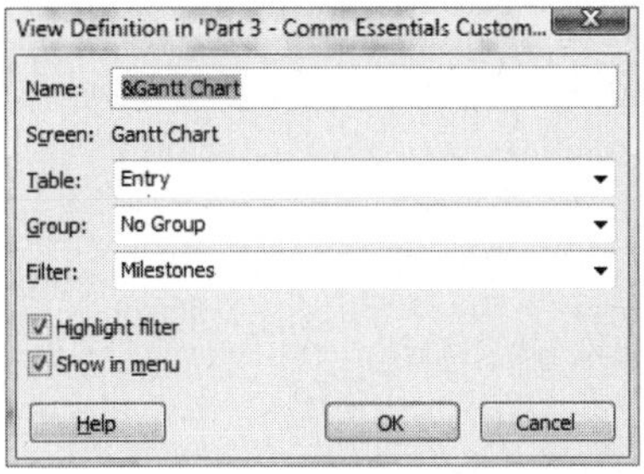

In addition to letting you give a view a name and select what type of view it is, such as Gantt, calendar, or network, the main choices in the View Definition dialog box include the following:

- Table selection (built-in or custom)
- Groups (built-in or custom)
- Filters (built-in or custom)
- Show highlights (for filters)

If you plan to create a custom view based on custom tables, filters, or groups, you need to create them first so they're available to be added in the View Definition dialog box. Custom fields can be added to any custom or built-in table, so you need to create them first if you plan to use them in custom tables that may be part of a custom view.

Creating a Custom View

In this section, we'll look at creating a custom view based on using custom parts such as tables and filters.

Custom View Example: Stakeholder Task View

In the previous chapters, you learned how to create custom fields, tables, and filters based on the scenario of communicating with stakeholders. If you need to refresh your memory about how to create custom fields and tables, refer to Chapter 11. You can also review how to create custom filters and groups in Chapter 12.

To create a custom task view (see Figure 13.2), follow these steps:

1. Select View tab ➢ Task Views group ➢ Gantt Chart drop-down list (or the drop-down list from any other task view button) ➢ More Views.

2. Click New, and select Single View.

3. In the View Definition dialog box, in the Name field, enter the name of the new view. In this example, enter **1-Key Stakeholder View**.

4. Beside Screen, select Gantt chart (it should be the default).

5. From the Table drop-down list, select 1-Key Stakeholder Table or another table. Note: This is a custom table that you must create before it will appear in this list.

6. From the Group drop-down list, select No Group. You aren't using a group for this view.

7. From the Filter drop-down list, select 1-Key Stakeholder Filter or another filter. Note: This is a custom filter that you must create before it will appear in this list.

8. Don't select the Highlight Filter check box.

9. Select Show in Menu to make the custom view appear in the drop-down list under Custom.

10. Click OK, and then click Apply.

FIGURE 13.2   View definition example for key stakeholder view

After you apply the view, the custom table and the custom filter run at the same time, as shown in Figure 13.3. To return to the default Gantt Chart view, click the Gantt Chart button on the View tab. Some of the bars and text may be formatted differently; this is covered later in this chapter. Not only are the tables, groups, and filters view-specific, but the formatting of the text and bar styles is as well.

As you can see in the Gantt Chart drop-down list in Figure 13.3, custom views are separated from built-in views, and the newly created 1-Key Stakeholder View is in the Custom section. You can switch from the Gantt Chart view to this new view by selecting it from the list. The primary benefit of this approach is that every time you need to generate communication to that stakeholder group, you don't have to remember to change the table, apply the filter, modify the text and bar styles, and so on. The view is ready to go at the touch of a button.

You can also display the View bar on the left side of the screen for easy access. In previous versions of Project, this was a plus, because views were often hidden under a File menu selection. However, the ribbon makes it easy to access various task and resource views. Also, in the status bar at lower-right, you can easily switch from one view to another, although the selection is limited. To display the View bar display on your screen as shown in Figure 13.4, follow these steps:

1. Right-click the view name at far left on the screen.

2. From the list that appears, select View Bar.

🌐 Real World Scenario

Three Common Custom Views

Over the years, I've worked with hundreds of organizations to set up and implement custom project-management solutions. I always start by trying to match their project-management methodologies and processes to the tools. In doing so, I've found that in most cases, you can focus on three custom views to help support better project management using Project.

One custom view should be tailored to the planning process. You can create a custom table with custom fields to support the way an organization plans projects. For example, if work is important, you can add a Work column to plan person hours. If it's important to flag specific tasks for reporting, then you add a custom Flag field. You then create a custom view called the Planning View, with the custom table and any associated custom formats for the text and bar styles.

Another custom view that is often needed supports the monitoring and controlling processes that cover updating and tracking. Based on the needs of the organization, you create custom fields (such as red, yellow, and green light indicators for status), add them to a custom table, and create a custom view for tracking. This also includes formatting to display baseline and other important information, such as variance.

Finally, create at least one custom view to enhance communication. For example, you may have a standard project-review meeting or committee that you communicate with regularly. Perhaps a filtered view on key tasks or milestones, complete with graphical indicators and status comments, is in order.

If you select Show in Menu when you create a custom view, the view is added to the View bar. The View bar makes it easier to switch from one view to another, but it takes up valuable screen real estate; the ribbon's organization already makes it simple to switch views.

As you think about how to be more effective with Project when you plan, track, and communicate, consider the types of custom views and custom components that make the most sense for your situation. These can be included in a template (see Chapter 4, "Getting Started and Setting Up the Microsoft Project Environment") so that when you start a new project, you automatically inherit these views. Later in this chapter, I'll introduce you to the Organizer tool, found in the backstage. It allows you to share views, tables, filters, groups, custom fields, and other components from one project with another.

FIGURE 13.3 Custom view for key stakeholders

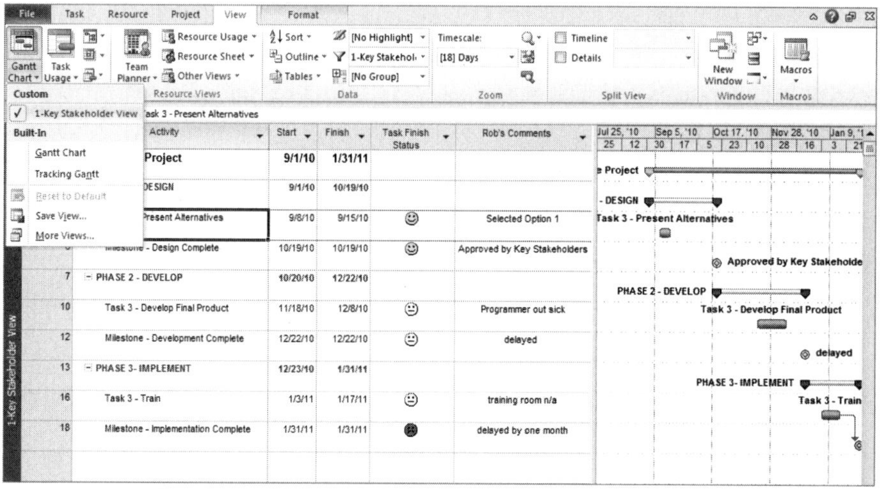

FIGURE 13.4 The View bar

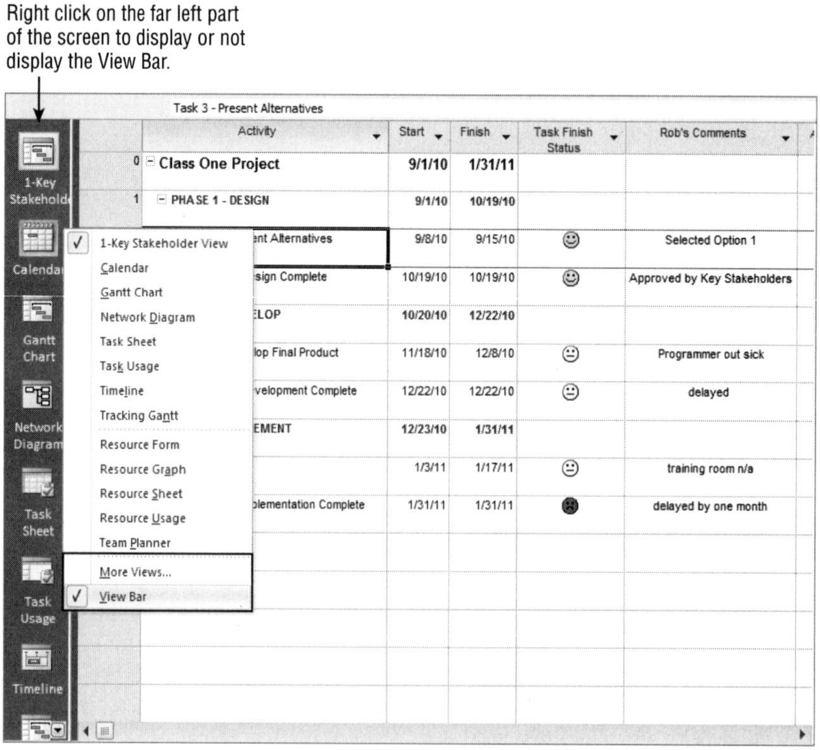

Right click on the far left part
of the screen to display or not
display the View Bar.

Formatting Text and Bar Styles

Communication and reporting are significant parts of what a project manager does, particularly during the planning and execution stages of a project. Learning how to enhance your schedule for presentations, reports, and email will help ensure your success. You can take advantage of the formatting tools available in Project to create higher-impact communication.

Formatting Text Styles

A Gantt chart consists of two separate parts on the screen. On the left is the text area, which contains the table of built-in or custom fields. On the right are the Gantt bars. You can format both sides to suit your needs.

One Line Item at a Time

In the text area, you can format one line item at a time. To change the look and feel of one item (or selected items), follow these steps (see Figure 13.5):

1. Select the task or series of tasks to format (remember, you can hold down the Ctrl key to multiselect tasks). To format an entire row, click the ID number on the left. You can also choose the specific cells you want to format.

2. Go to Task tab ➤ Font group.

3. Apply the appropriate font options.

FIGURE 13.5   Formatting text for specific line items

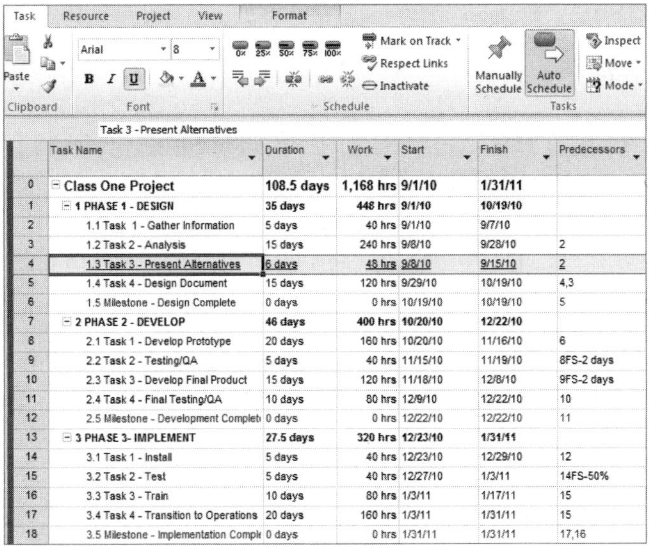

Figure 13.5 shows only one task highlighted in yellow and underlined. This allows you to call attention to that specific task. In this case, it highlights the fact that this task is coming up and that appropriate stakeholders should be aware of it. You can use this approach for both task-type views and resource-type views.

View-Wide Text Formatting

You may want to enhance the appearance of your schedule by making view-wide changes. For example, perhaps you want to call out the appearance of milestones, critical tasks, or summary tasks for the entire view and not just one task at a time. You can accomplish this by taking advantage of the Text Styles command, as shown in Figure 13.6, by following these steps:

1. In the Gantt chart, go to Format tab ➢ Format group, and click the Text Styles button.

2. In the Text Styles dialog box, click the Item to Change drop-down list.

3. Review the items that you can modify for the entire view.

4. Make a selection from the list, and choose the appropriate font settings such as size, color, and background.

FIGURE 13.6 Applying view-wide formats with text styles

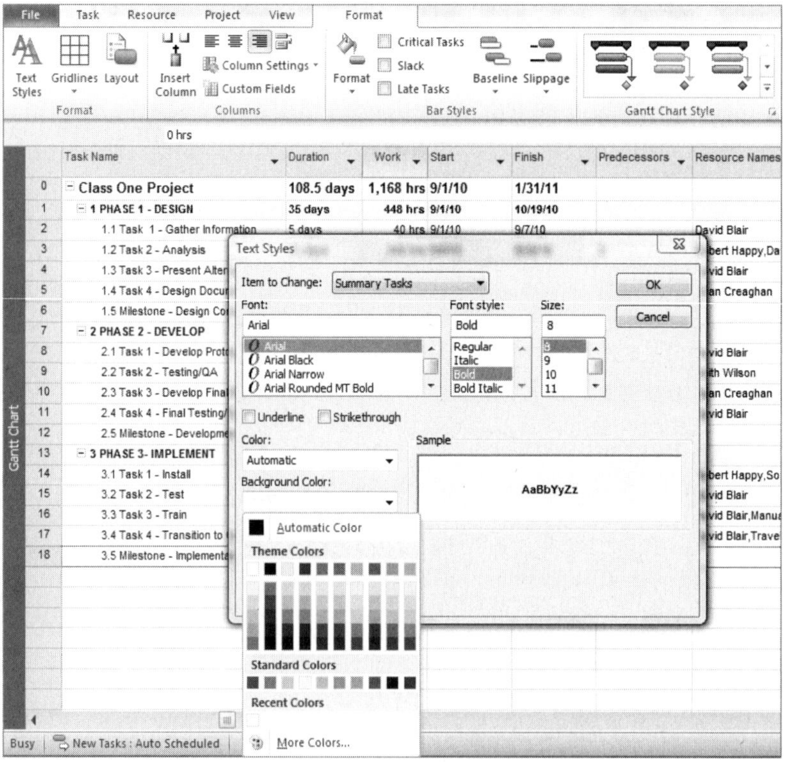

Figure 13.6 shows the selection for summary tasks with a background color of light yellow.

The text formats you select are view-specific. As you switch from one view to another, the formatted text changes as well. This makes it even more valuable to create custom views so you can apply custom text formatting to suit the needs of different stakeholders in each view without having to reformat each time.

Formatting Bar Styles

Formatting the look and feel of the Gantt bar area is also very useful. You can modify the look and feel of summary tasks, tasks, and milestones, including attributes such as progress lines for percent complete, delay lines, and so on. Not only can you change the appearance of the bar, but you can also add text around the bar. Any of the fields available to be added to a table is also available to be added on top of, below, to the right of, to the left of, or inside a bar. This allows for richer communication of schedules.

Formatting One Bar at a Time

Just as in the text area, you can choose to format one bar at a time or make view-wide changes to your Gantt bars. Sometimes you may want to focus on one task or one milestone and change its look and feel either by changing the color or by adding text around it.

Figure 13.7 shows the two choices you have when formatting bars. Bar applies format changes only to the specific line item or items you've selected, and Bar Styles makes view-wide changes to all the bars in the Gantt Chart view.

FIGURE 13. 7   Accessing format bar styles

To make changes to one bar, follow these steps:

1. In the Gantt Chart view, select Format tab ➤ Bar Styles group ➤ Format ➤ Bar.
2. Choose the appropriate shape, type, or color.
3. Click OK.

After you select the Format Bar option, you can choose the appropriate settings and style for that specific item or selected items. The example in Figure 13.8 shows the single selected milestone formatted with a different shape and a different color.

View-Wide Bar Format Changes (Including Adding Text)

You can also make view-wide changes to the look and feel of the Gantt bars by selecting Bar Styles from the Format list:

1. In the Gantt view, select Format tab ➤ Bar Styles group ➤ Format ➤ Bar Styles.

2. Under Name, select the item to change, and choose the appropriate bar shape, type, or color.

3. Click OK.

FIGURE 13.8 Formatting bar styles, shapes, and text

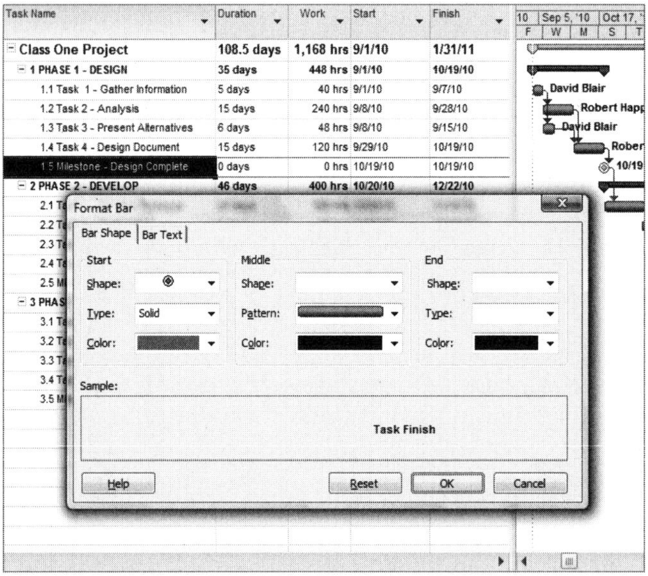

As shown in Figure 13.9, you can now make view-wide changes to the way bars are displayed in the Gantt view. For example, if you click Milestone and change the shape and color, the change affects all the milestones in the chart.

FIGURE 13.9 View-wide format changes to bar styles

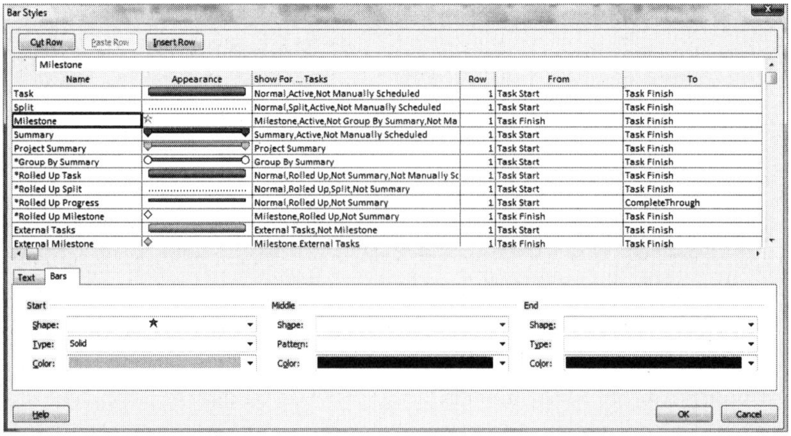

Using this approach, you can make view-wide changes to your Gantt bar area for any type of item or line that appears in the chart. You can also add text to your bar area, applying it to any of the fields that are available for a table. To do so, click the Text tab in the Bar Styles dialog box. You can then add text above, to the right of, to the left of, below, or inside a bar by selecting from the drop-down list. Figure 13.10 is an example of a modified Gantt bar based on applying text fields in the bar area.

FIGURE 13.10   Adding text to bars

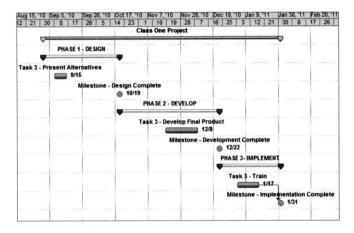

Figure 13.10 shows the Name field on top and the finish date to the right of the tasks, milestones, and summary tasks, including the project summary. This makes for another effective way to communicate a project schedule.

Formatting the Timeline View

The Timeline view is a concise roll-up of the entire project into one bar that can be easily formatted and shared (see Chapter 10). Because it's such a powerful communication tool, it's worthwhile reviewing the unique formatting options available. As with the Gantt chart, you can apply specific formats to enhance your communication.

By default, the Timeline view appears on top of the Gantt chart. You can turn the Timeline view on or off as follows:

1. Go to View tab ➤ Split Screen group.

2. Click the Timeline command on or off.

You can also add tasks or milestones to the timeline by right-clicking an item in the Gantt chart table and clicking Add to Timeline. You can remove items in a similar fashion.

After items are added to your Timeline view, you can format the items and the timeline bar itself for more effective communication. You can also display only the Timeline view without the Gantt chart by following these steps:

1. Go to Task tab ➤ View group, and click the Gantt Chart button.

2. From the list, select Timeline.

The Timeline view displays by itself, ready for additional formatting, as shown in Figure 13.11.

FIGURE 13.11   Formatting the Timeline view

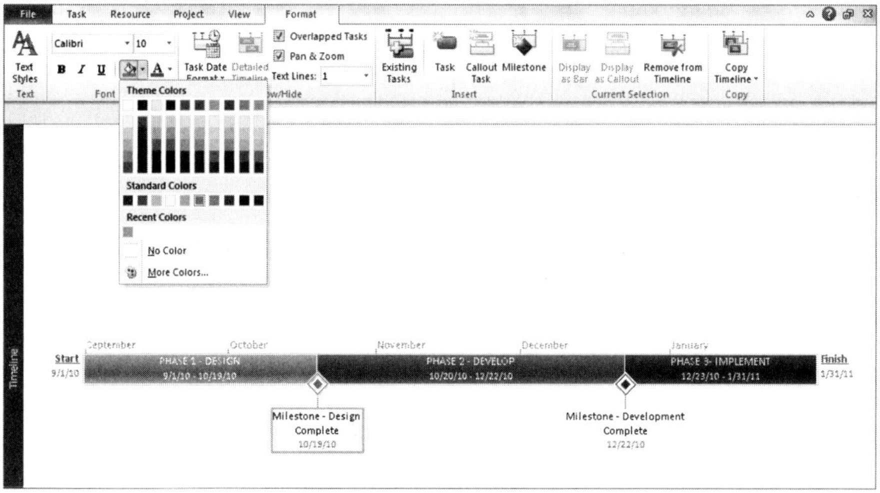

To format the Timeline view, click the Format tab, remembering that the format tools are different depending on which view is applied. In this case, you can use each of the group areas to modify the Timeline view in different ways. For example, you can change the font or color of a task or milestone by selecting it in the view and using the tools in the Font group or clicking the Text Styles command in the Text group to make view-wide changes to the text.

You can also add line items to or delete them from the Timeline view as shown in Figure 13.12, by following these steps:

1.   In the Timeline view, go to Format tab ➢ Insert group, and click the Existing Tasks button.

2.   In the Add Tasks to Timeline dialog box, select the items you want to include in the view.

Figure 13.12 adds to the view not only the milestones but also the three main summary tasks, which you can see in Figure 13.11. You're now free to format each of these items for more effective presentations.

You can also take a task or summary task that you've added to your timeline and make it a callout instead of embedding it in the timeline bar. Figure 13.13 illustrates using callouts for the summary tasks. To create a callout, follow these steps:

1.   In the Timeline view, click the task or summary task item you want as a callout.

2.   Go to Format tab ➢ Current Selection group, and click Display as Callout.

You can format the callout names by either using the Text Styles option for view-wide changes or using the Font group for individual item changes.

FIGURE 13.12   Adding items to or deleting them from the Timeline view

FIGURE 13.13   Adding a callout to the Timeline view

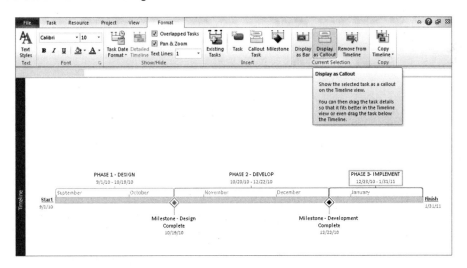

When you're ready to share the Timeline view, right-click, as shown in Figure 13.14, and select For E-Mail, For Presentation, or Full Size. You can also follow these steps:

1. In the Timeline view, go to Format tab ➢ Copy group, and click the Copy Timeline button.

2. Select For E-Mail, For Presentation, or Full Size.

3. In the target application (for example, Outlook or PowerPoint), select Paste.

FIGURE 13.14 Sharing the Timeline view

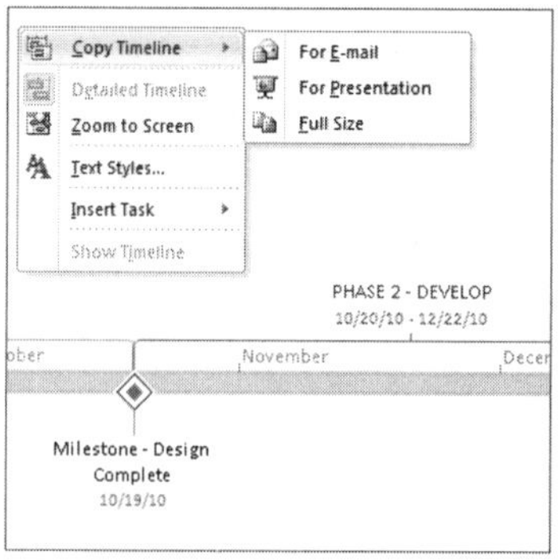

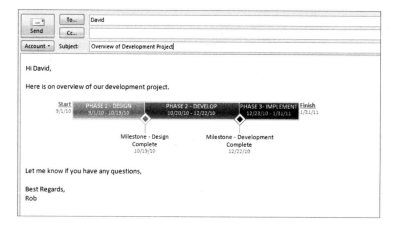

Figure 13.15 is an example of what it looks like if you paste a copy of the Timeline view into an e-mail.

FIGURE 13.15 Timeline View in an e-mail

As you can see, the Format tab in the Timeline view lets you share project information with stakeholders more effectively.

Sharing and Sending Project Information and Reports

This section describes how to share and send project information. I cover simple tools from enhanced copy and paste to synchronizing data with SharePoint. I also explain how to use the Organizer tool to swap components such as views, tables, filters, and so on from one project plan to another. You can also save changes to the default global.mpt file.

Enhanced Copy and Paste

Project 2010 lets you copy and paste information from one application to another while maintaining important schedule format characteristics such as the indenting and outdenting of tasks and column headings. You can quickly share project information in other applications, such as Word, PowerPoint, Outlook, and Excel.

As shown in Figure 13.16, when you select a section of a schedule, the column heading are automatically selected too, even though you haven't highlighted them. After you select the items, click Copy on the Task tab in the Clipboard group (or press Ctrl-C).

FIGURE 13.16   Selecting content to copy

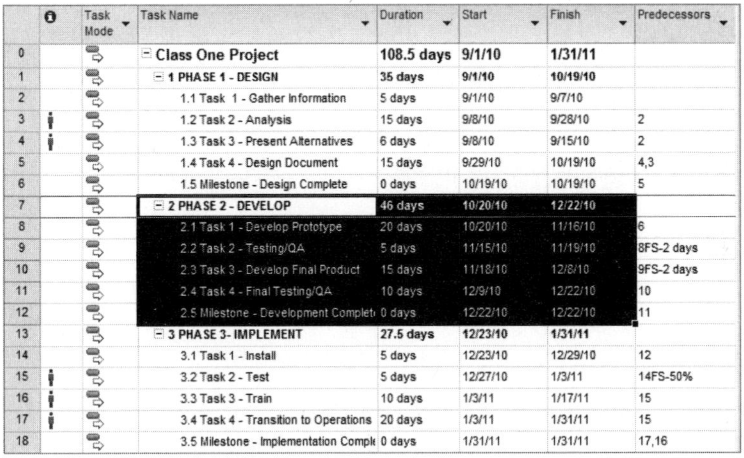

	🛈	Task Mode	Task Name	Duration	Start	Finish	Predecessors
0			⊟ **Class One Project**	**108.5 days**	**9/1/10**	**1/31/11**	
1			⊟ **1 PHASE 1 - DESIGN**	**35 days**	**9/1/10**	**10/19/10**	
2			1.1 Task 1 - Gather Information	5 days	9/1/10	9/7/10	
3	👤		1.2 Task 2 - Analysis	15 days	9/8/10	9/28/10	2
4	👤		1.3 Task 3 - Present Alternatives	6 days	9/8/10	9/15/10	2
5			1.4 Task 4 - Design Document	15 days	9/29/10	10/19/10	4,3
6			1.5 Milestone - Design Complete	0 days	10/19/10	10/19/10	5
7			⊟ **2 PHASE 2 - DEVELOP**	**46 days**	**10/20/10**	**12/22/10**	
8			2.1 Task 1 - Develop Prototype	20 days	10/20/10	11/16/10	6
9			2.2 Task 2 - Testing/QA	5 days	11/15/10	11/19/10	8FS-2 days
10			2.3 Task 3 - Develop Final Product	15 days	11/18/10	12/8/10	9FS-2 days
11			2.4 Task 4 - Final Testing/QA	10 days	12/9/10	12/22/10	10
12			2.5 Milestone - Development Complete	0 days	12/22/10	12/22/10	11
13			⊟ **3 PHASE 3- IMPLEMENT**	**27.5 days**	**12/23/10**	**1/31/11**	
14			3.1 Task 1 - Install	5 days	12/23/10	12/29/10	12
15	👤		3.2 Task 2 - Test	5 days	12/27/10	1/3/11	14FS-50%
16			3.3 Task 3 - Train	10 days	1/3/11	1/17/11	15
17	👤		3.4 Task 4 - Transition to Operations	20 days	1/3/11	1/31/11	15
18			3.5 Milestone - Implementation Complete	0 days	1/31/11	1/31/11	17,16

After you've made your selection and clicked Copy, go to the target application and paste. Figure 13.17 illustrates what happens when you paste into an e-mail.

FIGURE 13.17   Enhanced copy-and-paste example

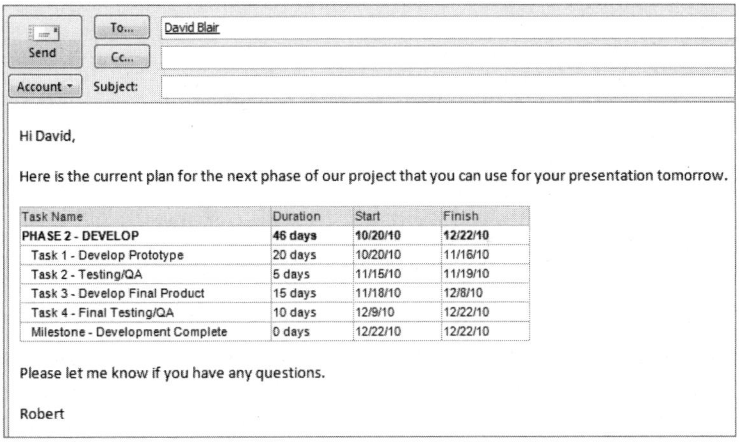

	To...	David Blair
Send	Cc...	
Account ▾	Subject:	

Hi David,

Here is the current plan for the next phase of our project that you can use for your presentation tomorrow.

Task Name	Duration	Start	Finish
PHASE 2 - DEVELOP	**46 days**	**10/20/10**	**12/22/10**
Task 1 - Develop Prototype	20 days	10/20/10	11/16/10
Task 2 - Testing/QA	5 days	11/15/10	11/19/10
Task 3 - Develop Final Product	15 days	11/18/10	12/8/10
Task 4 - Final Testing/QA	10 days	12/9/10	12/22/10
Milestone - Development Complete	0 days	12/22/10	12/22/10

Please let me know if you have any questions.

Robert

As you can see in Figure 13.17, the column headings are automatically included in the paste, and the formatting of the schedule stays intact, for more effective sharing and communication of project information.

Copy Picture

If you want to include the Gantt bars when you copy all or part of your project schedule, you can take advantage of the Copy Picture command. Based on whatever formatting, table, filter, or highlight you've applied in a Gantt view, you can share that information, including the Gantt bars, by following these steps (see Figure 13.18):

1. Select Task tab ➤ Clipboard group ➤ Copy ➤ Copy Picture.

2. In the Copy Picture dialog box, under Render Image, choose For Screen.

3. Review the other options available, and click OK.

4. In the target application, select Paste.

FIGURE 13.18   Copy picture

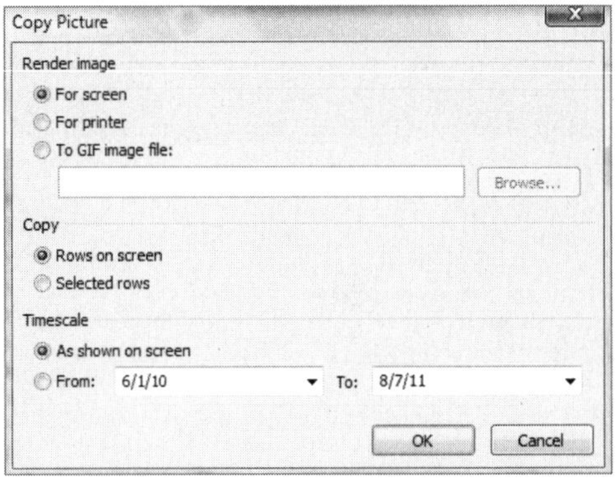

You can also control what you select by first highlighting the line items you want to include and choosing Selected Rows in the Copy Picture dialog box. Figure 13.19 shows what the picture looks like when you paste into PowerPoint.

The Organizer and the Global.MPT Template

Now that you know how to apply and create custom fields, tables, filters, groups, views, and calendars, you can share these elements with other project files. You may need to make them part of the default settings when you launch Project and start a new project file, which is based on a file known as the Global Template (global.mpt).

To share these elements using the Organizer, you must have both the source and target files open at the same time. For example, if you have Class One Project open and you start a new blank project, you can copy the custom view over by following these steps (see Figure 13.20):

1. Click the File tab to get to the backstage.

2. On the Info tab, click the Organizer button.

3. In the Organizer dialog box, click the View tab.

4. From the Views Available In drop-down lists, select the source and target files.

5. Click the view you want to copy, and click Copy from one side (the source file) to the other (the target file)

6. Click the close button in the upper-right corner. The view is now available in the target file.

FIGURE 13.19 Using Copy Picture to paste into PowerPoint

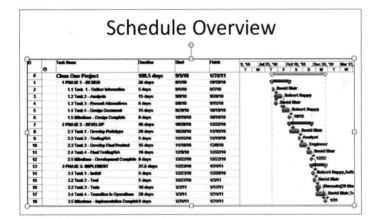

Sharing Views with the Organizer

A custom view is made up of filters, groups, and tables (which may have custom fields). If any of these components are custom, they have to be copied over into the target file. For example, if you have a custom view with a custom table based on custom fields, you must use the Organizer to move over all of these components.

You can repeat this process for any other type of element you want to copy over, such as calendars, custom fields, and so on. If you want any of the project elements to start up automatically when you launch Project, so they're included in all files (existing or new), you can add them to the `global.mpt` file. You can use the Organizer to swap elements between two files or between a file and the Global Template.

FIGURE 13.20 Using the Organizer

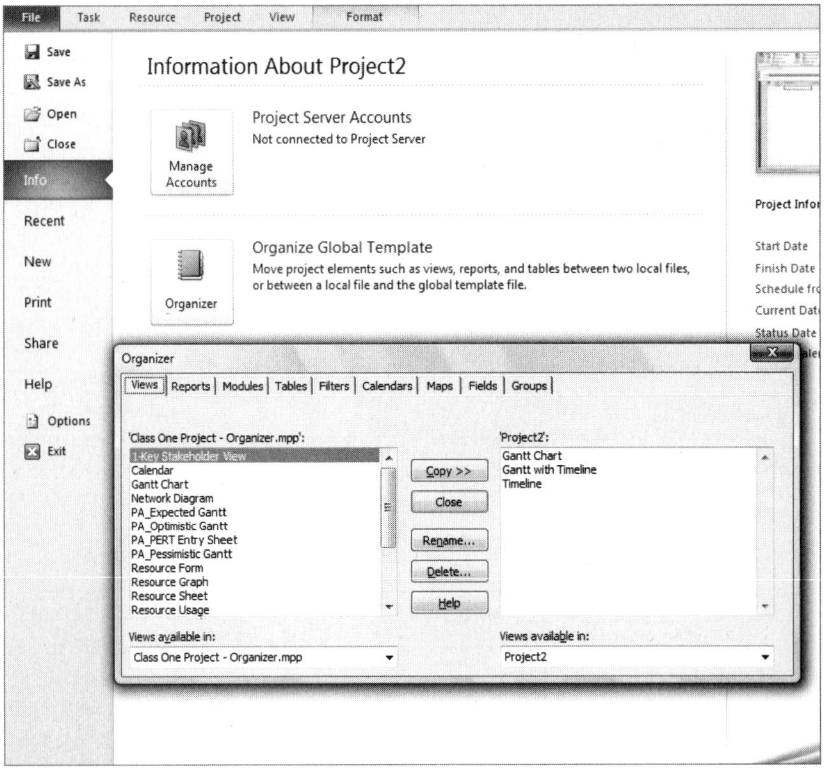

This is also the place to delete or rename project elements. For example, if you save a table with the wrong name, and it keeps appearing in the Table list's Custom section, you can either rename or delete it in the Organizer. This type of maintenance is particularly useful if you have a significant amount of customization.

Global.MPT and Other Project Templates

You can make custom views, fields, calendars, and other elements automatically start up when you launch Project by placing them in the global.mpt file. This means they're part of any existing or new project files you working on.

On the other hand, if you create your own project template files, you can include custom project elements that launch only when you start a new project plan from that specific template. For example, if you create a template for a development project, it may contain a standard list of tasks and milestones as well as custom views, fields, and calendars. For more on saving templates, see Chapter 4.

SharePoint Synchronization

You can share project information using SharePoint Server or SharePoint Foundation 2010. With the touch of a button, you can sync your data with SharePoint for better collaboration with project stakeholders, such as team members or senior management.

Users can view information in a Gantt chart–like Project task list in SharePoint and even provide updates. This synchronization is bidirectional, so project managers can both send project schedule information to and receive it from SharePoint, keeping all members of the project team informed with up-to-the-minute updates.

SharePoint Sync Requirements

You must have SharePoint Server or SharePoint Foundation 2010. It only works in manual scheduled task mode (auto-scheduled tasks are changed to manual) and with links that are finish-to-start (FS) with no lags. Also, if you have resource assignments on tasks, then in order for them to be accepted into the SharePoint task list the resources must be set up in SharePoint as users, with the same names used in the Project resource pool.

As shown in Figure 13.21, to set up the initial task list to sync with SharePoint, follow these steps:

1. Click the File tab to get to the backstage.

2. Click the Share tab, and click the Sync with Tasks List option.

3. At right, be sure the Site URL is correct, and click Validate URL.

4. Either select an existing Project task list or enter the name of a new list that will appear in SharePoint.

5. Click the Sync button.

FIGURE 13.21   Syncing a task list with SharePoint

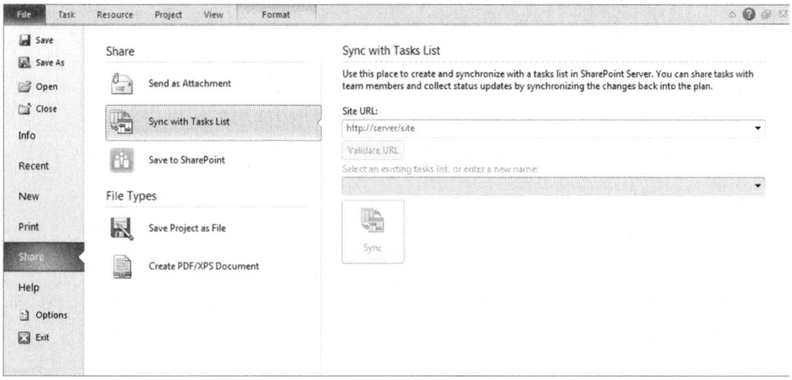

This automatically sets up a new Project task list in SharePoint in a simple Gantt chart format. You can now view the task list in SharePoint at any time and synchronize it with Project, including syncing updates from team members such as revised dates or percent complete.

After the task-list sync is set up, you can keep it in sync or update the sync at any time in Project. For example, when you make changes to your schedule in Project, or to receive updates from the task list in SharePoint, follow these steps:

1. In the backstage, click the Info tab.
2. Click the Sync button.

Project defaults to synchronizing the following fields: Name, Start, Finish, % Complete, Resource Names, and Predecessor. You can add more built-in or custom fields for synchronization as well. As shown in Figure 13.22, to add fields for synchronization, follow these steps:

1. In the backstage, click the Info tab.
2. In the Sync to Tasks List area, click Manage Fields.
3. Click Add Field.
4. In the Add Field dialog box, select the fields you want to add.
5. Click OK, and then click OK again.

FIGURE 13.22   Adding fields for SharePoint synchronization

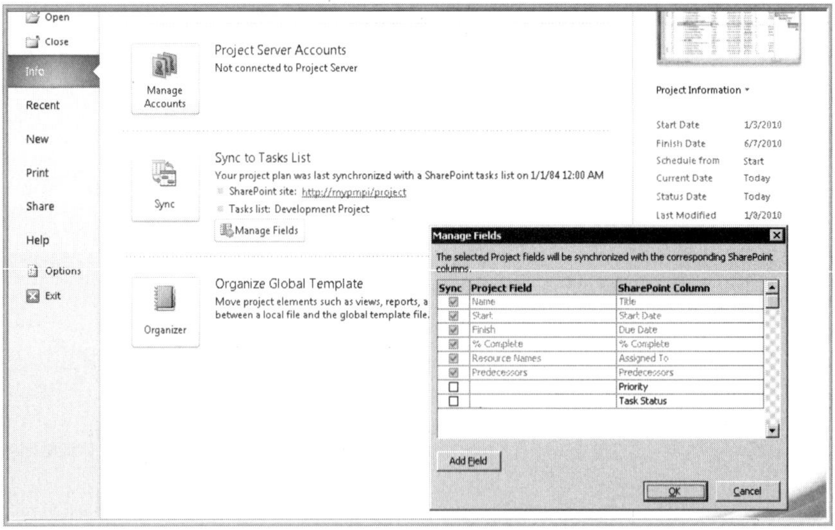

File Types

You can save project files in a variety of different formats. For example, maybe you want to save your plan as an Excel Workbook; or you may want to share it as a PDF for easy distribution.

To save your file in a different type or format, follow these steps (see Figure 13.23):

1. Click the File tab to get to the backstage.

2. Click the Share tab.

3. Under File Types, click Save Project as File. Or, choose Create PDF/XPS Document.

4. Review the various file-type options at right.

FIGURE 13.23   Saving a project as a file

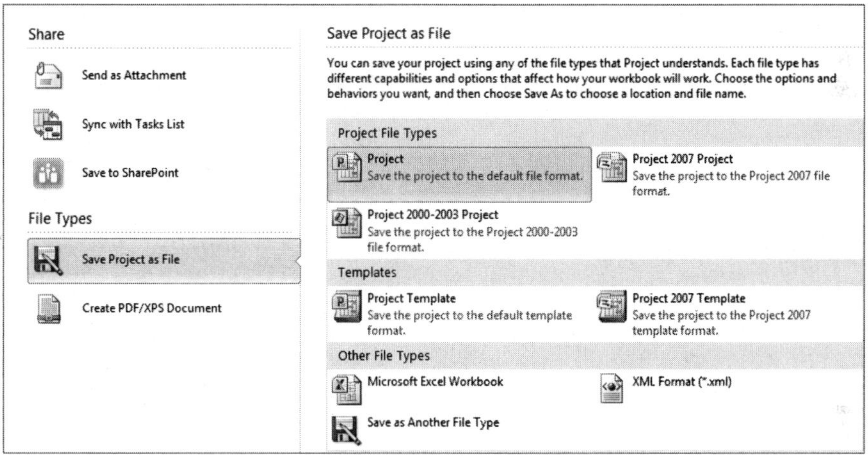

You can save the file in a previous version format, as a template for future reuse, or as another file type such as an Excel Workbook or XML format. Select Save as Another File Type for more options.

Visual Reports

Project can create graphical visual reports in either Excel or Visio. This lets you manage and communicate project information in an enhanced fashion compared to what is available in Project. For example, you can create a pie chart or bar chart outlining how costs or work is broken down.

As shown in Figure 13.24, creating visual reports is easy. Follow these steps:

1. Go to Project tab ➤ Reports group, and click Visual Reports.

2. In the Visual Reports dialog box, select either Microsoft Excel or Microsoft Visio.

3. Choose the report type you want to create.

4. Click View.

The report is automatically created in Excel or Visio. You can modify the various template settings with Edit Template to tweak the report or modify the level of usage data from weeks, to months, to quarters.

FIGURE 13.24 Creating visual reports

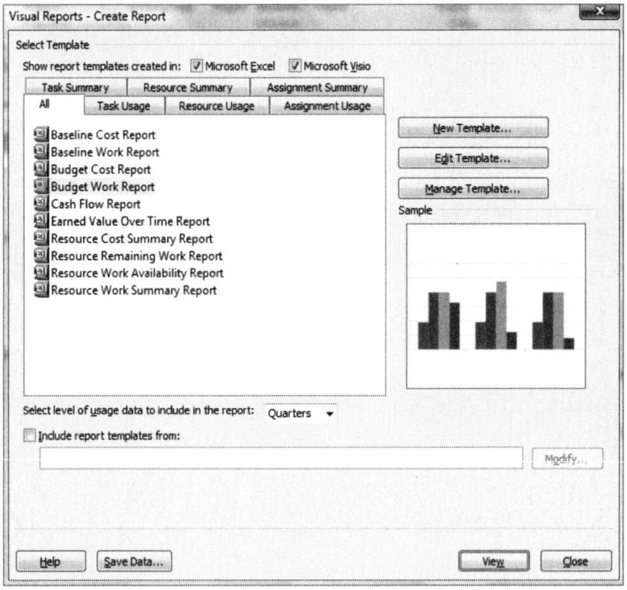

The generation of the report is based on building a local OLAP cube, which further allows you to modify the data after it's in Excel. It generates a pivot table field list in which you can pick and choose additional fields to add to the table in the report.

Next to the Visual Report button in the Reports group is a Reports button. It offers a list of predefined text-based reports that you may find useful when you need to look at things like the overall project summary or the Who Does What When report. These reports can also be edited to include filters, tables, and various other items, similar to selecting components in views.

To generate the Who Does What When Report (see Figure 13.25), follow these steps:

1. Go to Project tab ➤ Reports group, and click the Reports button.

2. Double-click Assignments.

3. Double-click Who Does What When, or click Edit to select options to include or exclude for the report. Print Preview automatically launches.

4. Click Print.

FIGURE 13.25   Printing predefined reports

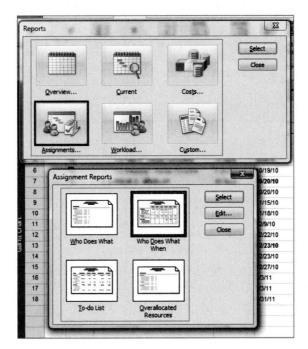

Summary

In this chapter, you learned how to use project elements such as custom fields, tables, filters, and groups to create custom views. I also covered how to format both text and bar styles, which are view-specific; as you switch from one view to another, formatting may also change.

I covered formatting the Timeline view in Project, because it's a new view and will no doubt by one of the most commonly used communication tools.

As you learn about customizing project elements, you may need to share them with other project files or the global.mpt template. To manage these elements, including deleting and renaming them, you can use the Organizer.

Finally, I covered important sharing tools found under the Share tab in the backstage. You can sync tasks with SharePoint Server or SharePoint Foundation 2010 and save plans in various file types such as Excel Workbook, XML document, PDFs, and others. Project also has a built-in Visual Reports tool that generates graphical reports in Excel and Visio. And you can take advantage of the predefined text-based reports, which you can find on the Project tab in the Reports group.

Hands-On Exercises

The following hands-on exercises are designed to test your understanding of the topics discussed in this chapter. We've provided files on the companion CD that will show you what your project file should look like as you perform these exercises.

EXERCISE 16

Creating a Custom View

1. Working with the Class One Project, select Task tab ≻ View group ≻ Gantt Chart ≻ More Views.

2. In the More Views dialog box, click the New button, click Single View, and click OK.

3. In the Name field, type in a custom name for the view, such as Key Stakeholder View.

4. The default Screen: Gantt Chart will be selected which is fine.

5. Select a table from the Table drop-down list--such as a custom table you created specifically for this stakeholder. In this example, I have selected My Planning Table.

6. From the Group drop-down list, select a group to apply or [No Group]. In this example, I have selected [No Group].

7. From the Filter drop-down list, select a filter to apply or [No Filter]. In this example I have selected Milestones.

8. Select Show in Menu.

9. Click the Apply button.

10. Go to Task tab View group, and click the Gantt Chart button to view the list of custom views and built-in views.

Save the Class One Project file.

EXERCISE 17:

Using the Organizer

1. Click the File tab to access the backstage.

2. On the Info tab, click Organizer.

3. Review the files that are open in the bottom section of the Organizer, under Views Available In.

The files default to the global.mpt file and the file you have open. You can change the files by clicking the drop-down list only if you have other files open.

4. Click the tabs across the top of the Organizer to view various elements such as tables, filters, groups, fields, and calendars. You can copy, delete, and rename each element under each tab.

5. Close the Organizer.

Chapter

14

Creating Master Schedules with Inserted Projects

IN THIS CHAPTER, YOU'LL LEARN ABOUT THE FOLLOWING:

✓ Working with the master schedule

✓ Using inserted projects

✓ Understanding cross-project, external dependencies

✓ Creating a critical path across a master schedule

✓ Including project information in a master schedule

Whether you're managing multiple projects or a program with subprojects, learning about how to create and manage master project plans with inserted projects is important. This chapter covers not only how to create and save master plans but also how to share resources across multiple projects. You'll learn how to view and analyze cross-project information, such as an integrated critical path, and how to apply filters to create high-level dashboard-type views.

Creating Master Schedules

This section explains what a master schedule is and how to create one. Master projects let you create rolled-up reports across multiple projects and create external dependencies between tasks in different projects.

Setting Up a Master Project File

A *master project* is a file that contains inserted projects from other source files that can be linked dynamically. If you choose to link to the source file, then every time the source file is modified or changed in any way, the master file is automatically updated to reflect those changes. You also have the choice to make changes to project information while in the master file; those changes are automatically reflected in the source file. In other words, this is a bidirectional dynamic link.

If you choose not to link the inserted project file, the current version of that file is inserted; there is no synchronization between the files if one changes.

To set up a master project file, you can either insert project files into an existing project file or create a new one from scratch. In this example, you'll create a new project file from scratch. Follow these steps to begin a new master project file:

1. Click the File tab to get to the backstage.
2. Click the New tab.
3. Under Available Templates, double-click Blank Project.
4. Click the File tab in the newly created project file.
5. Click Save As, and save the new blank project with an appropriate name, such as Master <_____> Project.

You now have a blank shell into which you can insert subprojects or existing project files. Instead of entering tasks into the Task Name column, follow these steps to insert existing project files into the master project file, as shown in Figure 14.1:

1. Go to Project tab ➢ Insert group, and click the Subproject button.

2. In the Insert Project dialog box, select the project file (or multiple files, using the Ctrl key) to be inserted.

3. Select the Link to Project option if you wish.

4. Click the Insert button to insert as read/write, *or* choose Insert Read-Only from the Insert drop-down list.

FIGURE 14.1   Inserting subprojects into a master project file

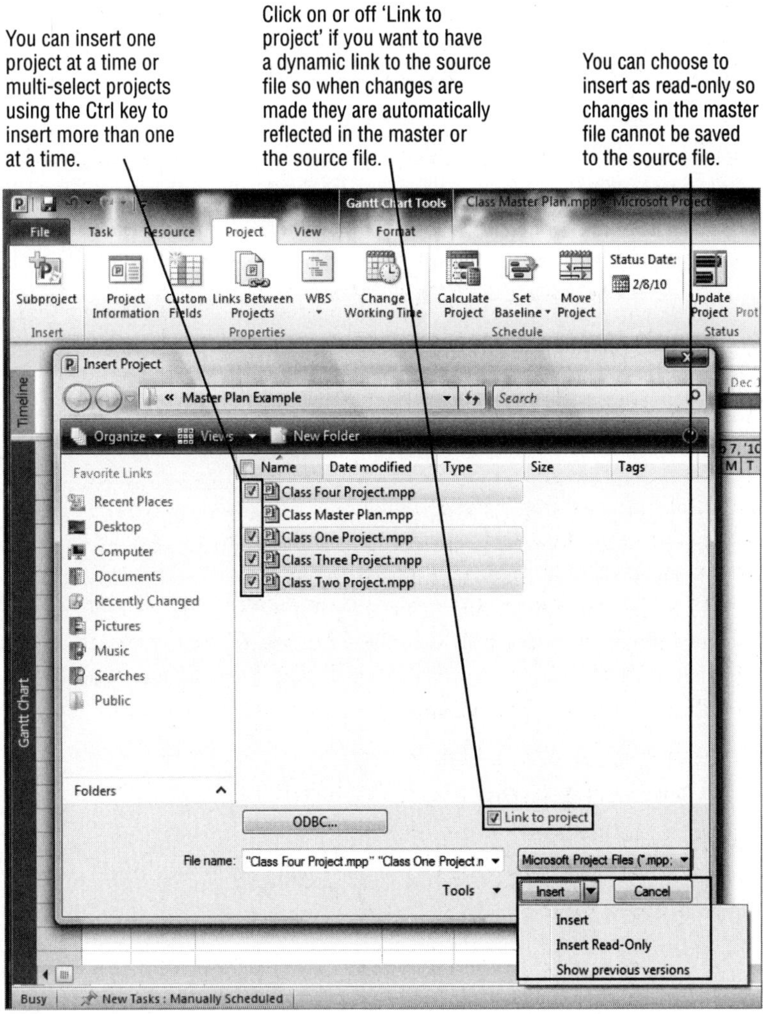

You can insert one project at a time or multi-select projects using the Ctrl key to insert more than one at a time.

Click on or off 'Link to project' if you want to have a dynamic link to the source file so when changes are made they are automatically reflected in the master or the source file.

You can choose to insert as read-only so changes in the master file cannot be saved to the source file.

As you can see in Figure 14.1, you have the choice to insert the project file as read-only. Doing so allows the dynamic link to exist but doesn't let users of the master file save any changes made to the source file. This is useful if you're using the master file for reporting and communication purposes and you don't want the users to make changes to the data in the source files.

Real World Scenario

Master Files for Dashboard Reporting

I worked with a biotechnology company that needed to track five milestones across each of its development projects. The client wanted to be able to capture an overview of these milestones in a one-page report. The company didn't want anyone to change the source data from the master file; only project managers were allowed to make changes to their respective project files. So, in this case, it made sense to insert the project files into the master file as read-only.

After the master file was set up, I created a filtered view specifically to display the five milestones across the projects. Because the client wanted the milestones to be automatically updated, project files had to be inserted with the Link to Project option: that way, when a project manager updated the source plan, the filtered view in the master file stayed in sync.

To generate the weekly milestones report across projects, the client opened the master plan, clicked the Custom Filtered view, and could quickly generate a report to print or copy into a presentation.

After you create the master file, you can save it with the inserted files embedded, so that the next time you open the master file it automatically finds the source files. Because the embedded files point to source plans in specific locations on your network or hard drive, it's important to keep the source files in a folder or location where they won't be moved. This way, when you open the master file, Project will find the source files when it searches for them using the embedded location. If you move the source files, Project will force you to search for the inserted project; if it can't be found, you'll get the message shown in Figure 14.2.

FIGURE 14.2 The file can't be found.

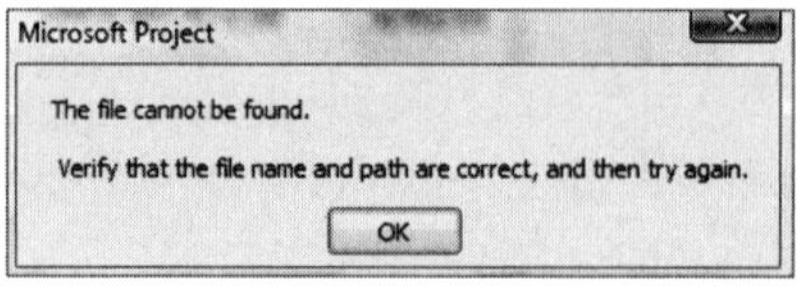

My recommendation is to keep the source files in the same location and avoid moving them, so the master file is stable. If you create a master file that isn't linked to the source file, then this is a moot point, because the master file won't search for the source files. This kind of master file, which doesn't link to source files, is a static snapshot of the inserted files that can be saved as a one-off file. Because master files are so easy to create in Project 2010, this option is useful for sharing consolidated plans.

When you save a master file, you're first prompted to save the master file, and subsequently you're prompted to save the inserted files. If you make changes to the source files in the master, you're prompted to save them; select Yes or No for each individual inserted project, Yes to All, or No to All, to save or not save all the projects at one time, as shown in Figure 14.3.

FIGURE 14.3   Saving master files

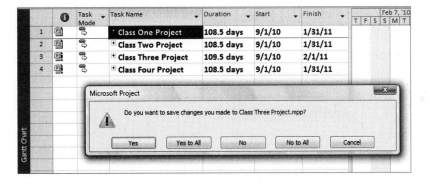

In Figure 14.3, two of the inserted projects have red exclamation marks beside them, indicating that they were inserted as read-only files. If you make changes and try to save them, you'll be prompted to save under different filenames.

Setting Up Cross-Project Links

After you've set up a master file with inserted subprojects, you can create links from one project to another. Cross-project linking enables project managers to link tasks in one project to tasks in another project. For example, you may have a task or milestone in one project that drives a line item, task, or milestone in another project. When you create a dependency between tasks in different projects this way, any changes to the start or finish date of the external task are automatically reflected in the successor task of the other project.

Review Chapter 7, "Setting Dependencies and the Critical Path," if you need a refresher on setting up links in a project. There are two basic ways to set up links between projects: You can manually type the path and filename in the Predecessors column, or you can use the Link tool, as shown in Figure 14.4.

FIGURE 14.4   Establishing cross-project links

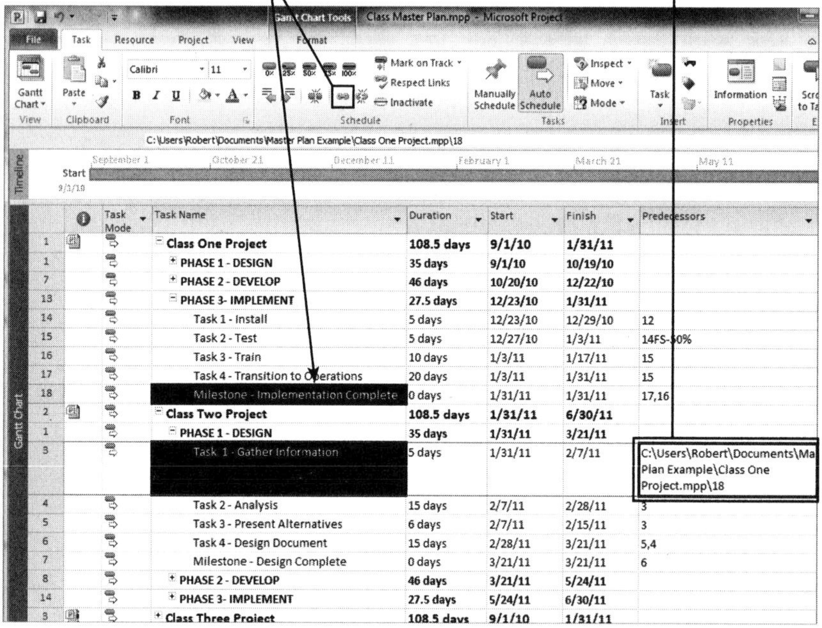

Have both project plans expanded in the master file and click on the first task and, holding the Ctrl key, click on the second task so they are both highlighted. Under the Task tab, in the Schedule group, click on the Link button.

You can also type the full path and file name with the ID number of the task directly into the predecessor column.

I've found that it's much easier to create a link using the Link button in the Schedule group rather than trying to remember the full path name and correct syntax to type into the Predecessors column. You also have the option to type directly into the Successor column if it's displayed in the table.

After cross-project links are established, you can view them in the source files as external links. *External* relates to those tasks outside of a project. These external tasks are sometimes called *ghost tasks*, a name that refers to an external (replicated) task, as shown in Figure 14.5.

External tasks aren't displayed in the master file if both tasks are expanded and displayed, because they're both in view. When either project is displayed alone (for example, doesn't contain the other as an inserted project), the external task is displayed with special light-gray ghost formatting so you can easily distinguish it from other tasks. If you're working in the source files, one project gets an external successor task and the other gets an external predecessor task.

If an external task is displayed as a ghost task in the active project, it gets its own ID in the active project (not necessarily the same ID it has in its parent project). A predecessor ghost task is inserted just before the corresponding internal successor task, and a successor ghost task is inserted just after the corresponding internal predecessor task. However, if a ghost task representing the external task already exists, then that ghost task is used to represent the external task in all the relationships it may have with tasks in the active project. In other words, if two tasks in the active project both have the same external predecessor, only one ghost task represents that external task in the active project.

FIGURE 14.5   External links (ghost tasks)

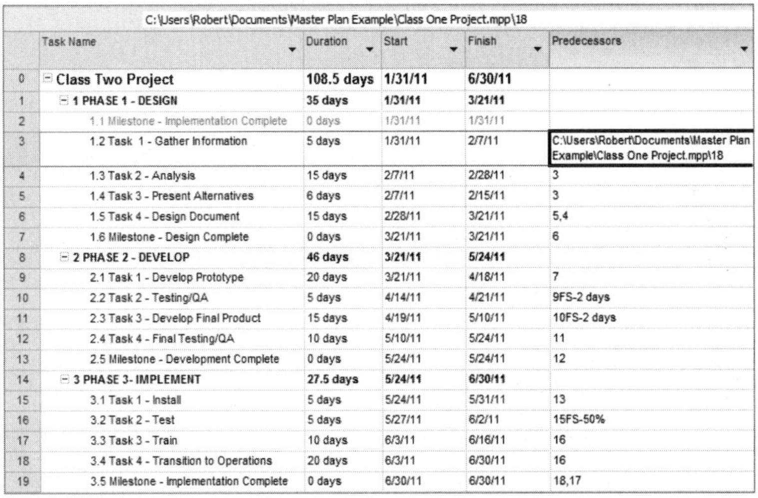

	Task Name	Duration	Start	Finish	Predecessors
	C:\Users\Robert\Documents\Master Plan Example\Class One Project.mpp\18				
0	⊟ **Class Two Project**	**108.5 days**	**1/31/11**	**6/30/11**	
1	⊟ **1 PHASE 1 - DESIGN**	**35 days**	**1/31/11**	**3/21/11**	
2	1.1 Milestone - Implementation Complete	0 days	1/31/11	1/31/11	
3	1.2 Task 1 - Gather Information	5 days	1/31/11	2/7/11	C:\Users\Robert\Documents\Master Plan Example\Class One Project.mpp\18
4	1.3 Task 2 - Analysis	15 days	2/7/11	2/28/11	3
5	1.4 Task 3 - Present Alternatives	6 days	2/7/11	2/15/11	3
6	1.5 Task 4 - Design Document	15 days	2/28/11	3/21/11	5,4
7	1.6 Milestone - Design Complete	0 days	3/21/11	3/21/11	6
8	⊟ **2 PHASE 2 - DEVELOP**	**46 days**	**3/21/11**	**5/24/11**	
9	2.1 Task 1 - Develop Prototype	20 days	3/21/11	4/18/11	7
10	2.2 Task 2 - Testing/QA	5 days	4/14/11	4/21/11	9FS-2 days
11	2.3 Task 3 - Develop Final Product	15 days	4/19/11	5/10/11	10FS-2 days
12	2.4 Task 4 - Final Testing/QA	10 days	5/10/11	5/24/11	11
13	2.5 Milestone - Development Complete	0 days	5/24/11	5/24/11	12
14	⊟ **3 PHASE 3- IMPLEMENT**	**27.5 days**	**5/24/11**	**6/30/11**	
15	3.1 Task 1 - Install	5 days	5/24/11	5/31/11	13
16	3.2 Task 2 - Test	5 days	5/27/11	6/2/11	15FS-50%
17	3.3 Task 3 - Train	10 days	6/3/11	6/16/11	16
18	3.4 Task 4 - Transition to Operations	20 days	6/3/11	6/30/11	16
19	3.5 Milestone - Implementation Complete	0 days	6/30/11	6/30/11	18,17

While you're in the source file viewing the external link, you can also edit it. If you double-click a cell in a ghost task, Project opens the external project and places the cursor at the proper task. The cross-project link can be edited in either project.

You can delete the ghost task from the internal task's project. Doing so removes the link and removes the ghost task from the internal project. This action has no effect on the external task in the external project except to remove the cross-project link (and the appropriate ghost task) when that project is updated.

Cross-Project Linking Options and Showing Links Between Projects

The Options area in the backstage lets you control how links are updated when files are opened, as well as whether external links are displayed as ghost tasks, as shown in Figure 14.6. To get to these option settings, follow these steps:

1.   Click the File tab to get to the backstage.

2.   Click Options, and select the Advanced tab.

3.   Scroll down to the Cross-Project Linking Options for This Project section.

The first two settings, Show External Successors and Show External Predecessors, determine whether ghost predecessors and successors are displayed as tasks or hidden in the current project. This setting doesn't affect the predecessor and successor fields of the linked internal task, which show the external links as text.

FIGURE 14.6 Cross-project linking options

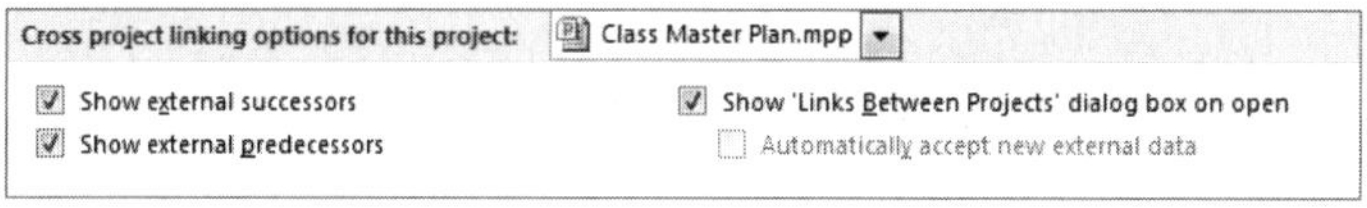

If you insert the parent project of an external task into the active project, then the external task isn't displayed as a ghost task but is instead displayed like any other task in an inserted project.

If you select the Show 'Links Between Projects' Dialog Box on Open option, then the Automatically Accept New External Data option is disabled and unchecked. If Show 'Links Between Projects' Dialog Box on Open isn't selected, then the Automatically Accept New External Data option is enabled and can be turned on or off.

If the Show 'Links Between Projects' Dialog Box on Open setting is selected, then Project displays the Links Between Projects dialog box whenever the file is opened, but only if there has been a change to an external task or link. If this setting is deselected, then Project doesn't display the dialog box on file open even if changes have been made to the external tasks or links. In that case, you can display the dialog box at any time by going to Project tab ➢ Properties group and clicking Links Between Projects.

If Automatically Accept New External Data is selected, then Project automatically accepts any new external link information without prompting you. If Project can't find the external link (because the link was removed or the project file was moved), then the external task is deleted.

Links Between Projects on Open

Suppose a link exists between a task in Class One Project and a task in Class Two Project, and you open Class Two Project. Here are two scenarios based on Class One Project being open or closed:

- If Class One Project is already open in memory, then the linked task in Class Two Project reflects the current information from Class One Project, and the ghost tasks reflect the current task data. Any open project reflects the current data of the external tasks and links.

- If Class One Project isn't currently open, then Project looks for the external data in the external project (which would cause the project to be loaded in the background). If this external data is different from the current data stored in the first project that's opened (Class Two Project), then Project displays the Cross-Project Links dialog box, which shows all external links. Links that have changed are shown in the Differences column.

The Links Between Projects dialog box (see Figure 14.7) displays all the cross-project predecessors and successors for the current project, with information about what changed in the current project. This dialog box also shows links whose source project can't be found or whose source task can't be found. From this dialog box, you can repair broken links, accept or refuse new data concerning a cross-project link, and edit or delete cross-project links (and thus ghost tasks as well).

FIGURE 14.7   Links Between Projects dialog box

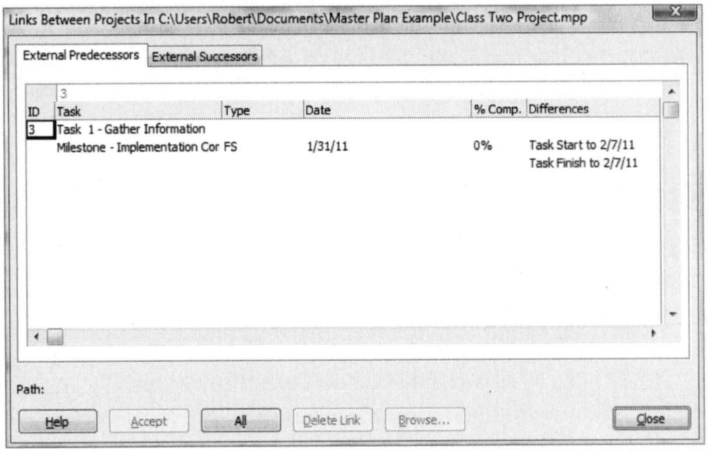

The dialog box has one tab that shows external predecessor tasks and another that shows external successor tasks. The following is a list of the fields in the Links Between Projects dialog box:

Task   Shows the internal and ghost-task pair that constitutes a cross-project link. The internal task is aligned to the left and has an ID number. The ghost task is indented under it.

Type   Shows the link type and any lag or lead information about the external link.

Date   Either the start date or the finish date of the external task. If the link is connected to the start date of the external task, then the date is the start date. If the link is connected to the finish date of the external task, then the date is the finish date.

%Comp   Shows the % Complete value for the external task.

Differences   Provides information about what has changed in the external task from the external project since it was last updated in the internal project, or lets you know that the external task or project file couldn't be found. If more than one piece of information changed, then the changes are listed on separate lines.

You also may have some choices to make regarding external links:

- The Accept button accepts all the changed information for the selected task.
- The All button accepts the changed information for all links in the dialog box.
- The Browse button lets you repair the path for an external project file that may have been moved or renamed.
- The Delete Link button deletes the selected cross-project link and removes the external task from the current project.

Critical Path Across Projects

Chapter 7 discusses the critical path, which allows you to see the controlling tasks that affect the end date of a project. This section shows how to view the critical path across multiple subprojects.

Default Settings

By default, after you create a master file with inserted subprojects, Project calculates one critical path, taking all the projects into consideration. The subproject or inserted project schedule with the last task or milestone drives what is on the critical path for all the other inserted projects. In Figure 14.8, Class Two Project finishes later than Class Three Project and therefore is on the critical path, whereas Class Three Project isn't.

When you insert a project into the master file, the source file inherits the characteristics of the critical path driven from the master. If Class Three Project isn't on the critical path and none of its tasks are in the master, then when you view it in the source file, it doesn't display any tasks on the critical path. In Figure 14.9, even though critical path formatting is turned on, no tasks appear on the critical path.

FIGURE 14.8   Viewing the critical path in a master file

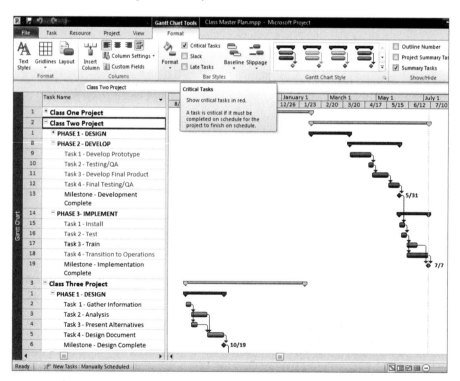

FIGURE 14.9 Viewing the critical path in a source file

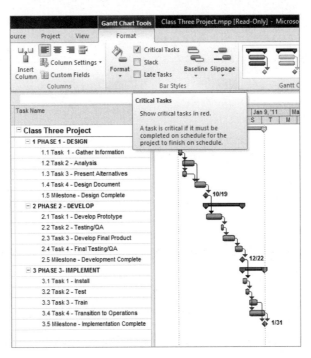

To display the critical path, select Format tab ➢ Bar Styles group ➢ Critical Paths.

Changing the Settings

The problem with inserting projects into a master is that by default, you lose the ability to view the critical path for an individual inserted project. However, you can change the settings so that you can do so.

By default, Project treats each inserted project like another summary task or phase. To change this setting, follow these steps:

1. Click the File tab to access the backstage.

2. Click the Options tab.

3. In the Project Options dialog box, click the Schedule tab.

4. Scroll down until you find Calculation Options for This Project.

5. Deselect the Inserted Projects Are Calculated Like Summary Tasks check box, as shown in Figure 14.10.

6. Click OK.

Class Three Project now has its own critical path, as will all the inserted projects. When you run the critical-path formatting in the source file, it also displays its own critical path. You can adjust the option setting depending on how you want to view the critical path.

FIGURE 14.10   Changing how inserted projects are treated

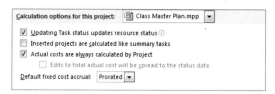

Real World Scenario

Integrated Master Schedules

Working with a large product-development company, I had to create a master plan that displayed the critical path across multiple projects. First, I developed an individual project schedule for each subproject that had a separate project manager who was responsible for maintaining the project file.

After creating the schedules, I created a master file with all the inserted subprojects. Then, I held an integration meeting with the project managers to establish the cross-project links in the master plan, with input from each of the stakeholders. Subsequently, each project manager could view the external ghost tasks in their source plans and immediately see the impact of slippage or change on any of the external tasks. This ultimately broke down barriers among the groups and allowed them to make quicker, more effective decisions based on changes and delays.

Everyone had read-only access to the master file so they could access the details of other project schedules if needed.

Reporting and Analyzing Across Projects

This section covers how to report and analyze information in a master plan. This includes looking at resource utilization across multiple projects.

Sharing Resources Across Projects

As you learned in Chapter 8, "Assigning Resources and Costs," you can set up a resource pool for sharing across projects. To do so, you create a separate file that contains only the resources used for assignments across multiple projects. This file typically doesn't contain any tasks or milestones—just resources in the resource sheet.

As shown in Figure 14.11, you can save the shared resources in a separate .mpp file and name it something like `Resource Pool.mpp`. Usually, I add the name of the organization, department, or group at the beginning of the name. This illustrates that the master file is a separate .mpp file that stakeholders can access or use to generate cross-project reports.

FIGURE 14.11   Master files and shared resources

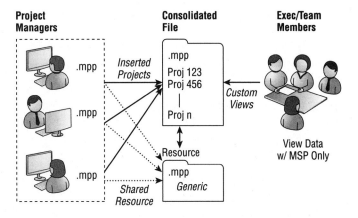

> If you're going to create a master file and a shared resource file, it's important to have one dedicated person responsible for owning and maintaining these files.

Each project manager who creates a new project file points to the resource pool, as shown in Figure 14.12, by following these steps:

1. Select Resource tab ➤ Assignments group ➤ Resource Pool drop-down list ➤ Share Resources.

2. In the Share Resources dialog box, under Resources For, select Use Resources.

3. In the From drop-down list, select the Resource Pool file (it must be open for this option to be available).

4. Click OK.

MPP files don't have multiuser access. This means only one person at a time can open each file as read/write. Whoever opens the master file may inadvertently open the source files by clicking the details of that project, which is why it's wise to insert projects as read-only—doing so keeps this from happening. If the project manager who owns the file tries to open it when the master file is open, they will only be able to open it as read only and essentially will be locked out from making changes.

FIGURE 14.12 Sharing resources across projects

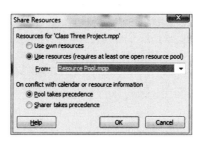

The resource-pool file behaves differently. When you open a file that shares resources, you're given the option to open the resource pool to see how the resource are being shared (see Figure 14.3).

FIGURE 14.13 Opening sharer files to view resources across multiple projects

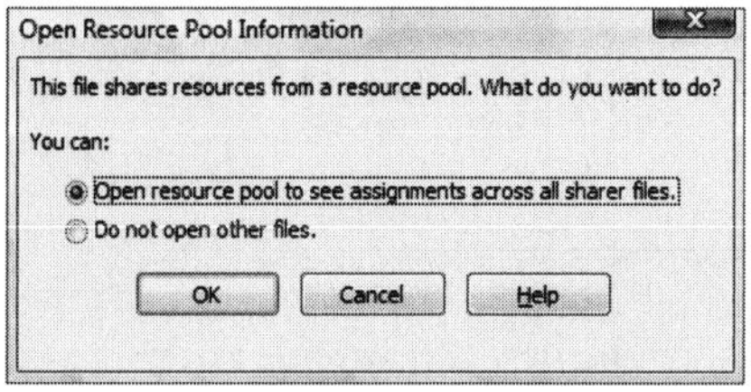

This option lets you view resource assignments across multiple projects. Also, as shown in Figure 14.14, when you open the resource pool file, you have three options: to open it as read-only, so others can continue to use it; to open it as read/write, so you can make changes but prevent others from using it; or to open the pool and all sharer files in a new master automatically.

FIGURE 14.14 Open Resource Pool dialog box

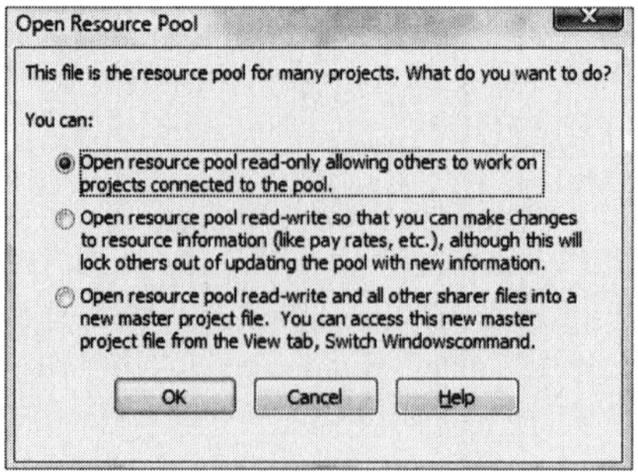

Analyzing Resources Across Projects

After you make assignments from a shared resource pool across projects, you can analyze how each resource is being used. In Figure 14.15, you can see that Engineer and David Blair are over-allocated on assignments across multiple projects. In this example, I clicked the Resource Usage view from the resource pool file (see Chapter 10, "Understanding Views," to learn more about changing views). You can access the same information from any of the source files, depending on how you open the resource pool.

FIGURE 14.15 Resource usage across multiple projects

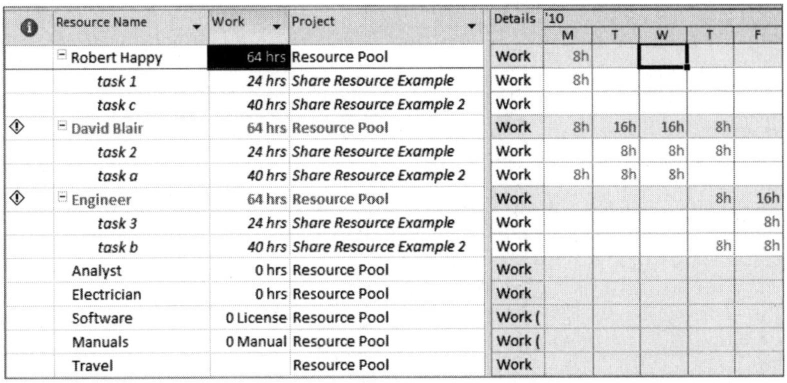

	Resource Name	Work	Project	Details	'10				
					M	T	W	T	F
	□ Robert Happy	64 hrs	Resource Pool	Work	8h				
	task 1	24 hrs	Share Resource Example	Work	8h				
	task c	40 hrs	Share Resource Example 2	Work					
◇	□ David Blair	64 hrs	Resource Pool	Work	8h	16h	16h	8h	
	task 2	24 hrs	Share Resource Example	Work		8h	8h	8h	
	task a	40 hrs	Share Resource Example 2	Work	8h	8h	8h		
◇	□ Engineer	64 hrs	Resource Pool	Work				8h	16h
	task 3	24 hrs	Share Resource Example	Work					8h
	task b	40 hrs	Share Resource Example 2	Work				8h	8h
	Analyst	0 hrs	Resource Pool	Work					
	Electrician	0 hrs	Resource Pool	Work					
	Software	0 License	Resource Pool	Work (					
	Manuals	0 Manual	Resource Pool	Work (					
	Travel		Resource Pool	Work					

In this view, I added the Project column to help distinguish where tasks came from. David and the engineer are being used across two projects, resulting in over-allocations for both resources. You aren't limited to the Resource Usage view; you can access all the other resource views, if needed, and make changes to the assignments. For example, Figure 14.16 applies the Team Planner view: you can analyze over-allocations and click and drag to change assignments.

FIGURE 14.16 Team Planner view across multiple projects

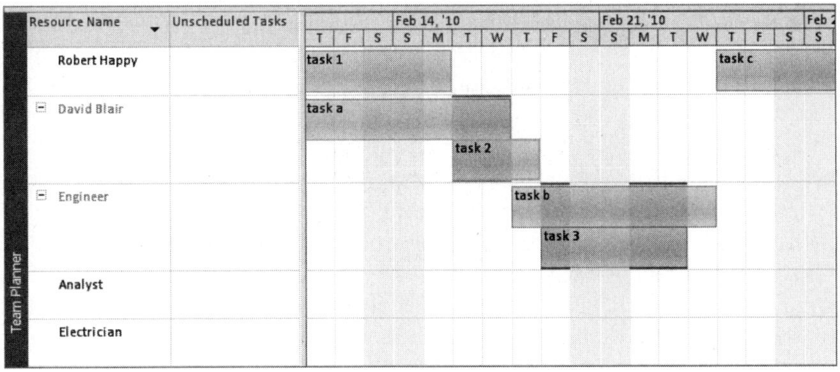

Roll-Up Reports

Having all your projects loaded in one master file lets you create more effective roll-up type reports (one pagers). Rolling up everything into one nice neat report can be very handy when you're communicating with stakeholders, particularly senior management.

With a master file, Project's powerful communication and reporting tools are still available. For example, you can use filtering to display milestones across projects, display only line items that need to be finished next week, or show only critical paths across the entire program. In the previous section, you learned how to view resources across multiple projects. Figure 14.17 shows an example of viewing milestones across multiple projects.

FIGURE 14.17   Filtering milestones across multiple projects

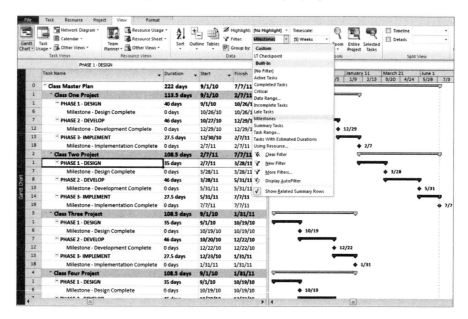

As shown in the figure, you can access the Filter tool in the View tab's Data group (see Chapter 12, "Using Filters, Groups, and Sorts"). You can use built-in or custom filters to zero in on a specific set of line items across projects, to create dashboard-type rolled-up views. Note that for filters to work across projects, they must be fully expanded. If you run a filter while certain projects are collapsed, then the filter doesn't apply to that section.

You can also apply other tools, such as grouping. As described in Chapter 12, you can access groups under via the View tab's Data group, much like the filtering tool. As shown in Figure 14.18, you can create a high-level overview of milestones across all projects.

All these filters and groups can apply to not only task views but also resource views. For example, in Figure 14.19 I clicked the Resource Usage view and applied the Resource group to roll up by department how many hours, dollars, and units are needed, by quarter.

FIGURE 14.18   Grouping milestones across projects

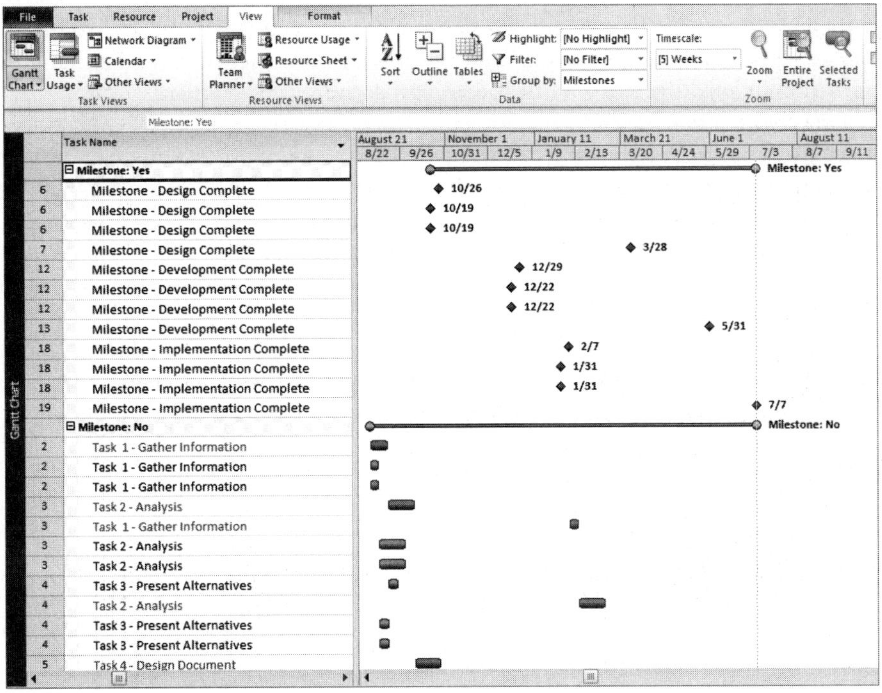

FIGURE 14.19   Grouping by department

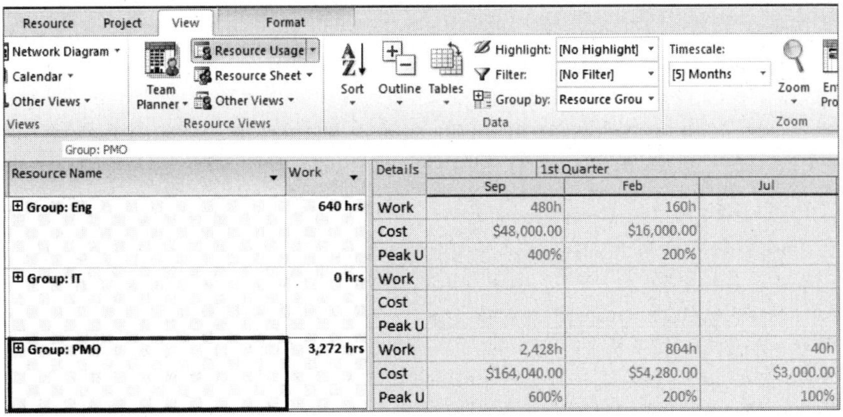

I added Peak Units and Cost to the time-phased portion of the view and changed the timescale to show months and quarters. Doing so lets you determine how many resources you need from each department across all the projects being shared. If you need a refresher on how to apply groups and filters, refer to Chapter 12.

Summary

In this chapter, you learned how to create master files by inserting subprojects (other project files) into a new or existing file. You can choose to insert projects as linked to the source file or not. If you insert subprojects in a linked manner, then as you update tasks in the source file or the master file, both are dynamically updated. It's wise to insert subprojects as read-only so that if you open the master files, you won't inadvertently open the source files and keep their owners locked out.

You also learned that it's possible to set cross-project dependencies referred to as *external links*. External links appear in the source file as ghost tasks (grayed out) so that the file's owner can see the externally linked task even though it's in another file and understand the impact it has on the project.

You can analyze task and resource information, taking advantage of Project's powerful communication and reporting tools while in the master file. For example, you can apply filters and groups across multiple projects to create roll-up type views and reports.

Hands-On Exercises

The following hands-on exercises are designed to test your understanding of the topics discussed in this chapter. We've provided files on the companion CD that will show you what your project file should look like as you perform these exercises.

EXERCISE 18

Creating a Master File, and View the Critical Path

1. Working with Class One Project, save it as Class Three Project to create multiple practice MPP files. You should now have three practice plans: Class One, Class Two, and Class Three Project.

2. Start a new project from Blank Project by clicking on the File Tab New tab Blank Project.

3. Go to Project tab ➤ Insert group, and use the Subproject command to insert the Class One Project, Class Two Project, and Class Three Project files.

4. Save as the file as **Class Master**.

5. Link the last milestone in Class One Project to the first task in Class Two Project.

6. Link the last milestone in Class Two Project to the first task in Class Three Project.

7. Select Format tab ➤ Bar Styles group ➤ Critical Tasks, and review the critical path.

8. Click the File tab to access the backstage, and click Options.

9. On the Schedule tab, under Calculations Options For This Project, click Inserted Projects Are Calculated Like Summary Tasks.

10. Under the Format tab, in the Show/Hide group, check Project Summary Task.

When you open up each source file individually you will notice that the external dependencies will appear as a greyed out tasks which are sometimes referred to as ghost tasks. These are the result of setting cross project dependencies from the master schedule.

Tracking and Analyzing Essentials

This part of the book covers how to effectively use Project to help track and analyze your schedule after a project has started. During the planning stages of the project-management process, you use Project to create a project schedule. This includes defining the phases, tasks, and milestones, when they should occur, and what resources and costs are required to accomplish them. After you've communicated with your stakeholders to obtain buy-in before the project starts, you move into the execution stage of project management, which includes the process of carrying out the work defined in your plan.

When execution begins on a project, you're responsible for monitoring and controlling each part of the plan; Project plays a significant role in enhancing your ability to perform at this stage. You can use Project to help with the following:

- Save an originally agreed-on plan by setting a baseline.

- Track project progress.

- Manage change and the impact of change on scope, time, cost, and resources.

- Analyze project variance and take corrective action.

- Revise the project as needed.

- Communicate and report on progress and status.

Understanding how to use Project for these tasks during execution helps you keep control of the project.

I've found that there is a tendency to use Project to create a nice-looking Gantt chart up front during planning, only to put it aside and forget about it during execution. This often happens because project managers don't know how to use the tools available in Project during a project's implementation stage.

Chapter

15

Setting and Maintaining Baselines

IN THIS CHAPTER, YOU'LL LEARN ABOUT THE FOLLOWING:

- ✓ Setting baselines
- ✓ Viewing baselines
- ✓ Maintaining baselines

The baseline is one of the most underutilized features in Project, yet it gives one of the greatest returns on investment. Understanding how to set a baseline is a key function in Project that will help you track and analyze your project much more effectively. In this chapter, you'll learn how to set and view baselines. In Chapters 16 ("Updating and Tracking Status") and 17 ("Comparing Results and Taking Corrective Action"), you'll learn how to use the baseline data to help track and analyze progress.

Understanding and Setting Baselines

Before you set a baseline, it's important to understand what a baseline is and what fields are incorporated into the baseline plan. In this section, you'll also learn how to set a baseline.

Understanding Baselines

You can think of a baseline as a snapshot of your original schedule. After you've created your plan and obtained buy-in from project stakeholders, and before you begin the project, you should set a baseline. Doing so will allow you to effectively compare your original plan to what actually takes place throughout the project execution stage, thus enabling you to make better decisions and take corrective action.

When you set a baseline in Project, it looks at what is in your current plan and copies it into the baseline plan. The following five fields are copied:

- Start
- Finish
- Duration
- Work
- Cost

Project includes time-phased data in the baseline in case you need to view work or cost in either task or resource views over a specific time period.

One way to better understand the core fields that are baselined is to view the Project Statistics dialog box (see Figure 15.1). You can access the Project Statistics dialog box as follows:

1. Go to Project tab ➢ Properties group, and click Project Information.
2. In the Project Information dialog box, click Statistics.

FIGURE 15.1 Project Statistics

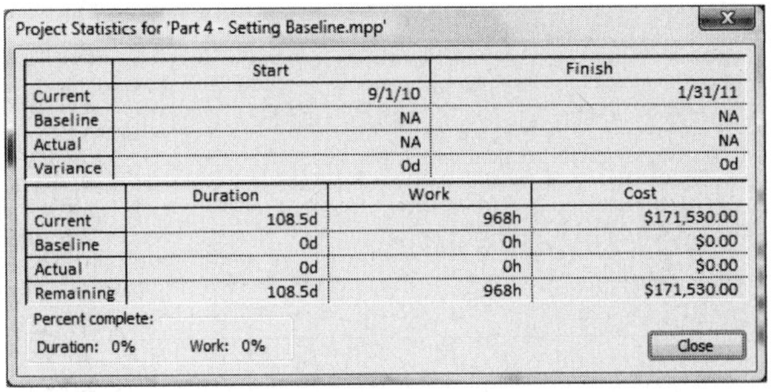

The Project Statistics dialog box provides an overview of the project from a current, baseline, and actual plan perspective. Notice that in Figure 15.1, the Baseline and Actual fields display have NA, because the baseline hasn't been set and no status has been recorded for actuals. When you set the baseline, the contents of your current schedule fields are copied to the baseline fields. At this time, the current plan and baseline plan are exactly the same—there is no variance between them.

After you start your project and begin to update the schedule, you can compare what takes place to the baseline. Your current plan will no longer be the same as your baseline plan, unless everything goes 100% as planned—which is rarely the case.

Project includes a comprehensive set of predefined baseline fields, tables, filters, and views that you can use for analysis; these are covered in the following two chapters.

You can always clear the baseline and start from a clean slate at anytime. You can also reset the baseline to match the current plan, and you can set multiple baselines. All of these scenarios are discussed later in this chapter.

Setting a Baseline

The default Gantt Chart view, which is based on the default Entry table, isn't formatted to display the baseline. To set a baseline (see Figure 15.2) follow these steps:

1. Go to Project tab ➤ Schedule group, and click the Set Baseline button.

2. Set Baseline is selected by default. For: Entire Project is also selected by default. Click OK.

You've now set your first baseline for the entire project.

If you click the Set Baseline drop-down list, in the Set Baseline dialog box, you see that you can set up to 10 other baselines in addition to the original (or core) baseline. Project allows up to 11 baselines to be set and stored in one project plan.

The original baseline is what most of the tables, views, and filters are based on. This is a key consideration if you decide to set multiple baselines (covered in more detail later in this chapter).

FIGURE 15.2   Setting a baseline

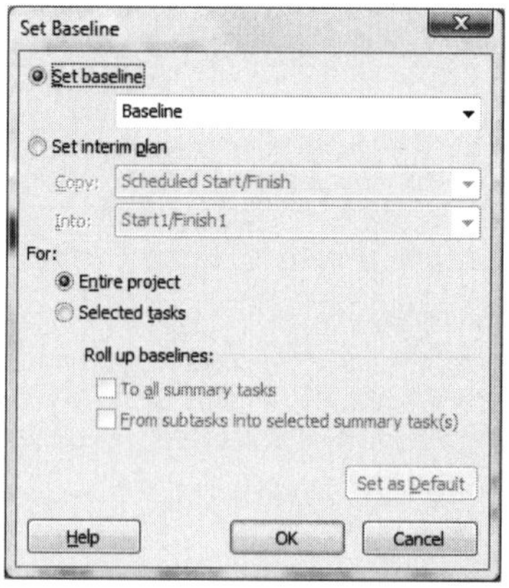

Viewing Baselines

After you've set the baseline—or before you set the baseline—switch views or format the existing view to allow for baseline data to be displayed. A typical task-based Gantt Chart view has two sides. On the left is the table or text area, and on the right is the bar area. Formatting one side doesn't format the other.

In other words, adding baseline fields to the table doesn't automatically change the Gantt bars to display the baseline. The reverse is also true: formatting the bars to display the baseline doesn't automatically add the baseline fields to the table or text area. You must format them separately (see Part 3 of this book, "Communicating and Reporting Essentials."

Tracking Gantt View and the Variance Table

Project includes predefined views and tables to display the baseline. One such view, which is formatted to display the baseline, is the Tracking Gantt view. Follow these steps to apply the Tracking Gantt view (see Figure 15.3):

1.   Select View tab ➢ Task Views group ➢ Gantt Chart drop-down list.
2.   From the list, click Tracking Gantt.

In the Tracking Gantt view, the Gantt bars are preformatted to display not only the baseline but also the critical path. After you set the baseline, you'll notice two sets of bars in the Tracking Gantt view. The bottom bars, which are gray, represent the baseline; the top bars, which are either blue (noncritical tasks) or red (critical tasks), represent your current plan. At first, these bars are the same length; but as you make changes to your current plan or record changes that are different from the baseline, the top bars move while the bottom baseline bars remain in place—unless you reset the baseline, as discussed later in this chapter.

FIGURE 15.3   Tracking Gantt view

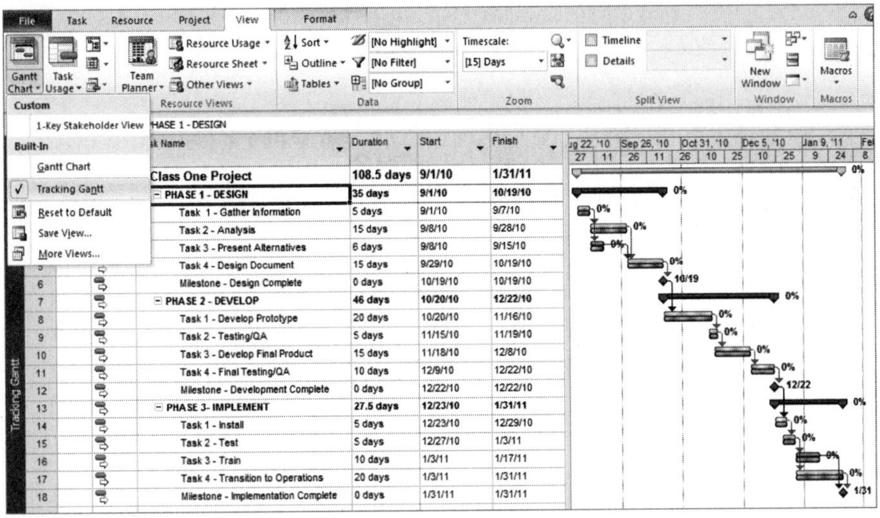

The Tracking Gantt view has the percentage complete to the right of each bar, which is useful when you start to record progress (as discussed in Chapter 16).

Because the Tracking Gantt view defaults to applying the Entry table, you may find it useful to change the table to the Variance table (see Figure 15.4): it includes the Baseline Start and Baseline Finish columns along with the Start and Finish Variance columns. Follow these steps to apply the Variance table:

1. Go to View tab ≻ Data group, and click the Tables button.

2. Select the Variance table.

When you set a baseline, the current Start is equal to the Baseline Start, and the current Finish is equal to the Baseline Finish; therefore, there is no Start or Finish Variance. This is because when you set your baseline, Project copies whatever is in your current plan into the baseline plan; they're exactly the same until you make adjustments.

You can add columns in the Variance table by using Add New Column, as shown in Figure 15.4. This allows you to customize the table to suit your tracking needs. For example, I like to add the following:

- % Complete
- Finish Status (custom field with graphical indicators)
- Duration (between Start and Finish)

You may find it useful to add other columns, such as Actual Start and Actual Finish, after you start recording data.

FIGURE 15.4 Variance table

	Task Name	Start	Finish	Baseline Start	Baseline Finish	Start Var.	Finish Var.	Add New Column
0	− Class One Project	9/1/10	1/31/11	9/1/10	1/31/11	0 days	0 days	
1	− PHASE 1 - DESIGN	9/1/10	10/19/10	9/1/10	10/19/10	0 days	0 days	
2	Task 1 - Gather Information	9/1/10	9/7/10	9/1/10	9/7/10	0 days	0 days	
3	Task 2 - Analysis	9/8/10	9/28/10	9/8/10	9/28/10	0 days	0 days	
4	Task 3 - Present Alternatives	9/8/10	9/15/10	9/8/10	9/15/10	0 days	0 days	
5	Task 4 - Design Document	9/29/10	10/19/10	9/29/10	10/19/10	0 days	0 days	
6	Milestone - Design Complete	10/19/10	10/19/10	10/19/10	10/19/10	0 days	0 days	
7	− PHASE 2 - DEVELOP	10/20/10	12/22/10	10/20/10	12/22/10	0 days	0 days	
8	Task 1 - Develop Prototype	10/20/10	11/16/10	10/20/10	11/16/10	0 days	0 days	
9	Task 2 - Testing/QA	11/15/10	11/19/10	11/15/10	11/19/10	0 days	0 days	
10	Task 3 - Develop Final Product	11/18/10	12/8/10	11/18/10	12/8/10	0 days	0 days	
11	Task 4 - Final Testing/QA	12/9/10	12/22/10	12/9/10	12/22/10	0 days	0 days	
12	Milestone - Development Complete	12/22/10	12/22/10	12/22/10	12/22/10	0 days	0 days	
13	− PHASE 3- IMPLEMENT	12/23/10	1/31/11	12/23/10	1/31/11	0 days	0 days	
14	Task 1 - Install	12/23/10	12/29/10	12/23/10	12/29/10	0 days	0 days	
15	Task 2 - Test	12/27/10	1/3/11	12/27/10	1/3/11	0 days	0 days	
16	Task 3 - Train	1/3/11	1/17/11	1/3/11	1/17/11	0 days	0 days	
17	Task 4 - Transition to Operations	1/3/11	1/31/11	1/3/11	1/31/11	0 days	0 days	
18	Milestone - Implementation Complete	1/31/11	1/31/11	1/31/11	1/31/11	0 days	0 days	

Formatting the Gantt Chart to Display the Baseline

Although the default Gantt Chart view doesn't display the baseline, you can reformat the view to display the baseline at any time. One quick way to do this uses the Format tab; follow these steps (see Figure 15.5):

1. In the Gantt Chart view, go to Format tab ➢ Bar Styles group.
2. Click the Baseline drop-down list, and select Baseline (the first option in the list).

Custom Tracking View

Over the years, I've worked with many clients to customize solutions using Microsoft Project. One of the key components to a successful implementation is to customize the tool to support the client's project-management processes, which include not only planning but also tracking and updating.

The solution typically includes developing a custom view for tracking and updating to support the project's monitoring and control stage. This includes adding custom fields such as the Task Finish Status indicator and the Needs Updating indicator (both included in the CD that come with this book).

The custom view also includes a custom tracking table that's based on the Variance table but modified to include % Complete and the two custom fields just described. The custom view also includes custom bar formatting to display the baseline in the Gantt bar area as well as custom gridlines to display both the current date in red and the project start date in blue. See Part 3 of this book for how to set these up.

This is similar to the Tracking Gantt view, except that you don't have to switch views to display the baseline. The baseline bars are the bottom bars, which are grey; they will stay in place as the current plan is adjusted. Having the baseline bars displayed in the Gantt chart makes it more effective for visually tracking and identifying variances.

You can add any of the baseline fields to any table at any time (see Chapter 11, "Using Tables and Custom Fields").

FIGURE 15.5   Formatting the Gantt chart to display the baseline

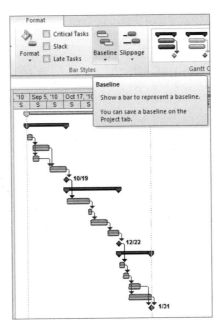

Maintaining Baselines

It's important for an organization to have well-defined baselining procedures in place for project managers to follow. These should include processes for the following:

- When to set a baseline
- When, if at all, it's acceptable to clear the baseline
- When it's appropriate to reset the baseline for the entire project or selected tasks
- When to save multiple baselines

Because the tool will allow you to do all these things, and there is no way to stop a project manager from resetting or clearing a baseline, this becomes a procedural issue. Organizations with mature project-management processes in place will have these types of procedures well defined.

After a baseline has been set, you may need to maintain it or keep it up to date. This section covers the following topics:

- Clearing baselines
- Rolling-wave planning with baselines
- Adding new tasks after a baseline has been set
- Setting multiple baselines and saving interim plans

Clearing a Baseline

At any time during a project's planning or execution stages, you can clear the baseline to make it appear as if it never existed. Clearing a baseline removes all data from all baseline fields and returns them to the state they were in before the baseline was set. In other words, the fields return to displaying NA for baseline data.

After a baseline is set and a project starts, you most likely won't clear the baseline as often as you'll use the option to reset the baseline or save multiple baselines.

However, I've found the feature useful at times, particularly early in the planning stage. For example, if a plan is partially built, and you're making adjustments to a specific section, you may want to set the baseline so you can see the impact of the changes you're making even though this won't be the formally agreed-on baseline. When you're finished with that portion of the planning, you can clear the baseline and set it at a later date, after you've obtained buy-in from your project stakeholders.

Follow these steps to clear a baseline (see Figure 15.6):

1. Select Project tab ➢ Schedule group ➢ Set Baseline drop-down menu ➢ Clear Baseline.
2. In the Clear Baseline dialog box, click OK.

FIGURE 15.6 Clearing a baseline

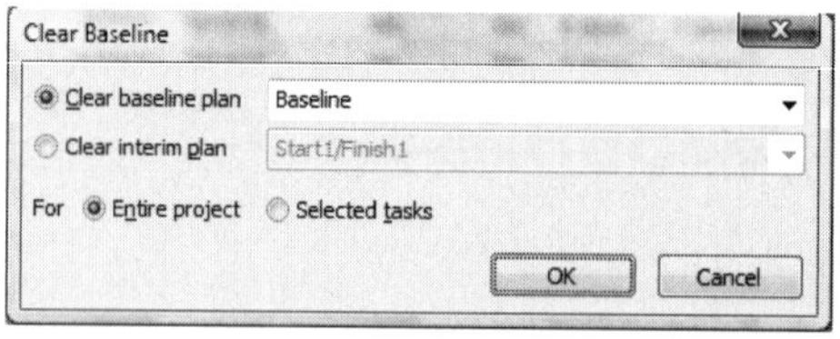

Figure 15.6 shows that you can clear any one of the other baselines or interim plans that you may have saved. There is also another option to clear the baseline only for selected tasks. The default clears the core baseline values for the entire project.

When you clear your baseline, the values in the baseline fields return to NA, as shown in Figure 15.7. Because there is no baseline to compare the plan with, any Start or Finish Variance returns to 0 days.

FIGURE 15.7   Clearing baseline values

Start	Finish	Baseline Start	Baseline Finish	Start Var.	Finish Var.
9/1/10	1/31/11	NA	NA	0 days	0 days
9/1/10	10/19/10	NA	NA	0 days	0 days
9/1/10	9/7/10	NA	NA	0 days	0 days
9/8/10	9/28/10	NA	NA	0 days	0 days
9/8/10	9/15/10	NA	NA	0 days	0 days
9/29/10	10/19/10	NA	NA	0 days	0 days
10/19/10	10/19/10	NA	NA	0 days	0 days
10/20/10	12/22/10	NA	NA	0 days	0 days
10/20/10	11/16/10	NA	NA	0 days	0 days
11/15/10	11/19/10	NA	NA	0 days	0 days
11/18/10	12/8/10	NA	NA	0 days	0 days
12/9/10	12/22/10	NA	NA	0 days	0 days
12/22/10	12/22/10	NA	NA	0 days	0 days
12/23/10	1/31/11	NA	NA	0 days	0 days
12/23/10	12/29/10	NA	NA	0 days	0 days
12/27/10	1/3/11	NA	NA	0 days	0 days
1/3/11	1/17/11	NA	NA	0 days	0 days
1/3/11	1/31/11	NA	NA	0 days	0 days
1/31/11	1/31/11	NA	NA	0 days	0 days

Rolling-Wave Planning with Baselines

If you're following a rolling-wave planning approach, you can use the baseline function and take advantage of the Set Baseline for Selected Tasks option. For example, if you have a stage-gate process, which includes planning the detail for the next gate prior to moving on, then this approach will work for you.

Perhaps you know the detail of only one phase and aren't ready to set the baseline for the next until it becomes clearer. For example, until the requirements are defined, you won't have the final details of how long the design stage will take; and until the design is completed, you may not have a clear understanding of how long development will take. In these types of situations, you can apply a rolling-wave planning approach and progressively elaborate on the details as you move from one phase to the next.

You can set the baseline for a specific phase or series of tasks as follows (see Figure 15.8):

1. Select the tasks in the Gantt chart for which you want to set the baseline.

2. Select Project tab ➤ Schedule group ➤ Set Baseline drop-down list ➤ Set Baseline.

3. In the Set Baseline box, make sure the Set Baseline option is selected.

4. Under For, select Selected Tasks.

5. Under Roll Up Baselines, select To All Summary Tasks. Click OK.

The option to roll up baselines to summary tasks is important if you want the summary-task baseline to change and reflect the impact of the baseline of the tasks. You also have a choice to manually select the summary tasks first and choose the second option, which rolls up baselines from subtask to selected summary tasks only. This option may be useful if you want to affect only one summary task without affecting others, such as the project summary.

FIGURE 15.8 Setting a baseline for selected tasks

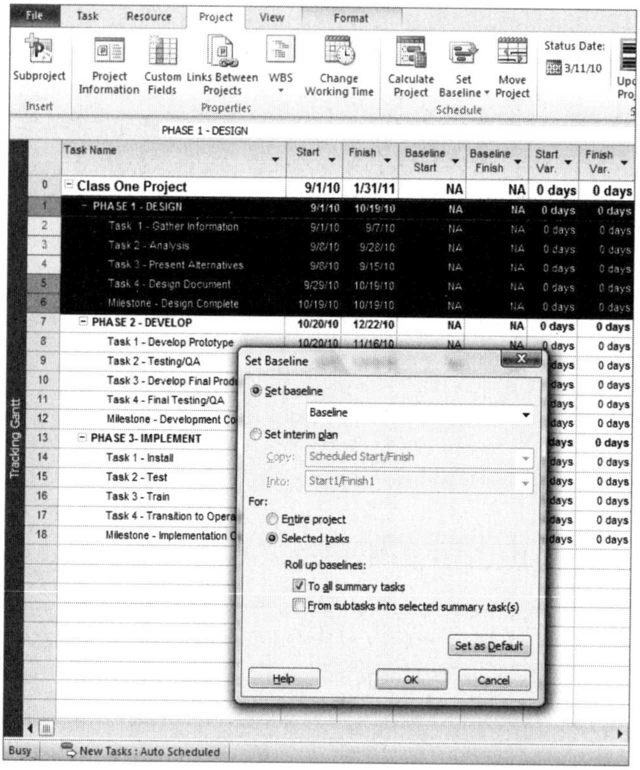

Adding New Tasks After a Baseline Has Been Set

Many times, after the baseline has been set and the project has started, you may need to add new tasks to your project plan. Perhaps you want to add details for more accurate tracking, or a change in scope results in the need for more tasks. When you add new tasks, you need to set the baseline for those tasks without resetting the baseline for the entire project.

As shown in Figure 15.9, when you add a new task, no baseline is associated with it until you follow the same steps as described in the previous section for Figure 15.8.

FIGURE 15.9 Adding new tasks after the baseline has been set

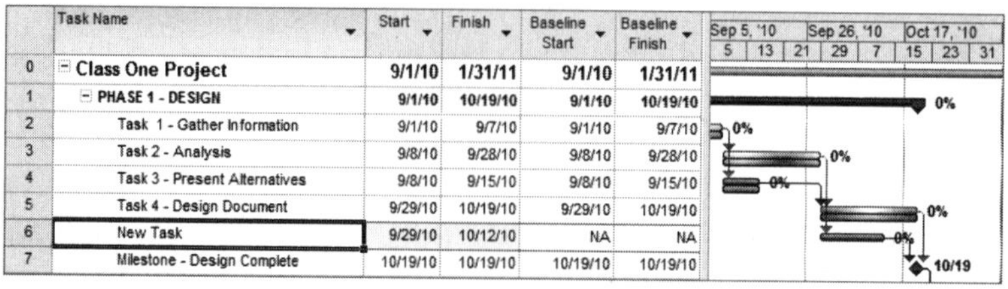

	Task Name	Start	Finish	Baseline Start	Baseline Finish
0	Class One Project	9/1/10	1/31/11	9/1/10	1/31/11
1	PHASE 1 - DESIGN	9/1/10	10/19/10	9/1/10	10/19/10
2	Task 1 - Gather Information	9/1/10	9/7/10	9/1/10	9/7/10
3	Task 2 - Analysis	9/8/10	9/28/10	9/8/10	9/28/10
4	Task 3 - Present Alternatives	9/8/10	9/15/10	9/8/10	9/15/10
5	Task 4 - Design Document	9/29/10	10/19/10	9/29/10	10/19/10
6	New Task	9/29/10	10/12/10	NA	NA
7	Milestone - Design Complete	10/19/10	10/19/10	10/19/10	10/19/10

Resetting a Baseline

At any time, you can reset the baseline. When you do this, the old baseline values disappear and are replaced with whatever values are in your current Finish, Start, Duration, Work, and Cost fields. The old baseline values are lost, unless you choose to save multiple baselines.

To reset the baseline, follow these steps (see Figure 15.10):

1. Select Project tab ➢ Schedule group ➢ Set Baseline ➢ Set Baseline.

2. In the Set Baseline dialog box, Set Baseline is selected by default (with the date the baseline was last saved in parentheses). The For: Entire Project option is also selected by default. Click OK.

3. A "Baseline has already been used" message appears. Click Yes.

The baseline has now been reset. A new date is now associated with the baseline and will appear in the Set Baseline field in the Set Baseline dialog box the next time you access it.

FIGURE 15.10   Resetting a baseline

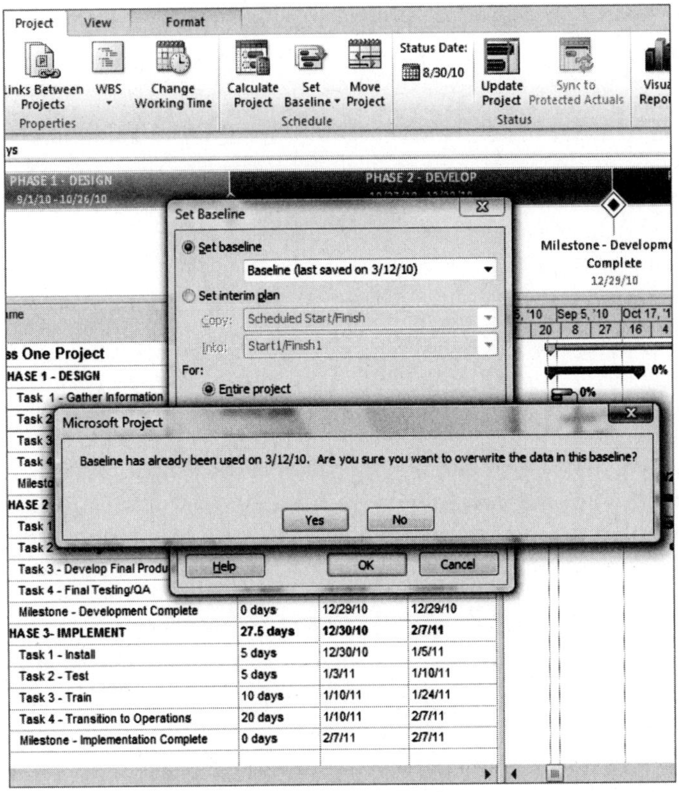

Multiple Baselines

You can keep multiple baselines for a project. Project allows you to maintain up to 10 baselines plus the core baseline. This comes in handy when you have a major change in scope—enough to warrant a baseline reset (a change significant enough to change the original agreement or intent of the project deliverables).

Another common occurrence is project reprioritization. Perhaps you started your project, but part way through, it was put on hold and pushed out to the future. When this occurs, and you restart the project, it may be necessary to reset the baseline. Instead of erasing the original baseline, you can save it to another of the baseline options.

Save the Interim Plan—Keep the Core Baseline Current

I recommend that you save an interim baseline into baselines 1, 2, 3, and so on before you reset your baseline. This allows you to keep the core (or original) baseline as the current baseline. This is important, because all the custom views, tables, filters, and earned value formulas default to using the core baseline values, not baseline 1 or baseline 2 or other baseline values.

To take advantage of the multiple-baseline option, you should follow a two-step process: first, save an interim plan; second, reset the core baseline. This way, your current baseline is always in the core baseline values; you have backed-up baselines in the baseline 1 through 10 values, depending on how many times you reset the baseline.

To save a backup or an interim baseline plan, follow these steps (see Figure 15.11):

1. Select Project tab ➤ Schedule group ➤ Set Baseline drop-down list ➤ Set Interim Plan.

2. In the Set Baseline dialog box, select Baseline from the Copy drop-down list.

3. Select Baseline 1 from the Into drop-down list. (For the second backup, select Baseline 2, and so on.)

4. For: Entire Project is selected by default. Click OK.

You've now backed up, or saved, your core baseline into the baseline 1 fields. You can repeat this process the next time you want to reset the baseline, but copy it into baseline 2, and so on. Saving an interim plan doesn't reset the baseline, nor does it change the baseline data in the view you've applied.

After you save an interim baseline plan, you can safely reset the baseline without losing the original baseline data, because that information is stored in the baseline 1 fields. To reset the baseline, follow the steps associated with Figure 15.10.

The Tracking Gantt view is formatted to display only the core baseline values and not baseline 1 through baseline 10 values. To view multiple baselines in the Gantt chart, select the multiple-baselines view, shown in Figure 15.12, as follows:

1. Select View tab ➤ Task Views group ➤ Gantt Chart drop-down list ➤ More Views.

2. In the More Views dialog box, click Multiple Baselines Gantt.

3. Click Apply.

FIGURE 15.11   Saving an interim baseline plan

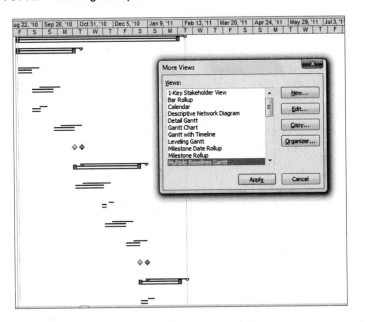

FIGURE 15.12   Viewing multiple baselines in the Gantt chart

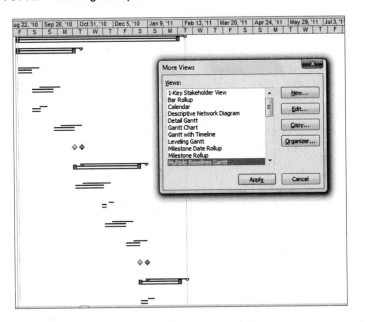

Each baseline is represented by a separate colored line in the Gantt chart, as shown in Figure 15.12. You can add any of the baseline 1 through baseline 10 fields to any table, create your own Variance fields using the other baseline fields, or add other baseline bars in the Gantt bar area by reformatting the bar styles.

Setting a Baseline on Manually Scheduled Tasks

If you set a baseline for manually scheduled tasks that don't have start date, duration, or finish date information, and the field is left blank, then the baseline information is blank as well. In other words, the baseline fields are also manually adjustable. However, the start and finish dates are internally recorded as the current date. So, if you later enter dates for a manually scheduled task, you still get a calculated variance. You can also manually enter different baseline information, and Project uses that to calculate variance. If you have text in the Start, Duration, or Finish field, it's copied into the baseline fields as well.

This also impacts how the variance is calculated, because the behavior is different depending on the values in each field. If you have incomplete schedule data for manually scheduled tasks, then setting the baseline and analyzing variance calculations won't be very useful.

Summary

In this chapter, you've learned what a baseline is and how to set one. I discussed the importance of having proper procedures in place to align with your project-management processes as you move from planning to execution. When you set a baseline in Project, the values in your current Start, Finish, Duration, Work, and Cost fields are copied into your baseline Start, Finish, Duration, and Cost fields. This includes time-phased data for both task and resource type views.

You can clear your baseline values at any time and return the baseline to NA. You can also reset the baseline, which copies whatever is in your current plan at the time into the baseline fields and erases all the old baseline values. Project can save up to 10 additional baselines, allowing you to back up your core baseline values before resetting and thus keep a historical record of previous baselines in one file.

Hands-On Exercises

The following hands-on exercises are designed to test your understanding of the topics discussed in this chapter. We've provided files on the companion CD that will show you what your project file should look like as you perform these exercises.

EXERCISE 19

Setting the Baseline in Tracking Gantt View

1. In Class One Project, select View tab ➤ Task Views group ➤ Gantt Chart drop-down list ➤ Tracking Gantt.

2. Select View tab ➤ Data group ➤ Tables.

3. Apply the Variance table.

4. Select Project tab ➤ Schedule group ➤ Set Baseline. Select Baseline for the entire project.

5. Observe the baseline values in the Variance table and the baseline bars in the Gantt bar area.

6. Select Project tab ➤ Properties group ➤ Project Information ➤ Statistics.

7. View the Current, Baseline, and Actual data. Why is there no actual data? (You haven't recorded any status yet.) Notice that the variance is 0 days.

8. Add five days to the duration of Gather Information. Observe the variance in the table under the Finish Variance column and in the bar area.

EXERCISE 20

Resetting the Baseline

1. Select Project tab ➤ Schedule group ➤ Set Baseline ➤ Set Interim Plan.

2. Save an interim plan by copying the baseline into Baseline 1.

3. Select Project tab ➤ Schedule group ➤ Set Baseline ➤ Set Baseline. Set the baseline for the entire project.

4. Select View tab ➤ Task Views group ➤ Gantt Chart drop-down list ➤ More Views ➤ Multiple Baselines Gantt.

5. Observe the baseline bar lines in the Gantt bar area.

6. Click back to the Tracking Gantt chart.

Chapter

16

Updating and Tracking Status

IN THIS CHAPTER, YOU'LL LEARN ABOUT THE FOLLOWING:

✓ Entering percent complete

✓ Capturing actual dates and duration

✓ Capturing actual hours and costs

✓ Understanding how percent complete is tied to actuals

After a baseline has been established for your schedule and the project begins, it's up to you to ensure that it stays on track. Instead of putting the plan aside and taking a fly-by-the-seat-of-your-pants approach to managing a project, you can use Project to help capture status and actuals and quickly understand and communicate the impact of change. This in turn will help you make better decisions.

Understanding and Entering Percent Complete

Percent complete is an essential part of tracking and updating, because it has a major impact on the calculation of your schedule and actuals. Learning about the different types of percent complete, how to enter percent complete, and the affect it has on your schedule is important for using Project successfully during all stages of project management.

Different Types of Percent Complete

Project has three basic types of percent complete:

- Percent complete
- Percent work complete
- Physical percent complete

Percent Complete

The default percent complete in Project is based on tracking the schedule task status. *Schedule status* refers to calculating percent complete based on a task's duration. For example, if a task is 10 days in duration and the % Complete value is 50%, then the Actual Duration value is 5 days and the Remaining Duration value is 5 days. If % Complete is 75%, then Actual Duration is 7.5 days and Remaining Duration is 2.5 days. If % Complete is 100%, then Actual Duration is 10 days and Remaining Duration is 0 days.

If any amount of time appears in the Remaining Duration field, then % Complete can't equal 100%. The Actual Duration and Remaining Duration values are tied to the calculation of % Complete.

As you enter % Complete values, Project automatically calculates the actual start and finish dates. If you enter 100% in the % Complete field, Project makes Remaining Duration 0; it also takes whatever values are in the current Start and current Finish fields (not your baseline start and finish) and copies them into the Actual Start and Actual Finish fields. It's up to you to enter values in the Actual Start, Actual Finish, and Actual Duration fields if they're different than planned (as discussed later in this chapter). Percent complete is tied to your actuals—what has actually occurred.

If you enter 100% complete for a task, the actual finish date is calculated automatically, because you must have an actual finish if the task is 100% complete. In the same manner, if you enter an actual finish date in the Actual Finish field, then Project assumes the task is finished and automatically calculates % Complete to be 100%. If, after the fact, you enter any amount of time into the Remaining Duration field, then the 100% complete you entered earlier is recalculated, and the actual finish date is removed and replaced with NA. As you can see, 100% complete, the remaining duration, and the actual finish date have an important interrelationship.

If you enter anything in the % Complete field from 1% to 99%, Project automatically copies whatever is in your current Start field into the Actual Start field. If, after the fact, you change % Complete to 0%, then the actual start date is removed and replaced with NA.

Percent Work Complete

Percent work complete is different from percent complete in that it's based on resource status for work hours or effort on a task. For example, if a task has an estimated 10 hours of work associated with it, and you spend 5 hours, then your percent work complete is 50%.

By default, updating percent complete automatically updates percent work complete. You only need to enter percent complete—Project automatically calculates percent work complete for you. Unless there is a compelling reason to calculate percent work complete separately, you don't need to pay attention to it.

However, if you do need to update percent work complete separately, you can add % Complete and % Work Complete columns to any table. You can also change the default for updating percent complete to automatically update percent work complete. Doing so lets you manually enter updates for task status such as percent complete, actual duration, and remaining duration separately from percent work complete, actual hours, and remaining hours (see Figure 16.1). Follow these steps:

1. Click the File tab to go to the backstage.

2. Click Options, and click the Schedule tab in the Project Options dialog box.

3. Scroll down to Calculation Options for This Project.

4. Clear the Updating Task Status Updates Resource Status check box.

5. Click OK.

I recommend that you not change the default setting unless you have a compelling reason to do so. Just be aware that % Complete and % Work Complete are two separate fields representing status for both tasks and resources.

FIGURE 16.1 Option settings for updating task status, which automatically updates resource status

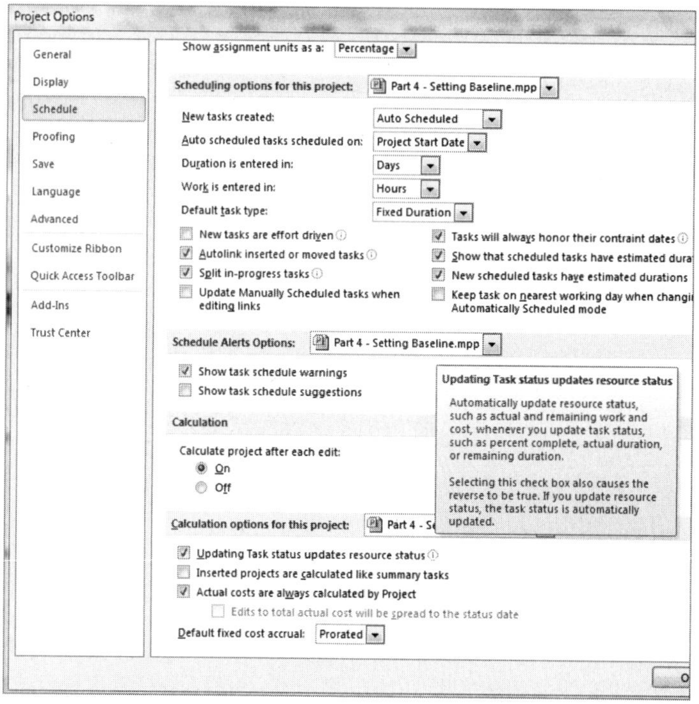

Physical Percent Complete

Project comes with earned value fields based on earned value formulas (see Chapter 17, "Variance Analysis and Taking Corrective Action"). Earned value (EV) calculations are based on percent complete. Project defaults to using the standard percent complete value when calculating EV. However, sometimes you may not want to use the standard % Complete field, because it's based on task status as determined by actual duration and remaining duration, whereas the Physical % Complete field is separate from these calculations. Instead, you can apply the Physical % Complete field to the EV calculation.

To change the EV calculation from % Complete to Physical % Complete, as shown in Figure 16.2, follow these steps:

1. Click the File tab to go to the backstage.
2. Click Options, and click the Advanced tab in the Project Options dialog box.
3. Scroll down to Earned Value Options for This Project.
4. Select Physical % Complete from the Default Task Earned Value Method drop-down list.
5. Click OK.

FIGURE 16.2   Changing the EV method to Physical % Complete

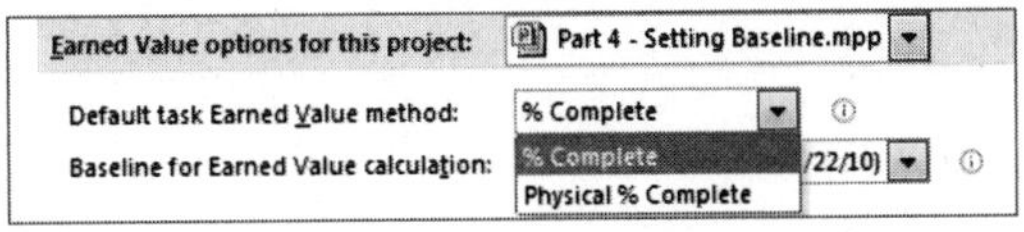

If you use Physical % Complete, you must enter it separately from % Complete. You have to add it to an existing table, but you'll find it in the tracking table as well. For more information about using tables, see Chapter 11, "Using Tables and Custom Fields."

Entering Percent Complete

Entering percent complete is easy. The hard part is determining what value to enter. 0% is simple—it means the task hasn't yet started. 100% is also simple—it means the task is finished. It's everything in between that becomes difficult to figure out.

Team members may have different ideas of what 25% means, so you may end up with different interpretations of a task's percent complete. To help simplify this decision-making process, some people only update tasks using 0% or 100%—nothing in between. This is referred to as the *0 or 100 method*. This may be fine if you have a sufficient work breakdown structure (WBS), because the summary task is calculated based on the weighted value from the roll-up of the task status, which may give you sufficient insight into the project's progress.

If this isn't sufficient, you may have to record percent complete while some tasks are works in progress. Another approach I've seen work effectively uses only 0%, 25%, 50%, 75%, and 100% complete, as follows:

- 0% = not started
- 25% = started but not halfway completed
- 50% = halfway completed
- 75% = more than halfway but not completed
- 100% = completed

This approach can help simplify entering percent complete.

Entering Directly in the Percent Complete Field

Percent complete appears in many places. For example, if you double-click a task and bring up the Task Information dialog box, you can enter percent complete on the General tab, as shown in Figure 16.3.

FIGURE 16.3   Entering percent complete in the Task Information dialog box

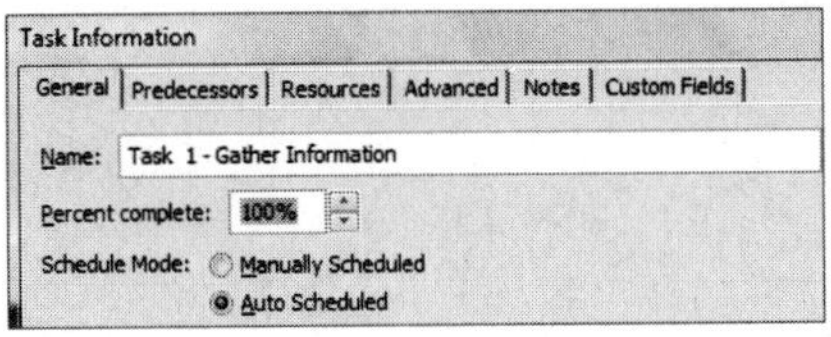

You can also add the % Complete field as a column to any task table. For example, Figure 16.4 shows the % Complete column added to the Variance table. See Chapter 11 to learn more about adding a column to an existing table.

FIGURE 16.4 Adding the % Complete column to a table

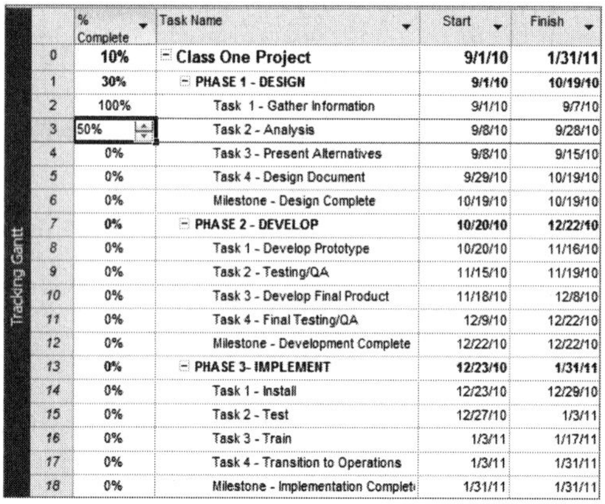

	% Complete	Task Name	Start	Finish
0	10%	− Class One Project	9/1/10	1/31/11
1	30%	− PHASE 1 - DESIGN	9/1/10	10/19/10
2	100%	Task 1 - Gather Information	9/1/10	9/7/10
3	50%	Task 2 - Analysis	9/8/10	9/28/10
4	0%	Task 3 - Present Alternatives	9/8/10	9/15/10
5	0%	Task 4 - Design Document	9/29/10	10/19/10
6	0%	Milestone - Design Complete	10/19/10	10/19/10
7	0%	− PHASE 2 - DEVELOP	10/20/10	12/22/10
8	0%	Task 1 - Develop Prototype	10/20/10	11/16/10
9	0%	Task 2 - Testing/QA	11/15/10	11/19/10
10	0%	Task 3 - Develop Final Product	11/18/10	12/8/10
11	0%	Task 4 - Final Testing/QA	12/9/10	12/22/10
12	0%	Milestone - Development Complete	12/22/10	12/22/10
13	0%	− PHASE 3- IMPLEMENT	12/23/10	1/31/11
14	0%	Task 1 - Install	12/23/10	12/29/10
15	0%	Task 2 - Test	12/27/10	1/3/11
16	0%	Task 3 - Train	1/3/11	1/17/11
17	0%	Task 4 - Transition to Operations	1/3/11	1/31/11
18	0%	Milestone - Implementation Complete	1/31/11	1/31/11

As you can see in Figure 16.4, when you enter the percent complete at the task level, the weighted average is rolled up to the respective summary tasks, including the project summary task. Project also allows you to enter percent complete at the summary task level, and it calculates percent complete for subordinate tasks. For example, if you enter 100% at the summary task level, Project automatically marks subordinate (indented) tasks as 100% complete as well.

Using the Buttons from the Ribbon

You can enter percent complete by taking advantage of the percent complete buttons in the Schedule group on the Task tab. As shown in Figure 16.5, you can click the 0%, 25%, 50%, 75%, or 100% button to quickly enter the status for a task or group of tasks. I use these buttons frequently.

FIGURE 16.5 Percent complete buttons on the ribbon

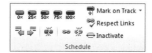

Using the Split View

You can enter percent complete if you have the split-screen view applied to the Gantt chart. To apply the split-screen view, follow these steps:

1. Go to View tab ➤ Split View group.
2. Select Details.

As shown in Figure 16.6, you can enter percent complete in the task-form portion of the split view, directly above the Predecessor Lag field. If you enter percent complete in the Task Form view, remember to click OK for it to register.

FIGURE 16.6   Task form in the split view

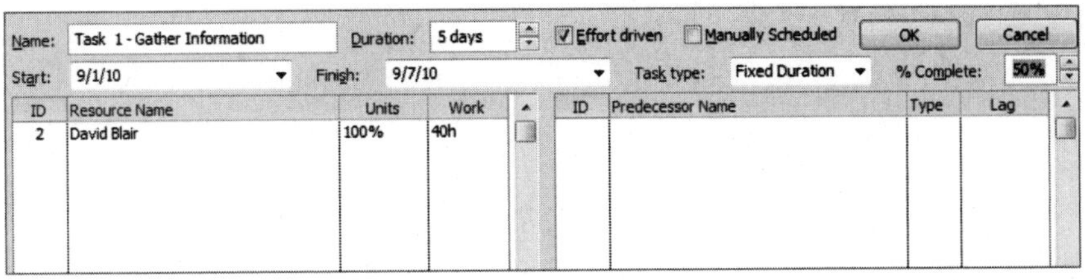

Name:	Task 1 - Gather Information		Duration:	5 days	☐	☑ Effort driven	☐ Manually Scheduled	OK		Cancel
Start:	9/1/10	▼	Finish:	9/7/10	▼	Task type:	Fixed Duration ▼	% Complete:	50%	☐

ID	Resource Name	Units	Work		ID	Predecessor Name	Type	Lag	
2	David Blair	100%	40h						

Understanding and Entering Actuals

Percent complete is just one part of the updating puzzle; you also need to understand how to manage what actually takes place in terms of dates, duration, work, and costs. When you record percent complete, Project automatically records actuals based on whatever is in your current plan at the time. It's up to you to input what really happens. The key components that you need to focus on for actuals are as follows:

- Actual start and finish dates

- Actual duration and remaining duration

- Actual work hours and remaining work

- Actual cost and remaining cost

This section explains how to enter actuals into Project and how they're linked to percent complete. It also covers the importance of understanding the current date and status date.

Current and Status Date

The *current date* is today's date. In the Gantt Chart view, this is represented by an orange vertical line that cuts through the timeline in the bar area, as shown in Figure 16.7.

Although the current date is nicely formatted in the default Gantt Chart view, if you switch views to, say, the tracking Gantt, it appears as a hard-to-see gray dotted line. As shown in Figure 16.8, you can change the format of the current date line in the tracking Gantt (or other Gantt Chart view) bar area by formatting the gridline as follows:

1. Go to Format tab ➤ Format group.

2. Click the Gridlines button, and select Gridlines.

3. In the Lines to Change list, click Current Date.

4. Under Normal, select a solid line from the Type drop-down list.

5. Under Normal, select red (or whatever color you prefer) from the Color drop-down list.

6. Click OK.

FIGURE 16.7   Current date in the Gantt chart

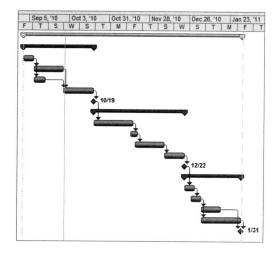

FIGURE 16.8   Formatting the gridline for the current date

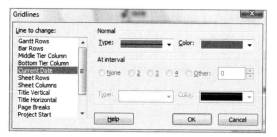

You can repeat this process for the project start date (making it blue, for example) and for other lines such as the project finish and the status date, discussed next. This type of formatting is view-specific, which means that as you change from one view to another, the formatting of items such as the gridlines can be different.

The current date is important because unless you intentionally fill in the status date, Project uses the current date as the default status date. In other words, the current date is used to determine whether a task should be finished. As you can see in Figure 16.7, everything to the left of the current date is in the past and therefore should be finished. Everything to the right is still in the future and therefore remains to be done. This is how Project determines whether a task needs to be updated. This is also the date Project uses to calculate EV components such as planned value, unless you fill in the status date.

You can modify the current date or add the status date in the Project Information dialog box on the Project tab, as shown in Figure 16.9.

FIGURE 16.9   Current and status date in the Project Information dialog box

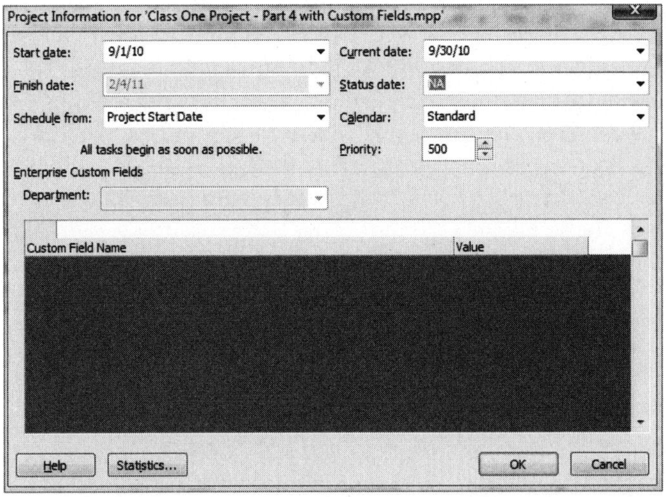

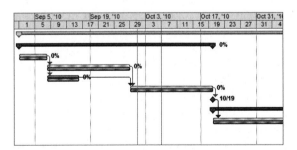

You can adjust the status date on the Project tab in the Status group by clicking the Status Date button.

Sometimes you need to have a status date that's different from the current date. For example, suppose you're preparing for a status-review meeting and you have updates until a specific date (say, the end of the month), and it's now a few days past. You can use the status date to reflect the end-of-the-month status. This allows you to capture status based on any point in time, past or present, without having to rely on the current date.

Figure 16.10 shows the Tracking Gantt view with the status date at the end of the month and the current date a week later. The gridline for the status date can be formatted with a different line type and color to stand out better in the Gantt bar area.

FIGURE 16.10   Displaying the status date and current date

The current date changes automatically based on your computer's system date, but the status date must be changed manually in the Project Information dialog box (see Figure 16.9).

Using the Status Date for Automatic Updates

Now that you understand more about current and status dates, you can take advantage of Project's automatic update functions. You can quickly update your project or tasks based on any status date you want, and Project calculates the appropriate percent complete.

For example, if a task is completely to the left of the status date, it's automatically updated to 100% complete. If the status date cuts exactly halfway through a task, then it's calculated to be 50% complete, and so on. Tasks in the future, completely to the right of the status date, remain at 0% complete.

Automatic Project Update

You can access the automatic update function as follows (see Figure 16.11):

1. Go to Project tab ➤ Status group, and click Update Project.

2. Accept the default for Update Work as Completed Through (notice that the date defaults to the status date; you can change it if needed).

3. Accept the default, For: Entire Project.

4. Click OK.

FIGURE 16.11   Automatic project updates

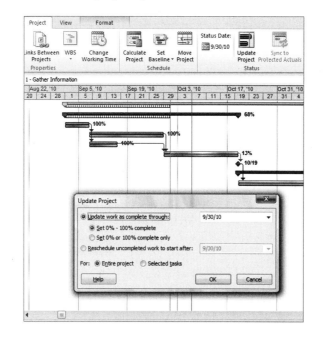

As you can see in Figure 16.11 you can also choose to reschedule uncompleted work to after the status date. Doing so moves all work that was supposed to be finished or started out to the future—to the right of the status date. This may significantly change your schedule. You also have a choice to update only for 0% or 100% and not update in-progress tasks (those for which the status date cuts through the task). This approach better supports the 0% or 100% update method. Finally, you can choose to update for the entire project or just selected tasks. This function is a very useful tool when you're updating project status.

Automatic Task Update

You can also select a task or group of tasks and click the Mark On Track button located on the Task tab in the Schedule group. As shown in Figure 16.12, when you click Mark On Track, Project automatically calculates percent complete based on the status date for each task you've selected.

FIGURE 16.12   Updating a task using Mark On Track

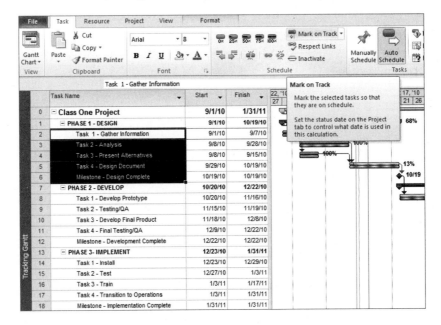

Move Incomplete Parts

As shown in Figure 16.11, you can use the Update Project function to move uncompleted work to the right of the status date. You can also use the Move command to quickly reschedule tasks to after the status date (see Figure 16.13). Follow these steps:

1. Go to Task tab ➤ Tasks group, and click the Move button.

2. From the list, select Incomplete Parts to Status Date.

FIGURE 16.13   Moving incomplete parts to status date

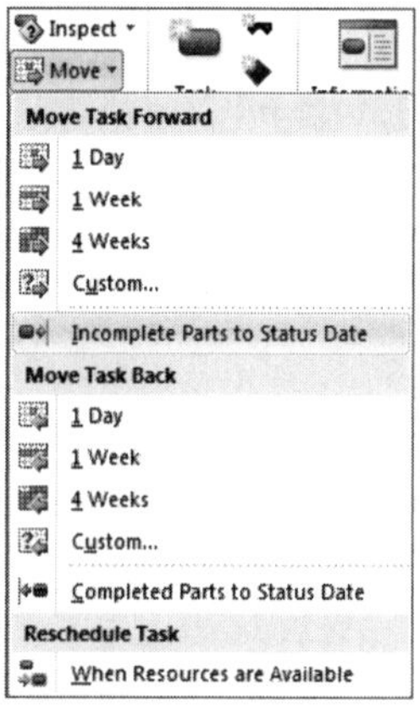

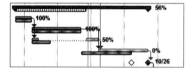

Doing so automatically reschedules tasks that are supposed to be finished but aren't, based on percent complete. This includes partially completed tasks—Project moves out the remaining part of the tasks. In Figure 16.14, a task was marked 50% finished and was supposed to be 100%; so, the remaining 50% was rescheduled.

FIGURE 16.14   Moving partially completed tasks

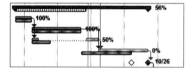

The next section talks more about splitting in-progress tasks.

Percent Complete and Future Tasks

Just because a task is in the future (or to the right of the status date) doesn't mean it can't have status. Project lets you enter percent complete for any task on your project, including those that are in the future or to the right of the status date. This doesn't usually make sense, but you're allowed to do it.

Entering Actuals

Percent complete is a key ingredient in updating tasks. Another major component is capturing actual information about dates, duration, work, and costs. In this section, you'll learn how to enter actuals in Project.

Percent Complete and Actuals, Joined Together

Percent complete and actuals are joined together. If you mark a task finished by entering 100% complete, Project automatically fills in the actual information. It does this by copying whatever is in your current plan fields (not your baseline fields) to the actual fields, including current start, finish, duration, work, and costs.

If you mark a task partially done, such as 50%, then Project automatically copies the current start to the actual start; spends half of the current duration, work, and cost; and calculates the remaining duration, work, and cost accordingly. Under this scenario, the actual finish date remains NA because you haven't completed the task.

A good way to view this is to apply the tracking table, which has many of the actual fields displayed. In Figure 16.15, I've applied the tracking table by selecting View tab ➢ Data group ➢ Tables.

FIGURE 16.15   Tracking table

Task Name	Act. Start	Act. Finish	% Comp.	Act. Dur.	Rem. Dur.	Act. Cost	Remaining Cost	Act. Work	Remainin Work
− **Class One Project**	**9/1/10**	**NA**	**10%**	**10.35 days**	**98.15 days**	**$15,210.00**	**$156,320.00**	**100 hrs**	**868 hrs**
− **PHASE 1 - DESIGN**	**9/1/10**	**NA**	**30%**	**10.67 days**	**24.33 days**	**$15,210.00**	**$44,230.00**	**100 hrs**	**228 hrs**
Task 1 - Gather Information	9/1/10	9/7/10	100%	5 days	0 days	$3,000.00	$0.00	40 hrs	0 hrs
Task 2 - Analysis	9/8/10	NA	50%	7.5 days	7.5 days	$3,210.00	$3,210.00	60 hrs	60 hrs
Task 3 - Present Alternatives	NA	NA	0%	0 days	6 days	$0.00	$3,600.00	0 hrs	48 hrs
Task 4 - Design Document	NA	NA	0%	0 days	15 days	$0.00	$6,420.00	0 hrs	120 hrs
Milestone - Design Complete	NA	NA	0%	0 days	0 days	$0.00	$10,000.00	0 hrs	0 hrs
− **PHASE 2 - DEVELOP**	**NA**	**NA**	**0%**	**0 mons**	**46 days**	**$0.00**	**$44,000.00**	**0 hrs**	**400 hrs**
Task 1 - Develop Prototype	NA	NA	0%	0 days	20 days	$0.00	$12,000.00	0 hrs	160 hrs
Task 2 - Testing/QA	NA	NA	0%	0 days	5 days	$0.00	$4,000.00	0 hrs	40 hrs
Task 3 - Develop Final Product	NA	NA	0%	0 days	15 days	$0.00	$22,000.00	0 hrs	120 hrs
Task 4 - Final Testing/QA	NA	NA	0%	0 days	10 days	$0.00	$6,000.00	0 hrs	80 hrs
Milestone - Development Complete	NA	NA	0%	0 days	0 days	$0.00	$0.00	0 hrs	0 hrs
− **PHASE 3 - IMPLEMENT**	**NA**	**NA**	**0%**	**0 mons**	**27.5 days**	**$0.00**	**$68,090.00**	**0 hrs**	**240 hrs**
Task 1 - Install	NA	NA	0%	0 days	5 days	$0.00	$12,140.00	0 hrs	40 hrs
Task 2 - Test	NA	NA	0%	0 days	5 days	$0.00	$3,000.00	0 hrs	40 hrs
Task 3 - Train	NA	NA	0%	0 days	10 days	$0.00	$40,000.00	0 hrs	0 hrs
Task 4 - Transition to Operations	NA	NA	0%	0 days	20 days	$0.00	$12,950.00	0 hrs	160 hrs
Milestone - Implementation Complete	NA	NA	0%	0 days	0 days	$0.00	$0.00	0 hrs	0 hrs

In Figure 16.15, I've added two columns using the Add Column approach: Remaining Duration and Remaining Work. I also took the liberty of hiding Physical % Complete because it wasn't being used. To learn more about tables and adding columns, refer to Chapter 11.

As you can see in Figure 16.15, when a task is marked 100%, such as Task 1—Gather Information, the Actual Start and Actual Finish fields are populated; Actual Duration, Actual Work, and Actual Cost are calculated with zero remaining.

When you mark a task 50% complete, the actual start date is automatically filled in; and half of the duration, work, and cost are spent, leaving half left in the remaining duration, work, and cost. Notice that the actual finish date is left as NA for all tasks that aren't 100% finished.

If you enter an actual finish date manually in the tracking table, then the percent complete automatically changes to 100%, and the remaining duration, work, and cost go to zero. You can't have an actual finish and not be 100% finished—they're tied together.

If you mark a task 100% complete and subsequently add any duration or work to the remaining duration or remaining work, Project automatically recalculates percent complete (to some value less than 100%) and removes the actual finish date.

Entering Actual Dates and Duration

When you mark a task finished by entering 100% complete, Project automatically fills in your actuals based on whatever is in your current plan. It stands to reason that if you keep your current plan up to date or update your current plan before entering percent complete, then when you enter percent complete, your actuals will reflect reality.

If you enter percent complete and your current plan doesn't reflect what actually happened, it's up to you to enter your actual start, finish, and duration. If a task is complete and you enter your actual start and actual finish manually before entering percent complete, then both percent complete and actual duration are calculated automatically. You can enter actuals directly into the tracking table, as shown in Figure 16.15, or you can use the Update Tasks dialog box.

Typically, if I have the Tracking Gantt view applied with the Variance table, I use the Update Tasks dialog box to capture actuals. You can enter actuals in the Update Tasks dialog box as follows (see Figure 16.16):

1. Select Task tab ➤ Schedule group ➤ Mark On Track drop-down list ➤ Update Tasks.

2. In the Update Tasks dialog box, enter percent complete or actual duration and/or remaining duration or actual start and/or actual finish dates.

FIGURE 16.16   Entering actuals in the Update Tasks dialog box

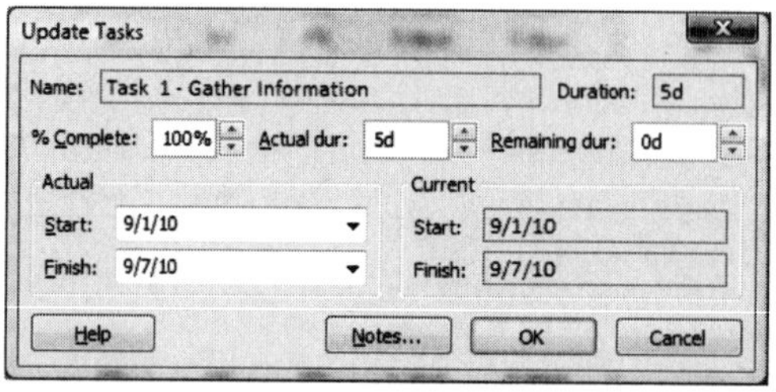

When a task is marked 100% complete, the actual start, actual finish, and actual duration become the same as the current start, finish, and duration. Therefore, when you're looking at the current start, finish, and duration in the Gantt Chart view, you're essentially looking at a copy of the actuals.

Entering Actual Hours

The same rules apply for percent complete and actual hours. Project automatically calculates actual hours spent and hours remaining based on what is in the current work estimates. For example, if there are 80 hours in the current work estimate and you mark a task 50% complete, then 40 hours of actual work is calculated, with 40 hours of work remaining. If you decide to increase the remaining work after the fact, that percent complete is recalculated accordingly, along with a new estimate for current work. The baseline work estimate stays the same.

One way to enter actual hours and remaining hours is to use the tracking table, as shown in Figure 16.15. The default tracking table only displays actual work—you have to add a column for remaining work. Another effective way to capture actual work is to create a split-screen view and change the Task Form view to display resource work. To apply the resource work form in a split view, follow these steps (see Figure 16.17):

1. Select View tab ➤ Split View group ➤ Details.

2. Right-click anywhere in the bottom view (the Task Form view).

3. In the list that appears, select Work.

FIGURE 16.17   Task form with work displayed

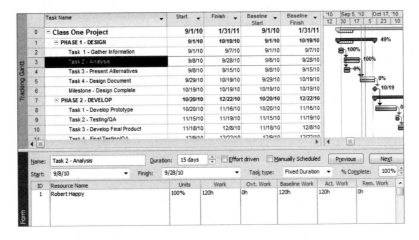

You can now enter actual and remaining work directly in the task form, in the Actual and Remaining Work columns. If you enter actual work after percent complete, the default value is based on whatever is in your Current Work field. If you enter actual work before entering percent complete, then percent complete is automatically calculated. For example, if you have a work estimate of 40 hours, and you enter 20 hours in the Actual Work field and click OK button (which will appear as Previous until you make a change that needs to be entered) in the task form, Project automatically calculates percent complete to be 50% and remaining work to be 20 hours.

When you enter 0 for remaining hours, percent complete is automatically calculated as 100%. Note that changing the remaining hours affects the calculation of percent complete and the total work estimate.

You can enter and modify actual work hours in any of the usage views as well. This may be useful if you need to track hours at a more granular or detailed level, such as day by day. Change views to either the Task Usage view or the Resource Usage view, and add the actual hours to the time-phased scale of the view. To learn more about changing and modifying views, see Chapter 10, "Understanding Views."

As shown in Figure 16.18, you can add actual hours in the usage views by right-clicking under Details and selecting Actual Work. You're now free to record actual work hours on a day-by-day basis. For example, in Figure 16.18, under the Task 1 – Gather Information, the actual hours for David Blair have been entered as 8 hours on Wednesday, 6 hours on Thursday and 3 hours on Friday, which is different from the 8-hours-per-day work estimate. To enter the hours, you can type them directly in each cell under each day for each resource.

FIGURE 16.18 Entering actual hours by day

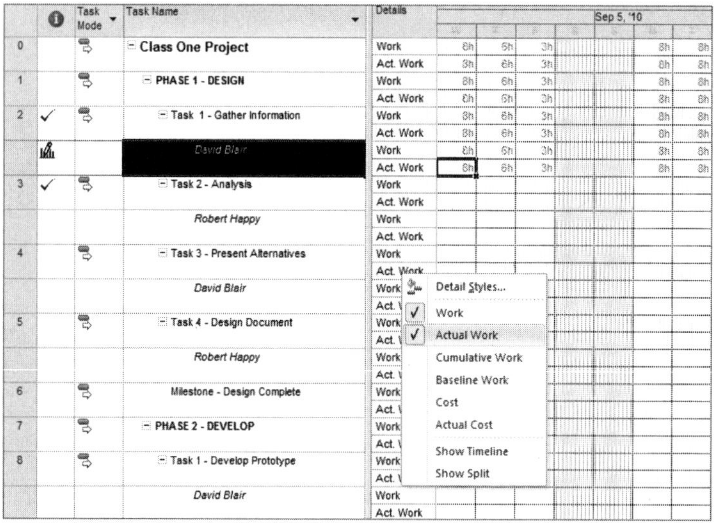

Capturing Overtime Hours

You can add the Overtime Hours column to any table; or, as in Figure 16.18, you can click on Detail Styles... to add overtime hours in the Details section in the Time Phase portion of the Task or Resource Usage view. In doing so, you can enter overtime hours on a day-by-day basis. The overtime hours need to be entered into the Overtime Work field, separate from the normal Work field.

Actual Costs

To review how to assigns costs, see Chapter 8, "Assigning Resources and Costs." Costs come from the following:

- Standard rates (or overtime rates) for work resources, which are related to work hours assigned to tasks.

- Standard rates for material resources, which are related to the cost per unit assigned to tasks.
- Cost per use, which is related to resources assigned to tasks. The Cost Per Use field represents a lump-sum fee, such as a setup cost.
- Cost resources, which are lump-sum costs associated with a resource. They're filled in at the time the resource is assigned to tasks (this has nothing to do with work hours, units, or standard rates).
- Fixed cost field, which you can use as an option to add costs to a task without assigning resources or using the resource pool.

Actual costs are automatically calculated as you enter status and percent complete. As shown in Figure 16.19, you can view this by applying the Cost table in a split-screen view by following these steps:

1. Select View tab ➤ Data group ➤ Tables ➤ Cost.
2. In the Split View group, make sure Details is selected.
3. In the bottom view, right-click anywhere, and select Cost from the list.

You can now review costs in the Cost table and in the Cost Form view in the bottom of the split view. You can enter actual costs for fixed costs or cost-type resources if needed. For hourly resources, costs are calculated automatically as you enter actual hours and resource status.

FIGURE 16.19 Applying the Cost table

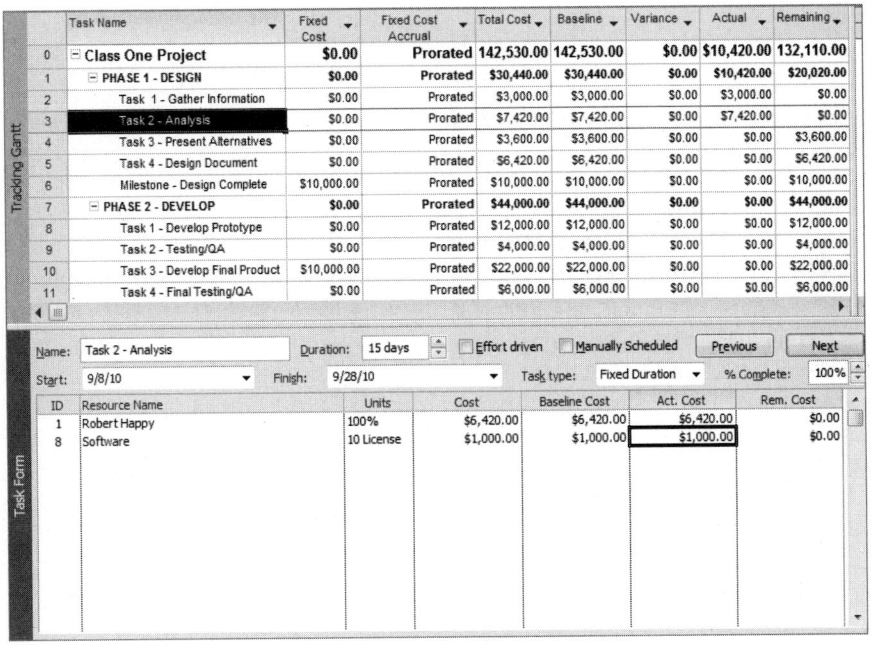

	Task Name	Fixed Cost	Fixed Cost Accrual	Total Cost	Baseline	Variance	Actual	Remaining
0	Class One Project	$0.00	Prorated	142,530.00	142,530.00	$0.00	$10,420.00	132,110.00
1	PHASE 1 - DESIGN	$0.00	Prorated	$30,440.00	$30,440.00	$0.00	$10,420.00	$20,020.00
2	Task 1 - Gather Information	$0.00	Prorated	$3,000.00	$3,000.00	$0.00	$3,000.00	$0.00
3	Task 2 - Analysis	$0.00	Prorated	$7,420.00	$7,420.00	$0.00	$7,420.00	$0.00
4	Task 3 - Present Alternatives	$0.00	Prorated	$3,600.00	$3,600.00	$0.00	$0.00	$3,600.00
5	Task 4 - Design Document	$0.00	Prorated	$6,420.00	$6,420.00	$0.00	$0.00	$6,420.00
6	Milestone - Design Complete	$10,000.00	Prorated	$10,000.00	$10,000.00	$0.00	$0.00	$10,000.00
7	PHASE 2 - DEVELOP	$0.00	Prorated	$44,000.00	$44,000.00	$0.00	$0.00	$44,000.00
8	Task 1 - Develop Prototype	$0.00	Prorated	$12,000.00	$12,000.00	$0.00	$0.00	$12,000.00
9	Task 2 - Testing/QA	$0.00	Prorated	$4,000.00	$4,000.00	$0.00	$0.00	$4,000.00
10	Task 3 - Develop Final Product	$10,000.00	Prorated	$22,000.00	$22,000.00	$0.00	$0.00	$22,000.00
11	Task 4 - Final Testing/QA	$0.00	Prorated	$6,000.00	$6,000.00	$0.00	$0.00	$6,000.00

ID	Resource Name	Units	Cost	Baseline Cost	Act. Cost	Rem. Cost
1	Robert Happy	100%	$6,420.00	$6,420.00	$6,420.00	$0.00
8	Software	10 License	$1,000.00	$1,000.00	$1,000.00	$0.00

Replacing Resources on a Task with Actuals

Sometimes you may need to replace a resource on a task that already has some percent-complete and actuals recorded but isn't finished. In this situation, you can replace the existing resource with the new resource in the Task Form view; Project automatically keeps the actual hours for the original resource and transfers the remaining hours to the new resource assignment. Follow these steps to replace a resource on a task with assignments in this manner (see Figure 16.20):

1. Select View tab ➢ Split View group ➢ Details to apply a split-screen view.

2. In the bottom Task Form view, in the Resource Name field, click the drop-down arrow beside the existing resource's name.

3. Select the new resource to replace the existing resource, and click OK (or press Enter).

    Project automatically assigns the remaining hours to the new resource and keeps the spent actual hours associated with the original resource assignment.

Actuals Are Hard-Coded, Date-Like Constraints

When a task has an actual start or an actual finish date, it acts like a hard-coded date with a constraint. These dates don't move to the left or to the right if there is a delay in a predecessor task.

🌐 Real World Scenario

Custom Tracking View

Most clients I work with have unique needs for tracking status on projects. Typically, this requires setting up a custom tracking view based on a custom tracking table. I start from a copy of the tracking Gantt chart, because it's already formatted to display baseline and current bars together. I also start the custom table from a copy of the Variance table, because it includes the Baseline and Variance columns. I then add columns such as % Complete, a custom text field for comments, and a custom Task Finish Status field that displays red, yellow, and green light indicators based on finish variance. I even use a custom Needs Updating field, which displays a red flag for tasks that are in the past and not marked as being finished. Both the Task Finish Status and Needs Updating fields are based on somewhat complex formulas that are included on the CD that comes with this book.

FIGURE 16.20   Replacing existing resources with new ones that already have status

Name: Task 3 - Present Alternatives	Duration: 6 days	☑ Effort driven	☐ Manually Scheduled	OK	Cancel
Start: 9/8/10 ▼	Finish: 9/15/10 ▼	Task type: Fixed Units ▼	% Complete: 50% ⬍		

ID	Resource Name	Units	Work	Ovt. Work	Baseline Work	Act. Work	Rem. Work
2	David Blair	100%	24h	0h	48h	24h	0h
6	Robert Happy	100%	24h	0h	0h	0h	24h

Splitting In-Progress Tasks

It's possible to split tasks in Project. The typical scenario is that you begin work on a task, stop for a time, and then begin again. In this case, you can use the Split Task command or the Move command. If a task has some status with percent complete and actuals, the actuals remain in place as if they were hard-coded constraints. If you use Split Task or Move, Project moves only the remaining work portion of that task. If needed, you can split a task within the actuals and even tasks that are marked 100% complete, but the Move function will only act on remaining duration or work.

To split an in-progress task with the Split Task function, as shown in Figure 16.21, follow these steps.

1. Go to Task tab ➤ Schedule group, and click the Split Task button.

2. Position the cursor over the portion of the task in the Gantt bar that you want to split.

3. Click and drag that portion to the new starting point.

FIGURE 16.21   Using the Split Task function

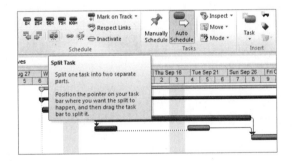

Figure 16.21 shows that if you split an in-progress task, the portion with the actuals and percent complete stays in place, and the remaining work is rescheduled based on where you drop it. The dotted line represents the portion of the task where no work is being done.

To split a task with the Move function, follow these steps:

1. Click the task you want to move.

2. Go to Task tab ⮞ Tasks group.

3. From the Move drop-down list, select the amount of time you want to move the task, such as one week.

Similar to the results in Figure 16.21, the portion of the task with percent complete and actuals remains in place, whereas the remaining work is moved out to the right, creating a split task.

Changing Percent Complete with the Click-and-Drag Approach

You can position the cursor at the end of the progress line in the Gantt chart bar area for a specific task and click and drag the progress line directly inside the Gantt bar to change percent complete. As you position your cursor inside the Gantt bar, the cursor changes to a percent sign combined with an arrowhead; when it does, click and drag.

The Tracking Decision Tree

To help with your updating process, Figure 16.22 shows a tracking decision tree. It guides you through the steps you may want to follow to update tasks in your project. Ask yourself these questions, and follow these steps in Project to keep your plan updated.

🌐 Real World Scenario

Using Enhanced Copy and Paste to Capture Actuals

I was using Project 2010 to keep track of a major project for a client. The group was distributed across many locations, and we held a team meeting once a week. We didn't have Project Server—just the desktop version. I had to present an updated plan for the meeting. Typically, I captured updates through conference calls, meetings, and email attachments. However, taking advantage of enhanced copy and paste, I ran a filtered view of what needed updating each week, highlighted only the cells I needed and copying and pasting them into an email.

With enhanced copy and paste, the formatting remained intact; team members could edit each cell in the table directly in the email, and reply—no attachments required. They could even add columns or comments and highlight their edits in yellow. Wow—copy and paste really is alive and well.

FIGURE 16.22   The tracking decision tree

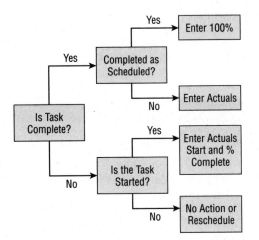

Summary

In this chapter, you learned about the different types of percent complete and how to enter status into Project. You can enter status for one task at a time or for a group of tasks. You also learned the difference between and the importance of the current date and the status date and how they play a role in updating status.

In addition to understanding and entering percent complete, you need to pay close attention to actuals. You can enter actuals for duration, start, finish, work, and costs. Actuals are closely tied to percent complete: if you enter 100% complete, Project automatically copies whatever is in your current start, finish, duration, work, and cost (not baseline) into the actual start, finish, and duration, work, and cost fields. You can make adjustments to actuals at any time.

The chapter also covered how to replace resources for in-progress tasks and how to split an in-progress task if work needs to stop for a time and start again later.

The next chapter will discuss how to analyze your plan for variances and take corrective action.

Hands-On Exercises

The following hands-on exercises are designed to test your understanding of the topics discussed in this chapter. We've provided files on the companion CD that will show you what your project file should look like as you perform these exercises.

EXERCISE 21

Entering Percent Complete and Actuals

1. Update all Phase 1 tasks to be 100% complete. Try using the 100% button on the Task tab in the Schedule group and entering **100%** directly in the table side of the Gantt chart (you may need to insert the % Complete column into the table).

2. Change the table to the tracking table. What happens to the actual fields in the Phase 1 tasks? Change a task's actual finish date so it finishes later. Add to a task's remaining duration—what happens to percent complete and the actual finish date?

3. Update Phase 2, Task 1—Develop Prototype to 100% complete but show the task completed two days early. Access the Update Tasks dialog box by clicking on the drop-down list by Mark On Track. (Remember, when actuals differ from the baseline, enter actuals and let Project calculate percent complete.) What happens to the actual duration? What happens to successor tasks?

4. Using the Update Tasks dialog box, update Phase 2, Task 2—Testing/QA to 100% complete but show that it takes four days more than estimated (four days late). What happens to the actual duration? What happens to successor tasks? Review the finish variance by switching to the Variance table or adding a new column to the tracking table.

5. Update Phase 2, Tasks 3 and 4, and the milestone to 100% complete. What technique did you use?

6. Update Phase 3, Task 1—Install to be 50% complete. What happens to the Gantt bar? What happens to the Actual fields? How complete is Phase 3? How complete is the project?

Chapter

17

Variance Analysis and Taking Corrective Action

IN THIS CHAPTER, YOU'LL LEARN ABOUT THE FOLLOWING:

✓ Understanding variance

✓ Understanding the impact of change: planned vs. actuals

✓ Taking corrective action

✓ Performing an earned-value analysis

Project can enhance your ability to perform during the execution stage of any project. It has powerful and easy-to-use tools that you can use to compare your original plan (baseline) to what actually occurs as you revise your schedule. It helps to communicate the impact of change and provides you with an effective tool for taking corrective action.

As a project manager, you're always juggling tradeoffs between scope, time, and resources, particularly after a project begins. Learning how to use Project's updating and tracking tools will help you make better decisions.

Understanding Variance

Now that you've learned how to set a baseline (as discussed in Chapter 15, "Understanding and Setting Baselines") and how to enter status for tasks and resources to capture percent complete and actuals, you can take advantage of performance measures to help you stay on track. At the very least, you can communicate more effectively why things are slipping or changing, to make better decisions and keep stakeholders informed.

Types of Variance

Project uses five basic types of variance:

- Start variance
- Finish variance
- Duration variance
- Work variance
- Cost variance

In addition to these variance fields, Project provides earned value fields, discussed later in this chapter. Variance depends on setting a baseline first, so you can compare what really happens (actuals or newly revised current estimates) to what was originally planned (baseline).

Variance values are calculated as follows:

Variance = (Actuals + Remaining) – Baseline

If nothing remains, such as when the task is 100% complete, then variance is the actuals minus the baseline values. This is the same for each of the variance fields calculated by

Project. For example, if you estimated a task to take 10 days, and it actually takes 12 days, the duration variance is 2 days. Positive variance is bad, because it indicates that you're late, you worked more hours than expected, or you're over budget:

> Duration Variance = 12 days – 10 days = 2 days (positive number indicates overage or slippage)

If variance has a negative value, this is favorable, because it indicates that you're early, you worked fewer hours than expected, or you're under budget, depending on which variance value you're analyzing. For example, if you estimated that a task would take 40 hours of work, you record 30 hours of actual work, and 0 hours remain (meaning the task is 100% complete), then the work variance is –10 hours (you finished with less work than originally planned):

> Work Variance = 30 hours – 40 hours = –10hours (negative number is favorable indicating under budget, ahead of schedule, or early)

If a standard cost rate is applied to the hours, you also have a negative cost-variance value and are under budget.

For in-progress tasks with status, Project not only looks at the actual values but also takes into consideration the remaining estimates. For example, if a task has a baseline duration of 10 days, the actual duration is 6 days, and 6 days remain, then you have a total new estimate of 12 days for that task, meaning your duration variance is 2 days. Because percent complete is tied to actual duration and remaining duration, Project calculates this task as being 50% complete. If you increase the remaining duration, Project will recalculate the duration variance and percent complete accordingly.

This also applies to work variance. As you enter actual hours worked plus remaining work estimates, Project automatically compares the sum of those values to the baseline to calculate work variance.

Viewing Variance

The easiest way to begin viewing variance in Project is to take advantage of some of the predefined tables and views. To learn more about changing views, please refer to Chapter 10, "Understanding Views"; to learn more about using tables, refer to Chapter 11, "Using Tables and Custom Fields."

Tracking Gantt and Variance Table

Switching to the Tracking Gantt view lets you see both the baseline and current Gantt bars in one view. You can also switch to the Variance table to view current schedule values and baseline values combined with both start and finish variance. Figure 17.1 shows the default Tracking Gantt view with the Variance table applied. In this example, you can see the impact of Task 1—Gather Information being rescheduled from originally taking one week to instead taking two weeks.

FIGURE 17.1 Tracking Gantt with Variance table

	Task Name	Start	Finish	Baseline Start	Baseline Finish	Start Var.	Finish Var.	'10	Sep 12, '10	Oct 31, '10	Dec 19, '10	Feb
0	Class One Project	9/1/10	2/7/11	9/1/10	1/31/11	0 days	5 days					0%
1	PHASE 1 - DESIGN	9/1/10	10/26/10	9/1/10	10/19/10	0 days	5 days		0%			
2	Task 1 - Gather Information	9/1/10	9/14/10	9/1/10	9/7/10	0 days	5 days	0%				
3	Task 2 - Analysis	9/15/10	10/5/10	9/8/10	9/28/10	5 days	5 days	0%				
4	Task 3 - Present Alternatives	9/15/10	9/22/10	9/8/10	9/15/10	5 days	5 days	0%				
5	Task 4 - Design Document	10/6/10	10/26/10	9/29/10	10/19/10	5 days	5 days	0%				
6	Milestone - Design Complete	10/26/10	10/26/10	10/19/10	10/19/10	5 days	5 days	10/26				
7	PHASE 2 - DEVELOP	10/27/10	12/29/10	10/20/10	12/22/10	5 days	5 days		0%			
8	Task 1 - Develop Prototype	10/27/10	11/23/10	10/20/10	11/16/10	5 days	5 days	0%				
9	Task 2 - Testing/QA	11/22/10	11/26/10	11/15/10	11/19/10	5 days	5 days	0%				
10	Task 3 - Develop Final Product	11/25/10	12/15/10	11/18/10	12/8/10	5 days	5 days	0%				
11	Task 4 - Final Testing/QA	12/16/10	12/29/10	12/9/10	12/22/10	5 days	5 days	0%				
12	Milestone - Development Complete	12/29/10	12/29/10	12/22/10	12/22/10	5 days	5 days	12/29				
13	PHASE 3 - IMPLEMENT	12/30/10	2/7/11	12/23/10	1/31/11	5 days	5 days					0%
14	Task 1 - Install	12/30/10	1/5/11	12/23/10	12/29/10	5 days	5 days	0%				
15	Task 2 - Test	1/3/11	1/10/11	12/27/10	1/3/11	5 days	5 days	0%				
16	Task 3 - Train	1/10/11	1/24/11	1/3/11	1/17/11	5 days	5 days	0%				
17	Task 4 - Transition to Operations	1/10/11	2/7/11	1/3/11	1/31/11	5 days	5 days	0%				
18	Milestone - Implementation Complete	2/7/11	2/7/11	1/31/11	1/31/11	5 days	5 days	2				

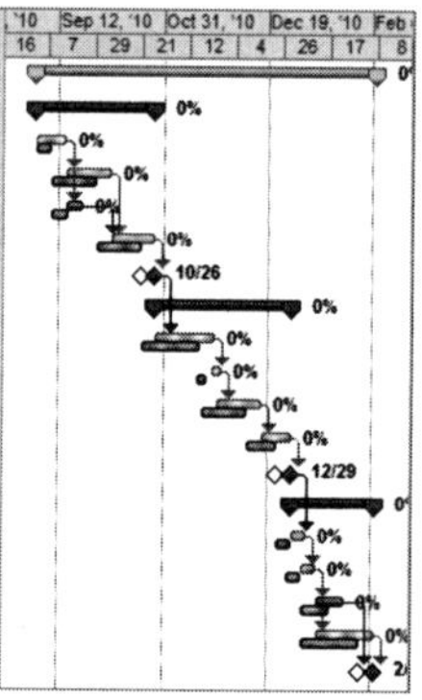

On further analysis, you can see the impact of changing this one task by looking at the following:

- Finish variance for each task

- Review change highlighting (or shaded tasks) under the start and finish date columns for all tasks impacted by the adjustment; the cells automatically change color to light blue;

- Gantt bar area showing the impact on the current plan versus the baseline plan

In this scenario, because Task 1 is on the critical path, the change affects the project finish date, which now has a finish variance of five days.

Tracking Gantt with Custom Tracking Table

My preference is to customize a new view by modifying a copy of the Tracking Gantt view and a copy of the Variance table to better match the tracking process. This includes using custom fields. In Chapter 11, you learned how to create custom fields with graphical indicators. Two of the fields I covered (which are also included in this book's CD) are as follows:

Needs Updating Field Marks with a red flag all the tasks to the left of the current date (tasks in the past) that aren't marked finished and therefore need to be updated.

Task Finish Status Uses a graphical indicator to display tasks that are early (green light), on time (green light), late by up to two days (yellow light), late by more than two days (red light), or complete (check mark).

Figure 17.2 shows the Needs Updating custom field based on three example tasks. You can access this formula on the CD in a file named Formula Needs Updating for 2010.mpp.

FIGURE 17.2 Needs Updating custom field

	ⓘ	Task Mode	Task Name	Needs Updating	Mar 21, '10	Mar 28, '10	Apr 4, '10
1	✓		Task 1				
2			Task 2	⚐			
3			Task 3				

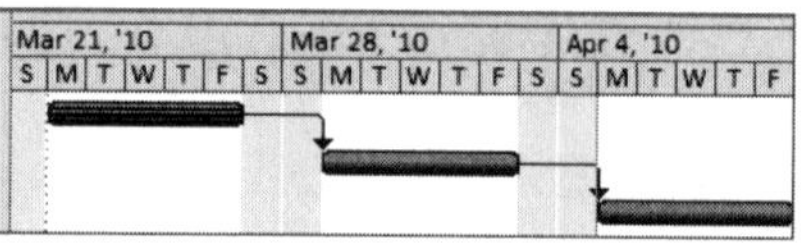

Using the orange line in the Gantt bar area as the status date in Figure 17.2, you can see that Task 1 is in the past but is marked 100% complete and therefore doesn't need updating. However, Task 2 is in the past but isn't marked done and therefore requires updating: it needs to be either marked complete or rescheduled to the future. Hence, a red flag is automatically generated. To review the formula and graphical indicator, go to Format tab ➤ Schedule group, and click Custom Fields.

The Needs Updating field is useful for reviewing and analyzing plans. Scan the project schedule for red flags, and focus on those tasks to be updated. You can use the auto filter for that column and quickly generate a needs-updating list of tasks to share with team members who are assigned to those tasks.

Figure 17.3 shows the Task Finish Status custom field, which you can find on the book's CD in a file named Formula Task Finish Status for 2010.mpp.

FIGURE 17.3   Task Finish Status custom field

		Task Name	Task Finish Status	Finish Variance		
1		Task 1 - On Time	●	0 days		0%
2		Task 2 - Early	●	-1 day		0%
3		Task 3 - Late Less Than 2 days	○	1 day		0%
4		Task 4 - Late Greater than 2 days	●	3 days		0%
5	✓	Task 5 - Completed	✓	0 days		100%
6		Task 6 - No Baseline	▭	0 days		0%

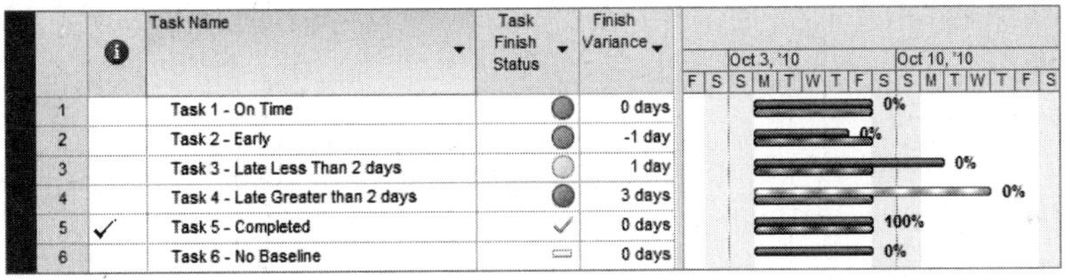

In this example, you can see that the tolerance level to change from a green light to a yellow light is anything less than two days late. For anything greater than two days late, a task automatically receives a red light indicator. You can modify the formula to change the tolerance of when a task should turn yellow or red based on the degree of lateness. To review how to change formulas, refer to Chapter 11.

 NOTE To swap or exchange custom fields from one file to another, use the Organizer tool in the backstage by clicking the File tab and then Info. You need to have both files open to exchange custom fields. For example, open the file Formula Task Finish Status for 2010 while you have your destination file open, to exchange fields. To learn more about the Organizer, see Chapter 13, "Creating Custom Views, Formatting, and Reporting."

Figure 17.4 is a custom view based on a modified copy of the Variance table, using the following fields:

- ID
- % Complete
- Task Name
- Start
- Duration
- Finish

- Needs Updating (custom field)
- Task Finish Status (custom field)
- Baseline Start
- Baseline Finish
- Finish Variance

FIGURE 17.4 Custom tracking table to analyze schedule

% Cmplt	Task Name	Start	Duration	Finish	Needs Updating	Task Finish Status	Baseline Start	Baseline Finish	Finish Var.
20%	− Class One Project	9/1/10	112.5 days	2/4/11			9/1/10	1/31/11	4 days
63%	− PHASE 1 - DESIGN	9/1/10	37 days	10/21/10			9/1/10	10/19/10	2 days
100%	Task 1 - Gather Information	9/1/10	5 days	9/7/10	✓		9/1/10	9/7/10	0 days
100%	Task 2 - Analysis	9/8/10	16 days	9/29/10	✓		9/8/10	9/28/10	1 day
100%	Task 3 - Present Alternatives	9/8/10	6 days	9/15/10	✓		9/8/10	9/15/10	0 days
0%	Task 4 - Design Document	9/30/10	16 days	10/21/10	◯		9/29/10	10/19/10	2 days
0%	Milestone - Design Complete	10/21/10	0 days	10/21/10	◯		10/19/10	10/19/10	2 days
0%	− PHASE 2 - DEVELOP	10/22/10	48 days	12/28/10			10/20/10	12/22/10	4 days
0%	Task 1 - Develop Prototype	10/22/10	22 days	11/22/10	●		10/20/10	11/16/10	4 days
0%	Task 2 - Testing/QA	11/19/10	5 days	11/25/10	●		11/15/10	11/19/10	4 days
0%	Task 3 - Develop Final Product	11/24/10	15 days	12/14/10	●		11/18/10	12/8/10	4 days
0%	Task 4 - Final Testing/QA	12/15/10	10 days	12/28/10	●		12/9/10	12/22/10	4 days
0%	Milestone - Development Complete	12/28/10	0 days	12/28/10	●		12/22/10	12/22/10	4 days
0%	− PHASE 3- IMPLEMENT	12/29/10	27.5 days	2/4/11			12/23/10	1/31/11	4 days
0%	Task 1 - Install	12/29/10	5 days	1/4/11	●		12/23/10	12/29/10	4 days
0%	Task 2 - Test	12/31/10	5 days	1/7/11	●		12/27/10	1/3/11	4 days
0%	Task 3 - Train	1/7/11	10 days	1/21/11	●		1/3/11	1/17/11	4 days
0%	Task 4 - Transition to Operations	1/7/11	20 days	2/4/11	●		1/3/11	1/31/11	4 days
0%	Milestone - Implementation Complete	2/4/11	0 days	2/4/11	●		1/31/11	1/31/11	4 days

Work Table and Split Views

If you need to focus on work variance, it's effective to apply the Work table with a split view that has the Work form applied. You can modify the split-view form by right-clicking the bottom part of a split view and selecting Work. To set up this view, follow these steps (see Figure 17.5):

1. In the Gantt Chart view, select View tab ➤ Data group ➤ Tables drop-down menu ➤ Work.
2. In the Split View group, make sure Details is enabled.
3. In the bottom view, right-click anywhere to bring up the list of forms, and select Work.

As you can see in Figure 17.5, Task 1 took 1 day longer to finish and a total of 48 hours of work instead of the baseline plan of 40 hours, resulting in a work variance of 8 hours.

Cost Table and Split Views

If you need to focus on cost variance, it's effective to apply the Cost table with a split view that has the Cost form applied. You can modify the split-view form by right-clicking the bottom part of a split view and selecting Cost. To set up this view, follow these steps (see Figure 17.6):

1. In the Gantt Chart view, select View tab ➤ Data group ➤ Tables drop-down menu ➤ Cost.

2. In the Split View group, make sure Details is enabled.

3. In the bottom view, right-click anywhere to bring up the list of forms, and select Cost.

FIGURE 17.5   Work table with split view applied

	Task Name	Work	Baseline	Variance	Actual	Remaining	% W. Comp.
0	⊟ Class One Project	1,008 hrs	968 hrs	40 hrs	224 hrs	784 hrs	22%
1	⊟ PHASE 1 - DESIGN	352 hrs	328 hrs	24 hrs	224 hrs	128 hrs	64%
2	Task 1 - Gather Information	48 hrs	40 hrs	8 hrs	48 hrs	0 hrs	100%
3	Task 2 - Analysis	128 hrs	120 hrs	8 hrs	128 hrs	0 hrs	100%
4	Task 3 - Present Alternatives	48 hrs	48 hrs	0 hrs	48 hrs	0 hrs	100%
5	Task 4 - Design Document	128 hrs	120 hrs	8 hrs	0 hrs	128 hrs	0%
6	Milestone - Design Complete	0 hrs	0 hrs	0 hrs	0 hrs	0 hrs	0%
7	⊟ PHASE 2 - DEVELOP	416 hrs	400 hrs	16 hrs	0 hrs	416 hrs	0%
8	Task 1 - Develop Prototype	176 hrs	160 hrs	16 hrs	0 hrs	176 hrs	0%
9	Task 2 - Testing/QA	40 hrs	40 hrs	0 hrs	0 hrs	40 hrs	0%
10	Task 3 - Develop Final Product	120 hrs	120 hrs	0 hrs	0 hrs	120 hrs	0%
11	Task 4 - Final Testing/QA	80 hrs	80 hrs	0 hrs	0 hrs	80 hrs	0%
12	Milestone - Development	0 hrs	0 hrs	0 hrs	0 hrs	0 hrs	0%

Name: Task 1 - Gather Information   Duration: 6 days   ☑ Effort driven ☐ Manually Scheduled   Previous   Next

Start: 9/1/10   Finish: 9/8/10   Task type: Fixed Duration   % Complete: 100%

ID	Resource Name	Units	Work	Ovt. Work	Baseline Work	Act. Work	Rem. Work
2	David Blair	100%	48h	0h	40h	48h	0h

Ready   New Tasks : Auto Scheduled

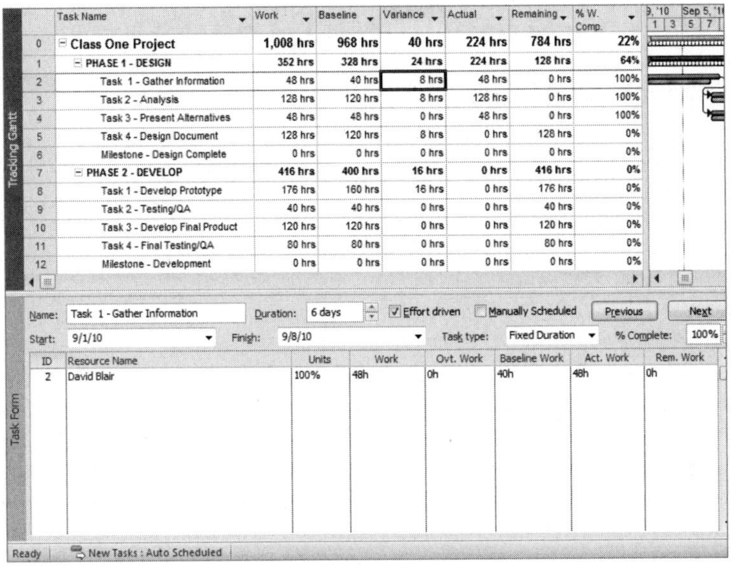

FIGURE 17.6   Cost table with split view applied

	Task Name	Fixed Cost	Fixed Cost Accrual	Total Cost	Baseline	Variance	Actual	Remaining
0	⊟ Class One Project	$0.00	Prorated	174,186.00	171,530.00	$2,656.00	$33,248.00	140,938.00
1	⊟ PHASE 1 - DESIGN	$30,000.00	Prorated	$60,896.00	$59,440.00	$1,456.00	$33,248.00	$27,648.00
2	Task 1 - Gather Inf	$0.00	Prorated	$3,600.00	$3,000.00	$600.00	$3,600.00	$0.00
3	Task 2 - Analysis	$0.00	Prorated	$6,848.00	$6,420.00	$428.00	$6,848.00	$0.00
4	Task 3 - Present Alt	$0.00	Prorated	$3,600.00	$3,600.00	$0.00	$3,600.00	$0.00
5	Task 4 - Design Doc	$0.00	Prorated	$6,848.00	$6,420.00	$428.00	$0.00	$6,848.00
6	Milestone - Design C	$10,000.00	Prorated	$10,000.00	$10,000.00	$0.00	$0.00	$10,000.00
7	⊟ PHASE 2 - DEVELOP	$0.00	Prorated	$45,200.00	$44,000.00	$1,200.00	$0.00	$45,200.00
8	Task 1 - Develop Pr	$0.00	Prorated	$13,200.00	$12,000.00	$1,200.00	$0.00	$13,200.00
9	Task 2 - Testing/QA	$0.00	Prorated	$4,000.00	$4,000.00	$0.00	$0.00	$4,000.00
10	Task 3 - Develop Fir	$10,000.00	Prorated	$22,000.00	$22,000.00	$0.00	$0.00	$22,000.00
11	Task 4 - Final Testin	$0.00	Prorated	$6,000.00	$6,000.00	$0.00	$0.00	$6,000.00
12	Milestone -	$0.00	Prorated	$0.00	$0.00	$0.00	$0.00	$0.00

Name: Task 1 - Gather Information   Duration: 6 days   ☑ Effort driven ☐ Manually Scheduled   Previous   Next

Start: 9/1/10   Finish: 9/8/10   Task type: Fixed Duration   % Complete: 100%

ID	Resource Name	Units	Cost	Baseline Cost	Act. Cost	Rem. Cost
2	David Blair	100%	$3,600.00	$3,000.00	$3,600.00	$0.00

Ready   New Tasks : Auto Scheduled

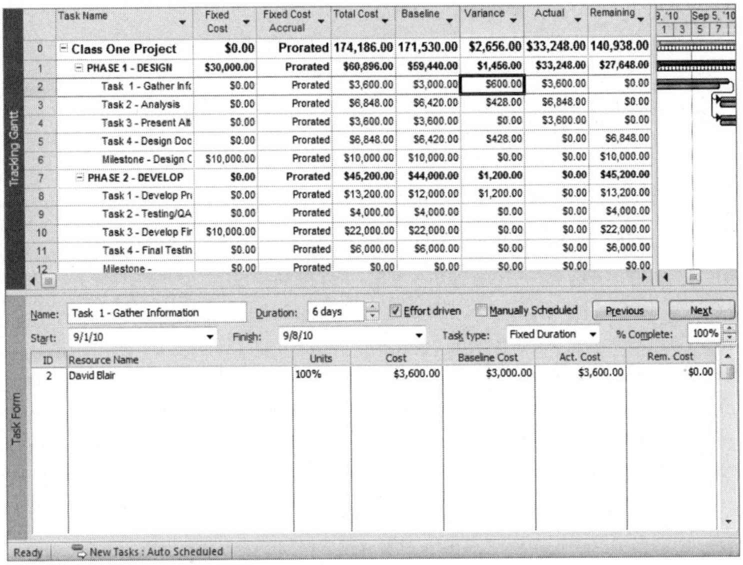

As you can see in Figure 17.6, Task 1 took 1 day longer to finish than planned and required a total of 48 hours of work instead of the baseline plan of 40 hours, resulting in a cost variance of $600 given the resource's hourly rate of $75.

Analyzing Variance and Taking Corrective Action

In this section, you'll learn about analyzing variance and how to use Project to make better decisions when you take corrective action.

Understanding Slippage

Now that you've learned how to set a baseline and capture status for percent complete and actuals, you can use the variance fields to help analyze your performance and make better decisions.

When you're viewing any one of the five standard variance values in Project (finish, start, duration, work, and cost variance), a positive number reflects an unfavorable position—it means you're late or over budget, depending on which variance value you're analyzing. For example, in Figure 17.7, you can see that Task 1 started on schedule but finished one day late and therefore has positive values in all variance columns except Start Variance. This reflects slippage both from a timing standpoint and from a budget standpoint.

FIGURE 17.7   Analyzing positive and negative variance values

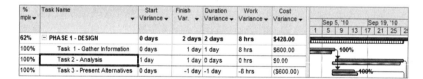

% mplt	Task Name	Start Variance	Finish Var.	Duration Variance	Work Variance	Cost Variance	Sep 5, '10 1	5	9	13	17	Sep 19, '10 21	25	2
62%	− PHASE 1 - DESIGN	0 days	2 days	2 days	8 hrs	$428.00								
100%	Task 1 - Gather Information	0 days	1 day	1 day	8 hrs	$600.00		100%						
100%	Task 2 - Analysis	1 day	1 day	0 days	0 hrs	$0.00								
100%	Task 3 - Present Alternatives	0 days	-1 day	-1 day	-8 hrs	($600.00)		100%						

Referring to Figure 17.7, you can also see that Task 3—Present Alternatives started on schedule and was completed one day earlier than planned (before the baseline), resulting in negative values in all variance columns except Start Variance. These negative numbers reflect a favorable position on the schedule because you're finishing ahead of plan, taking less work to do it, and in this case doing so for a lower cost as well.

Tracking variance is useful even if you aren't tracking costs. Many of the clients I work with don't use Project to track costs, because they don't have access to that type of information or don't have a requirement to do so because it's done in other systems. Some clients only use Project to track timelines for dates and duration, not needing to track effort for each resource. At whatever level of depth you apply the tool, understanding the variance fields helps you to make better decisions and communicate the impact of change more effectively.

Using Filters and Groups to Help Take Corrective Action

You learned a lot about using filters and groups in Chapter 12, "Using Filters, Groups, and Sorts," and you can use that knowledge to analyze your plan for slippage and take corrective action. You can use filters and groups together to create views that help you make better decisions as a project manager or with other project stakeholders such as team members.

For example, you can set up a view that displays tasks that are slipping, grouped by critical path, so you can see the tasks that impact your end date and that may need to be pulled back on schedule. The Slipped/Late Progress filter will filter for tasks that have a later finish date than the baseline finish or for tasks on which less work has been performed than planned to this point. To set up a view like this (see Figure 17.8), follow these steps:

1. In the Tracking Gantt view, select View tab ➢ Data group ➢ Filter drop-down menu ➢ More Filters.

2. In the More Filters dialog box, select Slipped/Late Progress, and click Apply.

3. Select Data group ➢ Group By drop-down list ➢ Critical.

FIGURE 17.8   Applying the Slipped/Late Progress filter with the Critical group to help take corrective action

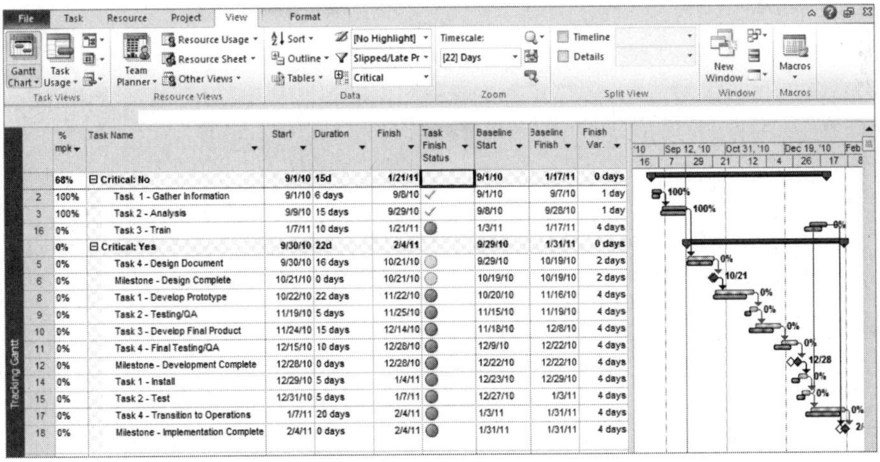

Figure 17.8 represents an excellent view you can use to work with team members to take corrective action and bring the end date back in line with the baseline. Options include the following:

- Decrease the duration of critical tasks.

- Add more resources to decrease the duration of effort-based tasks.

- Modify the dependencies (links between tasks) to make them overlap or be more concurrent.

- Modify scope such that you can remove one or more tasks or make a task inactive.

Keeping Notes for Schedule Changes and Slippage

Whenever a task is late or you change a task after the project has started, you can use the Notes field to keep track. On a large project, I record changes in a change log, but I also keep notes directly in the schedule in Project. You can access Project's Notes field by double-clicking any task to open the Task Information dialog box and then clicking the Notes tab. You can also access the notes under the Task tab in the Properties group.

As shown in Figure 17.9, you can record when a note is entered and capture notes not only for slippage but also for corrective action. For example, if you shave off time for future tasks to bring a project back on track, you can document it in the Notes field and explain why and how this occurs. If the project is late or over budget, it's easy to view the history and the notes to explain decisions along the way—particularly the effect of scope creep.

FIGURE 17.9 Keeping notes to track slippage and changes

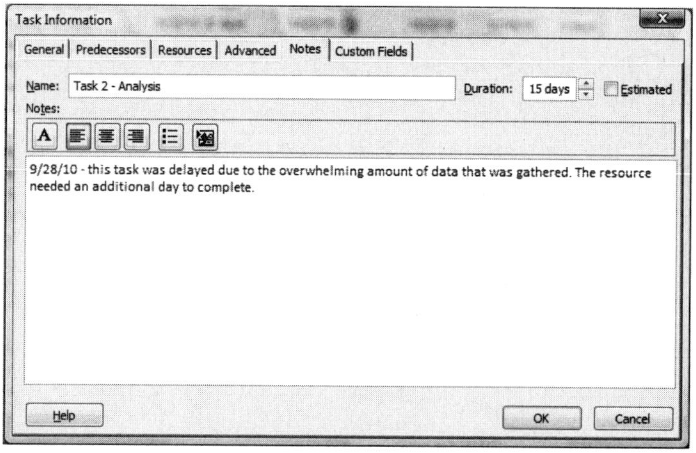

If you use the Notes field effectively to track the impact of changes and reasons for slippage in your schedule, you'll have an effective record of events at the end of the project. The Notes field can be included in tables and in the Gantt bar area. Notes can also be printed out as a separate report. If you need to print notes out in a hard copy, follow these steps (see Figure 17.10):

1. Click the File tab to get to the backstage.
2. Click Print, and then click Page Setup.
3. In the Page Setup dialog box, click the View tab.
4. Select the Print Notes check box.
5. Click Print. The notes report is printed in conjunction with the view you're printing.

FIGURE 17.10   Printing a notes report

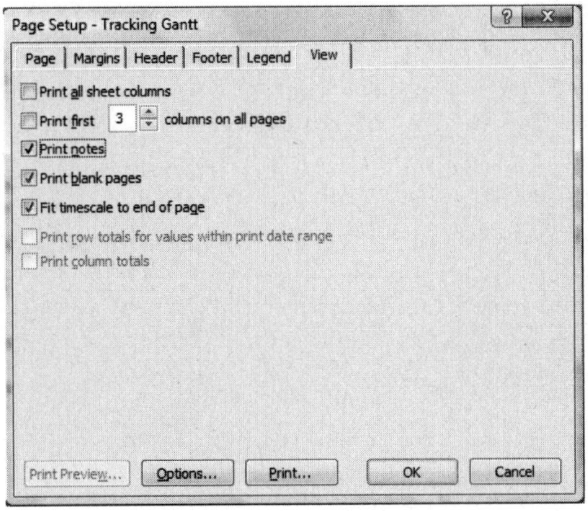

Visual Reports

Visual reports allow you to focus on project data in a more graphical manner using pivot charts and tables. These reports are useful to analyze project information as it pertains to work and costs for your project. Visual reports are based on building local online analytical processing (OLAP) cubes that present multidimensional data in a graphical format. The data is served up in either Microsoft Excel or Microsoft Visio.

You can choose the fields you want to display in an ad hoc manner in Excel or Visio after the cube is generated, because these programs connect directly to indexed data within the cube. To generate a visual report, follow these steps (see Figure 17.11):

1. Go to Project tab ➢ Reports group, and click Visual Reports.
2. In the Visual Reports—Create Report dialog box, click the All tab.
3. Select the visual report you want to generate from the list.
4. Under the list, select the level of usage data to include in the report; this dictates the level of granularity you want.
5. Click the View button.
6. Review the chart and data in Excel.

Project includes many good templates that you can use to generate visual reports in Excel or Visio, but you can also modify an existing template by clicking Edit Template in the Visual Reports—Create Report dialog box shown in Figure 17.11. You can also create a new template for a visual report by clicking New Template in the same dialog box.

FIGURE 17.11 Creating a visual report

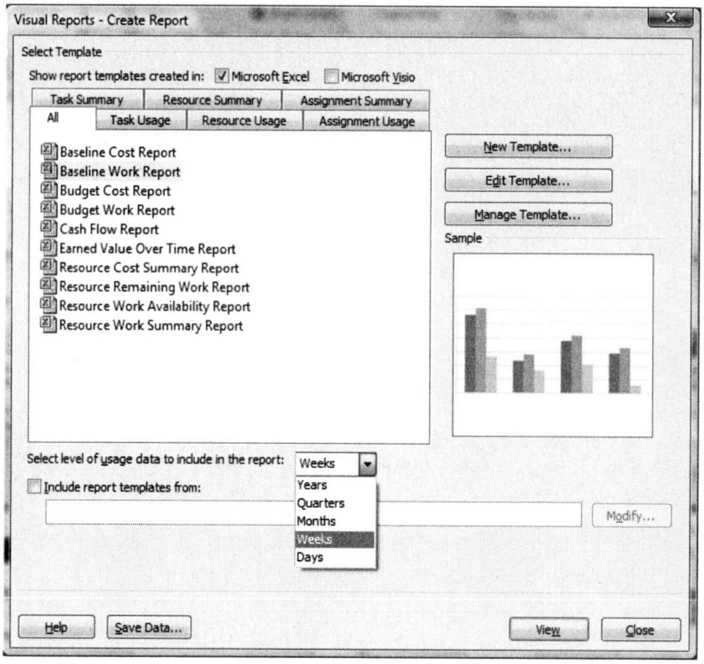

Earned-Value Analysis

Earned-value analysis helps you determine the cause and magnitude of a variance and decide whether corrective action is required.

Understanding Earned-Value Techniques and Values

Earned-value analysis is a technique that's primarily used for the following:

- Measuring performance throughout the project's life cycle
- Progress reporting that helps forecast the future performance of a project based on performance to date (useful for cost and resource management)
- Assessing progress relative to baseline data, and calculating the magnitudes of the variances

Earned-value analysis boils down to comparing what was earned against what was planned to occur up to a given point in time (status date) and against what actually took place.

The core components of earned-value analysis are as follows:

Earned Value (EV)   What was earned is based on budgeted cost of work performed (BCWP) from the original budgeted amount, now referred to as *earned value* (EV):

EV = BAC (budget at completion) × % complete

Planned Value (PV)   What is currently planned is based on the budgeted cost of work scheduled (BCWS) up to a given point in time, now referred to as *planned value* (PV):

PV = baseline costs up to status date

Actual Cost (AC)   What actually took place is based on actual cost of work performed (ACWP), now referred to as *actual cost* (AC):

AC = cost of actual work reported

The key EV variances are as follows:

Cost Variance (CV)   This represents the amount that cost varies between what has been earned and the actual cost to date. The CV at the end of the project is the budget at completion minus actual cost:

CV = EV − AC

CV% = (CV/EV) × 100

- CV < 0 means over budget.
- CV > 0 means under budget.

Schedule Variance (SV)   This is based on comparing the value difference between earned value and planned value:

SV = EV − PV

SV% = (SV/PV) × 100

- SV < 0 means behind schedule.
- SV > 0 means ahead of schedule.

Variance at Completion (VAC)   This is the difference between the baseline cost and the estimate at completion, to predict whether you'll be over or under budget:

VAC = BAC − EAC (estimate at completion)

- VAC < 0 means projected cost is over budget.
- VAC > 0 means projected cost is under budget.

The earned-value performance indexes are as following:

Cost Performance Index (CPI)   This represents the cost efficiency of work performed on a project:

CPI = EV ÷ AC

- CPI < 1 means over budget (cost overrun).
- CPI > 1 means under budget (cost underrun).

Schedule Performance Index (SPI)   This represents the scheduled efficiency of work performed versus the work scheduled:

SPI = EV ÷ PV

- SPI < 1 means behind schedule.
- SPI > 1 means ahead of schedule.

To Completion Performance Index (TCPI)   This is the ratio of the work remaining to be done to funds remaining to be spent, as of the status date, to help predict whether you'll have excess funds or run out of money:

TCPI = (BAC – EV) ÷ (BAC – AC)

- TCPI < 1 means performance can decrease to stay within budget.
- TCPI > 1 means performance needs to increase to stay within budget.

Earned-value analysis involves these forecasting measures:

Budget at Completion (BAC)   This represents the original agreed-upon budget (baseline cost) for completing the project:

Task Baseline Cost = (Work × Standard Rate) + (Overtime Work × Overtime Rate) + Resource per Use Cost + Task Fixed Cost

Estimate at Completion (EAC)   This represents the current estimate at a given point in time based on actual cost to that point in time plus what remains:

EAC = AC + Remaining Budget ÷ CPI

Note: Remaining Budget = Baseline Cost – EV

Estimate to Complete (ETC)   This represents the estimated cost to complete the work based on a given point in time to the end of the project:

ETC = EAC – AC

No Need to Memorize Earned-Value Formulas for Certification for Microsoft Project 2010

There is no need to memorize Project's formulas for earned-value analysis for the Microsoft certifications exam for Project 2010. However, this isn't the case if you plan to take the Project Management Professional (PMP) exam sponsored by the Project Management Institute (PMI).

Physical Percent Complete and the Status Date

To use earned value in Project 2010, you must understand the role of physical percent complete and the status date.

Physical Percent Complete

Project gives you an option to use the standard percent complete when calculating earned value or to use a separate field called Physical Percent Complete. This may be useful, because the standard percent complete is linked to actuals and remaining duration in a manner that may not reflect your need to calculate earned value. Physical percent complete provides an alternative that gives you more freedom to enter values not tied to these standard values.

The earned-value calculation method field lets you choose whether to use the Percent Complete (the default) or Physical Percent Complete field to calculate earned value. You can also choose which of the 11 available baselines should be used for earned-value calculations. Follow these steps (see Figure 17.12):

1. Go to the backstage by clicking the File tab.
2. Click Project Options, and select Advanced.
3. Scroll down to Earned Value Options for This Project.
4. In the Default Task Earned Value Method drop-down menu, choose either % Complete or Physical % Complete.
5. Click OK.

You can also set the earned-value calculation method on a task-by-task basis if you need to vary your approach. To do so, double-click a task to open the Task Information dialog box, click the Advanced tab, and select an option from the Earned Value Method drop-down menu (see Figure 17.13).

Status Date

Project applies the earned-value analysis based on a certain point in time, which is determined by setting the status date. You can access the status date in the Project Information dialog box, which you reach via Properties group ➤ Project tab (see Figure 17.14).

Typically, when you define the status date, it represents the end of the reporting period you want to use for earned-value analysis. It's important to reset the status date each time you wish to report on earned value.

Current Date

If you fail to define your status date, Project defaults to using the current date in the Project Information dialog box to calculate relevant earned-value fields. After you set the status date, Project continues to use that date for future calculations. Therefore, it's important to reset the status date for each reporting period.

FIGURE 17.12 Changing the earned-value calculation method for the project

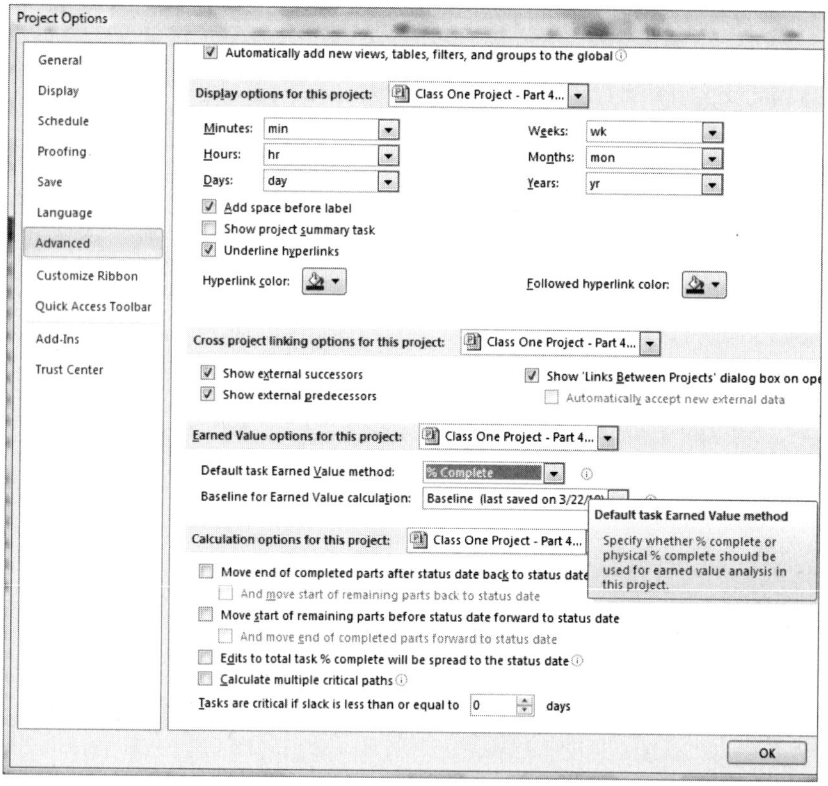

FIGURE 17.13 Changing the earned value calculation method for a task

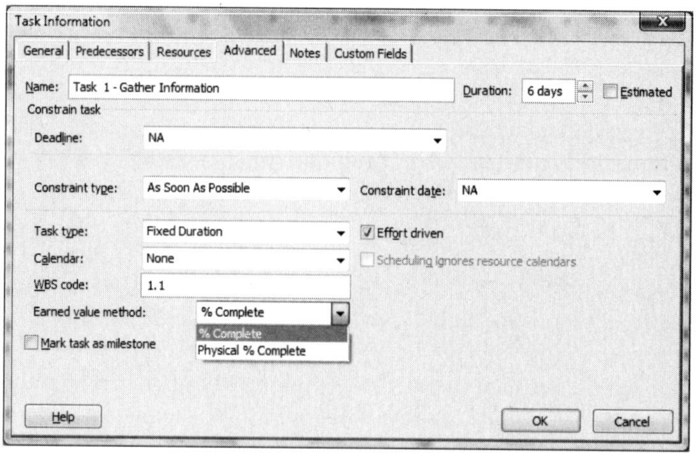

FIGURE 17.14 Setting the status date

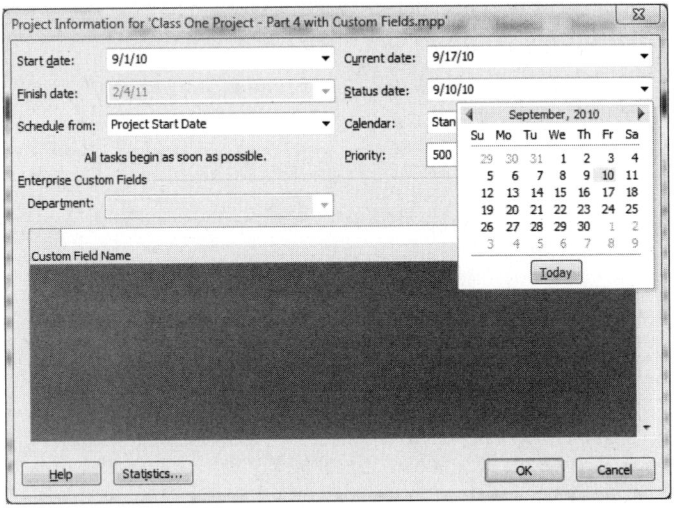

Using Earned-Value Analysis in Project

Project includes three earned value tables:

- Earned Value
- Earned Value Cost Indicators
- Earned Value Schedule Indicators

You can access these tables by selecting View tab ➤ Data group ➤ Tables ➤ More Tables (see Figure 17.15).

Earned value in Project is based on the fact that resources with costs have been assigned to tasks and a baseline has been set. It also relies on the status date being set and percent complete and actuals being recorded.

FIGURE 17.15 Accessing earned-value tables

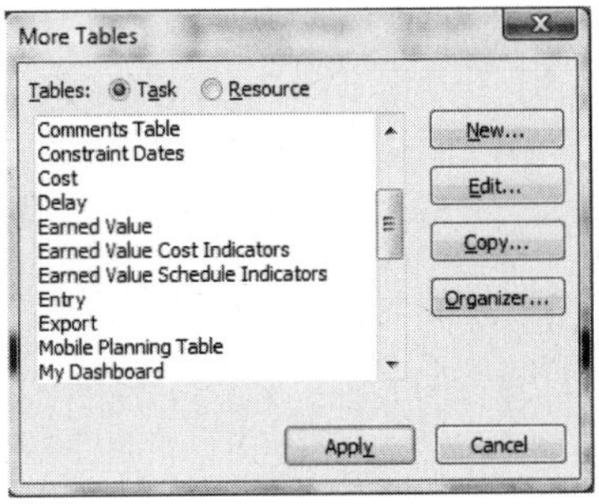

Earned Value Table

The Earned Value table provides an excellent synopsis of the primary earned value fields. Figure 17.16 shows an example of the Earned Value table, which is based on actual progress being entered for the first three tasks; the status date has been set and is represented by a vertical red line.

FIGURE 17.16   Earned Value table with progress

Task Name	Planned Value - PV (BCWS)	Earned Value - EV (BCWP)	AC (ACWP)	SV	CV	EAC	BAC	VAC
− PHASE 1 - DESIGN	$26,330.59	$23,310.00	$23,910.00	($3,020.59)	($600.00)	$61,409.00	$59,868.00	($1,541.00)
Task 1 - Gather Information	$3,600.00	$3,600.00	$4,200.00	$0.00	($600.00)	$4,200.00	$3,600.00	($600.00)
Task 2 - Analysis	$5,136.00	$3,210.00	$3,420.00	($1,926.00)	$0.00	$6,420.00	$6,420.00	$0.00
Task 3 - Present Alternatives	$3,000.00	$3,000.00	$3,000.00	$0.00	$0.00	$3,000.00	$3,000.00	$0.00
Task 4 - Design Document	$0.00	$0.00	$0.00	$0.00	$0.00	$6,848.00	$6,848.00	$0.00
Milestone - Design Complete	$0.00	$0.00	$0.00	$0.00	$0.00	$10,000.00	$10,000.00	$0.00
− PHASE 2 - DEVELOP	$0.00	$0.00	$0.00	$0.00	$0.00	$45,200.00	$45,200.00	$0.00
Task 1 - Develop Prototype	$0.00	$0.00	$0.00	$0.00	$0.00	$13,200.00	$13,200.00	$0.00
Task 2 - Testing/QA	$0.00	$0.00	$0.00	$0.00	$0.00	$4,000.00	$4,000.00	$0.00
Task 3 - Develop Final Product	$0.00	$0.00	$0.00	$0.00	$0.00	$22,000.00	$22,000.00	$0.00
Task 4 - Final Testing/QA	$0.00	$0.00	$0.00	$0.00	$0.00	$6,000.00	$6,000.00	$0.00
Milestone - Development Complete	$0.00	$0.00	$0.00	$0.00	$0.00	$0.00	$0.00	$0.00
− PHASE 3 - IMPLEMENT	$0.00	$0.00	$0.00	$0.00	$0.00	$68,090.00	$68,090.00	$0.00
Task 1 - Install	$0.00	$0.00	$0.00	$0.00	$0.00	$12,140.00	$12,140.00	$0.00
Task 2 - Test	$0.00	$0.00	$0.00	$0.00	$0.00	$3,000.00	$3,000.00	$0.00
Task 3 - Train	$0.00	$0.00	$0.00	$0.00	$0.00	$40,000.00	$40,000.00	$0.00
Task 4 - Transition to Operations	$0.00	$0.00	$0.00	$0.00	$0.00	$12,950.00	$12,950.00	$0.00
Milestone - Implementation Complete	$0.00	$0.00	$0.00	$0.00	$0.00	$0.00	$0.00	$0.00

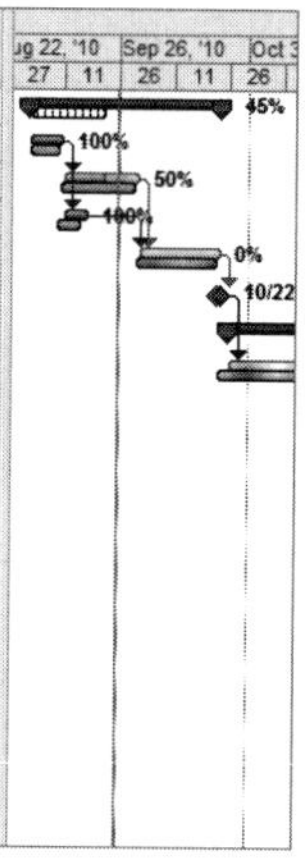

From this example, you can derive the following analysis:

Task 1   Gather Information has a CV value that is less than 0 and therefore is over budget. It also has a VAC value that is negative; therefore, the project cost will be over budget unless corrective action is taken.

Task 2   Analysis has an SV value that is less than 0, meaning that this task is behind schedule. This is because the percent complete is reported at 50% but should be higher based on the status date.

Task 3   Present Alternatives from a cost perspective is right on schedule because there is no variance and EV, PV, and AC are equal.

You can apply the Earned Value Cost and Schedule Indicator tables for further analysis. In addition, you can apply any of the earned-value fields in the new or existing tables and customize your own earned value views.

Summary

In this chapter, you learned about the importance of Project's variance fields when you're trying to analyze performance. Understanding variance and the impact of change provides you with more effective tools to make better decisions during the execution stage of your project.

Using predefined tables, groups, and filters that support analyzing slippage or schedule problems makes it easier to take corrective actions when a project begins to go off course.

Finally, I provided an overview of earned-value analysis and how it works in Project. Earned-value analysis measures performance based on a status date to determine how you're doing by comparing baseline and actual progress using core earned-value fields.

Hands-On Exercises

The following hands-on exercises are designed to test your understanding of the topics discussed in this chapter. We've provided files on the companion CD that will show you what your project file should look like as you perform these exercises.

EXERCISE 22

Analyzing Project Schedule

1. In Class One Project, review the Finish Variance field while in the Tracking Gantt view with the Variance Table applied.

2. Apply the filter for Slipped/Late Progress.

3. Apply the group for Critical.

4. Review tasks that are slipping that are on the critical path.

5. Shave off time on one or more of the critical-path tasks that has a finish variance until you bring the final milestone finish variance back to 0. In this example, I decreased the duration on the Transition To Operations task until the finish variance for the project was back to 0 days.

Appendix
A

Microsoft's Certification Program

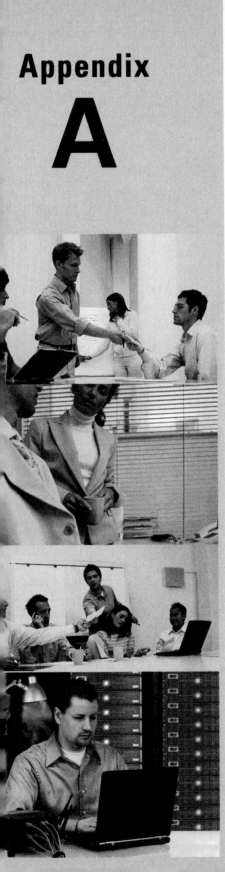

Since the inception of its certification program, Microsoft has certified more than 5 million people. As the computer network industry continues to increase in both size and complexity, this number is sure to grow—and the need for *proven* ability will also increase. Certifications can help companies verify the skills of prospective employees and contractors.

Microsoft has developed its Microsoft Certified Professional (MCP) program to give you credentials that verify your ability to work with Microsoft products effectively and professionally. Several levels of certification are available based on specific suites of exams.

Microsoft Certified Technology Specialist (MCTS)   The MCTS can be considered the entry-level certification for Microsoft certifications. The MCTS certification program targets specific technologies instead of specific job roles. You must take and pass one to three exams.

Microsoft Certified IT Professional (MCITP)   The MCITP certification is a Professional Series certification that tests network and system administrators on job roles rather than only on a specific technology. The MCITP certification program generally consists of one to three exams in addition to obtaining an MCTS-level certification.

Microsoft Certified Professional Developer (MCPD)   The MCPD certification is a Professional Series certification for application developers. Similar to the MCITP, the MCPD is focused on a job role rather than on a single technology. The MCPD certification program generally consists of one to three exams in addition to obtaining an MCTS-level certification.

Microsoft Business Certifications   Microsoft launched the Business certifications in 1997, with the release of the Microsoft Office User Specialist (MOUS). The program was later rebranded as Microsoft Office Specialist (MOS) and then, with the release of Office 2003, was changed to Microsoft Certified Application Specialist (MCAS). These certify Microsoft application professionals in their ability to use the Microsoft Office products, including Project.

Microsoft Certified Architect (MCA)   The MCA is Microsoft's premier certification series. Obtaining the MCA requires a minimum of 10 years of experience and passing a review board consisting of peer architects.

How Do You Become Certified on Project 2010?

Attaining Microsoft certification has always been a challenge. In the past, students have been able to acquire detailed exam information—even most of the exam questions—from online "brain dumps" and third-party "cram" books or software products. For the new generation of exams, this is simply not the case.

Microsoft has taken strong steps to protect the security and integrity of its new certification tracks. Now, prospective candidates should complete a course of study that develops detailed knowledge about a wide range of topics. It supplies them with the true skills needed, derived from working with the technology being tested.

Microsoft certification programs are heavily weighted toward hands-on skills and experience. It's recommended that candidates have troubleshooting skills acquired through hands-on experience and working knowledge.

To get your certification on Project 2010, you must pass one exam: Microsoft Project 2010, Managing Projects (77-178).

This exam uses a live-application, performance-based approach focused on measuring your skill based on outcomes and not necessarily on how you perform the tasks.

> The detailed exam objectives, and the chapters in which those objectives
> are discussed, can be found in the section "Certification Objectives Map"
> later in this appendix.

For a more detailed description of the Microsoft certification programs, including a list of all the exams, visit the Microsoft Learning website at www.microsoft.com/learning.

Tips for Taking a Microsoft Exam

Here are some general tips for achieving success on your certification exam:

- Arrive early at the exam center so that you can relax and review your study materials. During this final review, you can look over tables and lists of exam-related information.

- Read the questions carefully. Don't be tempted to jump to an early conclusion. Make sure you know *exactly* what the question is asking.

- Answer all questions. If you're unsure about a question, mark it for review and come back to it at a later time.

- On simulations, do not change settings that are not directly related to the question. Also, assume default settings if the question doesn't specify or imply which settings are used.

- For questions you're not sure about, use a process of elimination to get rid of the obviously incorrect answers first. This improves your odds of selecting the correct answer when you need to make an educated guess.

Certification Objectives Map

Table A.1 provides an objectives map for Exam 77-178.

TABLE A.1 Exam 77-178 Objectives Map

Objectives **1.0 Initializing Project**	**Chapter**
1.1 Create a new project.	4, 5
This objective may include but is not limited to: creating a template from a completed project, and creating a project from an existing template, an existing project, a SharePoint task list, or a Microsoft Office Excel workbook.	
1.2 Create and maintain calendars.	4
This objective may include but is not limited to: setting working or non-working hours and days (exceptions and work weeks) for calendars; setting a base calendar, a resource calendar, or hours per day; and applying calendars at the project, task, and resource levels.	
1.3 Create custom fields.	11
This objective may include but is not limited to: creating basic formulas, graphical indicator criteria, lookup tables, and task and resource custom fields.	
1.4 Customize option settings.	4
This objective may include but is not limited to: using default task types, manual vs. auto-scheduling, project options, calendar options (for example, working hours per day and hours per week), a customized ribbon, and the Quick Access Toolbar (for example, settings to share with others).	
2 Creating a Task-Based Schedule	
2.1 Set up project information.	4
This objective may include but is not limited to: defining the project start date, applying calendars and the current date, entering project properties, and displaying the project summary task on a new project.	
2.2 Create and modify a project task structure.	5
This objective may include but is not limited to: creating and modifying summary tasks and subtasks, rearranging tasks, creating milestones, manually scheduling tasks, and using outlining tools.	

Objectives **1.0 Initializing Project**	**Chapter**
2.3 Build a logical schedule model.	6, 7
This objective may include but is not limited to: using date constraints, setting deadlines, setting or changing the task mode (manual or auto), and using dependencies (links).	
2.3 Create a user-controlled schedule.	5, 6, 7
This objective may include but is not limited to: entering duration, estimated durations, and user-controlled summary tasks.	
2.4 Manage multiple projects.	14
This objective may include but is not limited to: using a shared resource pool, creating links between projects, and inserting sub-projects.	
3 Managing Resources and Assignments	
3.1 Enter and edit resource information.	8
This objective may include but is not limited to: using max units, resource types, a cost rate table, cost per use, availability, resource groups, and generic resources.	
3.2 Apply task types and scheduling calculations.	8 (and 4)
This objective may include but is not limited to: creating effort-driven tasks, using formulas (work = duration x units), and choosing a task type.	
3.3 Assign resources.	8
This objective may include but is not limited to: assigning multiple resources, and assigning resources to tasks using units that represent part-time work (vs. full-time work).	
3.4 Edit assignments.	8
This objective may include but is not limited to: understanding task usage, resource usage, and task forms, and editing assignments by setting the appropriate task type.	
3.5 Manage resource allocation.	8
This objective may include but is not limited to: viewing availability across multiple projects, changing assignments, leveling, replacing resources (for example, resolving over-allocation, and replacing generics with specifics).	

TABLE A.1   Exam 77-178 Objectives Map *(continued)*

Objectives 1.0 Initializing Project	Chapter
3.6 Manage resource allocations by using Team Planner.	8, 10
This objective may include but is not limited to: displaying current resource allocations and assignments, managing unassigned tasks, resolving resource conflicts, leveling resource over-allocations, and substituting resources (moving task assignments from one resource to another).	
3.7 Model project costs.	8, 9
This objective may include but is not limited to: using resource-based costs (work, material, cost), cost per use, fixed costs, and the accrual method.	
4 Tracking and Analyzing a Project	
4.1 Set and maintain baselines.	15
This objective may include but is not limited to: baselining an entire project, baselining selected tasks, using multiple baselines, and updating a baseline (for example, rolling up to summary tasks, and resetting the baseline).	
4.2 Update actual progress.	16
This objective may include but is not limited to: entering percentage completion, actual or remaining duration, actual work, remaining work, status date, and current date; rescheduling uncompleted work; entering actual start and actual finish; using actual work and usage views; and cancelling unneeded tasks (for example, deactivating a task, setting the active flag, or zeroing out remaining work).	
4.3 Compare progress against a baseline.	17
This objective may include but is not limited to: using date variance, work variance, and cost variance; showing the variance of the current plan against a baseline (tracking Gantt); understanding task slippage; and selecting a view to display variance.	
4.4 Resolve potential schedule problems by using the Task Inspector.	7, 17
This objective may include but is not limited to: using warnings and suggestions, entering task drivers, and identifying resource over-allocations.	
4.5 Display critical path information.	7

Objectives **1.0 Initializing Project**	**Chapter**

This objective may include but is not limited to: using single or master projects, viewing total slack, and displaying progress against deadlines.

5 Communicating Project Information

| 5.1 Apply views. | 10 |

This objective may include but is not limited to: applying views, grouping, filtering and highlighting, auto-filtering, sorting, and using tables.

| 5.2 Customize views. | 11, 12, 13 |

This objective may include but is not limited to: customizing views, grouping, filtering and highlighting, sorting, using tables, and sharing a view (using the Organizer).

| 5.3 Format views. | 13 |

This objective may include but is not limited to: using gridlines, bar styles, Gantt chart styles, text styles, the timeline, and cell formatting.

| 5.4 Share data with external sources. | 13 |

This objective may include but is not limited to: creating visual reports, using enhanced copy and paste, copying pictures, syncing to SharePoint (for example, uploading a schedule, syncing with a SharePoint list, and e-mailing a timeline), attaching or linking to supporting information, and exporting data to Excel.

| 5.5 Print schedules and reports. | 13 |

This objective may include but is not limited to: reporting progress status; saving to PDF or XPS; printing Gantt information, a schedule, or a timeline; and printing based on a date range.

Exam objectives are subject to change at any time without prior notice and at Microsoft's sole discretion. Please visit Microsoft's website (www.microsoft.com/learning) for the most current listing of exam objectives.

Appendix

B

About the Companion CD

IN THIS APPENDIX:

✓ What you'll find on the CD

✓ System requirements

✓ Using the CD

✓ Troubleshooting

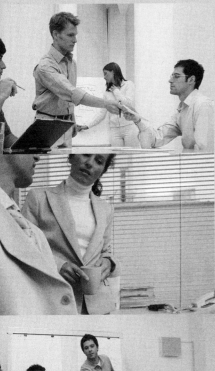

What You'll Find on the CD

The following sections are arranged by category and summarize the software and other goodies you'll find on the CD. If you need help with installing the items provided on the CD, refer to the installation instructions in the "Using the CD" section of this appendix.

Video Walkthroughs

The CD contains over an hour of video walkthrough from author Robert Happy. Robert shows you how to perform some of the more difficult tasks you can expect to encounter on the job.

PDF of the Book

We have included an electronic version of the text in .pdf format. You can view the electronic version of the book with Adobe Reader.

Adobe Reader

We've also included a copy of Adobe Reader so you can view the PDF files that accompany the book's content. For more information on Adobe Reader or to check for a newer version, visit Adobe's website at www.adobe.com/products/reader/.

System Requirements

Make sure your computer meets the minimum system requirements shown in the following list. If your computer doesn't match up to most of these requirements, you may have problems using the software and files on the companion CD. For the latest and greatest information, please refer to the ReadMe file located at the root of the CD-ROM:

- A PC running Microsoft Windows 98, Windows 2000, Windows NT4 (with SP4 or later), Windows Me, Windows XP, Windows Vista, or Windows 7

- An Internet connection

- A CD-ROM drive

Using the CD

To install the items from the CD to your hard drive, follow these steps:

1. Insert the CD into your computer's CD-ROM drive. The license agreement appears.

> **NOTE**
>
> *Windows users*: The interface won't launch if you have autorun disabled. In that case, click Start ➤ Run (for Windows Vista or Windows 7, Start ➤ All Programs ➤ Accessories ➤ Run). In the dialog box that appears, type D:\Start.exe. (Replace *D* with the proper letter if your CD drive uses a different letter. If you don't know the letter, see how your CD drive is listed under My Computer.) Click OK.

2. Read the license agreement, and then click the Accept button if you want to use the CD.

The CD interface appears. The interface allows you to access the content with just one or two clicks.

Troubleshooting

Wiley has attempted to provide programs that work on most computers with the minimum system requirements. Alas, your computer may differ, and some programs may not work properly for some reason.

The two likeliest problems are that you don't have enough memory (RAM) for the programs you want to use or you have other programs running that are affecting installation or running of a program. If you get an error message such as "Not enough memory" or "Setup cannot continue," try one or more of the following suggestions and then try using the software again:

Turn off any antivirus software running on your computer. Installation programs sometimes mimic virus activity and may make your computer incorrectly believe that it's being infected by a virus.

Close all running programs. The more programs you have running, the less memory is available to other programs. Installation programs typically update files and programs; so if you keep other programs running, installation may not work properly.

Have your local computer store add more RAM to your computer. This is, admittedly, a drastic and somewhat expensive step. However, adding more memory can really help the speed of your computer and allow more programs to run at the same time.

Customer Care

If you have trouble with the book's companion CD-ROM, please call the Wiley Product Technical Support phone number: (800) 762-2974.

Index

Note to the reader: Throughout this index boldfaced page numbers indicate primary discussions of a topic. Italicized page numbers indicate illustrations.

G

H

I

Wiley Publishing, Inc.
End-User License Agreement

READ THIS. You should carefully read these terms and conditions before opening the software packet(s) included with this book "Book". This is a license agreement "Agreement" between you and Wiley Publishing, Inc. "WPI". By opening the accompanying software packet(s), you acknowledge that you have read and accept the following terms and conditions. If you do not agree and do not want to be bound by such terms and conditions, promptly return the Book and the unopened software packet(s) to the place you obtained them for a full refund.

1. License Grant. WPI grants to you (either an individual or entity) a nonexclusive license to use one copy of the enclosed software program(s) (collectively, the "Software," solely for your own personal or business purposes on a single computer (whether a standard computer or a work-station component of a multi-user network). The Software is in use on a computer when it is loaded into temporary memory (RAM) or installed into permanent memory (hard disk, CD-ROM, or other storage device). WPI reserves all rights not expressly granted herein.

2. Ownership. WPI is the owner of all right, title, and interest, including copyright, in and to the compilation of the Software recorded on the physical packet included with this Book "Software Media". Copyright to the individual programs recorded on the Software Media is owned by the author or other authorized copyright owner of each program. Ownership of the Software and all proprietary rights relating thereto remain with WPI and its licensers.

3. Restrictions On Use and Transfer.
(a) You may only (i) make one copy of the Software for backup or archival purposes, or (ii) transfer the Software to a single hard disk, provided that you keep the original for backup or archival purposes. You may not (i) rent or lease the Software, (ii) copy or reproduce the Software through a LAN or other network system or through any computer subscriber system or bulletin-board system, or (iii) modify, adapt, or create derivative works based on the Software.
(b) You may not reverse engineer, decompile, or disassemble the Software. You may transfer the Software and user documentation on a permanent basis, provided that the transferee agrees to accept the terms and conditions of this Agreement and you retain no copies. If the Software is an update or has been updated, any transfer must include the most recent update and all prior versions.

4. Restrictions on Use of Individual Programs. You must follow the individual requirements and restrictions detailed for each individual program in the About the CD-ROM appendix of this Book or on the Software Media. These limitations are also contained in the individual license agreements recorded on the Software Media. These limitations may include a requirement that after using the program for a specified period of time, the user must pay a registration fee or discontinue use. By opening the Software packet(s), you will be agreeing to abide by the licenses and restrictions for these individual programs that are detailed in the About the CD-ROM appendix and/or on the Software Media. None of the material on this Software Media or listed in this Book may ever be redistributed, in original or modified form, for commercial purposes.

5. Limited Warranty.
(a) WPI warrants that the Software and Software Media are free from defects in materials and workmanship under normal use for a period of sixty (60) days from the date of purchase of this Book. If WPI receives notification within the warranty period of defects in materials or workmanship, WPI will replace the defective Software Media.
(b) WPI AND THE AUTHOR(S) OF THE BOOK DISCLAIM ALL OTHER WARRANTIES, EXPRESS OR IMPLIED, INCLUDING WITHOUT LIMITATION IMPLIED WARRANTIES OF MERCHANTABILITY AND FITNESS FOR A PARTICULAR PURPOSE, WITH RESPECT TO THE SOFTWARE, THE PROGRAMS, THE SOURCE CODE CONTAINED THEREIN, AND/OR THE TECHNIQUES DESCRIBED IN THIS BOOK. WPI DOES NOT WARRANT THAT THE FUNCTIONS CONTAINED IN THE SOFTWARE WILL MEET YOUR REQUIREMENTS OR THAT THE OPERATION OF THE SOFTWARE WILL BE ERROR FREE.
(c) This limited warranty gives you specific legal rights, and you may have other rights that vary from jurisdiction to jurisdiction.

6. Remedies.
(a) WPI's entire liability and your exclusive remedy for defects in materials and workmanship shall be limited to replacement of the Software Media, which may be returned to WPI with a copy of your receipt at the following address: Software Media Fulfillment Department, Attn.: *Microsoft Project 2010 Project Management: Real-World Skills for MOS Certification*, Wiley Publishing, Inc., 10475 Crosspoint Blvd., Indianapolis, IN 46256, or call 1-800-762-2974. Please allow four to six weeks for delivery. This Limited Warranty is void if failure of the Software Media has resulted from accident, abuse, or misapplication. Any replacement Software Media will be warranted for the remainder of the original warranty period or thirty (30) days, whichever is longer.
(b) In no event shall WPI or the author be liable for any damages whatsoever (including without limitation damages for loss of business profits, business interruption, loss of business information, or any other pecuniary loss) arising from the use of or inability to use the Book or the Software, even if WPI has been advised of the possibility of such damages.
(c) Because some jurisdictions do not allow the exclusion or limitation of liability for consequential or incidental damages, the above limitation or exclusion may not apply to you.

7. U.S. Government Restricted Rights. Use, duplication, or disclosure of the Software for or on behalf of the United States of America, its agencies and/or instrumentalities "U.S. Government" is subject to restrictions as stated in paragraph (c)(1)(ii) of the Rights in Technical Data and Computer Software clause of DFARS 252.227-7013, or subparagraphs (c) (1) and (2) of the Commercial Computer Software - Restricted Rights clause at FAR 52.227-19, and in similar clauses in the NASA FAR supplement, as applicable.

8. General. This Agreement constitutes the entire understanding of the parties and revokes and supersedes all prior agreements, oral or written, between them and may not be modified or amended except in a writing signed by both parties hereto that specifically refers to this Agreement. This Agreement shall take precedence over any other documents that may be in conflict herewith. If any one or more provisions contained in this Agreement are held by any court or tribunal to be invalid, illegal, or otherwise unenforceable, each and every other provision shall remain in full force and effect.

The Perfect Companion for all Project 2010 Professionals

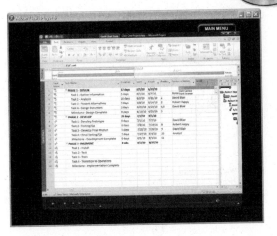

Contains over an hour of video walkthroughs with author Robert Happy

- Robert walks you through some of the more complex tasks you can expect to face when managing a project with Project 2010.

- See firsthand how to set-up key options for your scheduling success; build a plan using manual or auto scheduling; communicating more effectively with powerful new views and track and analyze your schedule once your project begins.

- An overview of the key features that are new to Microsoft Project 2010 such as the new ribbon interface, user controlled scheduling, Timeline view, Team Planner view, new team collaboration tools and the inactive task function.

Search through the complete book in PDF!

- Access the entire *Project 2010 Project Management*, complete with figures and tables, in electronic format.

- Search the *Project 2010 Project Management* chapters to find information on any topic in seconds.

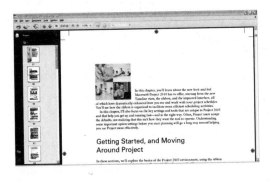

For Certification candidates, book maps to the exam objectives for the following exam:

- MOS: Microsoft Project 2010, Managing Projects (77-178)

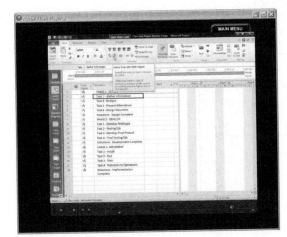

Special Video Training Offer

Dear Reader,

Thank you for purchasing my book.

Get the most out of Microsoft's popular project management tool, **Project 2010**, with my video-based, on-demand training course from Project Management Practice, Inc. and KeyStone Learning Systems, LLC.

This course is the perfect companion to my book and will equip you with the knowledge you need to effectively plan, track, and execute projects in **Project 2010**.

Special Offer

Visit

www.pm-practice.com/learnproject2010

and save $50 on your purchase of **Project 2010 Core Essentials**.

Best Regards,

Robert Happy, PMP, MCT

PROJECT MANAGEMENT PRACTICE INC.
Infinite Possibilities – Measurable Results

KeyStone
Learning Systems

This coupon is offered by Project Management Practice, Inc. and KeyStone Learning Systems, LLC.